CHILD PSYCHOTHERAPY, WAR AND THE NORMAL CHILD

Child Psychotherapy, War and the Normal Child

The names of Anna Freud, Melanie Klein and Donald Winnicott are well known as pioneers in child psychotherapy throughout the Western world. Margaret Lowenfeld was as influential before and after the Second World War. A leading figure in the history of the treatment of emotionally disturbed children, she developed a form of therapy and an approach to children's minds which remain unique.

While researching infant feeding and the problems of child care, Lowenfeld recognized the significance of children's play, both for what it revealed about stages of development and as a process in itself. Unlike her contemporaries within psychoanalysis, Lowenfeld viewed play not only as a medium through which children could work through their emotional conflicts, but also as a cognitive process – giving access to a child's mind. Her starting-point was always the meaning given to its playing by the child, and this collection introduces Lowenfeld's work for the first time in a systematic way.

In a thoroughly researched introduction and critical assessment, Cathy Urwin situates Lowenfeld's work within the history of psychoanalysis, the Child Guidance movement, and developmental psychology. She goes on to compare Lowenfeld's observations of preverbal states of mind with the work of psychoanalytic innovators in the Kleinian tradition in understanding the origins and functions of thinking and symbol formation.

Cathy Urwin is a research fellow in the Child Care and Development Group at the University of Cambridge. The late John Hood-Williams was a child psychotherapist, trained by Margaret Lowenfeld, with wide clinical experience.

CHILD PSYCHOTHERAPY, WAR AND THE NORMAL CHILD

Selected Papers of

MARGARET LOWENFELD

Edited by

Cathy Urwin and John Hood-Williams

sussex
ACADEMIC
PRESS
Brighton • Chicago • Toronto

First published in Great Britain 1988 by Free Association Books, London; reprinted 2013, with a revised cover, by
SUSSEX ACADEMIC PRESS
PO Box 139
Eastbourne BN24 9BP

Distributed in North America by
SUSSEX ACADEMIC PRESS
Independent Publishers Group
814 N Franklin St, Chicago, IL 60610, USA

Errata: page 243, para 3, line 4, for British Psycho-Analytical Society read British Psychological Society; page 272, fig. 2 has been reversed from left to right; page 282, fig. 14 is reproduced upside-down and has been reversed from left to right.

British Library Cataloguing in Publication Data
Lowenfeld, Margaret
Chid psychotherapy, war and the normal child.
1. Children. Psychotherapy
I. Title. II. Urwin, Cathy III. Hood-Williams, John
618.92′8914
ISBN 978-1-84519-084-2

Typeset and designed by Sussex Academic Press, Brighton & Eastbourne.
Printed and bound by CPI Group (UK) Ltd, Croydon, CR0 4YY
This book is printed on acid-free paper.

CONTENTS

Acknowledgements

John Hood-Williams, the co-editor of this book, sadly died while it was being printed. He was Director of Studies at Margaret Lowenfeld's clinic (The Institute of Child Psychology) and became a Trustee from the creation of the Margaret Lowenfeld Trust.

His experience and enthusiasm contributed significantly to the evolution of Dr Lowenfeld's ideas in both the United Kingdom and the United States. The Trustees hope that this book will commemorate both his contribution and their appreciation of it.

The editors are very grateful for the financial support for the publication of this book provided by the Margaret Lowenfeld Trust, which holds the copyright on Margaret Lowenfeld's previously unpublished writings.

Along with the publishers we would like to thank the following for permission to reproduce copyright material written by Margaret Lowenfeld, which first appeared as shown here:

Lancet (1927) 'Organisation and the rheumatic child', p. 1177; *Journal of Obstetrics and Gynaecology of the British Empire* (1928) 'Researches in lactation', by Margaret Lowenfeld and Sibyl Taite Widdows, 35, 1:14–30; *British Journal of Medical Psychology* (1931) 'A new approach to the problem of psychoneurosis in childhood', 1,3:194–227; *Medical Women's Federation Newsletter* (1934) 'Psychogenic factors in chronic disease in childhood', July: 1–18; *British Journal of Medical Psychology* (1939) 'The World pictures of children', 18:65–101; *Psychotherapy and Psychosomatics* and the publishers S. Karger A.G., Basel, Switzerland (1956) 'The structure of transference', published in *Acta Psychotherapeutica Psychosomatica e Orthopaedagogica*, 3:502–7.

Thanks are also due to the Margaret Mead Archive, in the Library of Congress, Washington, for making available the correspondence cited in Chapter 5.

Every effort has been made to obtain permission to reproduce copyright material throughout this book. If any proper acknowledgement has not been made, the copyright holder should contact the publishers.

Many people have contributed to the historical research giving rise to Part One of this book by providing reflections, memories, correspondence and other documentation on Margaret Lowenfeld's life and work. Cathy Urwin wishes to express the special debt she owes to the late John Hood-Williams. She would also like to thank other Trustees for support and encouragement, and several of Margaret Lowenfeld's colleagues, former students, friends, and individuals who had reason to be involved with her professionally. These include Ville Andersen, Dermot MacCarthy and Kate MacSorley, who are unfortunately no longer living, and Helen Bender, Hugh Clegg, John Davis, Madeleine Davis, Mollie Dundas, Rhoda Metraux, Gianna Williams, Margarita Wood, Thérèse Woodcock and many others. Special thanks are due to the following, for providing invaluable comments on earlier drafts of Part One or who contributed in various ways to the thoughts behind it: Madeleine Davis, John Davis, the late John Hood-Williams, Martin Richards, Sasha Rosen, Ann Scott, Deborah Thom, Valerie Walkerdine, Margarita Wood, Thérèse Woodcock and Beric Wright.

In moving the book as a whole into production, we want to thank Bob Young of Free Association Books for initial encouragement and inspiration, and Ann Scott, Selina O'Grady and others at Free Association for considerable patience and support through the later stages. Finally, special thanks to Jill Brown, Sally Roberts and Alison Harrison for secretarial assistance and what seemed like endless typing and retyping, and to Elaine Sharland for her careful work in organizing the Margaret Lowenfeld Archive and producing the bibliography.

PART ONE
Margaret Lowenfeld
by Cathy Urwin

1 INTRODUCTION

Given their concern with the history of individuals, the practices of child psychotherapy and related disciplines have paid remarkably little attention to their own history. Within psychoanalysis, of course, there is a strong tradition of returning to Freud in introducing theoretical and technical innovations. But the focus on internal forms of historical inquiry, or on what John Forrester (1986) has described as 'psychoanalytic' histories, has been at the expense of asking what may be prior questions: How was a place produced or carved out for recognizing and treating emotional problems in childhood? How did the social context influence the development of theory and technique? How, too, has the study of emotional dynamics associated with the therapeutic professions become so sharply divided from the so-called normal development studied by academic developmental psychologists?

These questions have become particularly pertinent over the last decade. Within academic developmental psychology, child psychotherapy and psychiatry, psychoanalysis, and allied disciplines, there is a growing interest in intellectual roots and the conditions of their production. Several factors have contributed to this interest. One may be related to a general preoccupation with history and heritage, reflected in films, literature, television and other aspects of popular culture at the present time; this appears to be associated with the marked social, economic and political upheavals of the last ten years (Raphael Samuel, 1987). Another factor may be put down to the age of the traditions of psychoanalysis, psychology and psychiatry. Within psychoanalysis, for example, sufficient time has elapsed to allow for the publication of new biographies, such as Phyllis Grosskurth's (1986) work on *Melanie Klein*, new accounts of influences on Sigmund Freud, such as Frank Sulloway's (1979) *Freud, Biologist of the Mind*, and re-examinations of old controversies, such as Jeffrey Masson's (1985) equally controversial account of Freud's abandonment of the seduction theory (Freud, 1896). Together these works broaden the basis for understanding the evolution of psychoanalysis to include not only the personalities of individual pioneers but also the social and political context of the times, and the effects of rivalries between different disciplines and professional groups.

Where children are the central focus, the evolution of the very idea of what a child is has itself demanded historical investigation. From the extreme form of the thesis that childhood is a social invention, particularly associated with Philippe Ariès's (1962) *Centuries of Childhood*, there has been a widespread acceptance of the idea that childhood itself is a concept with a history. That is, what children are taken to be varies between cultures and across historical epochs (Hoyles, 1979; Pollack, 1983). Within complex Western societies, specialized knowledges on child development have played a particularly important role in producing generally shared assumptions about children's emotional, physical and intellectual needs and notions of normal development. Recent analyses of particular social practices suggest that these effects are achieved through the intimate relation between the production of specialized knowledges and the ways in which institutions associated with such professions as social work, psychiatry, and education function in social regulation and the management of deviance (Donzelot, 1979; Foucault, 1977; Ingleby, 1986; Rose, 1985; Urwin, 1985a; Walkerdine, 1984).

A fourth factor promoting interest in history is more obviously related to the current political and economic climate. Restrictions in available resources and cuts in public expenditure have direct effects on professionals involved in such child-centred professions as child health, education and social work. These professionals include child psychotherapists working in the public sector who may be called upon to justify their existence. Paradoxically, economic restrictions are occurring just as developmental psychology may be beginning to recognize a lack of adequate tools for conceptualizing the contribution of emotional processes to cognitive development and symbolic functioning, raising questions about whether research psychologists can engage productively with, for example, the theory and practice of psychoanalysis (Boston, 1975, 1987; Stern, 1985;

Sylvester Bradley, 1988; Urwin, 1986). The relative reduction in or pressure on existing resources is also occurring in spite of the apparently overwhelming evidence indicating persistent if not increasing emotional problems in children and young people. This is illustrated, for example, in the media coverage given to child abuse, drug dependency, depression and violence inflicted on the self or others.

As Dilys Daws (1987) has pointed out, the profession of child psychotherapy has always been a relatively small one and, perhaps because of this, it has probably always regarded itself as under threat. But whether or not the profession could or should make claims about understanding or ameliorating such manifestations of emotional turmoil cannot be answered by referring to what goes on in the consulting room between child and therapist, or even to what constitutes relief or cure in any absolute or timeless way. If it is recognized that what counts as a problem, or the forms in which emotional problems manifest themselves, vary historically and socially, then it becomes imperative to ask not only what the relation is between socially defined manifestations of unhappiness or maladaptation and the inner world of the child, but also, what role is played by the psychotherapeutic tradition in the social construction of norms of normality and pathology, either independently or through its relation to other agencies, such as medicine, education, social work and the law.

In examining how and why child psychotherapy became possible, the period between the two world wars stands out as particularly significant. At that time a number of social and administrative changes associated with the post-war reconstruction brought the twentieth-century child into the centre of the stage. These changes included developments in medicine and welfare provision aimed at infants, young children and their mothers. Concern over high infant-mortality rate and the health of children had, in fact, become marked at the turn of the century when the poor state of health amongst a large proportion of the population had been demonstrated through the large number of potential recruits who had to be turned down for service in the Boer War because of ill health (Lewis, 1980). This concern was increased after the First World War when, in addition to the considerable loss of young men, the national population was declining (Rose, 1985). The response took the form of active research into infant feeding and nutrition, the widespread dissemination of 'mothercraft' and the instigation of a large number of epidemiological studies. These aimed to demonstrate or uncover links between diseases such as tuberculosis and correlates in the social environment and, ultimately, the family. Within medicine this marked the beginnings of a shift of focus on to community care, providing a point of entry for the philosophies of early detection and prevention (Armstrong, 1983; Lewis, 1980).

Over the same time period, parallel changes were taking place in education. Though compulsory education was introduced in the last century, the educational reforms and expansions promised in the 1918 Education Act occurred in the face of overcrowded conditions in schools and limited economic resources (Simon, 1974). School inspectors, welfare workers and teachers were directly confronted with the problem of how to deal with children who would not easily fit in, and who had earlier been described as the 'potentially imbecile', the 'potentially criminal' and the 'potentially insane' (Warner, 1890; Keir, 1952). It was, of course, in the context of the problem of identifying and possibly treating the child who did not fit that the educational psychology promulgated particularly by Cyril Burt over the first decades of the century found a foothold, giving rise to the concepts of educational subnormality, delinquency and maladjustment (Burt, 1917a, 1917b, 1925; Keir, 1952; Rose, 1985).

These developments occurred at a time when for many individuals in the population a major task was to recover from the disillusion and horrors of the First World War. It was also a time when the implications of the Russian Revolution of 1917 were felt internationally. Preoccupations with Empire and with problems of social control were clearly behind many government interventions. So, too, was the deliberate aim of inculcating positive attitudes towards British democracy (Simon, 1974; Walkerdine, 1984). Yet it was also a time of potentially radical intervention, and of educational reforms directed not just at who should get taught, but what and how. This was the 'New Era' in education, the era of experiments, the foundation of Summerhill, Dartington Hall, Bedales, and the Caldecott community, and the introduction of Montessori's methods. By 1933 the government-commissioned Hadow report had endorsed the 1918 Education Act's insistence on the need for widespread expansion in nursery education (Consultative Committee of the Board of Education, 1933). Though there were substantial

 differences in the positions of the new generation of 'progressives', they shared a commitment to moving away from old-style, rigid and autocratic teaching methods. For many, these were associated with Prussianism or the Germanic tradition, and were seen as playing a causative role in the instigation and course of the First World War. Within this movement, providing environments which would foster emotional as well as intellectual growth became a priority. This was linked, as for Froebel and Pestalozzi, with explicitly libertarian or democratic political ideals, fuelled by a concern to promote world peace. Among the new progressives, many drew explicitly on psychoanalytic assumptions (Selleck, 1972; Walkerdine, 1984).

Though apparently radical, the idea of freeing children from oppression and repression was not entirely lost on a population increasingly exposed to discussions on 'nerves' and coping with stress. Over the first two decades of the twentieth century psychological ideas to some extent became part of everyday parlance. Of particular importance in the British context was the relatively successful treatment of victims of shell shock sustained during the war by, broadly speaking, psychodynamic methods (see Crichton-Miller, 1920). Some success had also been claimed in the elucidation of psychological concomitants to malingering, or the reluctance to return to industrial work as well as to the front. In 1920 Hugh Crichton-Miller, a doctor and psychiatrist by training, established what later became the Tavistock Clinic, London, with the idea of expanding the possibilities of psychodynamic work in peacetime into the wider community. As Dicks (1970) has emphasized, one of the first patients treated in this clinic was, in fact, a child. A children's department was rapidly established, its development fuelled in part by the relative success that could be claimed in treating children exhibiting various forms of antisocial behaviour (Dicks, 1970). By 1927, the first experimental Child Guidance Clinic had been established in this country, and the National Child Guidance Council had been founded (Burke and Miller, 1929; Keir, 1952).

The work of Crichton-Miller and his colleagues and of the Child Guidance Council was theoretically eclectic. For example, many of Crichton-Miller's associates drew their ideas from the British dynamic psychology movement rather than from psychoanalysis *per se*. This movement reflected a shared commitment to the idea of 'deep' strata of the mind and the power of unconscious mental forces which demanded expression, whether in adaptive behaviour or in symptomatology. The membership varied in how far they accepted Freud's tenets, such as the importance of infantile sexuality. Nevertheless, the foundation of the new clinics marked some degree of receptivity to psychoanalytic ideas. By 1926 Melanie Klein had established residence in London. Donald Winnicott began using psychoanalytic ideas within his paediatric practice at around the same time, and Anna Freud arrived in this country as a practising child psychoanalyst in 1938, shortly before the outbreak of the Second World War.

The names of these pioneers in child psychotherapy are well known throughout the Western world. A much less well-known figure is the paediatrician and child psychiatrist, Margaret Lowenfeld. Yet, in the history of child psychotherapy in the United Kingdom, her role was particularly interesting if not of crucial significance. In the inter-war years she was at the spearhead of many of the shifts of emphasis mentioned above, but always maintained a position that was tangential. This eventually allowed her to develop a form of therapy and an approach to children's minds which remains unique. Here her route was not through psychoanalysis, though she was strongly influenced by the 'New Psychology' associated with the shell-shock work mentioned previously. Rather, Lowenfeld's first commitment was to medicine and to the health of children. After training in medicine through the First World War and further wartime experience in Eastern Europe, by the mid 1920s she had moved into epidemiological research and medical practice as a paediatrician. Through this route, she was one of the first to make explicit links between emotional and physical processes as they emerge in the psychosomatic disorders of childhood (Lowenfeld, 1930). In general terms, opening up relations between mind and body was a major influence in widening the acceptance of the importance of psychological processes by the medical profession, contributing to changing the face of modern medicine and psychiatry (Armstrong, 1983; Dicks, 1970). It was while she was engaged in research on infant feeding and the problems of child care that Lowenfeld began to make observations which led her to recognize the significance of children's play. By 1928 she had founded a Children's Clinic for the Treatment and Study of Nervous and Difficult Children, a venture which was both therapeutically and research-oriented.

Following Freud (1920), at this time the child psychoanalysts were also insisting on the importance of children's play. But for Lowenfeld, major influences included the progressive educationists, the early work of Piaget, and of other proponents of the child study movement, or the movement committed to the scientific study of child development (Riley, 1983; Urwin, 1986; Walkerdine, 1984). This movement had flourished throughout Europe and the United States since the turn of the century. It actually began in the last century under the influence of Charles Darwin, whose biographical sketch of his own infant served as a kind of rubric for future researchers (Darwin, 1877; see Urwin, 1986). But by the 1920s the push to discover the regularities of child behaviour, growth and development had been fuelled by the assumption that such knowledge could provide an appropriate basis for management and intervention. The introduction of mothercraft and the rationale behind psychological testing are obvious examples of this.

Initially Lowenfeld shared a commitment to the value of recording behaviour and development according to methods which had proved so successful in the biological sciences. However, her sensitivity to what she was observing rapidly led her to the emotional life of the child. From here she developed a form of psychotherapy which differed in emphasis from psychoanalytic therapies in that play was viewed not only as a medium through which children can work through or master emotional conflicts and confusions, but also as a cognitive process, giving access to the ways in which children think. In therapy itself the emphasis was less on using the emotional relationship between child and therapist than on enhancing the child's ability to organize and make sense of his or her own experience. Similarly, in interpreting symbolic material, Lowenfeld prioritized understanding the meaning from the point of view of the child currently producing it, and stressed the need to suppress pre-existing theoretical prejudices.

Lowenfeld's emphasis was related to what was later described as the belief that 'the child's relation to himself and to the universe provided as important a key to human development as the exploration of interpersonal relationships within the family, which she had got from psychoanalysis' (Margaret Mead, 1974). It also led to distinctive theoretical contributions. These included the identification of a primary form of thought which she later called the 'protosystem'. This exists before words, is multimodal and multidimensional, and cannot be translated into language. She linked it to a fundamental drive to pattern, giving rise to a primitive aesthetic awareness, and regarded the possibility for creative expression as essential both to the health and development of individuals, and to the survival and cohesion of cultural groups.

Central to the development of Lowenfeld's theory and practice was the World technique, in which children used a sand-tray to make imaginary worlds with facsimiles of real life and/or fantasy objects. This technique allowed for the exploration of both the inner world of the child and, simultaneously or on other occasions, the nature of his or her relation to a particular social reality. In its potential for emphasizing the cultural location of the child's symptomatology and experience, again Lowenfeld's approach may be contrasted with that of the psychoanalytic tradition. Though this interest in the cultural location of psychological experience and symbolic functioning was present throughout Lowenfeld's work, it is most obviously illustrated through the use made of the Lowenfeld Mosaic Test. Designed in the early 1920s, this consists of a set of coloured geometric shapes with which the individual child or adult is asked to make 'anything you like' on a flat board. It was used originally as a diagnostic and therapeutic tool in clinical contexts, but after the Second World War, its value in cross-cultural research was also recognized, as a means of exploring characteristic patterns of thought across cultures and historical epochs (Lowenfeld, 1954; Metraux, 1976; Metraux and Abel, 1957, 1975).

During the late 1920s and 30s, when the psychoanalytic tradition became more firmly established in Britain and the Tavistock and other Child Guidance Centres were also expanding, Lowenfeld's clinic was far from unsuccessful, both in recruiting popular support and in demonstrating positive effects of treatment. In 1931, as the clinic shifted premises to cope with an ever-increasing demand, its name was changed to the Institute of Child Psychology. By 1935, Lowenfeld and her colleagues had opened the first child psychotherapy training in this country. After the Second World War psychoanalytically oriented child-psychotherapy trainings were mounted at the Tavistock Clinic and at Anna Freud's Hampstead Child Therapy Clinic. Though her own work had been considerably disrupted during the war, in the late 1940s Lowenfeld made a major contribution to establishing what is now the Association of Child Psychotherapists, the administrative and political organ of the profession. Since that time a Jungian training has been added and, more recently, a child-psychotherapy training mounted under the auspices of the British Association of

Psychotherapy. This training is also psychoanalytic in orientation.

Margaret Lowenfeld died in January 1973. Within six years of her death the Institute of Child Psychology was closed and the training which she had mounted was discontinued. Today, remarkably little is known about a figure whose work and personality were once so central and influential. She left behind her two published books, *Play in Childhood* (London: Gollancz, 1935) and a volume on *The Lowenfeld Mosaic Test* (London: Newman Neame, 1954), and a manuscript on the World technique itself, which was edited and published posthumously under the title *The World Technique* (London: George Allen & Unwin, 1979). She also left behind a number of published and unpublished papers. Part Two of this volume presents a selection of her more theoretically oriented papers, some of them previously unpublished. The selection is intended to supplement, rather than replace, the account of her work and its development given in *The World Technique*. The chapters which follow in the remainder of Part One situate her life and work and describe her intellectual journey, with the dual aims of illustrating the contemporary relevance of historical inquiry and the idea of history on which her approach depends.

2 Growing up through Culture

In the first half of this century for a woman both to sustain a career and break new ground required considerable commitment and force of character. Margaret Lowenfeld has been described by those who remember her as authoritative, awkward, dogmatic and sometimes egocentric, with a determination to go her own way. She could be dismissive of others' opinions and inclined to moods, and yet as easily 'charm the birds down from the trees'. Though personal relations could be difficult, she none the less commanded considerable respect amongst colleagues of differing views for the strength of her commitment, her originality, and even brilliance, though she often found the nature of her ideas almost impossible to express in verbal form.

For those who shared Margaret Lowenfeld's commitments, the force of her personality held her in a position of authority less through domination than what Rachel Pinney, the founder of a method of 'creative listening' to children, has described as 'something more charismatic'. She could be an inspiring teacher, holding the attention of her students less through the logic of well-structured argument than through the sheer rapidity with which rich ideas would be associated into a multifaceted web of connections. Here she would draw clinical experience and observation together with ideas not only from medicine and psychology, but from philosophy, history, the visual and literary arts and anthropology. This reflected a dual commitment to understanding emotional disturbance in childhood and a lifetime's preoccupation with relations between individuals and cultural forms as organizing of human experience. She was also deeply concerned with identifying what could constitute conditions for human liberty.

For those who knew Margaret Lowenfeld more closely the occasionally brusque manner concealed a healthy suspicion of convention for the sake of it, and an area of fragility related to a life which had involved considerable emotional and mental pain. Throughout her life she was often dogged by physical illness, in part related to a tendency to work herself into the ground, and a bit further. Particularly in her later life she could be chaotic and disorganized, needing more businesslike colleagues to keep the administrative and practical side of the work going. For Margaret Lowenfeld herself, sustaining power came through a commitment to relieving unnecessary pain in others, with whom she in part identified, and through what she described herself as a strong if not insatiable intellectual curiosity. All are agreed that she was a highly creative, innovative thinker, with an acute sensitivity to pattern and meanings inherent in cultural forms; and that she was an exceptional clinician with an extraordinary capacity for relating to the most disturbed, difficult and unhappy of troubled children.

Though Margaret Lowenfeld had no children of her own and never married, she had some important and influential relationships. One of the most significant was with the British philosopher, Robin Collingwood (1889–1943), which spanned a large part of the 1920s and early 30s and which was crucial in crystallizing Margaret Lowenfeld's particular approach to development and developmental inquiry. Robin Collingwood is best known for his sustained critique of the realist tradition which dominated Oxford philosophy through the first decades of this century. His thesis was that the truth or otherwise of a proposition can only be ascertained after first establishing the question to which the proposer intended the proposition as an answer. This led him to the position that all philosophical inquiry is necessarily historical, and to a philosophy of history which stresses that it is the science of history which provides the foundation for a science of human affairs. Over the time when Collingwood was working out these ideas he was simultaneously trying to comprehend the significance of political and social events taking place in Europe before the outbreak of the Second World War. His death followed an illness which had dogged his later working life.

For Margaret Lowenfeld, from the late 1940s onwards, relationships with two women stand out as being particularly important. One was a friendship with the anthropologist Margaret Mead, whose work she was well acquainted with already but whom she did not actually meet until the World Federation for Mental Health Conference, held in London in 1948. After this they became friends, collaborating in cross-cultural and other research. One consequence of this was a tempering of some of the hostility and suspicion which Margaret Lowenfeld had held towards psychoanalysis since the end of the 1930s, the reasons for which will become clear. The other relationship was with Ville Andersen, whom she also met in the same year in Copenhagen, Denmark, Ville Andersen's country of residence. Ville Andersen was a Froebel-trained infant-school teacher, at that time running a children's club in Denmark. She had spent some years in business before moving into teaching. She was persuaded to come to England to the Institute of Child Psychology, and was one of the first students to train there after the war. After completing her training, Ville Andersen stayed on in London to work at the clinic as a psychotherapist, research worker and assistant to Margaret Lowenfeld, remaining with her as a colleague, living companion and confidante until the time of Margaret Lowenfeld's death. Since she was not employed in the United Kingdom nationality laws required that she return to Denmark.

Ville Andersen herself died in 1986. However, before this she made available various materials on Margaret Lowenfeld's life and work. These include part of a chronological reconstruction which Margaret Lowenfeld had compiled herself from a childhood diary, correspondence, and her family's recollections. Ville Andersen was also able to share memories of what Margaret Lowenfeld had told her of her childhood and early years. This information confirms the view of many of Margaret Lowenfeld's colleagues that the source of her particular empathy with disturbed children might lie in her own childhood experiences. It is also clear that the eventual direction of her intellectual work had precursors in early life, including her interest in questions of culture and community. Indeed, the conditions of her upbringing necessitated it.

CHILDREN OF TWO NATIONS

Margaret Lowenfeld was born on 4 February 1890 in Lowndes Square, London, as the younger of two sisters. Her sister Helena, born three years earlier, later became well known as Dr Helena Wright, one of the pioneers in the birth-control movement. She played a particularly important role as a doctor centrally involved in the setting up of the Family Planning

Association in the 1930s. As a gynaecologist she continued to contribute to international committees on birth control and to publish more or less controversial material on sexuality and sexual freedom up to the time of her death in 1981.

Although Helena and Margaret were both born in England and were British citizens by choice, neither regarded herself as unambiguously British. Margaret once described herself as 'of two Nations'. Her mother, née Alice Evans, was of Welsh origin, the daughter of a naval captain who came from a nonconformist Protestant background. Margaret's father, Heinz Lowenfeld, was Polish. His family were wealthy landowners and, though many had married out, his forebears were Jewish by race and religion. Heinz himself was the third of four brothers and spent his childhood on a family estate in Chrzanow, near Kraków, in what was then the Austrian part of Poland. His own mother, Rosa, was by all accounts a powerful force within the family, described as an independently minded and unusual woman, who came from an intellectual Prussian family of artists and writers. She had spent a large part of her own childhood in England and spoke fluent German, French, Italian and English, and laid particular emphasis on creating something of a cosmopolitan atmosphere within the household. For example, she encouraged the children's interest in art, music and drama, even putting on plays and concerts at Christmas time for the cousins and other relatives who lived in the vicinity.

Though for a considerable time the Lowenfeld family lived in comfortable prosperity, this was not uninterrupted. In part, the financial stability was affected by military operations taking place as the then divided Poland struggled for the independence that was not achieved until 1918. It was also threatened by Heinz's father's ill health. He eventually died in 1880 after a series of strokes. It then became clear that the sons would have to earn their own living, to avoid selling off the estate.

It was soon after this that Heinz came to England. While his three brothers remained in Europe, Heinz arrived in London with very little money, no particular training and very few contacts. One of these was his future wife Alice, who had stayed with the family in the previous year, convalescing after illness. The trip had been suggested to Alice's father by Rosa Lowenfeld's brother, who worked in the British Museum. Alice was then seventeen, Heinz six years older. According to Barbara Evans's (1984) biography of Helena Wright, which is to date the only published biographical account of this rather remarkable family, Alice was strongly infatuated with Heinz, and fell in love totally and uncritically. They were married in 1884.

By this time Heinz had changed his name to Henry, and proved remarkably successful at making money, buying and selling almost anything that could be bought cheaply and sold at a profit. Initially he dealt in Swiss cuckoo clocks and jewellery, but other projects soon followed. These included setting up a business for brewing and marketing a non-alcoholic beverage called Kops Ale. Eventually he tired of this, and moved on to other ventures, including the buying and managing of hotels and eventually London theatres. In 1893 he acquired the lease of the Prince of Wales Theatre, held a financial stake in the Lyric Theatre and in 1900 built the Apollo Theatre as his own. As with many of his projects, by 1904 he had somewhat lost interest in this, putting in a manager but retaining ownership until 1920.

This financial success meant that within six years Henry had recouped the losses of the Chrzanow estate, bought out all his brothers, and established an annuity for his mother. As sole owner he became responsible for the Chrzanow outgoings. This necessitated frequent trips to Poland. As young children Margaret and Helena would often go too, travelling the vast distances across Europe through several countries by train. The conditions at home in England also changed dramatically as luxury goods, art treasures, servants and other accoutrements associated with affluence were acquired to keep pace with the rise in social status and position of the family in London society. However, these external signs of progress masked considerable tension at home and in the marriage. According to Barbara Evans (1984), from the outset there was a considerable distance between Alice's background and Henry's and, despite Alice's devotion, they had relatively little in common. On the other hand, Alice appears to have had considerable social ambition, was pleased to be the wife of an important public figure, and in 1897 gained the satisfaction of being presented at court. Since servants were recruited in large numbers, including footmen and a butler as well as a Swedish cook and other indoor servants, Alice's chief occupations in the early years included collecting cuttings of Henry's achievements or acquisitions, and playing the role of a society hostess. Her Thursday afternoon 'at-homes' became a well-known London social event, and she was noted in society magazines for her indefatigable attentions as a hostess and excellent taste (Evans, p. 21).

 In Margaret Lowenfeld's own reconstruction of this period,

mentioned previously, she gives a note of her mother's activities when she herself was nearly ten years old. Her mother 'Entertained a good deal, giving musical at-homes at which I handed round ices'. At the same time she also noted her mother's new interest in spiritualism. 'There always seem to be seances going on in the house.' Otherwise, Helena and Margaret were seeing relatively little of their mother, and spent much time in the care of the servants. If social activities permitted, they would lunch with their mother and see her for half an hour at 4 o'clock.

This kind of scenario would not, of course, have been untypical of wealthy families in the late Victorian era. But it is clear that Margaret felt the lack of contact between herself and her mother particularly acutely. As a child she was often ill, spending long hours in bed at the top of the house, alone. Later she recalled having night terrors and screaming fits and not being able to break the habit of sucking her thumb, and instances the lingering pain of her mother drifting in in a silk dress to tell her that 'someone' would be up later (Ville Andersen, personal communication). Her mother's exasperated, 'Is that child ill *again*?' was a criticism which haunted her.

In addition to dealing with her loneliness, Margaret also felt that she was constantly being compared with Helena, who appears to have been the more resilient of the two children, as well, of course, as being older. As for her relation to her father, as a young child Margaret admired him greatly, though surviving letters suggest a rather wistful idealization characteristic of relations at a distance. Eventually she took from him a lifelong interest in the arts and in collecting things, and shared with him a tendency to want to move on to new projects once success had been demonstrated. Through her father she also became strongly attached to Poland and to the family establishment there, though the long journeys travelling by night, the shunting of trains in the dark, were described by her in later life as if they held a nightmarish quality. Once in Poland, on the fringes of family activity, with people talking in foreign languages, one gets the impression that the little girl was alternately confused or frightened, or powerless to make herself understood. Apparently grandmother Rosa was particularly important in noticing the child's curiosity and giving her credit for it. 'I wonder why . . .' Margaret would often say – 'What is it that you would like to know now, little one?' was Rosa's reply, reaching for the child to include her (Ville Andersen, personal communication).

Later, like Rosa, Margaret herself became fluent in four languages. Nevertheless she held that a scepticism about the adequacy of language as a medium for expressing emotion or clarifying thought stemmed from these childhood experiences of confusion or frustration, when there was so much talk and so little comprehension. Many people who knew her felt that her particular sensitivity to or empathy with disturbed children stemmed from her own emotional isolation in an environment in which materially she was very well catered for. One might also speculate that this contributed to her emphasis in therapy on harnessing adaptive processes inherent in children themselves rather than on reworking past relations with parents. But Margaret's scepticism about the reliability of parents was no doubt exacerbated by her own parents' separation and divorce, which took place in her early teens, the aftermath extending over a number of years.

The precipitating cause of the parents' separation was Henry's infidelity. According to Barbara Evans (1984), Henry had told Alice when they first married that fidelity was not to be part of the contract, that he might keep mistresses in the continental fashion, but that his wife would never meet one of them. No affair would last longer than a year because after that it would become something else. Initially the arrangement appeared to work well on Henry's side, the women involved mainly being actresses associated with his theatrical interests. The storm broke when Margaret was eight, when a particular affair came to her mother's attention and there was the first talk of a separation. Although the parents were reconciled Margaret noted that, by the following year, the day nursery had been permanently arranged as her father's bedroom, and that her mother was putting more and more time and energy into spiritualism. She had also started her own business, buying and selling bicycle saddles. The marriage finally broke over an affair with a woman called Frania Permutter who was, in fact, Henry's widowed Polish cousin. Henry was serious enough to approach Alice for a divorce. This Alice refused, declaring divorce a sin and wanting to try once more to make the marriage work. Although Henry at first agreed to this, he changed his mind. By the end of 1911 he had filed a nullity suit through the Viennese courts, basing his claim on the grounds that he was a Jew and Alice a Gentile. Henry eventually married Frania in 1902 as soon as the nullity proceedings had gone through.

In the meantime, the distress and confusion that Alice and the girls were thrown into was, of course, considerable. Alice was immediately ill, one of a series of illnesses which recurred again and again over the following years, particularly around times of negotiation with Henry. On the children's part, there was the more or less inevitable pressure to take sides. Margaret noted of herself as a desperately upset eleven-year-old, 'I write my mind to Papa.' At that time antagonism between Helena and her father was, perhaps, stronger. For example, reacting to the most trivial altercations which were simultaneously taking place between the parents, such as Henry's lawyer contacting Alice and asking if she wished him to raise his hat to her if they met, Helena on one occasion met him while riding in the park and hit him over the head with her horsewhip. The legitimacy of the nullity suit was, of course, contested. Indeed, on Henry's marriage to Frania, the press showed considerable interest in whether or not he had committed bigamy. Alice had no alternative but to instigate proceedings for divorce in London, to establish her daughters' legitimacy and protect her own position. The divorce finally went through in the autumn of 1903, leaving Alice with a large settlement and the custody of the two girls.

Based largely on Helena's retrospective view, Barbara Evans's (1984) account presents Alice as a weak woman, immature and unable to accept Henry's departure without anything other than a sense of bitterness. This was accompanied by strong demands on her children that they should make up for her sense of abandonment and emotional turmoil (Evans, p. 45). From Margaret's reconstruction it is clear that Alice attempted to cling to her daughters through the divorce and the ensuing years, and that Margaret in particular was in some ways bound up with her. Alice would become ill after some altercation or failed negotiation with Henry, to be followed by illness in Margaret. On the other hand, Alice herself made some vitally important decisions affecting the girls' future life. One of the most significant of these concerned their education. Here, Alice held as progressive ideas as Henry, if not more so.

Both girls began their education at kindergarten, attending the Froebel Educational Institution in Talgarth Road, West Kensington. This is said to have been the first Froebel school in England (Evans, 1984). In keeping with the emphasis on fresh air and the importance of the creative use of the body, they had also had a string of governesses since early childhood, whose major responsibilities were to take them skating, to dancing classes and to gym, although one taught Polish for a year. At the time of the divorce, Margaret was still attending the Church of England High School in Graham Street, London, which she had attended since the age of eight. But Helena had moved on to Cheltenham Ladies' College. Alice had negotiated this move in July 1901 with the then headmistress, Miss Dorothea Beale. In choosing this school, Alice was selecting an institution then run by one of the pioneers of women's education who, along with her colleague Mary Buss, had been responsible for laying bare restrictions on opportunity for middle and upper class women imposed by the private educational system. For Helena, who had hitherto found school trying if not difficult, the move to Cheltenham Ladies' College was a tremendous relief, providing her with an environment with relatively few rules in which she could enjoy lessons for the first time. It also freed her from the difficult home situation (Evans, 1984).

No doubt Alice always intended to send Margaret to Cheltenham too, which she did when the latter was twelve years old. But this was preceded by a year of Margaret and her mother living alone together, apart from servants, in the house in Lowndes Square. Alice had borrowed money to buy the property outright shortly before the divorce. But with dwindling rather than unlimited means, she decided to move to Cheltenham so that the two girls could go to school daily. Up to now, Helena had been living in a school boarding-house and the move, to Oakfield in Cheltenham, did not please her. She was already consciously oppressed by her mother's problems and voiced her anger. Margaret, of course, was three years younger and made of rather different stuff, reacting in contrasting ways. At home without Helena in many of the periods of most disruption between the parents she was also exposed to the direct effect of her mother's illnesses and to the more or less constant reverberations of negotiations and failed negotiations and trips up to town. As she noted in her diary, '1903, November. Mother perpetually moving'.

Once the move had taken place, Alice set about trying to establish herself locally with various social projects, running events for the local Conservative Party. She also aimed to model her household on something like the Polish pattern, attempting to patent her home-made horsehair lotion and to keep bees. Whereas Helena reacted with disgust and disdain at these new projects, Margaret developed a phobia of bees. Differences between the two girls' reactions encouraged their parents to use them differently. For instance, over a period of several years Henry appeared to express his annoyance at Helena by lavishing presents or sums of money on Margaret while giving Helena short shrift. However, it is clear that, like Helena, Margaret felt the school at Cheltenham released her in many ways and opened new doors. Like Helena she was particularly inspired by a Miss Margery Reid, a teacher who was in charge of the school museum and whose father had been a contemporary of Wallace and Darwin. Apart from helping her in the museum, this relationship extended to helping her in her own garden on Saturday mornings, Margaret noting in her diary for March 1905 'Helena's and my friendship with and rivalry over Miss Reid' as one of the significant events of the month.

Over this time contact between Margaret and her father persisted, while there was relatively little contact between him and Helena. Margaret was now preparing for her senior Oxford examination, which she took in July 1905, doing particularly well in English literature. The latter success seems perhaps surprising, given her later decision to do medicine and her apparent preference for visual as opposed to literary art. What is also interesting was that in her diary she noted that at the time of the examination she was 'very tired'. This was not relieved by a holiday trip to Holland. Just before the start of the new term and Margaret's matriculation year, a crisis was precipitated after Henry returned a pot of honey sent by Alice, along with a note saying he was 'not at home'. On the following day Margaret was taken by her mother to Dr Cargill, a woman doctor, who prescribed rest. A fortnight later, on 9 October, Margaret noted in her diary 'I break down'. Although Dr Cargill ordered a month without school work, her condition deteriorated. Helena stepped in to impress her mother with the seriousness of the situation and Henry was contacted. He sent money to pay for a journey of some sort at Alice's request. In the meantime, though writing back to her father on 26 October, Margaret took herself, alone, to Dr Cargill, and described the experience as 'my first move of revolt'. Margaret clearly developed some trust in Dr Cargill, but this did not totally ameliorate the situation. Where Margaret's father's panacea for all appears to have been money, Alice's was travel. Margaret was taken on a global trip to the West Indies, returning in time for Christmas, but she was intermittently still 'sick' over the rest of that holiday.

If Margaret's breakdown in 1905 was an indication of a crisis in her emotional–mental state, the New Year brought various attempts at self-restitution. One of the most significant of these was the discovery of religion, or what she described later as her first primitive conversion. In January 1906, she joined a newly formed Christian Society at Cheltenham which later became affiliated to the Student Christian Movement, and began attending Bible classes regularly. At the beginning of February, just before her sixteenth birthday and the age at which children of divorced parents could choose which parent they wished to live with, Margaret's father wrote to her asking her to live with him. Margaret refused.

By this time Helena had made her first attempt at matriculating. She had apparently decided on doing medicine when she was only six years old (Evans, 1984). Her mother did not block this move, but none the less planned that at the age of eighteen she should 'come out' before beginning her training. Helena fell in with these plans. Being introduced at court necessitated renting a house in town, Margaret and Alice travelling up and down to 84 Eltham Road in West London. Although social events were organized for Helena's benefit, they also increased Alice's opportunities for social contacts. Amongst her male friends was Frank Quicke, whom she later married. In the meantime, Margaret increased her activities with the Student Christian Movement with furious enthusiasm. By September that year, she noted in her diary, 'For the first time papa had no letter from me for his birthday.' However, links were not severed. By the beginning of the term Alice had decided to let the house at Oakfield, leading to correspondence between Alice and Henry about houses. A few days later, Alice was suddenly very ill in the night, choking, though she was better the next morning without treatment. In her notes, Lowenfeld suggested a diagnosis of 'Globus hystericus'. A week later Margaret herself was ill and was attended by Dr Cargill. At that time, Alice and Henry began discussing the disposal of income from trust after the parents' deaths, Henry insisting on giving £750 per annum to Margaret and £250 to Helena. Four days later Margaret broke down again.

Over the rest of the term, Margaret made various attempts to go back to the College on half time. Henry, as usual, sent Alice money for Christmas presents and the holiday. In spite of the divorce, the girls were still encouraged to make more or less annual trips to Poland, and to keep in touch with Henry's brother Willi and various cousins. Alice would generally go too.

Soon after they came home from a trip in January 1907, Frank Quicke arrived to take Alice to the local hospital ball, staying over for several days. Frank discussed marrying Alice with Helena. In turn Helena discussed it with Margaret. Though neither of the girls particularly liked Frank, 'Both felt that if they wanted it we had no right to interfere.' Within a few days Frank proposed to Alice, who at first refused, but then accepted. The engagement was announced on 3 February, the day that Margaret's birthday was kept. Alice, however, refused Frank's request that they should marry at once, and he 'rushed out of the house without hat or coat'. Though he apparently relented, and was pacified by Helena on his return, Alice remained in a 'fearful state of nerves'. As Margaret noted, 'Mother v. unhappy came to my room and took me in to sleep with her and said she did not want to marry Frank. I too tired to take much in. v. confused.'

In spite of Alice's ambivalence, the wedding took place sooner rather than later, on 15 March 1907. However, far from improving the situation, their mother's marriage to Frank made things more difficult for the girls, particularly since there was now a tendency for Frank to be drawn into taking sides. Helena, too, began to show the strain. By the end of the summer of 1907 she was herself on the verge of a breakdown. After much discussion between Margaret and Henry, the latter agreed to pay everything for Margaret and Helena to have six months' quiet. Margaret wrote of her mother's reactions, 'she is very unhappy and weeps'. Henry wanted to take the further initiative of settling an annual income on each of his daughters, but Alice refused because she thought that that would mean their leaving her. Although eventually Alice found a house for the girls, Henry refused to go along with her suggestion, leading to further argument. By the end of the year Frank was apparently drinking heavily and Alice was ill or crying most of the time.

Fortunately, by February 1908, Henry had found an acceptable second home for the girls for six months, at 'Sultanpore', Little Brickhill. It consisted of a small house with a garden on the Woburn estate. There the agreement was that the girls were to have six months' respite aided by their father's money. They were accompanied by 'Smuttles', originally a nurse, who had stayed longer than most of the family entourage, as well as village servants. In spite of the relative isolation, this arrangement apparently worked extremely well for Helena. Unsurprisingly, she was now more reconciled to what she had considered her father's treachery. Alice took this shift of loyalty badly, as she did the whole Little Brickhill episode. She eventually refused to visit them in Little Brickhill and tried to press them into choosing between living with her or their father. At this time Henry attempted to persuade Alice to allow the girls to live alone permanently, but failed. Although Margaret's health appears to have been relatively stable, in May 1908 she was taken by her mother to the well-known gynaecologist and eugenist, Dr Mary Scharlieb, who diagnosed a retroverted uterus. This was replaced in position by Dr Frances Stoney, the woman doctor who had attended Helena during her own mental breakdown. Frances Stoney was to have an important influence on both girls.

By June of that year, they had returned to Cheltenham, but preparations were already made for their final departure from school. In September, Helena celebrated her twenty-first birthday, and in the beginning of October she took up her place at the London School of Medicine for Women to study to be a doctor. She could have gone earlier, but returned to Cheltenham Ladies' College to take the pre-science course, which enabled her to enter medical school in the second year. Alice sold Oakfield, and bought a house in Hounslow which was to be the family's next home. In the meantime trouble brewed between Alice and Frank, who told her that she must choose between her daughters and him. Margaret's health deteriorated again, and she began to have nightmares. Shortly after Helena's start at medical school, 'A worse than usual nightmare sent me to sleep in mother's room.' Dr Stoney intervened, and tried to persuade Alice that Margaret's health demanded that she should be allowed to get away from her family, and that the two young women should live alone. Alice alternately wept or would not believe it, while Margaret continued to have nightmares and periods of illness. Eventually, a bargain was struck in February 1909, such that Margaret was to remain with her mother for a trial period of one year, after which time she could be 'released of all duty' towards her mother and would be allowed to make up her own mind about whether to live apart from her parents.

Margaret reluctantly agreed to postpone leaving. She started taking elocution lessons and a few classes at Bedford College for Ladies, London University, which she had begun but then broke off in the autumn of the preceding year. By March she had added fencing to the list of occupations. Alice and Frank were continually quarrelling, and Margaret became prone to fits of vomiting. In March that year, a row between Helena and Frank prompted Frank to walk out until Alice went and fetched him. In June the move to Hounslow was completed. The summer of that year was punctuated by the customary trip abroad. Helena and Margaret met their father in Trieste and later joined Alice and Frank in Venice. As usual, Alice had periods of illness including a suffocation fit on returning home to Hounslow. By the end of October, Margaret was noting, 'I seem to have spent a good deal of this time being ill and in bed,' and by 4 December, 'I fainted in the skating rink.'

By the turn of the New Year, 1910, it was finally settled that Helena and Margaret should live alone. Henry took over the lease of 49 Great Cumberland Place, London, a five-storey mansion near Marble Arch. To support what was socially an unusual arrangement, he engaged as chatelaine Lady Alice Leslie, who was then about sixty, an aristocrat and eighteenth in line to the throne. Lady Alice proved very popular with the girls. They were allowed to get on with their own studies and other pursuits, Helena bicycling every day to the hospital and Margaret continuing to attend classes at Bedford College. She took her matriculation in July of that year and failed in Latin. Her mathematics, apparently, also needed polishing. She retook the examination in January 1911, and achieved first-class results as she approached her twenty-first birthday.

MEDICAL TRAINING THROUGH THE FIRST WORLD WAR

By this time Margaret had also decided to study medicine. What led to the decision is not entirely clear, in that she did not seem to have had the childhood conviction of Helena, who had apparently decided on this career at the age of six (Evans, 1984). There may have been something inevitable involved in 'following Helena'. Nevertheless, Margaret's interest in science and studying more broadly had been fired at school. Along with horse riding, this interest was very important to her in sustaining her through the troubled times after her mother's move to Cheltenham (Ville Andersen, personal communication). More specifically, she regarded her contact with Dr Cargill as highly formative, if not life-saving. Her contacts with the Student's Christian Movement inspired her adolescent idealism and had involved her in active campaigning on behalf of the sick and destitute. Her own frequent illnesses perhaps also entered into her personal choice.

In providing the daughters with their particular education at Cheltenham Ladies' College, Alice clearly made their choice of a professional career possible, and made no objection to their pursuit of medicine. This was in spite of the considerable social aspirations which she felt for them. Henry initially appeared to accept the decision indulgently, but had considerable difficulty in adjusting to the idea that he had two 'modern' daughters bent on following a profession. Henry clearly recognized their aptitude. Later he was wont to say that 'Madge has the brains and originality, but Helena the capability': that is, Margaret was an innovator, Helena an ingenious adaptor of the original ideas of others (Evans, 1984, p. 183). However, he had hoped that they would marry into the world of banking, bypassing the issue of a career altogether, let alone medical training which at that time still presented tremendous obstacles to women. Given that neither persuasion nor outright opposition would work to shift their determination, in 1911, before Margaret actually began, Henry made a final attempt to loosen the hold of this ambition. Stressing that it was important that they knew what they would be giving up, he extracted from them the promise that they would each do a 'London season', the agreement being that they could pursue medicine if after this conventional social life did not satisfy them; in other words, if they had resisted the attractions of marriage. Helena and Margaret kept to the bargain, though it did little to sway their determination. It also had its uses. For instance Evans (1984) notes that over this year Helena and her father got to know each other better and a new closeness developed between them.

Eventually Henry reluctantly accepted that his elder daughter was not to be dissuaded and that, for the present at least, Margaret should be allowed to go her own way. Henry's business interests were taking up more time abroad and in the winter of 1912 he and Frania moved to live permanently in Paris, a move which was also considered better for his health, which was now less stable. At this time Margaret, following Helena, was finishing her first year at the London School of Medicine for Women, associated with the Royal Free Hospital and recently affiliated to the University of London. This was the first teaching hospital for women open in the United Kingdom and, in the Lowenfelds' time, the only possible place of training in the country. Unlike Helena, Margaret took the pre-science course at the hospital rather than at school and 'came down in biology' at the first attempt, in July 1912. She retook it, and passed in

February 1913, but had already been allowed to begin the Intermediate medical course, which included anatomy and physiology.

In addition to pursuing medical training, Margaret remained actively involved in the Student Christian Movement. She had become a close friend of Rena Carswell, whom she had met on a summer camp in 1906, and who was now the SCM Secretary for women's colleges. Helena had also joined and become very active in the SCM and in the summer of 1913 went as a delegate to the World Student Christian Federation meeting at Lake Mohonk in the USA. This was one of a set of experiences which eventually led Helena to take up medical work in China. During the conference she met Jim Wallace, a Canadian student, and triumphantly announced her engagement to him, even taking him to Paris to meet her father. However, the engagement lasted less than a fortnight. In November of that year, Henry summoned Margaret. Perhaps fuelled by his disappointment over Helena, a long struggle ensued about Margaret's wish to study medicine. In the end Margaret persuaded him to allow her to continue until she had finished her Intermediate course. But by that time events way outside the family's control had intervened.

Margaret took her Intermediate MB examination in July 1914, and passed. That summer Margaret and Helena were due to travel to Bayreuth for the festival. Henry was already in Marienbad taking one of his regular cures. On 31 July they went to Somerset House for passports, and on 1 August Helena applied to Thomas Cook's for tickets (the idea being, on Henry's suggestion, to meet him in time for the *Parsifal* in Marienbad), only to be told that no tickets were being issued. The next day, Germany declared war against Russia, and on 5 August England declared war against Germany – the outbreak of the First World War. Had they bought tickets a few days earlier, Helena and Margaret would have been trapped in Europe for the duration of the war. As it was Henry, holding an Austrian passport, returned to Austrian Poland where he was to base himself for the next four years, though his daughters were able to meet him occasionally in neutral Switzerland.

Though debarred from returning to Paris, Henry was far from inactive during the war years. He established a major antiques collection in Vienna, profiting from the confusion of the war years. But in addition, travelling between Vienna, Kraków and Chrzanow, he became the leader of the Society for the Foundation of Polish Legions. In Kraków he set up 'Zalal' or the 'Society to Help the People'. Under his direction, this society bought clothing and scarce wartime food such as sugar and jam, mainly from Russia, and sold it to the rich at 30 percent above market price, and to the poor at 100 percent below this figure. One of the uses made of the large profits was to extend the boarding section of the high school in Kraków and to establish bursaries (Evans, 1984).

The increase in Henry's active involvement with Polish affairs proved important to Margaret later on. In the meantime, indicative of the changed relationship, it was to Helena that Henry wired, in October 1914, 'Manage all my businesses.' By this time this included the management of the Apollo Theatre, the domestic and other expenses of 49 Great Cumberland Place, and the financial support of three of Henry's ex-mistresses. This administration apparently came easily to Helena, who qualified in 1915 and took up her first of the three required training positions in the Outpatients Department of the Camden Town branch of Hampstead General Hospital.

As for Margaret, if she had had any serious qualms about continuing medicine, the war instantly scotched them. At that time some adaptations were made in the training of women doctors in order that they should be able to take the place of men who were required for the armed forces. Though she had only just completed her Intermediate, Margaret started work at the Royal Free Hospital as a doctor in November 1914. Though Christmas of that year was spent in Hounslow, in the summer of 1915 Helena and Margaret managed a trip to Lucerne to meet their father. In the meantime, Margaret had some experience of working in surgery and casualty wards in the Royal Free Hospital, and in October of that year she held a short placement at Great Ormond Street, the well-known children's hospital. By November of that year she had taken up an assistant position at Endell Street Military Hospital, which counted as her second surgery post. By January 1917 she had taken her Conjoint Surgery Examination, but failed in the practical component. In April that year she took her Conjoint Medicine and Mid Examination, and passed.

As for most medical students, there were times when Margaret found the training exhausting. But medical training, and the particular experiences associated with working long hours in a military hospital in wartime, were not her only occupations. Her contact with the SCM, and with Rena

Carswell in particular, had continued. In October 1915, Rena sailed to India, and in May 1916 when one of Rena's colleagues arrived from India, Margaret became his temporary private secretary. She was involved in organizing a campaign to raise money and recruits to support Rena and the Indian YWCA. She eventually held a position as Commanding Officer for foreign women within the organization.

Though she had taken special coaching for surgery, perhaps the failure or perhaps the general exhaustion disenchanted her, and she decided not to retake surgery then. Her diary indicates that her first serious forays into the study of philosophy began at that time. In the meantime, Helena had announced her engagement to Peter Wright, who had 'appeared' in the spring of 1916. He was a strikingly good-looking young army captain, an RAMC officer on sick leave from a casualty clearing station in France, who had been sent to take up light duties at Bethnal Green Military Hospital where Helena was now working. In the event Peter was invalided out of the army, and he and Helena were married in August 1917. Margaret herself had started work again on surgery by the end of 1917, retaking and passing her examination in January 1918. By this time, she had obtained the minimal qualifications entitling her to practise medicine as a Member of the Royal College of Surgeons (MRCS) and Licentiate of the Royal College of Physicians (LRCP). Although she had completed work for her MBBS (Bachelor of Medicine, Bachelor of Science) she did not in fact take the examination. Her work was required immediately, owing to a shortage of doctors. She took up a post at the South London Women's Hospital as house surgeon and, according to her notes, 'worked nineteen hours a day'. She left this post in April 1918, becoming more involved in family activities. Helena's first child, Beric, was born in June of that year, and a month or so later the Wrights travelled to Land's End for a holiday. A decision was made to pack up 49 Great Cumberland Place for letting, the organization of this being Margaret's responsibility, though quite what her plans were at this point is not clear. At some point in the summer she cracked her head, suffering delayed concussion. She went on holiday with friends to a farm on Dartmoor but the effects of the injury remained. She was taken to a nursing home in Penzance, where she collapsed completely. Eventually she joined the Wrights at Carbis Bay, staying on there after their return to London.

It was while Margaret was staying in Carbis Bay that

Armistice was declared, in November 1918. Within the month this news was followed by the arrival of a message for Margaret from the family village in Poland. The message consisted of a desperate plea for help from the people from the family estate and surrounding locality, where the destruction and hardship caused by the war had been considerable. It was brought by W. R. Rose, who later became Professor of Slavonic Languages, London University. He was himself a refugee, recently released from internment. Whether the request was initiated by Margaret's father, or from the villagers who knew her or who had heard of her, is not clear. But in any event there was a marked congruence between the request and the kind of direction Margaret's work was already taking, as her contribution to the war effort had involved an increasing commitment to overseas aid, originally through her support of the Student Christian Movement.

FURTHER EXPERIENCE OF WAR

By December 1918, Margaret had decided to go to Poland. Once the decision had been made, the negotiations required were considerable. One difficulty was that Rose had already returned to Poland. The obvious route in was through her father, whom she joined in Switzerland in April 1919. However, by this time relations between Henry and Frania were particularly strained over the arrival of a Polish schoolteacher, a Miss Gadomski, who had been Henry's constant companion on his return to Chrzanow at the outbreak of the war. Eventually Frania was displaced by Miss Gadomski, whom the family had rechristened 'Gnaus', or 'The Serpent', and sometimes the 'Black One'. While Frania returned to Warsaw, Henry set Miss Gadomski up in a small cosmetics business in Paris. To Helena and Margaret it was recognizably a situation of history repeating itself. But to the Lowenfeld family, back in Poland, Miss Gadomski was a simple, modest woman, genuinely attached to Henry. Though thirty-five years younger than Henry, she remained with him until his death in 1931. Nor did she inherit a vast fortune from him. As he himself had anticipated, with his flamboyant and long blessed approach to financial affairs, the good fortune could not last for ever and he was caught by the devaluation of money in Germany and Austria after the war. Towards the end of his life, against Helena's advice, he had invested the bulk of his assets in Poland and was forced to live in comparative poverty. The daughters inherited a small amount through the estate of their mother, who died in 1930. But on Henry's death, as certified by probate, 'the net value of the personal estates amounts to nil' (Evans, 1984, p. 87).

In the meantime, in 1919, Margaret secured entry into Poland not through her father but via contacts gained in her philanthropic work with student organizations and through her medical training. Initially bogged down in Paris for the lack of a guide and interpreter, by mid August she had reached Warsaw as a medical officer with a League of Friends Typhus Mission. From there she travelled to Kraków and Chrzanow, to the family estate and village from which the request for help had originally come. Meeting appalling dereliction and despondency, she put the *gartenhaus* of the estate straight and became particularly involved in working with local children who had become orphaned and with refugees. Making new contacts, she organized the collection of supplies, even arranging a Christmas feast and a concert in the manner of the old days when Rosa had managed the social activities of the estate.

None the less the work was hard, exhausting and at times dispiriting. Illness intervened, as typhoid, dysentery, cholera, tuberculosis and epidemic influenza raged all round her. There were no medical stores to speak of and travel was difficult if not impossible. In addition to the relief work in the village, her position with the Typhus Mission meant moving to and from Warsaw and leaving many projects unfinished. In April 1920 she left Warsaw for Paris, feeling ill and wretched, and returned to London to buy stores and raise money for drugs and apparatus necessary for a return visit. In May 1920 she went to Truro to the Community of the Epiphany and made her first confession, before returning to London and later Oxford to promote links between Oxford and Polish universities, in her capacity as an officer in the SCM, now linked to the YMCA. In the meantime, following the enthusiasm generated by the 1918 settlement, an outburst of Polish nationalism led to skirmishes across the borders. In retaliation a Bolshevik army invaded Poland. This marked the outbreak of the war between Poland and Russia, which continued until 1921. Margaret noted in her diary – 'finish and arrange everything so that it is all right if I never come back'.

By September 1920, she had returned to Poland, first to Chrzanow and then to Warsaw, where the conditions demanded the creation of a medical department specifically concerned with prisoners of war, and in which Margaret was in charge of sanitation. Her job also involved general welfare work for troops along a battlefront extending over some four hundred miles. By January 1921 she had acquired an additional role dealing with thousands of demobilized Polish students and refugees from Russia who required food and clothing. A European Student Relief Organization was started to which Margaret became secretary. Though at times the medical work and student work pulled in opposite directions, eventually the roles were co-ordinated with the arrival of both money and a secretary for the student relief work. Margaret began a report on the student work, which she eventually left in the charge of the secretary as the work was now running relatively smoothly. Margaret resigned her post with the student organization to concentrate on her medical work, and on social and family obligations in Chrzanow.

In future years, Margaret Lowenfeld stressed the formative effect of her experience in the Russo–Polish war, both in leading her into developing psychotherapeutic method, and on the particular form of her theoretical orientation (Lowenfeld, *The World Technique*, 1979, p. 1). One account, repeated in her post-Second World War lectures for the benefit of students, first appeared in a public context in 1948 in a paper reprinted as the second paper in Chapter 10. Another appears in an unpublished history, 'The Institute of Child Psychology', written by Margaret Lowenfeld in 1969. This describes how, in the course of delivering supplies to institutions run by the Polish Government, she and her colleagues were required to visit a stone house, which received surviving children brought in cattle trucks that had been slowly moving towards Warsaw, the dead being thrown out along the way. Apparently, the house contained about forty boys between the ages of ten and fourteen. As she understood the situation, 'these children had lost everything a human child can have, language, nationality, family, "roots", and anyone with whom to share their childhood experiences' (Lowenfeld, 1969, p. 1). Because of other demands of the work, she had had to move on. Sometime later, however, this house was again on her list. In her account Margaret Lowenfeld described, with shock, her discovery that the children had not only survived, but organized themselves. She remembered a pleasant interior, the addition of furniture, even locks on the door, made by the children and adults in charge. Interestingly, she also recalled the addition of a theatre which the children had made, with footlights, scenery and costumes, and a cheerful sense of community. She asked if she could stay a while to watch. Without psychiatric experience at the time, after a day's observation, 'unlikely as it seemed . . . a substantial number of the boys I had been watching were cheerful and normal' (p. 2). To her account she added, as a question that for her demanded explanation, 'How could this have come about?'

In citing this question from 1948 onwards Margaret Lowenfeld was retrospectively justifying her quest for an explanation or theory of psychic processes which could account for how individual children were enabled to survive such traumatic experiences. She contrasted her position with one which she suggested stemmed from current psychoanalytic thinking: that early experiences had potentially devastating effects on psychic development. From her understanding of this thinking, not only would it have predicted that many of the children she had encountered would not have survived but, as important, it could not account for the reverse; that some children, if not many, do cope with quite appalling circumstances. What is it in the human psyche that makes this possible? But her question also has a social dimension, in that it is directed too at the survival of a social group and its ability to challenge adversity and muster resources under conditions which were later recognized as amongst the worst in Europe, everywhere tipping the nation towards extreme fragmentation if not despair. Here, Lowenfeld also later recognized, the exposure to the horrors of war, coupled with the effects of being called on to play numerous roles, opened within her something like the analytic experience of the therapist in training.

> That is, it opened doors on to an interior world I would not otherwise have reached. Later, when reflecting upon this experience, I realized that living in a constant atmosphere of fear, and with a lack of any overall direction, is of the essence of the experience of unhappy children and the black misery of prisoners of war is very like the depressions of infancy. (Lowenfeld, 1979, p. 2)

Bruno Bettelheim (1960) has drawn similar parallels, in describing how his experience in a concentration camp during the Second World War eventually contributed to his psychotherapeutic work with children. But what of the immediate impact of Margaret Lowenfeld's experiences, when she returned to

England in 1921 in her early thirties? In July 1921 Margaret left Poland, travelling back through Berlin. In her role as representative from Poland, she went to the annual SCM conference at Swanwick to report on the work. There she found it impossible to convey to her audience, in words, the extensiveness and nature of the atrocities she had seen. This difficulty, she later stressed, enhanced her view that verbal language is inadequate for expressing the full depths of human experience.

For Margaret, this war had divided one part of her family from the rest. Her father's domestic situation had again changed dramatically, and she was clearly exhausted if not traumatized and deeply disillusioned by her war experiences herself. In addition, Helena was in the throes of leaving England for China, along with her husband and, now, two children. After leaving Swanwick, Margaret stayed with her mother at Sidmouth, on holiday. She spent a large amount of time in bed, recuperating, although she continued correspondence and necessary negotiations about Poland, since at that time no one else was available to take over the work. By the beginning of October she was still complaining that she was 'not much good at anything' and a few days later chronic appendicitis was diagnosed. She was eventually put in the charge of the surgeon Wilfred Trotter and sent to Bowden House, a private London nursing home. Here, the significance of the choice of surgeon and nursing home may have been profound. Wilfred Trotter was the Dean of Westminster Hospital, a pioneer in neurosurgery and one of the first to interest Ernest Jones in psychoanalysis (Kohon, 1986). But he was also famous for a book of his own, *The Instincts of the Herd in Peace and War*. First published in 1916, with a new edition in 1920, this was an early essay on group psychology which was discussed critically and at length by Freud (1921) in his *Group Psychology and the Analysis of the Ego*. Amongst other things Trotter's essay was concerned with psychological factors predisposing nations to war, and the differences between psychological characteristics uppermost in British and German peoples, influencing, by his account, the course which the war eventually took. By 1921 Trotter was already one of the founder members of the Medical Advisory Board of what later became the Tavistock Clinic. As mentioned earlier, the major force behind the inception of the clinic in 1920 was Hugh Crichton-Miller, who established it as one of the first out-patient clinics in Great Britain 'to provide systematic major psychotherapy on the basis of concepts inspired by psychoanalytic theory to out-patients suffering from psychoneurosis and allied disorders who were unable to afford private fees' (Dicks, 1970, p. 1). To Margaret Lowenfeld the significance of this link was that Bowden House was, in fact, Crichton-Miller's private nursing home. Many of the staff who provided their services to the Tavistock on a voluntary basis were drawn from this establishment. In addition to the fact that the idea of dynamic psychology must have been available to her at this time, it is likely that the inspiration for what Margaret later referred to elliptically as an 'electric personal analysis', which she undertook some time in 1922, stemmed from these contacts, if she was not actually advised on particular personnel.

Thus, Margaret Lowenfeld may well have been one of the many whose first personal contact with psychotherapy was precipitated by wartime experiences. But at the end of 1921 her stay in Bowden House was for less than three weeks. She remained in contact with Wilfred Trotter, sharing many of his intellectual commitments. Eventually, too, there were a number of similarities between Crichton-Miller's vision and her own. But her move into psychotherapy was neither immediate nor direct. It came, first, through further medical work in the community.

MEDICAL RESEARCH IN THE COMMUNITY

In later years Margaret Lowenfeld stressed that when she returned from Poland there was as yet no discipline or profession of child psychiatry and precious little conception of it. Nor was there much by way of child psychotherapy. As noted previously, one of the first patients to attend Hugh Crichton-Miller's clinic was a child and, by the time he wrote the first major report on the progress of the clinic in 1927, Crichton-Miller was using the clinical vignette of a twelve-year-old boy referred by his school for persistent pilfering. Through a course of six interviews, the unconscious cause of his misdeeds was revealed, 'to wit his hostility towards his new stepmother' (Dicks, 1970, pp. 18, 19). Freud's theories, of course, had made copious references to childhood and, since the analysis of Little Hans, the opening was there for psychoanalytic work with children (Freud, 1909). On the Continent, Hermine von Hug-Hellmuth had presented a case of a child in treatment which established the possibility of this kind of work, and we now know from Phyllis Grosskurth's (1986) biography of

Melanie Klein that Klein had begun analysing her own children as early as 1919. But although it is tempting to focus on contrasts and similarities between Margaret Lowenfeld's eventual approach and psychoanalysis, beginning here misses the significance of her entering through a different route.

Margaret Lowenfeld was committed to medicine and to the training which she had had to struggle to begin and complete. When she returned from Poland a good few years after the close of the First World War, she found it difficult to obtain a job. Although women doctors were readily employed in wartime to release men doctors for military work, at the end of the war available positions were first filled with doctors returning from the forces and there were no longer obvious places for women. She had only just qualified before going to Poland, had no recognized speciality, and by her own account she had gone to Poland with but one medical and one surgical house post behind her (Lowenfeld, 1969, p. 1). However, the war work in general, as well as the specific incident with the cattle-truck boys, had involved her in a good deal of work with children, focusing attention on emotional and mental conditions as well as on physical states and relations between development and communal life. Given the lack of availability of medical posts, she aimed towards a research career which itself involved further training in development. After her period of analysis, as a preliminary in 1923 she became a postgraduate research student at the Mothercraft Training Centre. This centre existed explicitly to encourage the dissemination of scientific principles of infant management and mothercraft, with the aim of improving the infant mortality rates and the quality of parenting amongst the poorer classes. Courses focused particularly on the work of Truby King, nowadays associated with an insistence on rather rigid routines and regimes, but popular amongst professionals at that time because of the success claimed for his methods in improving infant mortality rates in New Zealand, his country of origin (Hardyment, 1983). While doing this course, Margaret Lowenfeld gained experience in handling ill or poorly nourished infants, both those who survived and those who did not. She began to notice in the faces and bodies of the children she was studying what she later described as 'expressions, postures and gestures that resembled those with which I had become familiar in prison camps and famine areas' (Lowenfeld, 1979, p. 2).

By the end of 1923, Margaret Lowenfeld had obtained a Medical Research Council (MRC) scholarship plus the Muirhead Fellowship to work under Professor Leonard Findlay at the Royal Hospital for Sick Children, Glasgow, on a study of the relations between acute rheumatism in children and home conditions. This study was one of the first epidemiological investigations to concentrate on illness in children and to attempt to relate it to life style and material circumstances. The first paper in Chapter 7 comes from this period of work. Ultimately the study gave rise to the monograph, *Social Conditions and Acute Rheumatism: MRC Child Life Investigations No. 114*, published in 1927. At that time rheumatic conditions were a major cause of school absence. Particularly significant, there was also a known association between rheumatic conditions in childhood and chronic heart disease. It thus had long-term consequences and, like tuberculosis, was a major threat to adult health. Although the aetiology was not well understood, there was a known relationship between the condition and poverty. It was also speculated that there might be relationships of various sorts between the condition and a variety of childhood ailments, from sore throats and persistent catarrh to conditions like chorea, a disturbance of the motor system resulting in disruptive gait and posture, relatively common in the 1920s but not observed in children nowadays. The study aimed to tease apart possible contributing factors and involved two cohorts of children and investigators, one centred round St Thomas's Hospital, London and the other in Glasgow where Margaret Lowenfeld was based. The methodology was relatively sophisticated. It included control groups, involving 100 families in each of the London and Glasgow samples. In addition to carrying out comprehensive clinical examinations which included assessing vision, height and dentistry, as well as recording eye colour in the search for possible genetic links, Margaret Lowenfeld was also required to participate in the social side of the investigation. This included making assessments and collating variables associated with such things as sanitary conditions, length of parents' marriage, income and work, eating habits, mothers' knowledge of mothercraft, and amount of time spent consuming alcohol per week. As Margaret Lowenfeld later acknowledged, this gave her insight into 200 families from the poorest parts of Glasgow (Lowenfeld, 1969, p. 2).

Although extensive, the findings of this survey were in some ways disappointing. It confirmed a general relationship between rheumatism and the kinds of poor living standards produced by poverty, and that there was no simple hereditary mechanism involved. But it was unsuccessful in pinning down specific factors which could be simply remedied. As in heart disease today, the aetiology could not be traced so conveniently. But aetiology does not appear to have been what interested Lowenfeld most. Her own major contribution, republished here, was concerned with demonstrating the effectiveness of an organized clinic, not only for detecting illness but also for providing a holistic approach to the treatment of children and their families. Ultimately these assumptions were central to the design of her own children's clinic, set up a few years later. Moreover, in many respects the findings which most intrigued Margaret Lowenfeld were precisely those which were incompatible with predictions drawn from orthodox medicine; nor did they fit in with the community-based aspects of the research. She became impressed with the curious anomalies that appeared in children's reactions to the same physical illness, and which could not be explained away in terms of social variables. As she reconstructed it later:

> From time to time during the clinical work carried out in the wards, I had been puzzled to observe that in some cases children with very severe cardiological conditions, who might reasonably be expected to die of these, recovered instead . . . On the other hand the reverse also occurred, in that every now and then children whose prognosis seemed good would unexpectedly die. (Lowenfeld, 1969, p. 3)

On the completion of her part of the research, in 1926, Margaret Lowenfeld returned south. She obtained the Alfred Langton Research Scholarship and took up a further research position under Professor Louise McIllroy and Professor Winifred Cullis in the obstetric unit of the Royal Free Hospital, working on a project concerned with infant feeding over the first ten days and the functions of the mammary glands. The second paper in Chapter 7 presents findings from this study. The study involved both observation of feeding activity and chemical analyses of milk content. It concerned, exclusively, infants born to women in hospital who at that time were generally from the poorer classes. Though a researcher, unsurprisingly, Margaret Lowenfeld became involved informally with the mother's side of infant feeding. Her training through the Truby King course obviously provided her with certain assumptions about appropriate management. But again, she was struck by variations in the infants themselves, in how strong or weak feeders they were, for instance, and by the fact that something indigenous to particular infants could help them offset considerable disadvantages in maternal health and social conditions and vice versa.

Since this study produced interesting results, it was continued for several more years. In the meantime Margaret Lowenfeld had gained sufficient experience to open a private practice, working in co-operation with obstetricians as an expert on infant feeding problems, and as a consultant concerned with a wider range of problems specifically associated with illness in childhood. She established her consulting rooms at 46 Queen Anne Street, London, in 1926, some two years before the official founding of the British Paediatric Association, of which Margaret Lowenfeld was one of the first members.

The consultancy, of course, provided an income. But Margaret Lowenfeld also took up another important post at this time. By and large up until the end of the Second World War hospitals and such public clinics as there were were supported by voluntary contributions. Medical staff customarily gave their services voluntarily. For a short period between 1926 and 1927 Margaret Lowenfeld was a medical officer associated in a voluntary capacity with the newly established Pioneer Health Centre in Peckham, London, which later became known as the Peckham Experiment. This centre was in part a response to the recommendations of the Dawson report of 1920, the *Interim Report on the Future Provision of Medical Services*, which was commissioned by the Ministry of Health. In many ways it was symptomatic of governmental concern over the nation's health after the First World War, which took the form of a shift in focus on to the community. The development of clinics was integral to this move (Armstrong, 1983). The report's chief recommendation was for the implementation of a concept of integrated health care which transcended the division that had hitherto existed between hospitals and consultant services, on the one hand, and the more communal or domiciliary aspects of health care on the other. In brief, the report proposed a division between 'primary' and 'secondary' health care.

The Peckham Experiment itself owed much to the commitment of George Newman, then Chief Medical Officer at the Ministry of Health. In addition to believing that 'all doctors, nurses, midwives, health visitors, sanitary inspectors and welfare workers should be missionaries of hygiene' (Newman,

1920a), Newman stressed that the general practitioner should have an especially important role in the new way of health, as 'the instrument, the outpost, the interpreter' (Newman, 1920b). The Peckham Experiment itself was set up in 1926 and is generally considered pioneering in the attempt to take these ideas into practice. However, after a screening programme revealed something of the extensiveness of the poor health amongst the people of Peckham, it was closed down owing to lack of funds and lack of means for implementing substantial changes. The centre was eventually reopened in 1935 with a new injection of funds and a new rubric, 'a social structure to be built with a new unit – not the individual but the family' (Pearse and Crocker, 1943, p. 13). But by this time Margaret Lowenfeld and the Peckham Experiment had long since parted company; she had established an experimental clinic of her own.

3 The Foundation of the Children's Clinic, 1927–31

The consultancy was the launching pad for a concept of children's medicine which prioritized what Lowenfeld would later loosely describe as the personality of the child (Lowenfeld, 1969). Like Hugh Crichton-Miller and Wilfred Trotter, Lowenfeld was committed to forging links in the study of mental, emotional and physical processes. She, too, had been profoundly affected by the British tradition of dynamic psychology. As for psychoanalysis itself, although she had some acquaintance with psychoanalytic theories, at this time she was not engaged by them. Nor does she appear to have been much touched by the arrival of Melanie Klein in London in 1926. Of more immediate significance was the child study movement, to which she had been introduced through her own research training, and in particular the tradition founded in Britain by James Sully, who had opened a psychological laboratory at University College, London, in 1896. Initially research which used children as subjects included recommendations to teachers and parents as one of its spin-offs. By the 1920s University College was putting on regular courses for teachers and social workers in principles of child development and observation. Increasingly these courses focused on problems of emotional adjustment, as well as on the principles of psychological assessment. From 1913, Sully's erstwhile student, Cyril Burt, had held the initially experimental post of 'child psychologist' within the school organization of London County Council, retaining a post at University College at the same time. Though references to emotion and volition had appeared in wartime publications, from the beginning of the 1920s Burt's published reports gave increasing attention to problems of moral defect, delinquency, and failures in adjustment (Burt, 1915, 1917a, 1917b, 1923a, 1923b, 1925).

Lowenfeld clearly knew of Burt's work. She was also personally acquainted with many professionals and voluntary welfare workers whose aim was to reach the child in the community. In particular, she knew of the work of Dr Alice Hutchinson and Miss Muriel Payne, who were in charge of the small and newly formed children's department within Hugh Crichton-Miller's clinic, then located next door to the University College Psychology Department. Lowenfeld was also directly involved in some of the discussions organized by the magistrate Mrs St Loe Strachey which eventually led to the formation of the Child Guidance Council in 1927, the same year in which Drs Noel Burke and Emanuel Miller started the East London Child Guidance Clinic under the auspices of the Jewish Health Organization (Keir, 1952; Lowenfeld, 1969; Rose, 1985).

But just as her starting-point was not psychoanalysis, neither was Lowenfeld strictly speaking part of the child guidance movement *per se* although her work later contributed greatly to it. To begin with, the movement drew its impetus from the apparently successful work of Drs Healey and Broner in Philadelphia in the United States (Rose, 1985). She was sceptical about the importation of ideas and methods which might prove inappropriate to this country. Second, in spite of the fact that the child guidance movement claimed to rest itself on the scientific principles of child study (Burke and Miller, 1929), even by 1927 the model which Lowenfeld had in mind was both more research-oriented, and more directed towards a persistent commitment to expanding medicine to embrace the psychological. Here she retained, or took further, Sully's holistic approach to relations between environment, body and mind which became diluted in many other attempts to take his ideas into practice (Sully, 1895). Thirdly, she objected to the child-guidance philosophy which in her view saw adjustment to environment in terms of the production of conformity. Such a viewpoint presupposed a satisfaction with current societal values and achievements which, for Lowenfeld, in the aftermath of the horrors of war, the devastation of Europe, the unequal distribution of wealth, and the clear evidence of the human capacity for cruelty, was untenable. Here Lowenfeld joined with a number of liberal thinkers and progressive educationists in the post-war period who saw understanding the causes of war and their prevention as a major task of the post-war reconstruction. One contribution to this was the scientific and therapeutic investigation of human minds. Here Lowenfeld's wartime experience and research observations had already led her into the belief that, in addition to the environmental considerations, there were processes inherent in children themselves which would enable them to find more adaptive solutions.

For Lowenfeld the key to these possibilities was play, a medium through which children do not simply discharge energy or master anxiety, but come to understand themselves and achieve a more or less productive relationship with their particular environments. The importance of play was, of course, stressed by the child psychoanalysts, following Freud (1920) himself. It was also given central significance by the progressive educationists who adhered to Froebel and Montessori's stress on play as a condition for inner harmony and freedom, and by most of the child study theorists on whom Lowenfeld later drew for theoretical refinement in delineating her own position (Lowenfeld, 1935). The centrality she gave to play was undoubtedly influenced by these traditions, but Lowenfeld's approach emerged as distinctive rather than derivative, in that she emphasized both process and content in play, and the contribution of both internal psychic processes and cultural forms, as is discussed at length in the next chapter. Furthermore her views were in the first instance fuelled through her acute observation and sensitivity to the emotional conflicts of her child patients. It was while she was working as a consultant that she first began to experiment with the provision of materials collected together in a box which came to be called the 'Wonder Box'. 'Now and then', she wrote, as she observed what they did, 'I came to understand what they were attempting to express' (Lowenfeld, 1969, p. 4).

It was this understanding that Lowenfeld wished to take further, with a broader-based population of children whose development could be studied and observed on many fronts at once. In retrospect Lowenfeld was inclined to describe the Children's Clinic as an 'experiment'. Indeed, the first published reports of the clinic, which were oriented towards both conveying discoveries and recruiting financial and popular support, noted that 'The Children's Clinic has been described as a great social experiment' (Children's Clinic for the Treatment and Study of Nervous and Delicate Children, *Annual Report 1929–30*). The reference to 'social experiment' aimed to imply a comparison with pioneering ventures like the Peckham Experiment, and the short-lived but highly influential Little Commonwealth establishment of Homer Lane, that claimed to have demonstrated the successful treatment of delinquent boys by the application of psychodynamic principles under conditions of complete freedom (see Selleck, 1972). In addition, in describing the clinic as 'experimental' Lowenfeld was emphasizing that in the early days she and her colleagues were in the business of finding out what could be achieved, what worked and what did not. Nevertheless, despite modifications, expansions and clarifications of direction in future years, in many respects the ground rules of Lowenfeld's practical and theoretical project were inscribed in the very beginnings of the Children's Clinic. These beginnings were both modest and awe-inspiring in their implications.

PRACTICAL BEGINNINGS

Given that in the 1920s any innovative venture within medicine would depend substantially on voluntary efforts, the first problem was not one of providing salaries but of obtaining suitable premises. The first initiative was taken in 1928 by Lowenfeld and an enthusiastic colleague, Miss Sorona Trew, a lecturer in science at Bedford College, London University, who approached the committee of the Women's Welfare Centre, 12 Telford Road, London W10. This resulted in permission to use two rooms in the centre one afternoon and one morning a week for a rent of eight shillings and sixpence per session. The clinic was opened in October of that year, and was advertised as a 'Clinic for Nervous and Difficult Children' through a poster (see Figure 1) which announced the purposes of the clinic, its address and opening hours, and which was displayed in local shops in the neighbourhood.

As can be seen from the poster, in aiming to reach children who were 'nervous', presented behavioural problems or were 'never quite well', the potential clientele included children likely to cause difficulties in placement for school authorities. But the assumption from the start was that they could all be reached through the same terms of reference.

One of the clinic's two rooms opened directly on the street and was used as the treatment room. The other was used for consultation with parents and keeping records. From the outset Lowenfeld aimed to combine observations of children's behaviour with physical examinations. Biochemical investigations, consisting of urine testing and estimations of acid ratio, were carried out in an empty washhouse at the back. The opportunities for play were never entirely random, though

CLINIC

FOR

NERVOUS AND DIFFICULT

CHILDREN

12 Telford Road, Ladbroke Grove, W.10

('Bus No. 15 or 52 down Ladbroke Grove, or 'Bus 18 or 46 down Harrow Road to Ladbroke Grove.)

All children are difficult sometimes, but
Some children are difficult all the time.
Some children seem always to be catching something and never to be quite well.
Some children are nervous and find life and school too difficult for them.
Some children have distressing habits.

This Clinic, which is in charge of a Physician, exists to help mothers in these kinds of trouble with their children, and also to help the children themselves.

TUESDAYS	THURSDAYS
10 a.m.	2 p.m.

NO LETTER NECESSARY.

Figure 1 *Poster advertising the opening of the clinic*

modifications in approach occurred later. By the time the clinic opened Lowenfeld had already designed the rudiments of what later became the Mosaic Test, an idea originally inspired by reflecting on variations in designs on traditional Polish dance dresses, each pattern identifying the area from which the dance troupe came (Lowenfeld, 1954). She had also become a collector of toys which had inspired her curiosity or her intuition about the possibilities they might open to disturbed children. Here she was both following Montessori's (1912) emphasis on the value of specialized toys, and explicitly recognizing toys as cultural artefacts which might have particular effects. However, at this time, the materials were not extensive, and were kept in the second room rather than being on display. Furniture too was sparse: a fireside chair by the small gas fire, a table in the centre, and later a second table for painting.

The poster proved effective in drawing in mothers and children, and sometimes just the children themselves, from the surrounding neighbourhood. The first child, in fact, came on his own. It was discovered afterwards that he had the reputation of being the bad boy of the neighbourhood, abominated by the shopkeepers. Lowenfeld had no recollection of ever meeting his mother. The child was defiant and silent. Lowenfeld provided a French painting book, water and paint brushes and withdrew. Half an hour later she returned to watch him absorbed in intense, excited concentration. Later she learned that the child had never painted before. Painting had yet to become a regular school activity. She also learned that the child was attending school extremely erratically. The attempt to get him there had been given up as he would meet any approach with absolutely silent resistance. At the clinic he became more talkative. He and Margaret Lowenfeld drew up a pact: more attendance at school when the clinic was not open, more paints and fresh material on clinic days. The child not only started attending school, but appeared altogether more co-operative and attentive, eventually bringing a friend along with him (Lowenfeld, 1969).

Though the children of the neighbourhood were clearly being reached, unsurprisingly the novel set-up aroused some suspicion as well as interest in the community, particularly since the project had been mounted with more enthusiasm than foresight about the political implications locally and in relative ignorance of administrative hurdles. One unforeseen hurdle, Lowenfeld later discovered, was that there was some concern amongst the local authorities about the opening up of the clinic in a building which was also used for giving advice on birth control. The suspicion was that there might be some connection between the two, the children being a front for some kind of birth-control propaganda. (Helena had as yet to achieve any notoriety.) Fortunately Lowenfeld found a strong ally in a Miss Nixon, the then secretary of the local branch of the Charity Organisation Society, which was particularly powerful in that neighbourhood, after Miss Nixon came unannounced into the clinic to investigate, and was moved and impressed by the sincerity of the enterprise. Miss Nixon proved invaluable in thinking through the relationship between the clinic and other neighbourhood schemes, and in smoothing differences of opinion or misunderstandings where necessary. It was Miss Nixon, too, who negotiated an agreement that the children involved could get their mark for school attendance on the days and times when they were at the clinic.

By the end of 1928, after having been opened for approximately three months, the Telford Road clinic could boast of a moderate clientele of ten children, and enough satisfied parents and children to justify expansion. Important lessons had been learned. One was that it was necessary to relieve Lowenfeld of some of the secretarial and administrative work. The other was that someone would need to work in greater depth with parents since it had become clear that 'A large factor in the psychological situation of the children was going to be presented by the psychological situation of the parents, especially where there were definite psychoneurotic or neurotic tendencies' ('Clinic for Nervous and Difficult Children', unpublished report, 1928, p. 3). An approach was made to Dr Isobel Wilson, associated with the adult department at the Tavistock. She agreed to open up a parents' department to support the work with children, though this was not actually established until six months after the clinic moved to new premises in the following year.

NEW PREMISES AND AN INSTITUTIONAL STRUCTURE

With the help of Miss Nixon as chief negotiator, by March 1929 the clinic was re-established in The Quest, 85 Clarendon Road, London W11. This was a large building in the charge of Miss Sophia Fry, from the well-known Quaker family, who ran the property as a kind of children's club. Lowenfeld and her colleagues were allowed the use of the club room, a waiting-room running along the first-floor front, a hall plus its piano, a paved yard and later a separate room for use as an office. Though these premises ensured that a good many more children could be seen, the rooms were only available on Monday and Thursday afternoons between 2.30 and 5 p.m. and everything had to be completely cleared away immediately afterwards.

The clinic reopened on 20 March 1929, now under the name of the Children's Clinic for the Observation and Treatment of Nervous and Delicate Children, thus preserving emphasis on observation with remediation, and the assumption of links between psyche and soma. The expansion required a firmer constitutional structure, a larger body of consultancy staff, as well as an active staff and, eventually, modifications in the selection and design of play equipment. Financial support largely came from voluntary donations or subscriptions in the first instance, though a small charge was made to most patients, the assumption being that 'parents tend to take more seriously advice they have paid for' (Lowenfeld, 1969, p. 13). The fee was adjusted to family income and varied between sixpence and five shillings and no child was ever refused on account of inability to pay. An executive committee, plus a salaried secretary, were recruited to oversee management and other issues, and an advisory council was appointed to monitor the aims and achievements of the work, which could be regarded as simultaneously medical, educational and social. Here there was not, apparently, any problem in recruiting support amongst clergy and lay workers committed to philanthropic work in the community. Support also came from the London County Council and from education. In the latter field members of the initial advisory council included John Bell, Professor Marcault and Miss I.M. Oakden. Other members joining included Sir Atul Chatterjee, the Reverend Herbert Gray, Lady Glenconner, Miss Irene Cooper Willis, Dr William Feldman, and the *Punch* cartoonist Charles Grave. The latter was responsible for adding cartoons to the leaflets produced to advertise the clinic and to canvas financial support (see Figure 2).

A number of these names are reasonably well known today, for their contributions to welfare work or education. So, too, are some of the members of the executive committee, where there was a striking overlap between some of the people involved with this project and with the Tavistock Clinic, which had also expanded its institutional framework in the same year (Dicks, 1970). Apart from Miss Nixon as chairman, the committee included in the first instance Dame Katherine Furze of the Red Cross, one of the vice-presidents at the Tavistock, Muriel Payne, mentioned earlier, and Dr Doris Odlum, again associated with the Tavistock. Even more striking were the overlaps in the honorary medical consultants. Under Margaret Lowenfeld as honorary medical director, the initial honorary medical and technical consultancy staff at the Children's Clinic included Dr H. E. Cameron, Dr Hazel Chodak Gregory, Dr Worster Drought, Dr Bernard Hart, Miss Gertrude Herzfield, FRCSE, Dr Hubert J. Normal, Dr E. Obermer, Dr Hamilton Pearson, Dr Elizabeth Sloan Chesser, Mr Scott Stevenson, MD, FRCSE, and Mr Wilfred Trotter, MD, MS, FRCS. Later this group were joined by Mr Kenneth Walker, FRCS, and Mr F. G.

Cruikshank, FRCP. Wilfred Trotter has of course figured before in this history, both in the context of his care of Margaret Lowenfeld and as a member of the medical advisory board of the Tavistock. But others in this group had strong connections with that clinic. For instance, Cruikshank had joined the Tavistock as consultant physician in 1928. Hamilton Pearson was on the original staff of Hugh Crichton-Miller's clinic, serving there as a director of the Children's Department until the outbreak of the Second World War. Another member of the initial consultancy staff was Cyril Burt, unsurprising given his strong connections with many child-centred projects at that time. By 1937 he, too, had become a vice-patron of the Tavistock Clinic, having served on its council between 1932 and 1936 (Dicks, 1970). At the Children's Clinic his presence on the consultancy staff opened

Figure 2 *Charles Grave's cartoons*

the possibility of links between the Children's Clinic and the University of London (though there is no evidence that he took part in the actual management of the clinic).

In addition to the medical consultants listed above, with the move to The Quest the Children's Clinic also established the posts of honorary dental consultant, honorary radiologist and honorary pathologist. These were filled, respectively, by Dr Bowdler, Dr E. J. Roth and Dr H.B. Hervey Wyatt. Similar posts were linked to the Tavistock in 1929. In Lowenfeld's case, this concern with many aspects of children's health reflected a holistic approach which never entirely disappeared even when the work was apparently more narrowly psychotherapeutic.

On a sessional basis, an active staff, consisting originally of three doctors and four other workers from various professions such as teaching and social work, was employed for direct work with the children. This population was less stable; new workers came and others left. But again, within this list there was some overlap with the Tavistock. For instance, Dr George Burns, who attended the Children's Clinic once a week until the early 1930s, also held a position in the Children's Department at the Tavistock between 1926 and 1934, when he became Director of Child Guidance in Birmingham (Dicks, 1970; Lowenfeld, 1969).

Also included in the original active staff was a speech therapist and a psychologist, Mrs T. Gosse. The main role of the latter was to administer intelligence tests. Lowenfeld probably thought that this was a useful addition to the research design and she was no doubt influenced by the new enthusiasm for Burt's work, gaining ground in many quarters. At roughly the same time, in 1928, a lecturer in psychology from University College, Constance Simmins, had been appointed to the staff of the Tavistock Clinic, establishing a formal link between the two institutions (Keir, 1952). She was joined by other psychological assistants in the 1930s though the psychologists' role always remained marginal to psychotherapeutic treatment *per se*. In Lowenfeld's clinic, a psychologist remained part of the team until the closure of the Institute of Child Psychology. But the role of the psychologist diversified, as did Margaret Lowenfeld's view of the contribution of psychology. Although she drew a number of theoretical ideas from the theory of measurable intelligence, and particularly from the work of Charles Spearman (1923, 1927, 1937, see Chapter 9), as will be shown her view of individuality departed in crucial respects from the science of individual differences promulgated by Cyril Burt.

FROM RESEARCH TO PSYCHOTHERAPY

From the outset the careful collection of observations within a research context was an integral part of Lowenfeld's commitment to building a psychological medicine of childhood. This was made explicit in the design of procedures regularly used at each session. For example, independently of whether or not experiences at the clinic proved beneficial for any particular child, a major objective was to record as far as possible, on pre-made case sheets, what was done in each session, including what kinds of conversations had taken place. This information was to be set against the results of intellectual, physical, and social assessments.

Intellectual assessment involved the psychologist, who was helped in the early stages of the clinic by another worker who happened to be a Froebel-trained teacher. Reports from school were also available in some cases. In making physical assessments Lowenfeld combined clinical examinations with detailed case histories, generally taken from parents. Though the influence of the research model used in the rheumatism study was clear, she was also influenced by theories derived from contemporary psychology. For example, as well as being concerned with disease or bodily dysfunction, Lowenfield hoped to demonstrate the value of assessing how far the child fitted or deviated from what might be expected for a child of that age, family background and social conditions. Here Lowenfeld was following the influence of Gesell's (1928) normative work, and the tradition embodied in psychometric testing. This, however, was several years before developmental screening became part of standard medical practice. In 1929, she was also interested in the theory of Kretschmer (1925) which proposed a relation between personality and body type. Lowenfeld's interest in this particular theory and Sheldon's (1940) development of it appeared to wane later on. But she retained her interest in physique, as one aspect of relations between psyche and soma.

A focus on the body gained in importance in the clinic from the latter half of 1929 through the inclusion of the Rhythm Department under the auspices of Mrs Vaux. The assumptions here were that extra opportunities for movement, from running, jumping, and wrestling to dance and movement to music, were particularly important to city children, and that in general movement provided an outlet for emotional energy as a means of communication or self-expression. This idea took on greater significance from the mid-30s when the team was joined by Miss Margaret Kirschner, a physical therapist from the Continent. Margaret Kirschner is an exponent of a Central European system of physical therapy somewhat akin to the Alexander technique. She approached Lowenfeld originally through family connections when she came to England in order to escape persecution by the Nazis (Evans, 1984). After the war she remained as a member of staff, and her approach was integral to the development of the clinic's holistic orientation. In the early days of the clinic, the intention to focus extensively on body function and physique is illustrated by the excitement produced as the clinic acquired a camera in its second year. The camera was not at first used to photograph play (let alone particular 'Worlds') but to record facial expressions and posture and as an additional means for recording changes before and after treatment.

In assessing the social situation of the child, although where possible contact was maintained with the general practitioner, again a large amount of information was obtained directly from parents in interviews which were intended to be sympathetic. Here the aim was to use the research framework to study and find out what was going on rather than to assume in advance any particular consequences of particular styles of upbringing. In the assessment of home background and home atmosphere, assumptions and prejudices were there, of course, as they had been in the rheumatism study. But Lowenfeld's emphasis was less on looking for simple causes in parental management than on making some estimate of the parents' expectations for the child's future, and of what the atmosphere was likely to be 'if his wishes were to deviate from those of his parents' (Lowenfeld, 1969, p. 11).

But from the outset Lowenfeld's own sympathies lay with the child. Increasingly, she allowed responsibility for work with parents and with the social aspects of the family situations to be delegated to other members of the team. The fruitfulness of this co-operative team-work can be seen particularly clearly in the early clinical papers (republished in Chapter 8). But for Lowenfeld, the main fascination lay in observing what the children were doing, as a means of gaining access to their feelings and fantasies. It was from these observations that her theories and distinctive therapeutic technique eventually evolved.

OBSERVATION AND FACILITATION OF PLAY AND COMMUNICATION

Lowenfeld wrote (1969) that she always believed that the opportunities offered by the design of the building were crucial in facilitating or limiting the form of her work. In retrospect she recognized that at The Quest a crucial asset had been the fact that the interconnection between the main play area and the room she took as her consulting room consisted of a small staircase and platform, slightly raised above the playroom itself, where she could stand and watch what was going on in the way that nowadays one might use a one-way screen. From here Lowenfeld was able to look down unobtrusively at a large group of children contained in a single play room (see Figure 3). Though this arrangement was forced by circumstances, it contributed to the possibility of a total environment, relatively free from constraints and separable from the world outside. This itself affected the ways of working with children which eventually evolved.

All the children taken on at the clinic were required to attend for the whole of both afternoon sessions each week. At the earlier diagnostic interview sessions it would have been explained to them that they were free to make use of anything that attracted their attention in the play room, that nothing they did

Figure 3 *The play room at The Quest*

or said would be repeated to their parents or teachers, that the adults working with them in the playground were there to help them and were interested in their ideas and problems, and that ordinary standards of speech and action did not apply in the play room. Finally, they were told that what they did with the material would be recorded and discussed with them from time to time.

Apparently, most of the children became rapidly absorbed in what they were doing. Aggressive behaviour occurred relatively rarely. When it did the policy was to direct it into activities in the paved outdoor space or into movement, games or dancing to music in the adjoining hall. The children's behaviour was monitored more or less constantly, ideally with a ratio of one child to each worker. This monitoring was intended less as supervisory and directive than as a form of careful observation. The staff were encouraged to watch, observe, follow, try to understand, but as far as possible to avoid imposing their own ideas.

Within this lack of structure Lowenfeld already held the view that play was not simply an outlet for energy release or tension reduction, but a medium through which children could express themselves or think. As previously noted, she believed that this could be facilitated through the careful selection or design of materials. Accordingly the play room was equipped with tables, chairs and occasionally a cabinet, plus a strong fixed play-pen with a mattress on the floor which made it possible to include quite small children in the room, or children who it was felt might do damage to others. In such cases, additional supervision was made as inconspicuous as possible. Shelves and cupboards along the walls were used to store play equipment when not in use. By this time Lowenfeld had developed an eye for play equipment used in other settings, educational as well as medical, and had already foreseen the need to find materials that would be suitable for work in a variety of contexts in many countries. In addition to the Mosaic Test, previously mentioned, there were toys in her collection that now ranged from tiny wooden people and houses which she remembered from her own childhood to large-scale construction equipment. In Berlin several years before she had established a connection with a firm of toy-makers and importers. This firm exhibited at the annual Leipzig Fair and used to boast that any toy in Europe could be found on their demonstration shelves. Though some of these had been available at Telford Road, at The Quest more items could be kept out in use at any one time. In addition, here, the children were provided with more opportunities for water play. Also included was a zinc tray and sand, the original purpose of which was to allow smearing and messing without reproof.

For the adults involved, making objective observations and recordings was not, of course, straightforward. They had been through different professional trainings and had varied experience of different schools of dynamic psychology. Since there was ultimately an insistence on differences between the role of the therapist within the Lowenfeld tradition and what the therapist was assumed to do in psychoanalysis (see in particular Chapter 11), it is important to consider how the workers understood their own roles.

In the first place, joining the clinic depended on accepting the collective emphasis on being as non-interventionist as possible, to support the child's view that this was a radically different context from the home or school, and that things could be expressed here that were not tolerated outside. Second, there was an emphasis on gaining experience of different types of children, and on comparing what was done by children of different ages, before coming to definite conclusions as to the significance of the play itself. To this end, all staff worked with all children, though a particular worker might be attached to a particular child throughout one session. On the one hand, this rotational system gave the staff experience with age-related changes in play, and with what Lowenfeld (1935) later identified as 'types' of play. At the same time, this system fostered the understanding of the uniqueness of each child, as his or her own system minimized the use of transference which, by 1931, was positively discouraged (see Chapter 8). But from very early on it was decided that no direct 'interpretation' should be given to the children of what they produced with material or said in the play room. Initially this appears to have been as much due to the considerable variation in the staff's experience in the psychoanalytic field as it was to fear of or antagonism towards psychoanalysis. In Lowenfeld's clinic, using interpretation was regarded as jumping the gun, and then as unnecessary because the clinic was having considerable success in its own terms.

From the surviving descriptions of the early work, the atmosphere in the clinic seems to have had less of a quality of bedlam or feverish excitement than of a commitment bordering on something passionate. The staff were, as it were, bowled over by the effect of the material on the children who worked, and by their intense concentration. Very little contact took place between the children themselves, though each child moved about freely with his or her particular worker of the day. Gradually, an approach evolved in which the worker discussed whatever a child brought up on his or her own level, using words, phrases and content emerging in the child's own communication. As Lowenfeld put it, 'Slowly an atmosphere was built, or rather built itself up, in which the children behaved freely and spontaneously, and keenly enjoyed discussing what they were doing with the adults with whom they were working' (Lowenfeld, 1969, p. 13).

Thus the principal aim of therapy became one of enabling the children to express ideas and fantasies and, where necessary or possible, to clarify for them in their own terms aspects of their personalities that were causing difficulty or conflict. But the ethos emerged through continued reflection on what worked and what did not, both in relation to play materials and the working relationships. It was clearly not the case that there were no tensions or disagreements between the staff, particularly since experience in other fields and considerable determination were characteristic of many of the team; there was a good deal of trial and error. Nor were the staff always non-interventionist. This is illustrated in a history of the World technique which Ville Andersen traced in 1959 in the course of helping to prepare the manuscript of the book, *The World Technique*, eventually published in 1979.

The World technique in fact began its development as early as 1929 with the inclusion of the sand-tray and a collection of Lowenfeld's small toy models of ordinary people, houses and other small objects. These were kept at that time in an old birds' nesting cabinet with small drawers. Apparently this cabinet was itself originally called 'the World' and when the children played with it they were deliberately encouraged to make realistic depictions of day-to-day scenes in the sand, depictions which could be regarded as more or less mature. However, inevitably from time to time elements of fantasy broke through, leaving the staff, as it were, running behind. When they stopped directing and concentrated on observing and recording the child's own product, then the potential of the technique began to dawn. As Ville Andersen noted, 'as soon as the workers (by chance or intention) refrained from . . . interfering or suggesting to the children, then something new and excitingly creative grew out of the children's constructions' (Lowenfeld, 1979,

p. 280). In this sense, the World technique was created by the children themselves.

This was within three months of the opening of the clinic at The Quest. From then on, in addition to extensive written descriptions, drawings of children's Worlds were included more frequently in the case records. At that time, as noted in the Introduction, Margaret Lowenfeld was involved with the philosopher, Robin Collingwood. Well known for his interest in archaeology and the philosophy and history of art, he was apparently particularly enthralled by these Worlds and would occasionally make drawings of the Worlds himself. Although Lowenfeld was already thinking about its implications, it was some time before 'World-making' became one of the central and best-known techniques of the clinic. In the first years of the clinic, it was perhaps one of a number of discoveries or opportunities for understanding children's minds which fuelled the enthusiasm of the clinic's workers and supporters. But in those early days, maintaining enthusiasm also depended on demonstrable success, seen in terms of popular demand for the clinic's services as well as the achievement of any desirable therapeutic changes. Not least among the clinic's preoccupations was that of ensuring a continuing supply of financial contributions.

FURTHER EXPANSIONS

By the end of the first financial year at The Quest (30 September 1929) fifty-five children had been seen under treatment, referrals now coming from London County Council, children's welfare societies, private doctors and consultants, parents and friends. By the end of the following financial year, there had been a further ninety-eight applications, although only fifty-four of these children were taken on. Though a few were regarded as unsuitable for treatment in various ways, the major problems in taking on new cases included the referral of children who lived too far away for treatment to be practicable, and the sheer limits on space and staff time available. The majority of referrals were local, but referrals occasionally came from outside London, even from as far as Devon. The range of sources from which referrals were received had also expanded to include a greater range of school care committees and education authorities. Table 1, taken from the *Annual Report 1929–30* (Children's Clinic, 1930), gives a breakdown of the kind of 'complaints' for which the children were first referred, categorized according to the parents' statements. The major complaint coming from parents was 'nervousness', a description explored more fully later, followed closely by the more obviously self-explanatory category, 'enuresis'.

Anxiety	1	Night terrors	7
Arson	1	Obstinacy	1
Backwardness	9	Pilfering	9
Cruelty	1	Post-concussion character change	1
Debility	1		
Enuresis	15	Screaming fits	2
Epilepsy	3	Sleep-walking	1
Fears	4	Spasms	1
Fighting	1	Speech defect	2
Hysterics	1	Sulkiness	3
Lying	6	Temper	1
Masturbation	2	Truancy	3
Mutism	1	Unmanageability	9
Nervousness	19	Voice loss	1

Table 1 *Primary classification of complaints from parents' statements*

Over the course of the year the total cost of the work per annum had risen from £275 2s 7d in 1929 to £1,069. The increase in demand for the clinic's work brought further expansions and some financial help from outside agencies. The Thomas Wall Trust sponsored a research fellowship, given to Miss A. T. Alcock who became responsible for co-ordinating play-room reports. There were also expansions in social work and in the parents' department. Follow-up work became possible as the Child Guidance Council loaned a psychiatric social worker, Miss Dorothy Lilley, whose salary was provided by the Commonwealth Fund. Lowenfeld noted, she 'not only took over the social side of the work but also gave us new insight into what could be done by trained workers in this field' (Lowenfeld, 1969, p. 16). Work with parents was now supported by Dr Marjory Edwards and Dr Evelyn Saywell, the latter associated with the Tavistock. Recommendations in 1930 included providing a library for parents, extending work with fathers, and opportunities for giving mothers advice on gynaecological conditions, since Dr Marjory Edwards was a gynaecologist with psychotherapeutic experience.

Amongst other changes in medical personnel was the appointment of Professor Leonard Findlay, Lowenfeld's supervisor in the rheumatism research, as senior physician to the clinic on his moving from Glasgow to London in September 1930. The proposal was that he would see all the children referred to the clinic, to diagnose any physical complaints which the children might suffer from, with particular emphasis on possible psychological concomitants. Some of the fruits of this collaboration are illustrated in the papers in Chapter 8. Another significant arrival was Dr Ethel Dukes, who became co-director of the clinic in 1931, and remained as a staunch supporter of Lowenfeld through difficult times during the Second World War.

Another important expansion was in the office and records department, supporting four paid and full-time members of staff, and eight voluntary workers. Their responsibilities included managing publicity and financial appeals, though a large part of this work was carried out by a voluntary committee. Eventually a full-time secretary took charge of publicity and public relations. Apparently Helena made a large contribution to the cost of this post. Lowenfeld's own contributions to publicity included two courses of public lectures, given in the summer of 1930 on 'Some Physical and Emotional Factors Causing Neurosis in Childhood' and 'The Study of Difficult Children'. Finally, but far from least, in 1930 the clinic initiated a one-year training course 'In the principles of modern dynamic psychology and in the carrying out of remedial work with difficult and neurotic children' (Children's Clinic, *Annual Report 1929–30*, p. 25). The course was intended for individuals who had already completed some recognized training in medicine, teaching, social work or some related field. Though students were required to attend lectures on psychology and education given in various departments in London University as well as in the clinic, the main emphasis was on practical work, supervised by Lowenfeld. It aimed 'to provide a unified method of handling each case, while allowing full scope for individual differences', and 'to foster insight into social conditions and administration as well as into psychological processes' (p. 25).

THE EXPERIMENT EVALUATED

Given that this proposal was put forward merely two years after the clinic was first opened, the achievements can only be regarded as impressive, indicative of the extent to which the clinic was gaining respectability in medical and educational circles. In retrospect, the overlap between supporters of Lowenfeld's enterprise and the Tavistock Clinic suggests that at this time a shared commitment to drawing together medical practice and psychology was more important than differences in theoretical emphasis. As already indicated, there were also strong parallels in the organization of the clinics, even down to the appointment of consultants from such apparently tangential fields as dentistry and radiology. This reflected the extent to which Hugh Crichton-Miller was also committed to the need to combine research and therapy, and to elucidating relations between psyche and soma (Crichton-Miller, 1920; Dicks, 1970).

An exploration of relations between 'psyche' and 'soma' was in fact one of the first public communications in which Lowenfeld used the clinic's findings. It was delivered at a meeting of the London Association of the Medical Women's Association on 25 March 1930, in an unpublished paper entitled 'The Interaction of Physical and Psychological Factors in the Causality of Neurosis in Children'. In using the term 'neurosis' Lowenfeld was accepting the diagnostic categories which had by now been admitted into adult psychiatry (see Armstrong, 1983). She was able to point out that at that time no psychiatric textbook gave an explicit entry to 'neurosis' in childhood. Where mental or emotional illness was discussed, the 'neurasthenic' child was trapped by his or her heredity. There was little to be done besides rest or a change in environment (the procedures which had been adopted by her own family during her troubled adolescent years). She pointed out that the textbooks did, however, describe physical characteristics of these children, including poor motor tone, limpness, and other physical characteristics which are now regularly associated with depression. Conversely, Lowenfeld argued, disturbances in the metabolic functioning, hormonal imbalances or dietary insufficiency also produce psychological dysfunction. With clinical examples she illustrated how improvements in one aspect of the condition could bring about changes in the other, and that in all cases this process was facilitated by opportunities for play. She also suggested that there were strong commonalities, in terms of underlying conflicts in emotional processes, between children who present their problems as learning difficulties or as conduct disorders. She ended by arguing the need for an approach which tackled the child's problem on all fronts, social, medical and psychological, an emphasis mirrored in the *Annual Report* for that year. 'The physician, the social worker and the psychologist must take the field as a team in which all the units combine and converge on the same goal' (Children's Clinic, *Annual Report 1929–30*, p. 10).

By 1932, Lowenfeld would have gained the satisfaction of seeing D. K. Henderson and R. D. Gillespie's well-known *Textbook of Psychiatry* include a separate chapter on child psychiatry for the first time. According to Ville Andersen, Lowenfeld regarded the effects of her initiatives upon opening up child psychiatry as one of her most significant contributions. In that chapter Henderson and Gillespie cite the growth of child guidance as showing 'that this topic must now be considered an important part of the psychiatric domain'. At this time Lowenfeld's team appears to have approximated what became the standard child-guidance pattern, in which doctors work closely with social workers and psychologists. As already noted, she acknowledged the value of the psychiatric social worker on loan from the Child Guidance Council. Given the heterogeneity in background amongst the staff, the links to other institutions, and the shared assumptions amongst referral agencies, overlaps and mutual influences would undoubtedly have occurred. However, even by 1930, there were emphases in the Children's Clinic which marked its distinctiveness from the child guidance movement. These also set the seeds for what ultimately became a rift between Lowenfeld's work and psychoanalytic approaches.

Compared to the child guidance tradition, Lowenfeld placed a greater emphasis on thorough physical examination and on combining research and therapy. In addition, her team approach was based less on the idea of a division of labour than on what eventually became a multifaceted holism co-ordinating contributions from different disciplines. Furthermore, Lowenfeld's clinic was distinctive in holding to a particular ideology of liberation against which, with some justification, she could claim that the child guidance movement was concerned with promoting conformity, or the removal of symptoms to adapt children to their environments, rather than promoting possibilities for transcending what Lowenfeld saw as some of the deleterious consequences of modern life and contemporary political systems.

Linked to the ideas of some of the progressive educationists, and implying a particular view of dynamic psychology, the clinic's orientation is well illustrated in the foreword to the

1929–30 *Annual Report*. Addressed to 'those to whom the tenets of psychology are new', this begins by stressing that amongst the casualties of modern life 'none is in greater danger than the child', and that whereas physical injuries cannot go unnoticed, 'Damage and disaster to the minds and sensitivities of children can and do', taking their toll in a considerable proportion of adult breakdowns; 'the child victim of the accelerated pace on the highway of life has in too many cases to endure increasing suffering without treatment for the remainder of its existence' (p. 9).

The foreword goes on to argue that psychological investigations have brought fresh knowledge not as a substitute for but as a supplement to the contributions of physicians and social reformers. The goal is not the production of better-adjusted citizens, but citizens who would create a better society.

> Society is the child grown up. Given warped, neurotic children, a perilously unhealthy society must follow; and no amount of mere education, physical training, or inculcation of high principles can avail to change it into a healthy society. The goal, we feel, in a universe so distraught as ours in 1930, should be to make possible the full development of liberated individuals capable of moulding society into a healthier and more beautiful form. (Children's Clinic, *Annual Report 1929–30*, p. 10)

This introduction was, of course, produced for public consumption with the aim of raising support and funds. Given its address to people to whom the tenets of psychology are 'new' it in fact assumes rather a lot; notably the idea that **'stress'** produces emotional problems with lasting effects, which should be minimized in childhood as far as possible. Later in that year a shortened version of the report was produced to support a fund-raising drive and this time the foreword bypassed psychological knowledge, moving straight to the issue of 'nerves'.

> The most urgent problem of modern life is the appalling increase – due to changed conditions of life – in the number of victims of what are commonly called 'nerves'.
>
> It is 'nerves' which produce the kind of panic that upsets international relations and causes international wars. It is 'nerves' which produce the kind of panic that upsets economic conditions and causes economic wars. It is 'nerves' which produce the kind of panic that upsets domestic

> relations and causes domestic disasters. It is 'nerves' which . . . causes war within the individual and disaster to the individual. (*The Children's Clinic*, 1930, p. 7)

The clinic's aim was to tackle the causes of the various forms of neurosis or 'nerves' in childhood with the 'object of producing stable citizens of balanced outlook and judgement and thus restoring stability to national and international life and relations' (p. 7).

These strong claims are indicative of the extent to which, by the end of the 1920s the discourse of 'nerves' had become public currency, entering into the ways in which parents described their children's complaints. The notion of stress as a major cause of 'wastage' in the labour force was commonly linked to an insistence on protecting the morale and development of the young in order to secure future law and order. One would assume that this connection would be a major reason for an interested public to support the initiatives of Lowenfeld and the child guidance movement. But Lowenfeld did not appeal in this way. Rather she chose to focus on the problem of aggression, here taking up the shell-shock work not simply for its demonstration of the effects of the stress of war on psychological function, but also for its explorations of the mentality of individuals in combat, and the psychological processes which were believed to be an integral part of conflict between nations. The final sentence of the pamphlet, which followed a request for financial support, appears almost embarrassing for its oversimplicity: 'What a chance for someone to go down in history as having secured the peace of the World' (p. 14).

In 1930 Lowenfeld was not of course alone in assuming a relation between psychological disturbance and war, and that freedom from the latter might be secured by appropriate upbringing. The pamphlet assumed an already converted audience: the point was to demonstrate the relevance of her enterprise to a pre-established set of priorities. The notion of freeing or liberating individual children, expecially through play, was integral to the philosophy of Montessori, for whom, 'the fundamental principle of scientific pedagogy must be, indeed, the liberty of the pupil' (Montessori, p. 28). According to Walkerdine (1984), after the First World War the progressive or child-centred tradition in education took particularly seriously the notion that producing free, liberated individuals might militate against further wars on the one hand and guard against the dangers of Russian totalitarianism on the other. This was in spite of the fact that the progressive movement drew the support of individuals from a variety of liberal or left-wing political persuasions, and included contributions from those as committed to social reform as the Webbs, Dora Russell and Margaret McMillan.

The congruence between Lowenfeld's approach and the work of these pioneers in education is partly a result of direct influences upon her, through her own educational experience (by contemporary standards she had been to progressive schools), her reading, and through some of her team. But it is also a reflection of commonly shared assumptions that were a product of the scientific orientation of the child study movement on the one hand and the way the effects of war had been felt, experienced or understood on the other. Nevertheless, within this complex Lowenfeld's position always remained distinctly different, largely because of the particular way she came to understand children's thoughts and feelings. Lowenfeld was clearly committed to social reforms and to creating the possibility for ridding the world of war. As we shall see, for Lowenfeld the need to tackle the relationship between social conditions and emotional disharmony within the individual remained an abiding conviction. Though not a socialist in the usual sense, in the 1920s and 30s she believed in a form of individualism that was radical, in the sense that this individuality was ill understood, was seldom expressed, and could not be 'liberated' without a clearer understanding of its nature and development. Like all writers who later became associated with progressive education through their emphasis on play and freedom of expression, Lowenfeld's thesis was often misunderstood; it was not a case of simply 'letting it all hang out'. (A similar case for the misappropriation or misunderstanding of tenets of progressive education has been argued by Smith, 1985, in relation to Susan Isaacs.)

A final way in which Margaret Lowenfeld's orientation was distinctive emerged through the multifaceted holistic approach itself, which was such that diagnosis and treatment belied any simple account of causation. Whether this was thought to lie in factors in the child's physique or temperament, in parental management, or in the social environment, Lowenfeld's methodology demanded a sustained commitment to multiple rather than singular causation. This can be illustrated by looking at the brief clinical vignettes appended to the

Annual Report of the Children's Clinic (1929–30, pp. 27, 28).

Interestingly, like the case described by Crichton-Miller in his first report on the Tavistock Clinic, mentioned previously (p. 35), Lowenfeld's team were confronted early on by a child with a step-parent, in this case a stepfather. In the Children's Clinic the child was a little girl, Jane, of nine years who had begun to steal, following this by truancy, lying and 'all kinds of untruthfulness until the mother brought her to the children's clinic in despair'. In this and in all the other four cases there is an implicit or explicit assumption that parental management or emotional adjustment is relevant to the child's condition, and that this requires modification in some cases. For example, all Jane's 'miseries' which came out in work and play at the clinic were 'explained' to the mother, who was 'quite unaware of them'. In the case of Ethel, a very anxious child with marked inhibitions in learning, who revealed layer on layer of fear and struggle in the play room, there was a young and apparently hearty mother, who, 'having no outlet for her practical emotions, had found it impossible to allow Ethel to grow out of that state of babyhood in which everything had to be done for her . . . Conversations with the mother modified her attitude towards the child.' There are also illustrations of how important family dynamics were assumed to be in the case of four-year-old Freddie, presenting uncontrollable fits of anger, night waking, bed-wetting and constipation, all of which were found to be associated with the birth of a new baby and his resentment in particular of the loss of his father's attention and his rivalry with him.

After extensive psychological work Jane had won a prize at school for good conduct, 'had ceased to steal and had become altogether reliable and trustworthy', Freddie's temper fits and enuresis had lessened or diminished and after a year of attendance, he had become 'a normal little boy'. Ethel's inhibitions slowly cleared away, so that from being a backward child, at her discharge she was 'equal in ability to any child of her age'. Tony, an epileptic child with a mother who applied very strict standards to herself and her child, returned to his old school where his headmaster reported that he was 'happy and doing well'.

Thus the clinic appears to have been operating according to principles promulgated by the child guidance movement, which emphasized a need for parent guidance, with the assumption that there were scientifically identifiable methods of good parenting, and it was assumed that inadequacy in this area played a causal role in the child's predicament. In describing the children's condition at discharge, there also seem to be normative notions in the emphasis on the removal of symptoms and such socially desirable qualities as improved school performance. It is also clear, in the brief descriptions of family dynamics, that the clinic was implicitly drawing on psychoanalytic theories. Interestingly, these included the work of Adler and his theory of the power complex (see Adler, 1928). In the case of the stalwart Freddie:

> Struggles with himself and struggles against his family led him to develop an identification with a power object, in this case a train, to such a degree that he could at no time be persuaded to answer or to carry out any action unless the command was put into the form of train symbolism, such as: 'Now it is time for the boiler to be filled up, come and sit by the teapot' – in which the teapot played the part of the boiler-feed – and then Freddie would consent to eat his tea. (Children's Clinic, *Annual Report 1929–30*, p. 28)

Adler's work also influenced the work of Burke and Miller over this time, and this may in part be related to the fact that Adler was present in London, lecturing regularly at Crichton-Miller's clinic through 1929 (Dicks, 1970). But whereas in Burke and Miller's work, as has applied in many interpretations of psychoanalytic theory, there was a tendency to assume direct causal links between parental handling and the child's symptomatology, a closer inspection of Lowenfeld's first published cases already suggests a more complex picture, perhaps reinforced by separating working with the parents from working with the children.

Though some of Lowenfeld's statements here and elsewhere on parental adequacy are at times pejorative or condescending, her main emphasis was on the parents' expectations or demands as more or less facilitating the child's own growth and unique temperament. Thus in Ethel's case, the problem posed by the mother's infantilization of her had an indirect effect on her symptomatology: it was 'the violent revolt of the child's nature [which] lay at the root of her fears' (p. 27). Furthermore, though modifications in the parents' attitudes or in their own emotional well-being contributed to improvements, in all cases the crucial agency to change came through the processes through which the children themselves worked through their own anxieties in play and, in the case of the older child, came to some understanding of their own natures. Thus 'Through the material at the clinic Freddie was able to work out in great detail and to get real satisfaction for all his desires for power', and Tony gradually learned 'to understand his own character and to bring different sides of himself into harmony'. Although Lowenfeld was clearly not free from pressure to remove socially undesirable symptoms, and the survival of the clinic depended on it, it would not be false to propose that she believed that the majority of the symptoms were an expression of the child's own unhappiness or confusion. That is, successful or complete treatment would leave the child in a position of greater harmony inside him or herself, and in relation to the environment; and increased curiosity and interest in learning would follow from this, as would also a greater aesthetic awareness. One of the outcomes for June, as important as the improvement in conduct, was a sense of artistry and form, reflected in a mosaic printed on the cover of the clinic report, and on all subsequent issues. This mosaic was probably one of the first systematic uses of the test within psychotherapy.

In 1930, Lowenfeld could with justification claim to be forging an approach which, though related to and drawing on other movements of the times, was none the less independent of them. On 25 March 1931 she gave the first account of the clinic work to be published, the first paper in Chapter 8. It is worth repeating some of the central tenets here. The first is Lowenfeld's interpretation of a commitment to holism, in which 'neurosis represents the reaction of the whole child to his total circumstances', such that any attempt at remediation 'must therefore concern itself equally with all the factors that make up the situation' (Lowenfeld, 1931, this volume, p. 178). The second expresses Lowenfeld's commitment to non-verbal media for expression and what increasingly appears as a sceptical attitude towards verbal communication. 'If we are to get in touch directly with a child's mind . . . we need to learn to understand the child's natural idiom, and that is not speech but play and action' (Lowenfeld, 1931, this volume, p. 180). The paper also refers to the problem of normality and conformity, concluding with the comments:

> I am in most profound disagreement with Dr Adler in his conception of the neurotic as lacking in courage. The qualities . . . that prevent him from fitting into the forms of society he knows are frequently precisely the qualities that, once realized

> and controlled, may ultimately enable him to do his part in the re-creation of social forms.
>
> What we hear called for on all sides today is creative ability and individuality. What we need is not a greater power to conform but a greater power to re-create our society . . .
>
> I have a profound belief in the neurotic child; well handled, I believe he is excellent material for the well-being of the next generation. (Lowenfeld, 1931, this volume, p. 214).

In her account of the history of the Institute of Child Psychology, written in 1969, referred to previously, Lowenfeld noted that this paper 'was not well received'.

4 Inauguration and Development of the Institute of Child Psychology, 1931–9

By the end of the 1920s, the clinic's premises at The Quest were stretched to breaking point. Children and parents were being turned away, older children put with younger ones were complaining that it was 'a place for babies' and there was a lack of adequate space outdoors for the 'expression of destructive tendencies . . . where noise can be made without distracting other children' (*The Children's Clinic*, 1930, pp. 13–14). Furthermore the cramped facilities had meant that a feature regarded as essential, the biochemical testing, had had to be sacrificed. Help came in the form of an anonymous offer of a leasehold on what was once Robert Browning's house in Little Venice, London. The house consisted of four storeys and faced on to Regent's Park Canal. A long walled-in garden running from the back door could be used for running games and noise, while the basement was arranged for mess, water-play, handicrafts and other experiments. The clinic could now open on any day of the week.

With the move, changes were made in the organization of staff. The clinic was supported by the new vice-presidents and, interestingly, none of the new medical staff joining at the time were formally linked to the Tavistock Clinic, though Dr Alan Maberley joined for a short period in the following year. It was at this time that Dr Ethel Dukes became co-director with Margaret Lowenfeld, and that the clinic changed its name to the Institute of Child Psychology (ICP). The ICP was launched with an appeal which described the aim of the treatment as 'the development of the child as an individual competent to face his own difficulties with understanding and courage' (Lowenfeld, 1969, p. 17). In July 1931 the ICP held its first conference under the theme, 'The Possible Contribution that the Study of

Difficult Children May Make to Education'. Appealing explicitly to educationists, sessions were chaired by C. W. Kimmins, Chief Inspector of Schools for London County Council, as well as by Professor Winifred Cullis from the Royal Free Hospital. In contrast to the reception given to Lowenfeld's paper in the previous year, the response given to the work *in situ* was positive and encouraging, the conference giving full support to the proposals for a training course mooted in the previous year.

However, this relative stability did not last. During the autumn of 1931 the national financial crisis hit the work of the ICP, as it did many other projects supported voluntarily. Donations and subscriptions shrank overnight or ceased altogether. With insufficient funds to cover the rent at Browning House, there was no alternative but to give the lease back to the original owner. Temporary premises were found in the ground-floor flat of the house next door, at 20 Warwick Crescent, premises which were considerably reduced in size. An arrangement of screens was used to divide up a single room into spaces for children's play, interviewing parents and carrying out medical examinations; the bathroom was given over to mess and water-play; and the conservatory became the office. Fortunately, by December 1931 arrangements had been made to rehouse the ICP in 26 Warwick Avenue, W9. Though not ideal, the new premises were larger and included a garden. The ICP remained there for four and a half years.

Despite the disruption produced by the moves, the newly inaugurated training persisted. The *Annual Report* of the ICP for 1933 looked back at that six months as a period of enthusiasm as 'the hall, the stairs and even the scullery were constantly invaded by small groups of children and workers anxious to try out some new and interesting experiment'. In the attempt to remedy the serious financial situation, in 1932 the ICP was registered as a friendly society under the Friendly Societies Act of 1896. Various functions were organized with the aim of raising money. Beginning in November 1932 these included the holding of two sets of public lectures per year at the Friends House, Euston Road, one in the spring and one in the autumn. The lectures covered such topics as 'The Mind of the Child', 'The Nature and Significance of Play in Young Children', 'Children in Trouble and the Way Out', and 'Common Difficulties in Normal Children' (Lowenfeld, 1969, p. 20). Though some lectures were given by Margaret Lowenfeld, many were given by other physicians who were well known at the time, such as Dr Sloan-Chesser, Dr Doris Odlum and Dr Donald Winnicott. Educationists also contributed.

While these talks were intended for the general public, they increased the clinic's reputation as well as its funds. Over the same time period regular discussion groups were held at the ICP for medical and other workers from specialist fields holding different views, the aim being to discuss current medical, educational and social problems. These discussions were consistently well attended. By 1934, a consultancy service had sprung up at the ICP, cases being sent for diagnosis, assessment or general advice rather than actual treatment. In the same year the ICP was asked to co-operate with the West End Hospital in establishing a play-therapy room under the medical direction of the hospital Child Guidance unit, and two helpers were sent there from the ICP.

While the ICP was expanding its sphere of influence outwards, the intensity of clinical work also increased. Though there are no data available on the number of cases seen, reports on the ICP for the years of work between 1933 and 1935 indicate a substantial increase in total number of attendances and hours of treatment (see Table 1).

	Attendances	Hours of Treatment
1933	590	1,157
1934	965	1,650
1935	1,355	2,081

Table 1 *Attendances at the Institute of Child Psychology, 1933–5**

*Figures abstracted from the Institute of Child Psychology, *Annual Reports*, 1933, 1934, 1935.

Given the financial and social hardship of the depression years, this expansion may seem surprising. On the other hand, comparable developments were happening in similar institutions. In his history of the Tavistock Clinic, Dicks (1970) describes the period up to the Second World War as the period of expansion, both adult and children's departments showing a steady increase in attendances and long waiting lists. The year 1932 saw the publication of the report on the Child Guidance Council's first Demonstration Clinic, set up in Islington in 1928. This experiment was funded by the Commonwealth Fund for five years on the understanding that the clinic would be taken over by the London County Council if it proved successful. It roughly paralleled the establishment of the East London Child Guidance Clinic, set up under the auspices of the Jewish Health Organization, where Emanuel Miller and Noel Burke were based, and of course Lowenfeld's establishment. Of the children seen at the Islington clinic the largest group were described as 'backward children', the second largest 'delinquent children' (chiefly accused of theft), and the remainder were referred for nervousness, being unmanageable, and such specific complaints as spitefulness, lying, stammering and the like. Forty-eight percent were reported as 'fully adjusted' at the end of the period (Keir, 1952, p. 24). Despite the judged success of the project, the unexpectedly high cost of maintaining it (£3,774 for the six months ending 31 March 1932) prevented the London County Council from taking it over. Nevertheless the Child Guidance Council continued to extend its work, setting up new clinics throughout the country as well as in London.

One could speculate on relations between increasing referrals to children's clinics and the social and material consequences of the economic depression. It seems likely that physical and emotional hardship in families experiencing unemployment and poverty would have created pressure for existing services to expand and develop strategies for containing social unrest, in so far as this was expressed in civil disobedience or maladjustment. Over this time the input of psychological services into education was also expanding, as consequences of unemployment were added to pre-existing problems in mounting an adequate secondary-school system (Simon, 1974). As previously noted, it was in 1932 that the new edition of Henderson and Gillespie's psychiatric textbook included its section on child psychiatry. Following the shifts in nosology and conceptualization which had taken place in adult psychiatry, the model of illness shifted so that 'neurosis' in children was reinterpreted not as a neurological problem or a disease but in terms of psychological processes. Thus, mental–emotional disturbance could, in principle, be found in all of us. Within a few years, as we have seen, the Peckham Experiment had been reopened as a health centre which now took the family as its basic unit (Armstrong, 1983).

Peckham's new rubric was symptomatic of a subtle shift of emphasis which occurred through the 1930s. Increasingly the focus of attention in administrative and social intervention moved away from the individual child patient or parent on to the family, and relationships in the family, and finally the mother and child (Armstrong, 1983; Riley, 1983). Though the latter shift was already taking place in the 1930s, its full implementation was linked to what, in her account of factors contributing to the closure of nurseries for infants after the Second World War, Denise Riley (1983) has called the 'popularization' of post-Kleinian psychoanalysis, notably the ideas of John Bowlby and Donald Winnicott. But this popularization depended on post-war social and administrative changes affecting medical and social-work practice and, first, these theories had to achieve some centrality.

Throughout its period of expansion, the theoretical backbone of the Tavistock Clinic remained relatively eclectic, influenced by exponents of the British dynamic psychology movement as well as by psychoanalysis (Dicks, 1970). Elsewhere, Melanie Klein was beginning to make her influence felt. Having arrived in England in 1926, after a somewhat rocky start she made a positive impression on a sufficient number of analysts at the British Psycho-Analytical Society to ensure her acceptance and a continuing respect for her work. By the early 1930s she had gathered around her a small group of devotees which included Nina Searl, Susan Isaacs, for a time, Klein's own daughter Melitta Schmideberg, and a little later Donald Winnicott. By 1932 Melanie Klein had published the English edition of her *The Psychoanalysis of Children*. Over the same time period Susan Isaacs had begun publishing observations and commentaries on the children in the Malting House School, her own experiment in progressive education, in her two books, *Intellectual Growth in Young Children* and *Social Development in Young Children*, published in 1930 and 1933 respectively. The second book in particular makes extensive use of psychoanalysis, drawing on the work of Melanie Klein. But the first book is particularly influenced by and indebted to the early work of Piaget, reflecting Isaacs's commitment to the Child Study tradition. Though increasingly involved in psychoanalysis, in 1933 she became head of the newly formed Department of Child Development in the Institute of Education, London University, remaining there until 1943.

Given that all these expansions in theory and practice were occurring over a time of restriction in resources and mounting uncertainty, one possible outcome would have been an increase in mutual support between similar but independent institutions and theoretical groupings. On the other hand, conditions were also ripe for rivalry. For the ICP, to some extent the latter alternative proved uppermost, such that it emerged with a distinctive philosophy and theoretical orientation. That is, through the 1930s, previously implicit theoretical and technical grounds for separating the ICP from the orientations of the Tavistock, the child-guidance clinics and the psychoanalytic movement became more clearly drawn. Though many factors contributed, a major impetus came from Lowenfeld's analysis of some of the considerable material accumulated from her child patients. This enabled her to go on to formulate theoretical tools with therapeutic implications.

THEORIES OF PLAY

A first and crucial step in this process was the publication of *Play in Childhood* (1935). As Lowenfeld noted in the preface to the first edition, the book was based around a series of lectures and discussions given at the ICP in 1934 to an audience including a large proportion of educationists, school inspectors, principals, members of training-college staffs, headmistresses and staffs of nursery schools. By this time the second and third reports of the Hadow Consultative Committee on Educational Provision, *The Primary School* (1931) and *Infant and Nursery Schools* (1933), both commissioned by the Board of Education, had included explicit recommendations for ample opportunities for play. Though official policy, there was actually a considerable time lag in the incorporation of these recommendations into standard infant-school practice. Indeed in Britain the child-centred movement did not really take hold until the publication of the Plowden report in the 1960s, when Lowenfeld took advantage of long-standing links with education (as is discussed in the next chapter). But in 1934, in speaking to her particular audience, Lowenfeld was almost certainly addressing the converted. In publishing *Play in Childhood* a year later the aim was to put forward views or conclusions about the nature and functions of play and its importance in development, based on what she had read and observations of children at the ICP. In addition she aimed to confirm the general application of her views, given that her observations of children were largely based on the clinic population.

In her retrospective account of this period, Margaret Lowenfeld stressed the laborious hours at the British Museum, 'using every moment that could be snatched to read . . . on the history of thought about both of the two words "play" and "child" and the fact of children at play' (Lowenfeld, 1969, p. 290). As an academic work, *Play in Childhood* is important in itself as the first full-scale survey of theories of play. Viewed historically her search was indeed relatively thorough, and in various ways the survey of theories has since been reproduced many times, for example, by Suzanna Miller (1968), and Garvey (1977). She gave a circumscribed and critical place to the work of Herbert Spencer, who emphasized play as 'discharge of energy', Karl de Groos, who regarded play as an expression of instinct, and to Stanley Hall, well known for his 'recapitulation' theory of play ('Ontogeny recapitulates phylogeny'). In contrast to contemporary developmental psychologists, she emphasized the influence of the spirit of Froebel, for whom play was 'the highest expression of human development in childhood', and 'the appropriate vehicle and helpmate of education'. She was particularly sympathetic to James Sully, a founder of child study in Britain, for his emphasis on objective detachment and appropriate humility in relation to the possible meanings of children's play to the cultured adult. However, she stressed that, although most of the theories were valuable in capturing one or more aspects of play, none embraced it in its entirety. That is, in spite of considerable variety in the methods used there was as yet no systematic classification of play, and 'no theory of play available which can be applied to all forms of play taken by the play of children' (Lowenfeld, 1935, p. 36).

For Margaret Lowenfeld play was an orientation, 'the expression of the child's relation to the whole of life, and no theory of play is possible which is not also a theory which will cover the whole of a child's relation to life'. Though this working definition appears extremely broad and all-embracing, readers of more recent or contemporary works on play may recognize the origins of an emphasis on functions of play, which may be worked through with different materials (e.g. Garvey, 1977) and on the idea that what characterizes play is not the behaviour itself but the manner in which it is carried out (Bruner, 1972; Reynolds, 1972). In Lowenfeld's terms, 'Play . . . is taken as applying to all activities in children that are spontaneous and self-generated; that are ends in themselves; and that are unrelated to "lessons" or to the normal physiological needs of the child's own day' (1935, pp. 36–7).

For Lowenfeld, play functioned as a form of thinking, in which the expression of emotions and feelings was integral. In this context, she gave a particular place to the contribution of psychoanalysis and quoted extensively from Freud's account of play given in *Beyond the Pleasure Principle* (Freud, 1920). This account stressed how the active repetition in play of previously unpleasurable experiences or events that had made a great impression on the child enabled him or her to gain mastery over the situation, diminishing the strength of the underlying anxiety. The emphasis on mastering anxiety by turning passive experiences into active ones has been particularly important in Anna Freud's psychoanalytic tradition (A. Freud, 1966). Interestingly, Lowenfeld also cited the way Freud linked the repetition compulsion in play with some of the intransigent phenomena revealed in the analysis of shell-shocked adults, phenomena which contributed to his hypothesis of the death instinct (Freud, 1920). She also referred explicitly to psychoanalytic discoveries in chapters which, appropriately enough, classified play as 'Repetition of Experience' and as 'Phantasy'. In using the term 'phantasy' she was distinguishing this form of thought from the kind of imaginative thought described as 'fantasy' in daily usage. However, Lowenfeld's use of the term phantasy was not identical with the unconscious phantasy described by psychoanalysts though there were similarities (see later). She went on to acknowledge, specifically, that the psychoanalytic tradition provided 'most' of the knowledge we have' on children's experience of emotions within the self, their attractions and their fears over the first two years, here referring to the work of Melanie Klein (Lowenfeld, 1935, pp. 103–4). She added that this work was virtually alone in attending to the infant's experiences of sensations, such as touch, sight, smell, and sound. However, she was also explicitly critical of Klein and her following for developing Freud's conception of play into a theory in which play is 'regarded exclusively as the representation in symbolic form of wishes, ideas and thoughts related to the theory of infantile sexuality' (p. 36).

In referring to papers published before 1935, Lowenfeld was encompassing the period before the differences betwen Melanie Klein and her daughter Melitta Schmideberg had surfaced to cause such contention and bitterness within the British Psycho-Analytical Society (Klein, 1932; Schmideberg, 1934, 1935; Searl, 1927, 1930, 1933; and see Grosskurth, 1986). Lowenfeld insisted that she did not deny the existence of the kind of play described by psychoanalysts. But she rejected the supposition that infantile sexuality accounted for the totality of the content and functions of play, and questioned any attempt to reduce the meaning of symbolic expressions to a universal set of categories derived from a pre-existent theoretical framework. Thereafter references to Klein's work were sparse. Though she gave extensive and acknowledged quotations from Susan Isaacs's work (1930, 1933), she seldom discussed Isaacs's interpretations. By and large, Isaacs's observations were used as further illustrations of assumptions crystallized through her own work, or to provide material from children not drawn from a clinical population.

Lowenfeld herself made extensive use of the early work of Piaget, particularly *The Child's Conception of the World* (Piaget, 1929). This emphasized young children's tendencies towards 'magical' views of causality and the assumption that the world revolves round them, contributing to confusions between phantasy and reality and, in Lowenfeld's rendering, a primacy of subjective over objective thought. She also drew upon the normative studies of Arnold Gesell and Charlotte Bühler, and of K. Banham Bridges, here referring to the largest available studies of 'normal' populations, though she noted that they were generally drawn from a narrow range of social backgrounds.

Thus Lowenfeld's forebears in her synthesis on play were not, on the whole, the analysts, but the child study movement, educationists and early developmental psychologists who insisted on objective methods of recording behaviour. Unsurprisingly, Lowenfeld's survey came out with a tentative developmental sequence reflected in the series of chapter headings following the Introduction, as follows:

Play as bodily activity
Play as repetition of experience
Play as the demonstration of phantasy
Play as realization of environment
Play as preparation for life
Group games
The comic element in play
Children who do not play

In each case the classification indicates predominant preoccupations, the emphasis being on the function of the form of play to the child engaged in it. How the child passes through each type of play will affect later manifestations. In brief, play as bodily activity refers to the young baby who, through the language-acquisition period, begins to 'realize experience', reproducing events or perceptions internally and repeating them with variations. Here, Lowenfeld in part followed Freud in assuming that 'it does seem to be undeniable that small children have a very strong and essential wish to reproduce their own experiences in play' (Lowenfeld, 1935, p. 107), including past experiences as a baby. But rather than assuming that this repetition was necessarily to master anxiety, Lowenfeld proposed that it also served a vital cognitive function, as 'There seems to be a strong inner drive in all human minds to externalize themselves, or to re-create their experiences *in order to be able to assimilate them*, and the small child is no exception to this rule' (p. 107, emphasis added). The implication is that knowledge of one's own experiences will generally precede knowledge of the external world as independent; the chapter concentrates on the bodily experiences associated with eating, urinating and defecating. Though similar to Piaget's ideas, this was considerably earlier than Piaget's theoretical link between play and assimilation in *Play, Dreams and Imitation*, which was published in 1951, and in which Lowenfeld's work was mentioned.

For Lowenfeld, the realization of one's own experience feeds into and is fed by the 'demonstration of phantasy' which follows it and to some extent depends on it. After distinguishing phantasy from imagination, which retains a definite relationship to reality, in Lowenfeld's account the essence of phantasy was that it rules in a world of imagery and is controlled by the individual's desires; it is as it were 'the stuff that dreams are made of' and is not necessarily unconscious. Lowenfeld used illustrative examples from Piaget's (1929) observations of magical thinking in four-year-old children in this section. But because she emphasized the dominance of desire, her account of their significance differed from his. Piaget saw the young child's fantasizing in terms of a cognitive deficit. Lowenfeld saw the emotionality as uppermost, but none the less stressed this as a process with cognitive effects which were developmentally necessary.

By five or six, the child, having 'made terms with his earlier experience, turns naturally outwards towards his environment' (Lowenfeld, 1935, p. 322). That is, in this scheme, children test out and explore relations between their inner selves and external reality which, as they discover, cannot be moved by phantasy. Realizing the environment through play is seen most obviously in doll play, where children work out relations between external reality, constraint and desire.

Doll play is also a vehicle for play as a 'preparation for life' as children take on board and reproduce roles or choices afforded by the culture. Role play and other manifestations of this form of play peak in middle childhood. Finally, group games were placed at the end of the sequence as a form of play carried forward to form a major element in adult life.

Lowenfeld's sequence is in many respects consistent with Piaget's scheme, or other sequences which stress a developmental shift from the egocentric or undifferentiated individual to the socialized individual. This is the most usual framework to follow from the child study tradition, and it carries with it certain assumptions about the 'normal' course of development (Urwin, 1986). However there were important emphases in Lowenfeld's account which cut across ways in which accounts of the normal course too easily lead to a normative reduction. First, Lowenfeld stressed that children's play has both internal and external aspects, producing both functional and expressive effects. Second, the functional components persist despite variation in form or mode of expression, accounting for instance for the comic element in play, and are governed by affectivity or emotional factors. Third, Lowenfeld insisted upon individual variation and the uniqueness of expression and, fourth, that although there would be age-related peaks in interest, children might use all forms of play at any age. However, she argued that it was particularly characteristic of neurotic children to show far more variation and inconsistency, or problems in playing at all.

These emphases on diversity had important and distinctive therapeutic implications. Of course, many psychoanalysts have recognized dangers in assuming a fixed developmental sequence. For example, one reason why Klein introduced the term 'position' in her accounts of paranoid-schizoid and depressive positions in infancy was to avoid the rigidity that had become associated with the term 'stage' (Klein, 1935, 1946; see Segal, 1986). However, a fundamental difference follows from Lowenfeld's emphasis on the many necessary developmental functions associated with children's play. It is this that underlay the provision of unconstrained opportunities for all types of play (from motor activity and messing to constructive play and group games) in the ICP. Furthermore once this developmental perspective was coupled with an emphasis on discovering the meaning of the play for the child engaged in it, then allowing that the child might be needing to play as a means of representing experience, reworking the social environment or preparing for a life event was as important as recognizing emotional conflicts to do with, for example, Oedipal wishes or internal ambivalence.

In recognizing that play expresses relations to the social world, Margaret Lowenfeld's developmental framework makes questions of social and cultural location as central to the therapist's task as it does to the child's. But at this point in the account, Lowenfeld has a theoretical and technical problem. The developmental necessity for play in part accounts for the extent to which opportunities for play are themselves therapeutic. But what of children who cannot or do not play, and how can this be ameliorated? More specifically, in terms of the developmental sequence, what impedes the development of play as the realization of early experience, which as she suggested affects all subsequent manifestations? The major theoretical contribution on this issue was not put forward until later in the 1930s. However part of the answer was already contained in *Play in Childhood*, as Lowenfeld began to struggle with the philosophical basis of her work and its place in history and culture.

PHILOSOPHICAL AND SOCIOCULTURAL FOUNDATIONS

In *Play in Childhood* for the first time Margaret Lowenfeld refers explicitly to Robin Collingwood's recently published *An Essay on Philosophical Method* (1933). In this work Collingwood was already moved towards an examination of relations between historical and philosophical method, which eventually led him to conclude that correct philosophical inquiry was necessarily historical. In brief, he arrived at this position through insisting that in order to evaluate the truth of a proposition one needs to know what question the proposer had in mind when supplying the proposition as an answer. From here he concluded that the proposition would need to be situated historically, just as historical inquiry necessitates attempting to understand relations between the artefacts, statements, military manoeuvres or other sources of historical evidence on the one hand, and the thoughts, intentions, purposes and meanings in the minds of the original users on the other.

As he described in his *Autobiography*, a passionate account of the story of his mental life, written in 1938 and published the following year, Collingwood's viewpoint was based as much on his reflections on historical method through his work in archaeology as on his work in the history of philosophy. He also delved deeply into the history of artistic expression and feeling (Collingwood, 1938). The autobiography neatly summarizes his view in three basic propositions. First, in his conception of history, 'all history is the history of thought', in so far as one is thinking historically when one is able to say, 'I see what the person who made this (wrote this, used this, designed this, and so on) was thinking' (Collingwood, 1939, p. 110). But how can one know the history of a thought? The thought must be expressed, in language, or in another form of expressive activity such as painting. Either way, Collingwood insisted that the historian must reach after the thought in the head of the initiator of the activity in the past: 'He must be able to think for himself that very same thought, not another like it', so that it follows that 'historical knowledge is the re-enactment in the historian's mind of the thought whose history he is studying' (p. 112). But thinking the thought of someone existing in the past is not the same, of course, as having the thought oneself *de novo*. There is a differentiation based on context, a past thought living in the present in one's mind, but encapsulated; thus Collingwood's third proposition was that 'Historical knowledge is the re-enactment of a past thought encapsulated in a context of present thoughts which, by contradicting it, confine it to a plane different from theirs' (p. 114). It was from this dialectical position that Collingwood drew perhaps his most radical conclusions. If the historian knows past thoughts by rethinking them,

> The knowledge that he achieves by historical inquiry is not knowledge of his situation as opposed to knowledge of himself, it is a knowledge of his situation, which is at the same time knowledge of himself. In re-thinking what somebody else thought, he thinks it himself. In knowing that somebody else thought it, he knows that he himself is able to think it. And finding out what he is able to do is finding out what kind of a man he is. If he is able to understand, by rethinking them, the thoughts of a great many different kinds of people, it follows that he must be a great many kinds of man. He must be, in fact, a microcosm of all the history he can know. Thus his own self knowledge is at the same time his knowledge of the world of human affairs. (Collingwood, 1939, pp. 114–15)

In his autobiography, Collingwood relates how this train of thought was completed in about 1930 and that by completing it, he had completed his answer to a question that had haunted him ever since the war: 'How could we construct a science of human affairs, so to call it, from which men could learn to deal with human situations as skilfully as natural science had taught them to deal with situations in the world of Nature?' (Collingwood, 1939, p. 115). For Collingwood the answer was not sociology, which he rejected for its ahistoricity and lack of contact with human purposes, nor psychology, which he criticized for its positivism masquerading as science, nor psychoanalysis, with which he had some sympathy. Rather, for Collingwood the answer now was that 'The science of human affairs is history', a thesis developed further in his final books, *The Idea of Nature* (1945) and *The Idea of History* (1947), both published posthumously.

Unsurprisingly Collingwood's work was considered highly controversial in his lifetime, and has since been variously criticized for being idealist or for a thoroughgoing relativist collapse. On the other hand, it has been pointed out that he was furrowing much of the ground that was later furrowed by the European tradition of hermeneutics, the most well-known example being representatives of the Frankfurt school flourishing after the Second World War. In spite of the criticisms of 'relativism', it was from 1930 onwards, having clarified his theoretical position, that Collingwood began a re-evaluation of his political position such that he moved from holding a faith in British democracy, and liberalism in the widest sense, to a position closer to socialism. Crucial to this shift were what he saw as changes in the function and content of the British press, and in particular the government's response to the Spanish Civil War, and what he regarded as a collusive support of Fascism. A vivid account of this change in consciousness was given in the last chapter of his autobiography, which concludes with a spine-chilling foreboding that a further outbreak of war was inevitable. In the year that the book was actually published, this prophecy had already become a reality.

The argument for the need for a philosophy of history was not yet fully developed in the *Essay on Philosophical Method*, cited by Lowenfeld. But given that he had already formulated his basic thesis by 1930 it is not surprising that there is a comparability between many of Collingwood's ideas and Lowenfeld's emphases. The most obvious is the continuing stress on understanding the meaning or function of the play for *the child actually doing it*, and on understanding the questions behind the child's own preoccupations. Here Lowenfeld could be said to be applying Collingwood's historical method to produce a unique explication of individual development and its sociocultural location, which became clearer in later work.

Collingwood's ideas also gave support to Lowenfeld's view of the nature of thought itself. In *Play in Childhood* she draws on his *Essay on Philosophical Method* in discussing the nature of early phantasy and the way in which it interweaves with the developmentally prior forms of representing experience. In Lowenfeld's view, these none the less constitute a form of thought. Here she quotes Collingwood in order to support the view that forms of thought exist within us prior to the language we use to express them.

> We speak well, in prose, only in order to say what we mean. The matter is prior to the form . . . The matter does not exist as a naked but fully formed thought in our minds before we fit it with a garment of words. It is only in some dark and half-conscious way that we know our thoughts before we come to express them. Yet in that obscure fashion they are already within us, and, rising into full consciousness as we find the words to utter them, it is they that determine the words, not vice versa. (Collingwood, 1933, p. 200; cited in Lowenfeld, 1935, pp. 152–3)

The challenge to the hegemony of language in this viewpoint has to be understood in relation to philosophical debates on relations between language and truth amongst Collingwood's contemporaries. Taking the idea further, Lowenfeld drew on Piaget (1932a) and other European educationists in insisting that before age eight or nine children do not use words to communicate their *ideas*. Yet before the first word is acquired the infant has a network of phantasies. For Lowenfeld this does not function simply for emotional expression or discharge but constitutes a form of thought. Even when the child has begun to acquire language, the expression of phantasy requires a multi-dimensional, non-verbal medium, unconstrained in advance, in order to capture the multiple use of the senses: 'The feel of a jug, the fact that it can hold fluids, the smell and taste of the glue on a wooden toy [interwoven] with its shape' (Lowenfeld, 1935, p. 156).

> Children appropriate the materials they find to hand, and invest them with imaginative qualities that make them a vehicle for the concepts, wishes and phantasies that surge within their heads . . . Having created the elements they need for their play they proceed to combine them in ways which

> enable them to express the underlying ideas they are trying to grasp. (Lowenfeld, 1935, p. 156)

This gives play a fluidity which, Lowenfeld suggests, parallels Collingwood's assumptions about thought that precedes verbal expression. Yet it is in the nature of the early 'pre-verbal' thought of the child that its multidimensionality and open-endedness cannot be simply translated into verbal expression, which is by and large culturally imposed, and constrained in form and time in accord with rules of grammar. Thus children do not set out with their thoughts fully developed. Rather,

> These thoughts grow as the play develops, out of the interplay between the material and the mind that is working on it. In very few cases does one find a completed synopsis in the mind, which is then expressed in material, but instead that the statement of the first stage of the play . . . suggests to the mind the next stage, and it is characteristic of children's phantasy play, if unchecked by an adult observer, that it will move forward simultaneously in several planes of thought at once. (Lowenfeld, 1935, p. 177)

Many clinicians from various traditions would recognize this fluidity as an essential feature of young children's play, which cannot be captured in any simple theory of stages. It was one of the characteristics which led Freud (1900, 1911) originally to draw parallels between children's play and the free associations and dreams of adults, contributing eventually to Melanie Klein's emphasis on play as the appropriate medium for child analysis. As will be discussed more fully later, there are some points of correspondence between Lowenfeld's pre-verbal thought and Klein's primitive phantasy (Isaacs, 1948). But for Lowenfeld, in therapy the issue would not simply be to follow the movement of anxiety, desires, or conflicts. Her primary interest in the shifting aspects of the play would be in the actual process of making links between different materials of expression, regarding this process as simultaneously both affective and cognitive. Moreover, in examining the material interwoven by the child, whether this was words, parts of a game, or pieces of remembered stories, she would assume a social and historical dimension.

In introducing *Play in Childhood* with an account of historical theories of play, Lowenfeld was of course doing a standard review of alternative points of view. But in carrying out her historical survey, she also came across the phenomenon which we have since come to associate with the work of Ariès (1962), de Mause (1974) and other investigators of the history of childhood: that what a child is and what, if anything, is regarded as interesting or particular about childhood has varied in accord with different cultural, economic and political systems. Using the idea of societies in different stages of development, which she would have become familiar with through the work of Trotter (1920), as examples she cited Margaret Mead's early work on child-rearing practices in non-Western societies (Mead, 1931) and, within British culture, the celebration of the child associated with Wordsworth's romanticism. But having noted cross-cultural and historical variation, Lowenfeld did not leave it at that. If the meaning of childhood must be situated historically and socially, following Collingwood, so must the questions which one has about it.

In her introduction, Lowenfeld sketched the background to her own study. Implicitly and explicitly, she continued the theme which preoccupied her since the First World War: bewilderment and terror at the destructiveness of humanity which seems to be 'exactly balanced' by the mounting demonstration of apparent power and control over Nature, set against what she took to be common experiences of misery and chaos associated with the First World War and a terror that these would repeat themselves. Fortunately, she noted, in the attempt to understand causes and sources of human misery, 'Seeds germinate in the dark, and it is in semi-darkness that this battle begins, the darkness of both mental misery and our own ignorance' (p. 10). Here, Lowenfeld was referring to the discovery of and possibilities in dynamic psychology, emphasizing both the conditions of its production as well as its content. In spite of an emergent emphasis on sociocultural variation in the content and context of children's play, Lowenfeld's views were clearly distinguishable from the kinds of social determinism which have since become associated with role theory and various versions of behaviourism. In contrast to the idea that children can be simply moulded, a view which she associated with the Germanic tradition in education and to some extent with the American ideal, for her what was distinctive about the contribution of dynamic psychology was that it had led to the view that there were certain unchanging aspects of a child's nature, persisting to form the background of all adult life. In consequence:

> The life of the child . . . comes to reveal itself as pregnant with greater issues; and the mind of the child to hold within itself clues to the understanding of corporate humanity. (p. 15)

From this point of view,

> From being a charming embroidery upon the normal purpose of man, conceived as growth and learning, the nature of play comes instead to occupy a prominent place in the problems of mankind. (p. 15)

Given this historical and social placing of play, its study should reveal mental and emotional dilemmas repeating themselves in the world at large. Against the background of the buildup of Fascism in Italy, Hitler's accession to power in 1933, and the beginnings of the Nazi purges, 'play' was viewed as containing keys both to sources of terror and destruction, and to solution:

> Play . . . expresses a child's relation to himself and his environment, and, without adequate opportunity for play, normal and satisfactory emotional development is not possible . . . If the author is correct in this view . . . then any individual in whose early life these necessary opportunities for adequate play have been lacking will inevitably go on seeking them in the stuff of adult life. (p. 324)

Unfortunately opportunities missed in childhood never present themselves again in the same form, and the tragedy and the danger is that individuals are compelled to seek satisfaction for something which they cannot identify.

> Forces unrealized in childhood remain as an inner drive for ever seeking outlet, and lead men to express them not any longer in play, since this is regarded as an activity of childhood, but in industrial competition, anarchy and wars.
>
> The less a man or a child is aware of the interior forces of his mind, the more irresistibly is he driven to express them. We have seen how fantastic is the content of much of this interior life of the mind in children . . . the nature of this logic is, however, at utter variance with the logic of the conscious mind, and man's disharmony with himself is due to the fact that he is unaware of this situation; that, once childhood is over, he takes his games for reality, his fantastic conceptions of the world for political sanity, and his momentary myths for considered thought. (p. 325)

Thus, there was a social imperative behind Lowenfeld's project, in which play emerges as a very serious business. Lowenfeld was not alone, of course, in seeing parallels between the play of children and the terrors and destructiveness of war. It was an emphasis shared by many of the early progressive educationists, and it re-emerged during the Second World War. For example, discussing how the care of children in the wartime nurseries was managed, Riley (1983) draws attention to a *British Medical Journal* leading article entitled 'War in the Nursery'. Published in 1944, the article discusses the staff's responsibility to contain the 'aggression natural to the nursery age' where 'destructive impulses let loose in war may serve to fan the flame':

> If the nerves of staff strained to breaking point cannot hold out, delinquency may ensue; the age of resistance may thus be prolonged to adolescence or adult life in the form of bitterness, irresponsibility or delinquency. (Riley, 1983, p. 95)

As Riley pointed out, the article reflects embryonically the theorization of the consequences of separation and maternal deprivation, associated with the work of Bowlby and Winnicott. By 1940, Bowlby had published one of his first papers on a relationship between early separation from the mother and delinquent behaviour, in this case stealing, reporting on work actually undertaken in the 1930s. Lowenfeld's book on play, however, attaches no special importance to mothers, and in fact rarely mentions relations between parents and infants and young children, save in so far as parental intolerance of reproof can be regarded as contributing to children's inhibition or lack of opportunities for expression (Lowenfeld, 1935, p. 107). Though emphasizing a propensity for aggressivity and destructiveness, a viewpoint which she later clarified, for Lowenfeld in 1935 dangers were less to do with specific negative forces themselves than with consequences of lack of opportunity for expression and reintegration. That is, for Lowenfeld what was crucial about play was not the laying bare of natural impulses, but the processes through which impulses and experiences, physical, social and emotional, were brought together or reworked. This brought to the forefront the problem of creativity.

NEUROSIS, NORMALITY AND CREATIVITY

Play in Childhood was an immediate success. At the time

Lowenfeld refused permission for the book to be published in the USA, on the grounds that 'the time was not yet ripe there' (Lowenfeld, 1969). This decision was eventually reversed in the 1960s. By the outbreak of the war the book had gone out of print. It was republished in 1965, running into several reprintings, including a specifically American edition with a new introduction, published in 1967. Later in 1935, the year that *Play in Childhood* was first published, the ICP held a conference on its work at Conway Hall, Red Lion Square, London, which was attended mainly by officials of educational and local-government bodies. The work apparently met with considerable approval.

That *Play in Childhood* and the work of the ICP found favour among educationists at this time is not surprising, given the many assumptions and commitments which Lowenfeld shared with her contemporaries in progressive education. For instance, even the official Hadow reports (1931, 1933) had explicitly linked the importance of play to the provision of freedom. But there were contrasting emphases which are particularly important in considering what aspects of Lowenfeld's work were actually taken up and what was disregarded. As Walkerdine (1984) suggests, in her essay 'Developmental Psychology and the Child-centred Pedagogy', the incorporation of child-centred ideas within the educational system inevitably involved selective uptake and transformation, by virtue of the regulatory function of the school. For example, the Hadow report (1931) had insisted that individual freedom 'is essential; and freedom only becomes dangerous when there is nothing to absorb the child's restless activity and provide an outlet for his experimental spirit'. But the relative freedom aimed at within the ICP could not by definition be reproduced, given the venture's status as a 'social experiment'.

Just as the uptake of psychoanalytic ideas within practices of social regulation in Europe and America has seldom, if ever, incorporated the idea of an 'unconscious' (Holland, 1977; Riley, 1983), applications of Lowenfeld's views on play have focused on the idea of matching a tailored input to a normal developmental course against which deviations can be pinpointed at the expense of infinite variation and open-ended investigation. The kind of emphasis this produced is illustrated in Lilian de Lissa's textbook for nursery teachers, written from the benefit of several years' experience of child study, and published in 1939:

> Not only is play the surest index of a child's character it is also an indication of the normality of his development and of his mental and emotional health. Every nursery teacher should continuously watch her children at play and make some record of it. She should also make as comprehensive a study as she can of play itself, for this will enable her to interpret and evaluate her observations, and give some insight into each child and the kind of help and guidance he needs. It will help her to understand when and how to come forward and when to leave him alone. It will also guide her in her choice of the materials and playthings most helpful for each particular phase of growth. (de Lissa, p. 191)

From the emphasis on observation to the provision of opportunities through suitable materials, the similarity with Lowenfeld's approach is clear. However, implicit in the above recommendations is the idea of a central core of normal development which the teacher can promote through knowing the right sequence and having the right tools. What is missing is the emphasis on the child's own way, so central to Lowenfeld. Furthermore, through her clinical work by this time Lowenfeld had clarified her own position on the nature of normality. One consequence was that within her overall approach the idea of a developmental sequence was of less central significance.

While Lowenfeld's work made inroads into education the clinical side of the ICP also expanded, despite the shifts in premises. The one-year training course, started in 1931, continued and in 1935 two further courses were added. One was another one-year course for medical men and women who wanted to acquire experience in the diagnosis and treatment of psychological disorders in children. The other was a three-year course, providing training in psychopathology and psychotherapy with children and leading to a diploma. This was the first training specifically for child psychotherapy. Candidates were not required to have had a medical training, but held degrees or diplomas in psychology or had extensive teaching experience. By 1930 Melanie Klein's influence had contributed to an increase in the number of people in this country wishing to work with children according to psychoanalytic principles, leading the British Psycho-Analytical Society to work out criteria for training in the psychoanalysis of children. These criteria were based heavily around training requirements for adult analysis (Grosskurth, 1986). In addition to undertaking a full personal analysis, trainees were required to take two adults as their first cases, each under supervision for at least a year. Only then could the trainee work with children and young people, one in adolescence, one in the pre-latency period, and one in the latency period, each case to be supervised for one year.

Lowenfeld's training operated from a broader base. Trainees undertook some form of personal analysis and were required to follow through individual cases. But a major emphasis was placed on working with a relatively large number of children across all age ranges and in all the contexts provided by the clinic, making diversity in development, in home circumstances and in temperamental characteristics particularly apparent. Eventually Lowenfeld explicitly criticized the desirability of assuming, as she claimed the analysts did, that one could work in depth with a single child of a particular age on the grounds that what one would be following was merely a variant of a universal developmental pattern.

Establishing the training both depended on and promoted the public recognition given to the clinic at that time. Open seminars and discussions continued, and in 1936 the institute launched a bulletin, the Institute of Child Psychology *News Bulletin*, published four to six times a year until 1940, with a special wartime issue published in 1945. Besides containing reports on the work of the ICP, advertisements for fund-raising activities, book reviews and discussions of meetings, it also contained contributions from people outside the clinic, working in related fields, in child guidance, psychology, medicine and education. Of particular interest here is the issue of October 1936, Number 3 in the first volume, which contained a detailed report on a conference discussion on the significance of 'neurosis' as applied to children.

Unsurprisingly, the conference proved to be less about what constitutes neurosis, than what is 'normality'. The bulletin's editorial stressed the recency of public knowledge of child psychopathology: children's natures were no longer just the concern of psychiatry and education; they were of concern to 'the magistrate, the children's physician, the novelist, and even the features' editor of the popular press' (ICP *News Bulletin*, 1936, p. 1). The editorial attributed this change not only to the work of Freud and Adler, but also to the increase in juvenile delinquency, and the changing outlook in education. It emphasized in particular the influence of the work on shell-shock and malingering, and the experimental ventures like the Little

 Commonwealth in England, the George Junior Republic in

America, and the progressive schools. Various contributions from psychology and education were cited, including the work of Cyril Burt, Charlotte Bühler, Jean Piaget and C. W. Valentine. Finally the editorial acknowledged the contribution of the child guidance movement and the concept of the child guidance team. But within the plethora of new approaches there were still problems in finding ways of accurately depicting children's predicaments. What, for instance, could the term 'neurosis' mean, when referring to children?

In retrospect, at the heart of the discussion about neurosis and what constitutes normality was the issue of who decided and provided treatment. The point was well made by the conference chairman, Professor Hamley from education, who introduced the problem of the day. He described an incident in which he had had to interview a small child who had been 'expelled from one school as an incorrigible delinquent, while in another school he had been described as a delightfully natural child'. Again, 'another child had been described as a lovely child, but a doctor had regarded the child as neurotic because he was so quiet' (ICP *News Bulletin*, 1936, p. 1). Summing up at the end of the day and feeling some light had been shed on the subject, he concluded: 'It was for those present to decide whether abnormality was something which could be treated by educational means, or whether the child concerned should be passed on to a doctor.' However, he confessed that he had once or twice been a 'little disturbed' during the discussion:

> For there seemed a danger of regarding a condition as abnormal when it was only a slight variation or variant from the normal. In fact, he thought some of the cases that had been described as abnormal, or even slightly above or below the normal, were in the statistical sense really normal. (Hamley, in ICP *News Bulletin*, 1936, p. 6)

In this context, Hamley's remarks were in part a response to the presentation of Charlotte Bühler, then based in London, whose studies of normal child development were taking her into the field of mental health, with the aim of demonstrating the appropriateness of psychology's increasing contribution to psychiatric medicine. At this time there was some active collaboration between Bühler and Lowenfeld, which eventually led Bühler to try to adapt the World technique into a research instrument. Since her adaptation involved trying to standardize choice of toys, Lowenfeld was keen to stress contrasting guiding principles; for Lowenfeld the World was not a 'test' (see discussion following 'The World Pictures of Children', 1939, this volume, p. 290). Here, Bühler's presentation on 'sorting children into types' was based on the assumption that it was possible to devise standardized tests which would discriminate between neurotic behaviour and similar-looking behaviour which was not neurotic but could reflect, for example, a critical period in normal development, slow maturation, feeble-mindedness, a primary deficiency, or environmental neglect.

Also of interest was Donald Winnicott's contribution at the conference. He spoke as a psychoanalyst, as well as a paediatrician. Winnicott stressed the complex question of what normality is, and that psychoanalysis made the classification of normality even less possible. What emerged from his considerations was the importance of recognizing the intensity of early feelings. From this it followed that it could be abnormal if children could not employ 'the whole range of neurotic symptoms', or if the symptoms were of the kind that produced a hostile or unfriendly environment (ICP *News Bulletin*, 1936, p. 4). Thus, for Winnicott, normal development depended on a considerable degree of parental tolerance; psychological abnormality emerged as a matter of degree, and was to be diagnosed 'not on the presence of symptoms, but on the degree and quality of the anxiety and compulsiveness behind the neurotic symptoms' (p. 4).

Lowenfeld's approach was apparently pragmatic, but with far-reaching implications. She delineated the approaches currently available to the unsuccessful child. Orthodox medicine still tended to regard the child as an organism, severing the study of diseases from the personality of the child, leading to the assumption that the 'neurotic child' could similarly be picked out by virtue of his peculiar characteristics. In education, the normal child was the one who fulfilled the rules of the school to best advantage, the abnormal one was the one who did not. 'So again, the neurotic child is an individual who does not do something somebody else does. He makes, as it were, his own diagnosis' (ICP *News Bulletin*, 1936, p. 3). Similarly, for the sociologist, the delinquent or problem child was one who behaved in a way which contravenes accepted social laws or rules of behaviour. And finally, one found the child who 'feels things and fears things unthought by others'. This child, the 'psychoneurotic child', was approached from the angle of psychiatry.

Within this definitional problem produced by the new

disciplines Lowenfeld stressed the cultural relativity of notions of normality. Furthermore, not only would similar behaviour be tolerated in one society and in one historical epoch and complained of in another, but in the present context parents and experts could disagree over what would be appropriate and healthy adjustment. 'Neurosis' was a popular and not a scientific term. It was possible, however, to use what was known about physical, intellectual and emotional growth and environmental necessities to rule out possible causative factors which could be ameliorated, arriving at the end of the day 'with certain conditions whose origin lies in the emotional life of the child, and I would submit that it is to these conditions that the term neurosis can be applied' (ICP *News Bulletin*, 1936, p. 3).

It might be objected, Lowenfeld argued, that this diagnosis was a residuary diagnosis. However, she stressed that this was something which was to some extent inevitable at present. The stumbling-block to any satisfactory definition of neurosis and, by implication, abnormality was that it was not possible to have such a definition in the absence of any satisfactory definition of health. Here she put forward a commitment to what health might consist of:

> It is my own personal conviction that life is biologically intended to be creative, and that health in an individual or society can only exist when the individual or society is creative. Health therefore is a type of existence that is positively creative, non-health the opposite of this. (ICP *News Bulletin*, 1936, p. 3)

The work of the ICP was intended as an attempt to work out this goal in practice. While every child referred, whether for asthma, reading difficulties, hitting the neighbour or night terrors, was subjected to routine medical, physical and psychological examinations, the aim was not to be constrained by the fact that these tools were the products of different traditions. Nor was it assumed that different symptomatologies necessarily represented different conditions. Rather, it was believed that they could arise from the same fundamental phenomena, an entanglement in the emotional life of the child, which affected his or her capacity for creative development. Furthermore:

> It seems to me that what we need is a breaking down of the concept that children's medicine, experimental psychology, probation work and education are separate entities, and to

> attempt instead to study each child as a child and not as a particular kind of child. (ICP *News Bulletin*, 1936, p. 3)

Thus the ICP had reached a position in which the aim was to capitalize on tools provided from different disciplines, without losing the commitment to the holism which emerged as central from its first inception. Because it functioned as a relatively independent unit, its structure enabled it to avoid parcelling out and carving children up, which Lowenfeld identified as a major danger in the development of separate professional bodies.

Several points emerged from this orientation. First, the ICP would need to maintain its relatively separate status. Second, the nature of co-operative work with contributions from different disciplines would lead to abandoning as inappropriate the search for convenient if oversimplified diagnostic categories, such as a nosology adapted from adult psychiatry. This would be a bypassing of issues to do with the complex relations between abnormality and health, as is implied in the acknowledgement of the central task as understanding the 'child as a child and not as a particular kind of child'. Third, Lowenfeld's orientation also implied that the aim of many of the protagonists of the child study movement, to chart the processes of normal growth and development, must be displaced in order to embrace both the possibility of universal laws or processes in development and infinite variety in developmental route or outcome.

THE THEORY OF THE PROTOSYSTEM

In 1937 Margaret Lowenfeld put forward what became her central and in many ways most interesting theoretical contribution: the postulation of a primary system, or 'protosystem'. This concept is discussed at some length in the introduction to Chapter 9, which opens with the paper in which Lowenfeld first put forward the working theory, 'A Thesis Concerning the Fundamental Structure of the Mento-emotional Processes in Children', given to a meeting of the General Section of the British Psychological Society on 18 April 1937. Briefly, the protosystem operates from birth, if not before, and refers to ways in which infants organize or regulate the stream of perceptual and sensory experience coming from their own bodies and/or the outside world. This regulation involves processes of grouping or link-making which constitute a form of 'thinking', with regular and assumedly lawful characteristics. However it results in products of a different sort than does the rational thought of adults or older children. These products of thought are by nature inexpressible in words and can themselves give rise to strong emotions. They are entirely subjective and, being formed from specifics of infantile emotional, perceptual and bodily experience, idiosyncratic.

As adults we are generally unaware of the existence of the protosystem, although it persists in all of us. It operates, for example, in the kind of 'thought before words' which Lowenfeld (1935) used Collingwood's observations and arguments to support, and some of its products can be seen in art and literature, notably in the work of Chagall and the stream-of-consciousness writers (see p. 312). But while these creative products are more than usually aesthetically pleasing, disturbances in the functioning of the protosystem can persist in apparently 'normal' individuals to result in breakdowns, depression or outbreaks of cruelty and violence in later life.

In proposing this system, Lowenfeld was beginning to answer the questions left open-ended in *Play in Childhood*: what was the nature of the processes through which the infant and young child repeats and assimilates to itself its own experience, and how could disturbances in this functioning contribute to later difficulties in play and other aspects of personality and intellectual development? (See this volume, p. 80.) On the one hand there may be some primary difficulty (environmental, constitutional or both) inhibiting the working of the protosystem in infancy. This would contribute to disturbances in social/emotional development, intellect and all aspects of symbolic functioning. On the other hand, just as the availability of suitable material within a relatively permissive environment could contribute to the development of a working-through with play, the cultural and interpersonal context in which the child was developing could also facilitate protosystem functioning.

But parental activities would in no sense simply determine the evolution of the protosystem. Since the products of the protosystem are necessarily subjective, its operations can result in considerable confusions and misconceptions when seen from the adult point of view. The consequences of these differing conceptions can be emotionally inhibiting or a source of pain and distress for the child. One of the tasks of therapy would be to provide a context, and a therapeutic input where necessary, which would enable the child to become aware of his or her own protosystem confusions and misconceptions. According to assumptions of dynamic psychology, these processes facilitate the release of the energy caught up or bound within the confused areas, which is then made available for dealing with reality situations. Under suitable circumstances the work of the protosystem eventually facilitates the move outwards towards external reality, paving the way for the development of rational cognitive activity and the use of language and explanation.

When Lowenfeld first put forward the theory of the protosystem, she in fact referred to it as the 'primary system'. She was persuaded to change the name to 'protosystem' in the early 1950s by Margaret Mead, who pointed out that there would be likely confusions with Freud's (1900) 'primary process'. Such confusions would be inevitable because there are clear similarities or overlaps between Lowenfeld's distinction between the primary system and the conscious, linearly organized rational thought of adults and older children and Freud's distinction between primary and secondary processes (see, for example, Freud, 1900, 1911). This overlap was acknowledged by Lowenfeld herself (Lowenfeld, 1944, 1948, this volume, pp. 315, 325). But in contrast to Freud (as she understood him), Lowenfeld gave no special privilege to infantile sexuality and the theory of the pleasure principle. Rather, she was advocating something more like a primary drive to pattern and grouping, and the synthesis and reproduction of experiences. Furthermore, the use she made of evidence obtained from Worlds and other sources led her to identify processes of synthesizing or link-making which pre-dated and differed in kind from the processes of 'association' then emphasized by Freudian psychoanalysis (Lowenfield, 1944, this volume, p. 315).

In the emphasis on a primitive mode of thought originating in infancy, Lowenfeld was raising the kinds of considerations inherent in Melanie Klein's (1932) postulation of an epistemophilic instinct, or a drive towards knowing. There are also a number of points of correspondence between the products of the protosystem and the primitive phantasy given centrality by the Kleinian psychoanalytic tradition, discussed particularly by Susan Isaacs (Isaacs, 1948; see also Segal, 1986). But particularly interesting are the similarities between Lowenfeld's focus on processes of link-making, which began as early as 1937, and the more recent postulation of 'proto-mental' events and primitive link-making described by the psychoanalyst Wilfred Bion. In addition to the usual emphasis on the instinctual life, unconscious processes and the organization of defences, Bion found it necessary and conceptually possible to develop a 'theory of thinking' within a psychoanalytic account of the emotional life of the baby (Bion, 1962, 1967). Although working within the Kleinian psychoanalytic tradition, interestingly Bion consistently emphasized the contribution of Freud's (1911) account of the two principles of mental functioning to his own thinking.

These developments or refinements within the psychoanalytic tradition clearly bring it closer to Lowenfeld's account of the mental-emotional life of babies. However, there remain fundamental differences. First, in attempting to delineate characteristics of the protosystem, Lowenfeld looked not to psychoanalysis or other dynamic theories, but first of all to contemporary psychology, and in particular the work of Charles Spearman, who had recently held a Chair in the Department of Psychology at University College, London University. (The use she made of Spearman's work is discussed in the introduction to Chapter 9.) Second, in contrast to the work of Klein and Bion, in Lowenfeld's scheme no *particular centrality* is given to the relation to the mother or mother's body; it is not a theory of object relations. It remained, like play, a theory of a relation to the totality of experience, which would include relationships with significant others.

In putting forward her theory of the protosystem, Lowenfeld had drawn together her central preoccupations. It was a theory which had at its core assumptions of relations between the development of bodily processes and the experience of these and the development of mind in the infant and young child; it enabled her to conceive unique variability and individuality in development, and yet at the same time the existence of universal processes; it enabled her to regard the availability of cultural products as fundamental to the expression of experience, and at the same time to view creativity not as a by-product of development but as a necessary component which made further development possible. She was thus in a stronger position to differentiate her work from other psychotherapeutic traditions, in theory as well as in practice.

The development of Lowenfeld's theory, however, was tied to the use of her methods, the World technique and the Mosaic Test, methods which she argued were particularly suitable for the expression of thought processes that were non-verbal, plastic and multidimensional. In preparing *Play in Childhood* considerable work had gone into studying the Worlds and Mosaics of particular child patients and their relation to other records of their behaviour. The fact that after moving from Browning House the staff were generally working under cramped conditions may also have contributed to the increasing centrality given to World-making within the clinic. In any event, from the second half of the 1930s onwards, many of Lowenfeld's presentations were largely given over to discussions of Worlds, generally illustrated with slides, with more or less theoretical elaboration. For example, following the presentation of the theory of the protosystem in Manchester, later in the same year she gave two papers in Europe, each of which was extremely well received. The first was 'The Value of Direct Objective Record of Children's Phantasies', given at the eleventh International Congress in Psychology, Paris, July 1937; the second was 'A Method of Direct Objective Representation of Children's Phantasy', given at the ninth International Medical Congress for Psychotherapy, Copenhagen, October 1937. Once the theory of the protosystem had been established she could claim with some justification the adaptability of World-making as both a research and a therapeutic tool. In each of these two papers the central thesis was the value of a method for making accessible the mental-emotional processes of children, such that they could be studied, compared, followed longitudinally and so forth, thus providing a window for the phantasy life of children without requiring the pre-given theories or particular expertise proposed by psychoanalysts; these could be as constraining as illuminating.

Now that relations between theoretical premises and technique were crystallizing, with public recognition and a successful record of treatment behind her, Lowenfeld felt freer to differentiate herself from psychoanalysis in particular, and to be somewhat cavalier in her criticisms. The paper given in 1937 to the General Section of the British Psychological Society was met with modest approval, since besides referring extensively to Spearman's (1923, 1927) work which would have been familiar to many of those present, it espoused the aims of objectivity, and voiced a number of commonly felt objections to or suspicions about psychoanalysis: nobody, after all, knows 'what goes on'. Unsurprisingly, such a line of argument also met with hostility and suspicion. Her next major presentation, the second paper in Chapter 9, 'The World Pictures of Children', was given in 1938 to the Medical rather than the General section of the British Psychological Society and was published in the following year. There were many child psychoanalysts in the audience, including Melanie Klein, Susan Isaacs, Nina Searl and Donald Winnicott. Lowenfeld was attacked vehemently for failing to acknowledge the work of Melanie Klein and other developmentalists, for misunderstanding psychoanalysis and central tenets of the psychoanalytic method, and for forcing the emotional dilemmas of children into an artificial framework for the sake of some semblance of scientific credibility.

The discussion which followed the presentation, including Lowenfeld's systematic reply to each point, is published in Chapter 9. Given the hostility of the reception, it is worth noting that Lowenfeld was confronting a group of Klein's followers at a time of mounting disruption and uncertainty about the future of the British Psycho-Analytical Society (see Grosskurth, 1986). It is also worth noting that the 'controversies' of the time were not simply between different groupings within psychoanalysis but were also about which grouping and what kind of approach held particular promise for the treatment of emotionally disturbed children, and who decides. Given the degree of hostility, the cogency of Lowenfeld's replies is striking. However, she was personally devastated by the attack, and the encounter led to an accentuation of differences and a lack of productive interchange. This was gradually somewhat ameliorated after the Second World War largely through the influence of Lowenfeld's friendship with Margaret Mead (Ville Andersen, personal communication).

More immediately, the need to preserve freedom to develop independently was imperative. One of the most important factors contributing to this was the acquisition of new premises. In 1936 an anonymous offer had been made to the clinic of the gift of a freehold house 'to accommodate the developing activities of the institute as soon as a suitable freehold house could be found' (Lowenfeld, 1969, p. 21). It took until 1938 to find suitable premises, a large Victorian house at 6 Pembridge Villas, London W11. The building was adapted to accommodate all the clinic's requirements. The ground floor contained offices, a waiting-room, interview rooms for parents and student quarters, while the first floor consisted of a board room, the psychologist's room and a room for a housekeeper. The basement, containing six rooms of different sizes and leading out to a garden at the back, was given over entirely to the children, and no adult was permitted down there except when engaged in the work.

The ICP's new home was opened amid great excitement and promise on Thursday, 23 June 1938. Within fifteen months the work was harshly disrupted with the outbreak of the Second World War.

5 Impact and Aftermath of the Second World War

War was declared on Germany on 3 September 1939. Since the ICP functioned as a teaching establishment as well as a clinic and this was the vacation, the building was taken over by the fire service immediately and the clinic closed down. However, within a matter of months evacuation quarters were found in a house in Berkhamsted, Hertfordshire. The house had been damaged in a civilian fire and the owner permitted the insurance money to be used for equipment and alterations. The clinic reopened under the name 'The Children's Clinic' and it is interesting that the pamphlet advertising the clinic locally proposed that the Berkhamsted population could become as proud of their clinic as the people of Peckham were of theirs.

The running of the clinic was carried out by a local committee, referrals coming from the immediate vicinity and, in some cases, London. Though financially the clinic ran at a loss, the clinical and research commitment continued. So too did the child-psychotherapy training, one student qualifying during the war and the other just afterwards.

Lowenfeld herself lived in rooms above the clinic, travelling back and forth to London and maintaining clinical commitments in both places. But despite these adaptations, the war years also hit Margaret Lowenfeld particularly hard. The outbreak of the Second World War followed the invasion of Poland, inevitably bringing reminders of her previous war experiences. There was a sense of having seen it all before, reinforced by having seen it coming. Unlike Collingwood, whose sense of the war's inevitability had been accompanied by a re-evaluation of political commitment, for Lowenfeld opting for a socialist world view was not open. It was too closely identified with the Russian invasion of Poland, and linked with the same limitations and dangers as Fascism: that is, that the imposition of a political regime on a people ill prepared for it would at best produce unrest and was as likely to produce the horrors and evils associated with Stalinism. With respect to the implications of Nazi domination, she was also of course dealing with fear for the lives of many of her Jewish relatives living in various parts of Europe. Her cousin Margaretta, for example, died in Auschwitz. In a state of near breakdown, in 1940, Lowenfeld went into a second analysis, this time with a Jungian. As with her earlier analysis, Lowenfeld did not make the name of her analyst known. Nevertheless she constantly expressed her personal debt to this analysis and, as will be illustrated later, the influence of the Jungian theory of symbols and archetypes is clear in her post-war work. Interestingly, a number of Jungian therapists have found aspects of World-making particularly compatible with their own approach (see, for example, Kalff, 1966). At the same time she continued to insist that her approach concerned processes which were not encompassed by any of the psychoanalytic or analytic schools, her work was a complement to them. Here Lowenfeld's way of working through the impact of the Second World War had productive as well as painful effects.

PSYCHOLOGY, CULTURE AND POLITICAL SYSTEMS

Work on clinical method and its relation to theory continued through the war years, including the production of the first paper in Chapter 10, on 'Direct Projective Therapy', given in 1944 to a General Section meeting of the British Psychological Society, held in Edinburgh. However, in many respects a more representative guide to Lowenfeld's major preoccupations is to be found in articles written for the general public and in unpublished manuscripts.

The former category includes popular articles on evacuation written in the early stages of the war. Lowenfeld was amongst those who had foreseen that a mass evacuation might be necessary if not desirable from way before the actual declaration of war. Once evacuation began, her response was to pose the question as to whether in fact this disaster should be regarded as an obstacle to normal living, or as a tremendous opportunity leading to new kinds of experiments and discoveries with social organization which could actually produce rather than inhibit creative innovation and adaptation. This view is, of course, in contrast to the idea that the evacuation of children was a likely cause of emotional trauma, associated with a general recognition of the dangers of separating children from their parents which came to dominate much of the popularization of psychoanalytic ideas in the post-war period. Although Lowenfeld modified her views on effects of evacuation and separation subsequently, these early articles raised a theme which remained central through the war years: the problem of locating individuals in a form of social organization most conducive to opportunities for creativity.

For Lowenfeld the Second World War brought to the forefront those issues concerning the relations between social systems, culture and psychological functioning that had been raised by her own experience of the First World War and the Polish–Russian wars, and that had gained intellectual significance through the early contact with Wilfred Trotter. As we have seen, to understand processes inimical to maintaining peace was a priority in the philosophy of the Children's Clinic and in the holistic approach to children's functioning. In many respects Lowenfeld's own way of working through the impact of the Second World War involved using her theories of individual psychology and understanding of the culture and politics of European countries to analyse what produced the rise of Fascism and Hitler's ascendancy. From this followed certain implications or speculations for a post-war world and the political organization of Europe. This vision of a future also dictated intellectual priorities.

The richest source of information on this central theme comes from notes which Lowenfeld made for herself on relations between social conditions and the psychology of individuals and groups likely to be more or less conducive to peace and stability. These notes were clearly written in a state of emotional turmoil, perhaps in the attempt to work something through. None the less they give insight into her distinctive position and the priorities which remained uppermost after the war. One of the most articulate remaining manuscripts, 'Factors Influencing "Peace" or Unrest in Countries', documents her thought processes and explores the kinds of reconstructive task that would await a post-war world. The answers which Lowenfeld arrived at were not simple political answers, nor simple psychological ones. Rather, to be successful any political organization would have to take account of and be compatible with the pre-existing forms of thought within the peoples the governments would seek to represent.

Like many, Lowenfeld attributed the instability of Europe in the inter-war period to an unsatisfactory political settlement after the First World War, which for her included a disregard of the organic processes through which boundaries between the peoples of Europe had been established over centuries. She also attributed an inevitable instability to the expansion of modern capitalism and the artificial production of desirables, putting forward the idea that the first aim of a post-war world should be to 'change the goal of civilization and to change it from power to creative achievement'. Actually implementing this, of course, would mean broaching questions of government. In contrast to the flavour of some of her earlier writing, here she explicitly separated herself from the liberatory philosophy of some of the progressive educationists, who had asserted that the provision of 'freedom' would allow the emergence of a 'natural' democracy (see Walkerdine, 1984). For Lowenfeld, freedom could not be imposed and is illusory in a social group, because constraints follow from any form of government and 'are necessary for the development of thought amongst its peoples and its individuals'. As for democracy,

> This is not a natural reaction. No one is born willing to hear the other point of view. The natural tendency if a view is held with any strength at all is to take this as the only view and to be willing to defend it with blood. (Lowenfeld, 'Factors Influencing "Peace" or Unrest in Countries', undated manuscript, p. 4)

It is true, Lowenfeld pointed out, that in some cases social and cultural practices had contributed to modifying this spontaneous reaction. This was particularly obvious in Britain where, from the organization of houses in schools to group games and inter-school rivalries, the preparation of the young reflected a social evolution directed to inculcating democratic attitudes. For Lowenfeld the result was that 'The whole life of the Englishman was typically orchestrated through committees, unions, and so forth, through which it becomes essential that in order to achieve any practical ends, one has to learn to bear and forbear and see others' points of view' (p. 4). While this has contributed to the relative stability of Britain, it has also had its limiting consequences.

> All this takes a lot of time; time that in other cultures is given to music or outdoor life. The Englishman cannot think of life

> without some communal activity and looks upon Parliament in normal times much as on a football match. (Lowenfeld, 'Factors Influencing "Peace" or Unrest in Countries', undated manuscript, p. 5)

This Lowenfeld contrasted with Continental countries:

> Here infidelity to thought patterns and thought conviction is identified with mental heresy. It is felt that to compromise is to betray one's own integrity to maintain a position incumbent on the honest man.

Referring to the system whereby, before the revolution, the Polish people elected their own kings, Lowenfeld added, 'The highest degree of belief in this thesis was the *Librum Veto* that killed the former Polish kingdom.' In south-east Europe, on the other hand,

> It is not so much a question of integrity of thought as loyalty to feeling. For a Hungarian to believe there is good, for example, in a Romanian proposition smacks of disloyalty to Hungary . . . Ideas are identified with feeling and compromise becomes impossible. There is lacking all scaffolding for democratic procedure.

Under these kinds of conditions, Lowenfeld argued, attempting to adopt or introduce a form of democratic rule could have results as disastrous as were the consequences of German republicanism. Either, under the guise of democratic rule, one group could seize control and force its views on the rest, or, under the appearance of stability, factions would split off, slowly take more power, eventually bursting through the bond of government in which no one could believe anyway. Thus, Lowenfeld concluded, 'To be stable a form of government must be chosen for each country which allows of expression in a traditional and so satisfying form of the strongest feelings of the people' (p. 7).

It was not, of course, in Lowenfeld's power to determine political settlements. Nevertheless, from her analysis she came to the conclusion that one of the central tasks facing the post-war world was to 'study and understand the normal ways of life and habits of emotional and mental behaviour of the peoples making up the countries'. For Lowenfeld, the route *par excellence* into 'habits of emotional and mental behaviour' eventually came through the study of culture. By this she meant both forms of high art and architecture and ceremonial ritual, and also the day-to-day patterns of behaviour, designs of dress and practical implements studied by contemporary cultural anthropologists.

In viewing the study of cultural products as also an opening to the study of thought, Lowenfeld was adopting the kind of historical approach to the study of mind advocated by Collingwood. It is interesting that his own views were influenced by reflecting on the methods involved in his archaeological studies. For Lowenfeld, cultural products both expressed thought patterns of a community, but also served to reproduce them over generations. In the same way that in play materials were essential in ensuring that children could reproduce and assimilate internal mental events, the appropriation of cultural forms into mental-emotional machinery was a necessary way in which children mentally formulated their relation to the social organization around them and their loci in relation to the universe.

Thus, what became theoretically interesting were the relations between protosystem functioning and the expression of creativity afforded by the culture of the community. In retrospect we must question the basis for a simplified view of a tie-up between patterns of thought and particular national characteristics, and the assumption of varying degrees of political naïvety amongst different European nations. To today's readership there is something unfamiliar about this kind of visionary political analysis, and even in her own time Lowenfeld was perhaps looking backwards. The idea of levels of development in political and social organization and their relation to national personality characteristics in part reflects the imperialistic content in which social anthropology first emerged. It played an important role in Wilfred Trotter's analysis of the First World War, and also figured in Lowenfeld's (1935) analysis of historical changes in the position of children in society, as noted earlier. The distinction between primitive and rational thought is also found in Freud and many of his contemporaries (Urwin, 1986). However, here it is important that Lowenfeld gave no particular priority to the expression of more primitive tendencies or aspects of the mind over the effects of more rational and apparently highly developed modes of thought characteristic of civilized Western societies, or vice versa. Nor in speculating for herself on the evolution of potential forms of political organization was she concerned with proposing in advance the rightness of one form of approach over another. Indeed, her speculations in this paper on the conditions in which Hitler came to power make it clear that her views of the processes involved were extremely complex and were influenced by a lifetime's knowledge of Europe. Lowenfeld based her arguments both on the unsatisfactory political situation left over after the First World War, and on the maintenance of an education system which in her view concentrated on intellect at the expense of feeling. The latter was left over for the family, which over generations had inculcated obedience and veneration to the father, and by implication, to king and country. The assumption was that this would now be transferred to the state. But since a democratic political system had been imposed on a people unfamiliar with democratic forms, in actuality the same attitude towards leadership and government re-emerged but 'now without the semi-magical outlet of adoration for caste and king which had given an expression to the primitive layers of personality before'. In consequence,

> Material misery . . . and . . . drabness of life threw into stark relief the emotional hungers that there was now no machinery to satisfy. It was inevitable that a Hitler should come. That is to say, it was inevitable that the demand for adoration, blind relief, fervour, ecstasy, blind drive to power should find a way out because these are all parts of the primitive personality and by 1923 I was already writing that this must happen. (Lowenfeld, 'Factors Influencing "Peace" and Unrest in Countries', undated manuscript, p. 10)

Unfortunately, the 1923 draft no longer survives. One of the consequences which Lowenfeld drew from this was that the post-war reconstruction would have to reckon with the fact that millions of people in central Europe had adopted a scale of values which were 'the reverse of the rest of the world'. The only way forward was to understand more fully the conditions through which this had occurred, and to acknowledge in addition the culpability of the Allied nations.

Thus, despite the considerable pressures of the war, for Lowenfeld the re-examination of the past which had been forced upon her had the effect of highlighting the analysis of culture as a major priority for the post-war period. Within this analysis, her interest in cross-cultural comparisons was not a simple relativism; she viewed the possibilities for the expression of human potential as both having been universally thwarted or skirted by historical and social processes, yet at the same time as necessarily incomplete. Here it is important to note a profound pessimism or realism in Lowenfeld's views which contrasted with the optimism behind much of the expansion of welfare and social improvements which heralded the new Britain of the post-war years.

> The main task of the post-war thinker is to keep in the forefront of all planning a picture of man as he is, not as one would like him to be, and to endeavour to fit plans to what *can* be not to what it would be nice to have. (Lowenfeld, 'Factors Influencing "Peace" or Unrest in Countries', undated manuscript, p. 11)

POST-WAR RECONSTRUCTION

As soon as the war was over, Lowenfeld set about recouping ground lost through the closure of the ICP. Problems presented themselves immediately, some of them relatively trivial and short-term. Since a skeletal management structure had been maintained throughout the war, formally the ICP was still in existence and 6 Pembridge Villas could now be reclaimed. However the building had suffered considerably. Given the statutory limit of £10 for domestic redecoration, it was some considerable time before the premises could be refurbished satisfactorily. Other problems were more serious, with long-term effects on the financial and institutional support of the clinic.

Lowenfeld took a principled stand against the National Health Service. Her argument, which was shared by a number of Liberal as well as Conservative thinkers at that time, was that a national and centrally controlled health service would interfere with the essentially and necessarily personal, individual contract between doctor and patient. Here the strides made in the role of the general practitioner were emphasized. It was also thought that nationalization would mean increased centralization, and that this would result in an imposed uniformity. Though she eventually modified her views on the Health Service in general, it was this emphasis on uniformity that Lowenfeld felt to be particularly inimical to the work of the ICP.

Accordingly, with the passing of the Health Act in 1948, the organizational form of the institute changed from that of a friendly society to that of a non-profit-making limited company. Although Lowenfeld continued to see private patients, the children attending the clinic came from a similar range of socio-economic backgrounds as before. This was achieved through an arrangement made with the North-West Regional Hospital Board whereby they paid for treatment on a per capita basis. Consequently, with the exception that in the post-war years the ICP tended to give particular emphasis to cases illustrating interactions between psyche and soma, on the whole the types of children attending the clinic were similar to those found in any child-psychiatric or child-guidance clinic at that time.

But by the late 1940s, the number of such clinics had expanded considerably. According to the *Annual Report* of the National Council for Medical Health, by 1944 there were more than seventy Child Guidance clinics in Great Britain. By 1952, this number had risen to 155 (Keir, 1952). In accounting for this expansion, most writers emphasize the effects of evacuation. Some accounts stress how the removal of children from impoverished city environments drew the attention of an otherwise oblivious or ill-informed middle class to the high incidence of poor physical health and emotional disturbance in such children, thus vindicating further the convictions of the between-war innovators (Wills, 1978). Other accounts also stress how the disturbed behaviour and unhappiness caused by loss of parents or evacuation during the war produced a general need to respond (Daws, 1987). Consistent with the first emphasis, the crucially important Feversham report, concerned with co-ordinating voluntary mental health services in Great Britain, was actually prepared in the 1930s and published in 1939 (Dicks, 1970). Though shelved in the war years, this report became the blueprint leading to the amalgamation of the previously separate bodies, the Child Guidance Council, the Central Association for Mental Welfare, and the National Council for Mental Hygiene, forming the National Association for Mental Health. This in turn set up a special Child Guidance Committee to monitor the treatment of behaviour problems in childhood, standards of training, and the provision of child-guidance facilities. This committee crystallized the still much contested division of labour between clinical and educational psychologists and psychiatrists, in which overall medical responsibility is required in cases of early emotional and psychological disturbance (Keir, 1952; Rose, 1985). In the post-war era, it was assumed that the activities of the child guidance movement could be extended more efficiently through the increase in welfare spending and co-ordinated administrative machinery.

In this sense, the effects of the war were first to slow down then to accelerate developments which were already taking place.

In addition to these developments, it is also true that for a population recouping from the war years a major effect of the distress produced by evacuation was an increasing interest in the particular theories or traditions which claimed to account for some of these effects: in short, those theories which emphasized the formative aspects of the relation between children and their parents, and the centrality of the family. Indeed, for a short period, Lowenfeld's own writing on evacuation shared the general and probably heartfelt rhetoric of the time; that what was required was a restitution of the family. It has previously been mentioned that a shift from the 'individual' to the 'family' as the focus for treatment or preventive intervention was already taking place in the inter-war years in some branches of child-guidance work and community medicine (pp. 72–3). Given that the theoretically eclectic child guidance movement had always linked the promotion of emotional harmony with the problem of social stability, the scene was set for the uptake of theories which had as their first focus the problems or dangers resulting from separation. In the British context this meant a gradual dominance of theories of the mother–infant relationship. Though the focus on this relationship originated in Klein's work, the emphasis on it as potentially causative of later emotional problems is particularly associated with the more environmentalist accounts of John Bowlby (1951, 1953, 1969) and Donald Winnicott (1964, 1979).

As Riley (1983) points out, it would be wrong to confuse the widespread use of ideas originally derived from psychoanalysis with psychoanalysis itself. The uptake and reapplication of psychoanalytic concepts always involves selectivity and transformation, and psychoanalysis and child psychotherapy have a developmental history of their own. Nevertheless, it remains true that the development and viability of child psychotherapy as a profession were greatly enhanced by the events of the post-war years. Here, just as in relation to child guidance, Lowenfeld's position was interestingly tangential.

DEVELOPMENTS IN CHILD PSYCHOTHERAPY IN BRITAIN

In some respects the developments in child guidance did not directly affect Lowenfeld herself. Since she was a recognized child psychiatrist, she did not have the problem of medical responsibility which bedevilled psychologists in the child-guidance tradition. Furthermore, though she and her erstwhile colleagues had been influential in introducing the idea of play and sand-trays into many clinics, she remained consistent in holding that her approach was distinct from the philosophy of the child guidance movement; she held a different emphasis on the role of environment and on the aims of treatment. She also differed in the relative depth of exploration offered in her form of therapy. Here she was considerably closer to the analysts.

By the late 1930s, Klein's work had become relatively well known in Britain, even if it was not generally accepted. During the war years her activities included some collaboration with Susan Isaacs (1941) on the Cambridge Survey into the effects of evacuation (see Smith, 1985). In the meantime Anna Freud had been in England since 1938, armed with considerable experience of working with children in educational settings in Europe. Along with Dorothy Burlingham she, too, began work on effects of evacuation through her influential studies of children in her wartime nurseries at Hampstead (see A. Freud, 1973). In 1947 she established a child-psychotherapy training based at Hampstead, using her own work as the theoretical base. Her first intake of students included those who had worked in the wartime nurseries during the war and who wished to take their understanding further through obtaining a deeper and more rigorous framework for understanding (Wills, 1978).

Work with children had, of course, continued from the Tavistock base throughout the war. John Bowlby, who became director of the Children's Department in 1945, had already gathered a large amount of his retrospective case material on effects of early separation on later psychopathy or 'affectionless character formation' before the outbreak of war itself, though the most influential if controversial article 'Forty-four Juvenile Thieves' was not published until 1944. Interestingly, a system of classification devised by Bowlby was used in the Cambridge evacuation survey. In 1948 Bowlby broadened his search for possible separation effects, beginning the series of separation studies with the Hampstead-trained psychiatric social worker James Robertson. This collaboration led eventually to the famous series of films that includes *A Two-year-old Goes to Hospital*. Coupled with his pre-war experience, it was on the strength of this work that Bowlby was commissioned by the World Health Organization to produce the monograph *Maternal Care and Mental Health*. Published in 1951, this put forward evidence on the importance of the child's tie to the mother, including the dangers of early separation. A popular version of this report, *Child Care and the Growth of Love* was first published in 1953 and rapidly became a best-seller (Hardyment, 1983). In the meantime, since 1948 the Tavistock had mounted a child-psychotherapy training. This was managed jointly by John Bowlby and Esther Bick, a close follower of Melanie Klein. It was Bick's initiative that was responsible for the distinctly Kleinian theoretical orientation of the training, though she eventually parted company with it.

As Doris Wills (1978) noted, it was apparent that a new profession, child psychotherapy, was being created. In fact it was through the British Psychological Society that first steps were taken towards creating a central organization. A subcommittee, established in 1947 to consider the professional status of non-medical people who were already working with children, approached Dr Kenneth Soddy, then medical director of the National Association for Mental Health, with the suggestion that a council be set up to represent the interests of the professionals involved, and to consider acceptable standards in psychotherapy and to develop schemes of training. Two working parties were appointed. One, under John Bowlby, drew up a document on training. The other, under the chairmanship of John Gibbs, a psychologist, formulated articles for the association. The outcome, in 1949, was the founding of a Provisional Association for Child Psychotherapy (Non-Medical) and a Provisional Medical Advisory Council, under the chairmanship of Dr Soddy. As Doris Wills also noted, it was not an easy move to establish a 'non-medical' profession for work with disturbed children. Indeed, at that time there was a motion before the Mental Health Advisory Committee to the London County Council proposing that lay psychotherapists should not be employed in the Health service. The support and argument of doctors committed to the value of child psychotherapy was therefore crucial. Along with John Bowlby, Kenneth Soddy, Donald Winnicott, and her colleague Ethel Dukes, Margaret Lowenfeld was one of the medically trained individuals who played a major role in the negotiations. Eventually she served on the first medical advisory committee. These negotiations were responsible for the association's appendage 'non-medical', which was eventually dropped.

But despite the need to counter criticisms from the medical establishment, it was also true that child psychotherapy could now be recognized as a body of expertise with something to contribute. In a recent account of the history of child psychotherapy, Dilys Daws (1987) has suggested that the formation of the Association of Child Psychotherapy gave official recognition to a profession that had existed informally since much earlier in the century. She adds:

> Two distinct inspirations came together to form this new profession, theoretically that of psychoanalysis, and practically that of the child-guidance movement. The tensions of this joint influence are experienced still today in different degrees by each child psychotherapist. (Daws, 1987, p. 3)

The tensions to which Dilys Daws is presumably referring are, on the one hand, the concern of the outside world with the problems posed by disturbed children and the social responsibility of the therapist, which is often accompanied by the need to accept a variety of working conditions; and on the other hand, a commitment to the particular methods and pursuit of truth supported by psychoanalysis, resulting, for example, in the apparent luxury of suspending a goal of removing symptoms and allowing children to work through in their own way. It is notable that in retrospect psychoanalysis is regarded as the theoretical bedrock of the profession. This raises questions about the effects of the formation of the association on Lowenfeld.

To begin with, in the immediate post-war years, the commonality of concerns and interests amongst the membership of the association and the values attached to professional recognition far outweighed any disadvantages. The formation of the association marked a vital step forward in bringing to public attention the values of in-depth work relating mental-emotional phenomena to a wide range of developmental difficulties. More problematic were the Association of Child Psychotherapy's responsibilities for monitoring standards of training, where one might anticipate pressure in the direction of requiring comparability across different trainings.

Lowenfeld's students were already required to undergo personal analysis, as in the other trainings (though the majority chose Jungian, Adlerian or Reichian analysts rather than orthodox Freudian). It also appears that in the early days there was a greater interchange between different trainings than at present. For instance, through the fifties students at the ICP would attend seminars at the Tavistock, and students from the other trainings would visit the ICP. Guest lectures for students for all courses were organized, and among the regular guest lecturers was Winnicott. Given the conditions of referral, there were also similarities in the types of children seen. In all courses, there was the assumption that therapy with children should proceed independently of parental involvement, to ensure confidentiality and facilitate developing the child's trust. By this time, as in the pre-war training, students at the ICP were required to follow through individual cases. But despite these broad comparabilities, there were also important differences, through which the ICP retained or took further the pre-war ethos.

First, although lectures given to the students at the ICP encompassed a range of psychoanalytic theories, Lowenfeld's own focus was on understanding processes of symbol formation. Her lectures were enriched by accounts of myth, fairy-tales and folk legends, references to the arts and anthropology, and by a continual emphasis on the importance of philosophy. Though references to Collingwood's work continued, after the Second World War Lowenfeld became particularly interested in the philosophy of Suzanne Langer because of her emphasis on mind as a symbol-making instrument. Her work on meaning, symbol systems and the philosophy of art is drawn together in her *Philosophy in a New Key* (Langer, 1942).

Second, although it was no longer practicable for all children to undergo a full medical assessment, the ICP itself retained a special interest in children who manifested emotional disturbance in physical complaints. The physical therapist Margaret Kirschner was still included in the clinic staff. Students were encouraged to become familiar with her work and were expected to have a grasp of basic rudiments of physical and motor development.

Third, as in most child-guidance clinics, a psychiatric social worker was responsible for working with the parents of children in therapy. Initially this position was held by Ada Jordan, who had been with the ICP before the war. But on her retirement in the early 1950s her place was taken by Kate MacSorley. Kate MacSorley was a refugee from Berlin who remained in the UK after the war. She originally trained as a psychologist before training as a social worker and had the additional virtue of being particularly attuned to Lowenfeld's philosophy and her approach to therapy. This was important in putting across the point of the work with children to their parents, for example. Her role was in some ways unique, and in this sense could be differentiated from the general system of social work employed in other clinics.

Fourth, although the use of play was central to all traditions, the ICP retained its emphasis on what could be achieved by working through with play itself and on the value of particular kinds of materials, including the World, Mosaics and other Lowenfeldian techniques. Finally, although each child had sessions with his or her own particular therapist, unlike in other child-guidance clinics the children were allowed to choose which room they wished to work in or to move freely from one room to another, followed by their particular workers. In addition to having supervision on individual cases, trainees also participated in 'corporate' sessions, in order to get a wide exposure to a variety of children and their activities. As in the pre-war period, the emphasis was on observing what the children did, the movements in their attention and involvement, and their reactions to other people's presence. In the 1950s, for the first year of training students at the ICP would participate in corporate sessions only, before pursuing follow-up work with five individual cases in the second and third years. The work with individual cases was still carried out in such a way as to minimize the role of transference, as is discussed particularly in Chapter 11. With a few modifications in the 1970s, the course retained this basic shape.

Thus, in spite of the formal linkage to the psychoanalytically oriented trainings, the ICP remained administratively distinct and retained its own unique ethos. It would be surprising, however, if this linkage had no effects on theory and practice at the ICP. One might also expect some influence from Lowenfeld's own Jungian analysis. An examination of case histories such as those published in *The World Technique* suggests that in the post-war period the Lowenfeldian therapists fairly frequently made psychoanalytically informed readings of the symbolic material expressed in the children's Worlds. Here, as elsewhere, Lowenfeld acknowledged the pertinence of psychoanalytic findings, repeating her position that the latter may be strengthened by being produced through an entirely different method which does not hold those theoretical assumptions as a starting-point. However, a closer reading of these case histories shows several major differences in technique and theoretical commitment. In the first place, the imagery and symbols produced in a child's world may strongly suggest particular preoccupations which are given a central place in psychoanalysis, and would be noted by the therapist. But interpretations were to be given sparingly, and always in a way which took the child's own current conscious preoccupations as a starting-point. Moreover, where interpretations were used, it was in order to clarify confusions, facilitate unblocking, or provide necessary information that the child had hitherto been too anxious or too confused to grasp; this process might or might not have been impeded by realities set by the environment, or non-adaptive expectations or confusions of the parents. Thus the aim of therapy remained to avoid imposing a theoretically based understanding on the children, and to facilitate their working through to produce their own solutions.

It may be useful to consider as an example the case of Mary Smith, a ten-year-old girl whose series of Worlds and treatment is described in *The World Technique* and who at referral was described as 'tense, noisy and babyish'. She had difficulties in school work, would attack her younger brother, and wet her bed occasionally. At the sixth session she made a World involving two houses with streams flowing from them, flowing under a pair of bridges before drawing closer together again (see Figure 1). Three vehicles, including an ambulance and a steam engine, stood between the two houses. Soldiers with rifles,

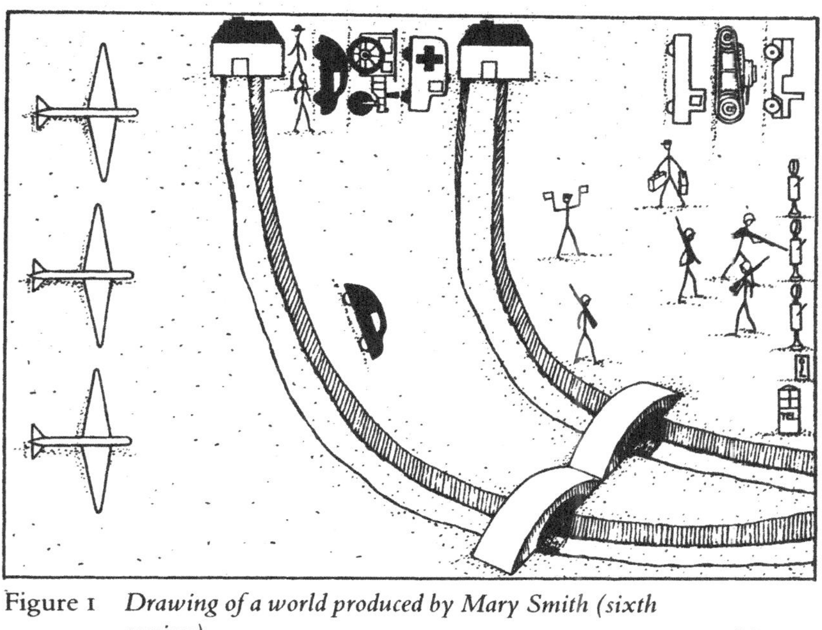

Figure 1 *Drawing of a world produced by Mary Smith (sixth session)*

petrol pumps and army tanks were arranged on one side. Three aeroplanes in a straight line stood on the other side. A single car was arranged between the streams, facing the bridges.

Lowenfeld described this World as 'frankly symbolic' as opposed to realistic; in the real world objects are not found arranged in this way. The assumption was that Mary was not constructing a realistic scene but was attempting to 'say something' through using realistic objects. Lowenfeld continued:

> In all schemata of symbols houses appear as symbols of femininity, 'the home', or, as is probable here 'the body'. The three vehicles between the two houses carry with them ideas of accident (or illness), pressure and movement. The two men beside them, the absence of women from the whole world, and the army vehicles and soldiers on the right all emphasize the maleness of the rest to the scene . . . From a psychoanalytic view this World is a symbolic statement of confusions between erection, coitus and damage, which is one way more obvious and direct than many attempts made by children and adults to express these ideas and fears in words. Bearing these ideas in mind the therapist said that houses were a bit like bodies and continued discussing the stages of the evolution of reproduction. (Lowenfeld, 1979, p. 40)

This discussion began with the fundamentals of reproduction in various animals. (Mary's earlier Worlds included a plentiful supply of horses, cows and ducks.) The therapist moved on to the situation in humans in the next session.

Out of context this account may appear cold-blooded or over-cognitive. It is as if the psychoanalytic framework is, after all, used to read the content of the child's mind, which is to be straightened out by providing correct information, thus repeating Lowenfeld's own criticism of psychoanalytic practice. However, the essential emphasis is on making an interpretation explicit only when it would clarify the child's own need for understanding. This depended on being in touch with the child's current preoccupation through following the mental-emotional process expressed through the World. Second, interpretation was not made 'within the transference'. That is, rather than relating the child's preoccupation or representation to some anxiety or phantasy set in play by the relationship to the therapist, no assumptions were made about what might be going on between them, other than what Lowenfeld used to describe as 'a normal atmosphere of trusted fellowship'. Instead, the focus was on understanding what was happening within the child's mind as expressed through the World, visible to both of them. These mental operations would extend beyond the boundary of psychoanalysis (see Chapter 11). In short, though psychoanalytically informed interpretations could be used to clarify an aspect of the child's current preoccupations, Lowenfeld rejected the psychoanalytic accounts of the developmental process in so far as they comprehended all psychic phenomena as products of personal relationships, whether these were actual environmentally driven experiences or the products of the child's own phantasies.

THEORETICAL DEVELOPMENTS AND THEIR RELATION TO PSYCHOANALYSIS

Despite the relative autonomy of the ICP, given the hegemony of the psychoanalytic tradition in the post-war years one would expect that the onus fell on Lowenfeld to clarify theoretically the nature of the mental-emotional processes which she felt that her approach and particular techniques could uncover or demonstrate. There was also increasing pressure to delineate more precisely the differences in the role of the therapist and the nature of the assumed therapeutic agency. To some extent the former task was taken on board, through two important theoretical developments.

In 1948, the year in which the Mental Health Act required a change in the organization of the ICP, the World Federation for Mental Health held an international conference in London for the first time. In the same month the ICP put on a conference of its own which included presentations from a number of workers using Lowenfeld techniques in various parts of Europe, as well as reports from ICP staff. Lowenfeld's own presentation on 'The Nature of the Primary System', reprinted here in Chapter 10, remained her fullest account of what she later referred to as the protosystem. This paper extended the line of argument first put forward in 'A Thesis Concerning the Fundamental Structure of the Mento-emotional Processes in Children', given in Manchester in 1937 (see p. 247). It was concerned essentially with the nature of pre-rational thought, and was an exploration of how and in what ways the young child links experiences and perceptions to provide cognitive but not conscious mental structures which peg the workings of infantile phantasy.

Apart from the inclusion of rich illustrative examples from art and literature, the major addition in the post-war paper was the introduction of the idea of 'clusters' to refer to the formation of primitive structures, linked together more or less loosely into a network, forming the mental products of the protosystem. In Lowenfeld's scheme, clusters have a sensorial or perceptual aspect, such as 'things which make me feel warm' or 'things which make me feel horrid'. But the items are linked together not by association but rather by a process through which they become identified or coalesce such that the original items now form part of a single whole.

There are similarities here between clusters and the complexes which proceed concept formation proper in the work of the Russian psychologist Vygotsky. At this time Lowenfeld was familiar with his ideas, though the account of his work most familiar to Western readers, *Thought and Language*, was not published in England until 1962. But in Lowenfeld's scheme, in addition to the sensorial or perceptual aspect, clusters have a dynamic aspect, each cluster being more or less highly charged, depending in part on the nature of the experiences drawn together and on the opportunities for energy release.

Both the entirely subjective basis on which these groupings are formed and the intensity of the energy bound within them contribute to idiosyncrasies within the system. In general these products and the actual experiences related to them are forgotten over the course of development. Opportunities for play and for creative outlets of various kinds and the gradual increase in contact with external reality, which modifies confusions and misperceptions, allow the energy bound up in clusters to find its way through to the secondary system. However, in some cases this does not occur or happens unevenly, and here Lowenfeld distinguished four broad patterns which could disable development, roughly corresponding to different types of children receiving treatment at the ICP.

First, energy remaining locked up in the primary system could produce the listless child, lacking in initiative or curiosity. Second, energy could be unevenly distributed throughout the protosystem, contributing to uneven discharge throughout the secondary system and its concentration in areas of the body, producing psychosomatic disorders. Third, children who become obsessed with rituals or who have phobias are generally projecting their clusters on to reality. Fourth, in some cases the secondary system is ill developed and there is an inadequate distinction between what is inside and what is outside, so that the two become confused. Depending on the specific content of the clusters, the child could be dreamy or detached, present an early psychosis, or show outbursts of delinquent behaviour.

Thus the idea of clusters was important therapeutically, particular constellations turning up again and again in the Worlds of particular children. It also had theoretical implications, enabling Lowenfeld to cross-refer to psychoanalytic and Jungian theories. Much of the material described in accounts of the Freudian or Jungian unconscious would be found as clusters in the protosystem, such as the archetypes described by Jung, or the introjected objects of psychoanalysis. Accounts of the origins of these mental structures would, however, differ. For Lowenfeld, similarities were due not only to similarities in the experience of infants everywhere, but to the nature of the immature infant's relation to his or her own body and perceptual apparatus at a time in development when the distinction between internal and external was not firmly established, and the fact that from the outset the human mind seeks resemblances, groups into patterns and creates mental representatives. From this source, too, stems the capacity and necessity for aesthetic awareness.

In 'The Nature of the Primary System' (1948), Lowenfeld described how, in a sensitive and intelligent child, the formation of clusters out of early experiences of intimacy and intensity could provide powerful and valuable resources which could be drawn on in later life. By the time that she came to draft *The World Technique* in the mid-1950s, Lowenfeld had come close to formulating the idea of a primitive aesthetic expression, which underpins aesthetic awareness in later life. This was implicit in her central conviction that the opportunity to be creative was fundamental to psychic health. After discussing the formation of pathogenic clusters and/or the thwarted or twisted opportunities for expression which had, in her view, contributed to the horrific events of the war years, in the published version Lowenfeld continued:

> Conversely, in the poignancy and immediacy of these early clusters and in their richness of expression lies hidden (in sensitive and gifted people) the germ of creative work; *absence of the possibility for expression of experienced beauty can be as productive of depression and strain as is emotional conflict.* (Lowenfeld, 1979, p. 26, emphasis added)

The latter observation itself depended on further theoretical clarification on the nature of the energy that required expression. Lowenfeld assumed that homeostatic principles were relevant to regulating mental stability, and in this sense her thinking was akin to that of the early Freud. However she consistently differentiated her view from a Freudian emphasis on infantile sexuality. Nor did she wish to swing her argument on the existence of a pleasure–unpleasure principle (Freud, 1900). Though this dimension was important, in Lowenfeld's systems effects of pleasure or unpleasure were linked to the formation and operation of the affective–cognitive structures of the protosystem. Nevertheless Lowenfeld needed to explain the mechanisms and effects of the location and unblocking of energy, and the nature of the impetus to development.

In the pre-war work, Lowenfeld had discussed these processes in terms of such concepts as 'energy' or 'force', loosely derived from dynamic psychology. Unlike some members of the British dynamic-psychology tradition, Lowenfeld rarely explicitly used the concept of 'instinct', and one must assume that she rejected the idea as inadequate in explaining the phenomena she was exploring. However, in many discussions, she did imply the existence of 'destructive tendencies' and 'dark forces' in the human psyche, apparently taking them for granted. This suggests that her model would assume the existence of both something like a destructive or aggressive tendency and a life-preservative or creative force. This would bring her view close to the oppositional model of love and hate which originated in Freud's (1920, 1923, 1930) account of life and death instincts, and which became pivotal in the work of Melanie Klein (Klein, 1935, 1946; Segal, 1986). But Lowenfeld differentiated herself from this kind of model. In her view it could easily collapse into the idea of emotion, independent of cognitive structure, being the driving force in development. It appears that this was among the theoretical problems that she was attempting to address in putting forward her 'theory of "E"'.

The theory of 'E' was discussed at the 1951 conference at which the material in the first paper in Chapter 11 was presented. In some respects it could be understood as an alternative to Freud's libido theory. But what was crucial about the theory was that it postulated the existence of a primary force, E, which was basic to growth and function, but which was neutral. That is, E was neither positive nor negative in itself. The mode in which it was manifested would be determined, not by its intrinsic nature, but by the nature of the structures through which it flowed. It was manifested in three distinguishable ways: through physical activity (EP), accounting for growth and the activity of the various systems of the body; through the intellect (EI), producing cognitive activity; and in feeling (EF), finding expression in the emotions and the affective life generally. If for any reason one of these functions was unusually highly charged, for example, in running a race, at the height of sexual experience, or in solving some difficult intellectual problem, the other modes of functioning would be simultaneously inhibited. Alternatively, the blocking of one channel would increase the discharge of E in other functions, thus implying some connection at source. If no appropriate channel for discharge were available, the effects could include intense anxiety, physical symptoms, inability to think rationally, or outbursts of anti-social activity (see also Lowenfeld, 1979, pp. 271–2).

The theory of E proved a useful construct clinically, enabling Lowenfeld and her colleagues to draw together observations on patterns of symptomatology, and changes occurring over the course of treatment. For example, while Worlds gave access to the distribution of E within the protosystem, the theory of E was useful in relating changes observed in treatment and the child's behaviour outside the treatment context, and could be used in considering what kind of play activity to offer a child at any particular point. But the theory also drew attention to phenomena, or interpretations of phenomena, inaccessible through other theoretical systems. This applied particularly in Lowenfeld's attempt to account for destructive and violent phantasies, feelings and actions without recourse to an aggressive instinct. In Lowenfeld's view,

> High charges of force, whatever its nature, tend to bring about explosion, the moment of explosion and its force depending upon the relation between the energy involved and the strength of the container. The effect is destructive and could therefore, in relation to what is destroyed, be regarded as aggressive. In fact in such a case, the resulting destruction is due solely to the absence of other paths of dispersion for the energy, once it has reached a certain pitch.
>
> Dammed-up E can and does frequently reach a point where some detensioning process must take place. These may take many forms, from an epileptic fit to hyperkinesis, or acute

> anxiety. Our experience with children suggests that it is not essential to postulate an aggressive instinct but that they also, in a certain proportion of cases, can be both understood and resolved through application of the theory of 'E'. (Lowenfeld, 1960, reprinted in *The World Technique*, 1979, p. 272)

It is interesting that Lowenfeld's postulation of the theory of E paralleled or followed extensive debate within the British psychoanalytic movement over the relative plausibility or adequacy of the concept of the death instinct in general, and the way it was understood by Melanie Klein and her followers in particular. One kind of response to Klein favoured by many analysts in the British object-relations tradition was a rejection of her concept of the death instinct in favour of models emphasizing aggression as a response to a frustration in reality (Kohon, 1986). This has tended to be accompanied by an increasing attention to the contribution of the environment, particularly as a result of Winnicott's work.

These theoretical discussions contributed to a displacement of the centrality given to aggression in popular versions of psychoanalysis or its derivatives in the post-war period. Bowlby's (1969) Attachment Theory, for instance, says relatively little about the role of aggression (Urwin, 1985b; Urwin and Sharland, forthcoming). Since Lowenfeld wished to suspend the idea of an aggressive instinct one might assume that the issue of aggression had become less central for her. In fact this is not the case. Understanding aggression remained a priority within a world-view that was decidedly pessimistic. In explaining why the particular case histories included in *The World Technique* had been chosen, she noted, 'In the opinion of the writer violence rather than sex is the crucial problem of this period in the world's history' (Lowenfeld, 1979, p. 27). One might also add that even compared with some of her contemporaries, as well as by today's criteria, her theory had rather little to say about gender (see Chapter 12).

Though Lowenfeld clearly drew on the theory of E in clinical work, as is illustrated, for example, in the cases in *The World Technique*, she actually wrote little about it. It remained as a set of descriptive postulates, valuable in linking observations and in conceptualizing developmental change as it occurred through Lowenfeld's therapeutic approach, but it is not clear whether the theory was intended to replace the contributions of psychoanalysis or to draw attention to phenomena which that scheme occluded. More crucially, Lowenfeld left unexplored the precise nature of the therapist's role in enabling the child to sort out protosystem confusions, or in facilitating a change in energy distribution. Even within Lowenfeld's own scheme, it is necessary to explore whether an intervention which takes place via an interpersonal relation is of the same sort as, for example, providing opportunities for specific types of play activity.

In retrospect, that Lowenfeld did not explore the therapist's role any further limits the dialogue to be had between the Lowenfeld tradition and psychoanalytic approaches. That Lowenfeld did not pursue these questions may reflect her determination to go her own way, or the need to avoid engaging in a dialogue which would itself have been indicative of the psychoanalytic community's unwillingness to allow the value of other approaches at that time. Given the reception accorded to her ideas by the psychoanalytic community in 1937, by her own account she was not willing to put herself up for personal attack again. Alternatively or additionally, Lowenfeld's resistance may have been based on a more profound recognition that focusing attention on the obvious importance of interpersonal relations, and in particular on the mother–child relation, which had come to occupy such a prominent place in the post-war era, was itself a distraction from what was for her the central task: understanding developmental relations between mind and body, culture and the universe, and the possibilities for creative thought and action to pitch against 'a terrific sense that time was running out for the Western world, if not for the entire world' (Mead, 1973).

FURTHER RESEARCH INTO CULTURE AND EDUCATION

It was in 1948 that Margaret Lowenfeld first met Margaret Mead, at the World Federation for Mental Health Conference held in London in the August of that year. Lowenfeld introduced herself and brought Mead to see an exhibition mounted at the ICP as a contribution to the Mental Health Congress. Lowenfeld had long been an admirer of Mead's work, and the opportunity to actually meet her appears to have produced an almost childlike excitement and reverence. For her part, Mead noted in a letter to Gregory Bateson written on 21 October of that year, 'I learned more from her in two days than from the whole rest of the summer put together', recognizing her as 'a brilliant person with masses of irreplaceable experience deposited in an ongoing project which if broken up will be virtually impossible to reassemble' (personal correspondence, Margaret Mead Archive, Washington, by courtesy of Rhoda Metraux).

In part, this mutual admiration was based on similarities in interests and priorities. Both women were committed to the idea that scientific research could potentially be relevant to social issues in the broadest sense, and identified the need to move across national boundaries as imperative in the post-war period. Both had a deep fascination in relations between social organization, patterns of daily living and the creative expression of cultural experience. As Rhoda Metraux, the anthropologist and colleague of Margaret Mead noted, 'Both had an extraordinary capacity for discerning and analysing pattern in very fine detail within a holistic context' (Metraux, 1986).

As forceful and determined women and independent thinkers, there were some obvious similarities in character. But there were also differences. Physically large, Lowenfeld conveyed her vulnerability and confusion and, as a clinician, her deep sensitivity to the position of the victim, and the need to identify the unique in the individual or the source of strength which could be released to ensure self-correction once areas of fragility had been understood. Mead was small, by comparison intensely energetic, and tended to think in terms of changes in social organization or child-rearing practices on a grand scale which would ensure a new kind of future for subsequent generations. A pioneer in the attempt to take findings from the study of cultural differences in child-rearing and personality development into child health and education, she lacked, of course, Lowenfeld's particular experiences of war and, as an American, she had never had first-hand experience of invasion. In the post-war years Mead was in a position of considerable influence, serving on numerous national and international committees on child health and education. Lowenfeld was clearly impressed by this, seeing Mead as someone who could increase her own access to international contexts. Encouraged by Mead, she also saw her as an important source of support in obtaining research money. Here, nothing changed to alter Mead's view of Lowenfeld's particular genius. But she could be exasperated by Lowenfeld's difficulties with organization and with expressing her ideas in written form. This could exacerbate Mead's tendency to impose her own view.

Despite these differences, the friendship between the two
 Margarets proved enduring and mutually valuable, leading to a

productive working relationship. It was through Mead that Lowenfeld secured her first visit to the USA in April 1950, returning on the liner *Queen Mary* at the end of June. The trip had been discussed between them as early as March 1949, when Lowenfeld wrote to Mead of 'The idea that [the] USA might allow me to unload some of the thought about cultures and about inter-communication by concrete methods that I have been working at all the war' (ML to MM, 18 March 1949, personal communication, MM Archive, Washington; by courtesy of Rhoda Metraux). At this time there was some hostility within the ICP to Lowenfeld's internationalist ventures, based on incomprehension or suspicion, or on the idea that they would detract from the important task of re-establishing the ICP itself. However Lowenfeld Mosaics were already in use in a number of clinical settings in Europe and, along with the Rorschach and a modification of the Thematic Apperception Test, they had, for example, been used in research in Jamaica by Madeleine Kerr. By the time the trip to the USA took place, Lowenfeld had received numerous requests to lecture in various universities and educational establishments. She had also amassed a large list of people who she wished to meet, including the child psychiatrists or analysts Erik Erikson and Leo Kanner and the psychologists Sibyl Escalona and Frances Ilg.

Of all the effects of this first transcontinental crossing on her work, perhaps one of the most significant was that it provided Lowenfeld with her first exposure, *en masse*, to a set of Mosaics produced by children who had grown up in America. This occurred on 26 May 1950, at an informal gathering at the offices of the Columbia University Research in Contemporary Cultures (RCC). Though Mead was in charge of this project, she was actually away at the time. The sample had been collected, in the form of coloured-in tracings of Mosaics, from a group of elementary-school children by a psychologist, Ursula Stewart. What was described by Rhoda Metraux, present at the time, and by Lowenfeld herself on subsequent occasions, was the profound sense of shock, which she put into the words, 'But these children must be very disturbed!' That is, characteristics which in British or European children would be associated with extreme immaturity or mental deficiency were present over and over again within the sample. Given that some of the children who had produced the Mosaics were actually known to those present, Lowenfeld re-examined her initial conjectures. By the end of that meeting her attention was focused on what it was that differentiated them from Mosaics produced by British children. That is, she recognized them as organized products coming out of a different cultural setting.

As an anthropologist, Rhoda Metraux (1986) has related Lowenfeld's shock to the kind of experience frequently confronting the anthropologist doing field-work in another culture when taken-for-granted assumptions about meaning, representation and salient dimensions of life are overturned. For Lowenfeld, the shock may have been less based on incredulity than on a recognition of evidence supporting a long-standing belief that effects of cultural location would be reflected concretely within the psyche. The anthropologists present saw the possibilities for the use of Mosaics in their own research. It had several advantages over the Rorschach Inkblot Test, the projective test used most frequently in the field at that time, the most important being that it relied on designs produced by subjects themselves.

Lowenfeld made a further trip to the USA in the early fifties, to give demonstrations and discuss findings on the use of her techniques within the USA, and in 1953 the Mosaic Test was used systematically in the field for the first time. In Manus, New Guinea, it was used in a study mounted by Margaret Mead, Ted Schwartz and Lenore Schwartz. Simultaneously Rhoda Metraux incorporated the use of Mosaics in her work in Montserrat, and provided life histories of the villagers for the clinical psychologist Theodora Abel, who joined her to carry out the psychological aspects of the research.

Some of the findings from this work were presented in *The Lowenfeld Mosaic Test* (Lowenfeld, 1954) or can be found in the references to the work of Abel, Mead and Metraux cited previously (p. 10). Perhaps more surprisingly, Lowenfeld's contact with Margaret Mead also influenced her in developing research in education, and in mathematical thinking in particular. In one of her many projects, Mead was involved in the dilemma imposed on American educationists concerning the relatively poor mathematical ability shown by many American children. This interest was prompted by the USA's attempt to explain its poor performance in space research in the 1950s when compared to their Russian rivals. Mead correctly identified Lowenfeld as capable of unravelling the difficulties experienced by many children in grasping mathematical concepts, and indeed she had already begun to explore this problem herself.

 In the 1940s Lowenfeld designed what later became the

Poleidoblocs Tests, G and A, each consisting of sets of blocks of basic geometric shapes, which were designed to enable children to discover through construction and experiment the basic structure of mathematics: reversability, composition and decomposition, equivalence and so forth. She had also designed the basics of the Kaleidoblocs Test, which was intended to act in the reverse direction from standard psychological tests and hence to supplement them. That is, instead of aiming to pinpoint a particular ability and detect a specific deficit, the Kaleidoblocs aimed to provide the child with the opportunity for expressing an understanding of relations, particularly in the area of space perception. Again, the test consisted of brightly coloured objects of various shapes (see Lowenfeld, 1979, pp. 273–4). Both Poleidoblocs and Kaleidoblocs were used in clinical work at the ICP, where the three-dimensional constructions produced spontaneously by the child were assumed to be comparable in origin to the two-dimensional responses given in the Mosaic Test. However, the widespread application of the techniques in educational assessment or in teaching depended on more extensive work with larger groups of children in educational settings.

It is important to stress that for Lowenfeld there was no necessary conflict between her clinical work and research into mathematical thinking. Both involved the exploration of developments in a form of thinking through which the mind represents to itself aspects of its relation to the environment, and its own thoughts. Just as the clinical work emphasized that affect and cognition worked together, difficulties in mathematical thinking could be related to disturbances in the protosystem, which were in turn related to the emotional life of the child.

None the less, these developments did not interest or please all members of the ICP. There were those who resented or were suspicious of the effects of Margaret Mead on the direction of the work, or who wished that it would remain more obviously clinical. There were also intense personal rivalries, which were reinforced by the continual financial pressures producing problems for the management of the clinic. In an attempt to ameliorate some of the conflict, in 1959 Lowenfeld opted to shift her main working base to her private consulting rooms in Harley Street. She continued to lecture at the ICP and remained director of the training component, the management now being chiefly in the charge of Phyllis Traill, who had trained at the ICP in the 1930s and had occupied a prominent position in child guidance in Birmingham and worked in Chesterfield before returning to the ICP after the war.

From her Harley Street base Lowenfeld continued clinical work with children and, as she became older, herself extended the use of the World technique into clinical work with adults (see Lowenfeld, 1979, pp. 253–70). Major efforts however went into research with and the perfection of the new techniques. Responsibility for establishing connections with local schools, liaising with teachers and assembling records of children's productions were largely in the hands of Ville Andersen. Although Mead was influential in encouraging this direction in Lowenfeld's work, which was at one time supported financially by a small grant from an American foundation, it also evoked interest and support amongst British educationists.

These were now the post-Plowden years in primary education when the aim was to put into practice a child-centred approach, and to encourage learning through discovery. Preparations were also being made for the introduction of the new mathematics. Thus the work on the Poleidoblocs and their dissemination into schools was supported by a grant from the Leverhulme Foundation, administered through the British Association for the Advancement of Science, and between 1960 and 1963 Lowenfeld became co-director with Dr Z. P. Dienes of the British Association Unit for Research into the Generation of Mathematical Insights.

THE LAST YEARS

From the mid-1960s onwards, Lowenfeld spent less and less time at the ICP itself. Though her methods and approach remained the fundamental source of inspiration at the clinic, as she got older, becoming more disorganized and apparently autocratic, productive collaboration became increasingly difficult. By the end of the 1960s, most of her energy was taken up with attempting to consolidate research findings and to complete written projects. Here, Margaret Lowenfeld was greatly aided by the organizational skills of Ville Andersen, who had left the ICP with her when she transferred her major base to Harley Street. One of Lowenfeld's last written projects was the unpublished history, 'The Institute of Child Psychology', completed in 1969 and referred to throughout these chapters. Interestingly, that history concluded with the hope that not only would her work continue to aid the treatment of disturbed children, but that it would contribute to prevention through research and the application of her tools in educational and clinical contexts.

Though considerable effort went into organizing records and research in the last years, Margaret Lowenfeld continued to give talks and lectures on subjects of perennial concern or contemporary relevance. The papers presented in Chapter 12 in this selection, 'The Adolescent's Search for Identity' and 'Communication with Children' are amongst her last public presentations. They are included here less for their contribution to the overall theoretical scheme than for their illustration of persistent priorities.

Margaret Lowenfeld continued to lecture at the ICP and to supervise senior students. But by 1970 her attendance was reduced to once a week. She and Ville were spending much of their time at Cherry Orchards, a house in Cholesbury, Buckinghamshire, which Margaret had bought on her mother's death, and which at first had only been used for weekends. By this time her ability to work had deteriorated and she suffered increasingly from delusions and alterations in mood. In April 1972, when she was already under medical surveillance, she fell out of bed and was found by Ville in a state of mental exhaustion, talking wildly in Polish about school days, matriculation and Latin grammar, returning to a question: perhaps I could have saved more? She appeared to be reliving terrifying wartime experiences (Ville Andersen, personal communication). From this time onwards she became increasingly difficult and the family felt there was little hope of recovery. Her sister Helena was still in good health. In spite of years of rivalry and intense ambivalence, she persuaded Margaret to move to a nursing home near the Wrights' flat. She spent Christmas that year with Helena and her husband and died in hospital the following February on the day before her eighty-third birthday. She was buried at the church of St Lawrence, Cholesbury, which is in fact only a short distance from Little Brickhill where the two girls had spent their first six months away from home. Helena was also buried there, nine years later.

Ville Andersen, still a Danish citizen and now without employment in Britain, returned to Denmark. From her retirement she contributed to the preparation of *The World Technique* book, collaborating with John Hood-Williams. The book was published first in a limited edition by the ICP itself, publication eventually being taken over by Allen & Unwin.

John Hood-Williams, who had trained at the ICP in the early

1950s, had been approached to take over the directorship of the ICP shortly before Margaret Lowenfeld's death. His appointment began in January 1973, when the economic resources of the clinic were already insufficient to ensure adequate development. On the one hand, many of the private donations on which the clinic continued to rely were no longer forthcoming. On the other hand, the system whereby local authorities in the London area referred children and paid for their treatment was put to the test with the expansion of child-guidance work in London and the increasing recruitment of cases by the Tavistock Clinic. Though the per capita system could keep pace with the running costs of the ICP initially, by the mid-seventies the running costs soared, with the spiralling inflation that followed the International Monetary Fund crisis and rising oil prices. This prefigured the first rounds of local-authority spending cuts in the late seventies. Coupled with this, an increasing proportion of the staff at the ICP were now salaried, where for many years after the war the majority of workers had continued to give their services on a voluntary basis, either because they had private incomes or held consultancies elsewhere. Many of Margaret Lowenfeld's own colleagues who had been central in establishing the viability of the work after the war had also died or retired, Phyllis Traill dying shortly after her retirement in 1975.

The loss of Margaret Lowenfeld as the figurehead of the ICP and the source of its inspiration and distinctive emphasis, of course, put a strain on the morale and commitment of those aiming to carry on. It also had effects on the outside world. Over the years, the psychoanalytic traditions within the Association of Child Psychotherapists had become more dominant. For example, the Tavistock-based child-psychotherapy training increased its annual intake of trainees considerably. One consequence was that the association came to identify itself as a psychoanalytic body. After Margaret Lowenfeld's death, suspicion and antipathy towards the ICP training began to be voiced more overtly. Criticism from the training council was directed at modifying the ICP training such that it resembled more closely the other trainings. Some of these changes reflected the need to ensure comparability in the credentials which could be presented by applicants for child-psychotherapy posts within the public sector. For example, agreement was reached on the length of training, the ICP training being extended from three to four years, and on the requirement of intensive personal analysis. Before this a minimum of two times a week was considered satisfactory. Up to now students from the ICP had not found it difficult to transfer to working in NHS clinics or other clinical or educational establishments (Thérèse Woodcock, personal communication). Nevertheless theoretical orientations or practical priorities in these settings were also open to modification. Thus other changes in the training reflected the need to adjust to changes in the likely demands of the various work situations in which trainees from the ICP would find themselves after qualification. For example, in the mid-1970s the ICP training included work with parents as a necessary component of the course, a similar move being made by the Tavistock and Hampstead trainings.

The pressure for these changes was in part based on the need to ensure the viability of the ICP training as a professional qualification. Other criticisms focused on the work itself, and in particular around the unresolved issue of the ICP's dismissal of the transference as necessarily the central therapeutic agency. Though the different psychoanalytic schools represented in the association traditionally differ in how transference is defined and used, the concept remains a defining feature of the psychoanalytic approach. For the new generation of psychoanalytic child psychotherapists, who had not been party to the pre-war developments and the initial founding of the association, the habit of defending psychoanalysis may have been compounded by incredulity and incomprehension as to what could happen therapeutically if the centrality of transference was displaced.

To some extent the need to update training requirements in line with work demands was a pressure which applied in all trainings, an example of what Dilys Daws (1987) has described as the 'tension' remaining within child psychotherapy as a result of its practical and theoretical heritage, discussed earlier. For the ICP, however, the implications of these pressures were more profound. If substantial adjustments were to be made in the preparation of trainees to equip them for work outside the ICP itself, the questions raised were ultimately about the viability of Lowenfeld's particular holistic approach, and the extent to which the philosophical, ideological and theoretical basis of the work could be maintained if the particular clinical model through which the work had evolved was forced to adapt.

In working through these issues, perhaps inevitably, the link with the professional body of child psychotherapists appears to have operated divisively rather than as a source of support, contributing ultimately to the demise of the Lowenfeld tradition. The major precipitating causes for this were, however, economic. As the economic recession began to bite in the late 1970s, the local Health Authority withdrew from the scheme whereby they paid for the treatment of children referred to the clinic. Since this comprised over 98 percent of the ICP's income, there was no alternative but to close down. In the same year the Association of Child Psychotherapists withdrew its recognition of what was now, apparently, regarded as an 'eclectic' training (Daws, 1987) on the grounds that it no longer fulfilled the association's training requirements, a major reason given being the lack of an institutional base. This occurred in 1978, some fifty years after the initial foundation of the Children's Clinic.

6 Retrospective

Though the ICP was closed, Lowenfeld left behind a good number of therapists trained in her approach. Although some have died or have retired, others are working in child-guidance clinics, children's centres of various kinds, or are in private practice, combining clinical work with research and teaching the use of Lowenfeld techniques. On the closure of the ICP a Trust was established. Amongst other things, this has supported a research post in Cambridge, England, which has made the present work possible, and an annual Day Conference which brings together clinicians and research workers from various professions and psychotherapeutic traditions concerned with emotional development in children. In this sense a commitment to a multidisciplinary approach to understanding children is carried forward. The conference also provides a forum for the presentation of clinical and theoretical papers based on Lowenfeld's approach and for the discussion of new research projects which utilize her techniques. These include research into the emotional-mental processes of children with reading difficulties, using Lowenfeld's Worlds (Wood, 1987, forthcoming) and a re-examination of the value of Mosaics in cross-cultural work, including the elucidation of developmental effects of Chinese culture (Woodcock, 1986a, 1986b). The conference has also drawn in visitors from the USA. On the West Coast there is a healthy tradition of clinical work continuing the use of Lowenfeld Worlds (Clegg, 1984). This owes much to the initiative of Robert Royeton. After graduating from the ICP in 1973, Robert Royeton returned to California, to set up an Institute of Child Psychotherapy for carrying out clinical work and training students along the lines set by Lowenfeld. Interest on the West Coast was originally encouraged by the uptake of the use of Worlds by the Jungian child analyst, Dora Kalff, who briefly worked with Lowenfeld at the ICP in the early 1950s and who was influential in introducing the idea of sand-play to American practitioners (Kalff, 1966). In addition, the recent publication of an American book on the Mosaic Test, by Eugene Perticone and Renée Tembeckjian, who presented their work at the conference in 1987, may renew interest in its clinical and research applications.

These are examples from many areas in which Lowenfeld's ideas are still being used or taken forward. Nevertheless, given that Margaret Lowenfeld was once so well known and so influential in the field of child psychotherapy and psychiatry, it is perhaps remarkable her work is so ill understood and little recognized. Few people know, for instance, how and why sand-trays are available in child-guidance clinics up and down the country and even less is known about the generation of ideas behind their application. Paradoxically, where her influence can be most easily pinpointed, in the child-centred movement in education and in self-directive play therapy, her theoretical ideas have been often oversimplified to the point where they almost reverse her own emphasis. For example, the emphasis on play and creativity is reduced to a simple formula: given space for discovery children will automatically learn according to a universal developmental pattern, and work through their difficulties to a harmonious solution, free from conflict. It is not surprising that Lowenfeld's ideas can be assimilated to this position, given that in her early work she identified herself explicitly with a liberatory perspective and with many in the Progressive Education movement (Walkerdine, 1984). Yet, as we have seen, the opportunity provided by the Children's Clinic and the ICP depended on establishing an environment distinct from the world outside. It may be that this recognition lay behind Lowenfeld's own observation that 'The Children's Clinic is, and must always remain, an experiment' (Children's Clinic, *Annual Report 1929–30*, p. 11). Moreover, as Lowenfeld's theoretical framework became more complex, the holistic approach insisted on diversity, defied any attempt to read off what constitutes normality, and belied any attempt to reduce it to a simple linear theory of causation. If the ascendancy of psychoanalytic approaches in the post-war period has had less to do with therapeutic efficacy than the widespread uptake of normative versions of psychoanalysis, then the fact that Lowenfeld's key ideas resist normative re-renderings may have been a major factor contributing to the eclipse of the work and the demise of the ICP.

The publication of the papers that follow, some fifteen years after Lowenfeld's death, provides the occasion for a re-examination of some of her ideas. From the present perspective, the interest is not in whether or not they express external or universal truths or have contemporary relevance in any simple way. Lowenfeld's scheme was incomplete, indicating problem areas rather than providing a coherent, overarching theoretical system. Often her ideas were poorly expressed. Sometimes this reflected her own difficulties in thinking and in using language. Sometimes it was due to the difficulty of putting non-verbal material in verbal form, as Lowenfeld suggested. Sometimes it is the difficulty of formulating something which as yet cannot be understood, and can only be described. Furthermore, as Suzanne Langer (1942) asserted of the history of philosophy, every age has its own preoccupations and its problems are peculiar to it. This process of change is partly social and political, but it has also to do with reasons of intellectual growth. Just as the preoccupations of the 1920s and 30s do not repeat themselves in exactly the same way in future years, changes in the kinds of intellectual tools available imply that solutions would not be sought again in the same places or in the same way.

It is for this reason that, here and in the introductory sections of the following chapters, to make Lowenfeld's work accessible it has been necessary to contextualize Lowenfeld's preoccupations and to elucidate intellectual sources no longer in current usage. But if intellectual growth is itself regarded as less of a teleological or evolutionary process than one of multifaceted determination, of sociocultural upheaval, personal struggle for integrity against compromise, self-interest and disillusion, it is as likely as not that new directions turn out to be blind alleys, and that apparent progress is at the expense of valuable areas which get forgotten or destroyed or are obscured by complementary and more powerful theoretical perspectives.

Thus re-examining Lowenfeld's ideas in the light of contemporary approaches may enrich our understanding of the formation and breadth of the latter and also pose a number of challenges. For instance, there are a number of questions for psychoanalysis. With hindsight it is possible to identify not only overlaps in areas of interest and priority, but influences of Lowenfeld's work within psychoanalysis. For example, in a detailed examination of play and symbolism, Madeleine Davis

(1988) has illustrated the extent of Lowenfeld's influence on Winnicott. This influence, which he eventually recognized explicitly (Winnicott, 1971), is particularly apparent in three of the most distinctive aspects of Winnicott's work: the broadened notion of what constitutes a symbol, the emphasis on accounting for creativity, and the importance of the play process as a thing in itself. The latter emphasis contributed to the idea that a goal of all psychotherapy, with children and adults, is to enable the patient to reach the point where playing is possible. Since this view has had widespread effects on psychotherapy technique in many traditions, even where the response is critical, it is particularly interesting that it originated from an influence outside psychoanalysis.

More recently, there have also been a number of developments within psychoanalysis which bring its priorities closer to Lowenfeld's. By a strange irony of history, this is particularly so in the Kleinian and post-Kleinian tradition. For example, Meltzer (1967) and his colleagues have given particular attention to the role of the psychoanalytic process in helping to clarify various zonal confusions, such as confusions between different body orifices. This interest is clearly parallel to Lowenfeld's observations on the way in which zonal confusions may be represented concretely in children's Worlds, as described on page 116. Similarly, descriptions given by Meltzer (1973) of what he calls 'mental geography' overlap with Lowenfeld's emphasis on working out relations between inside and outside the body as a prerequisite for the development of mind as a mental space. But perhaps the most significant parallel is with the work of the psychoanalyst Wilfred Bion. As already mentioned in discussing Lowenfeld's first formulation of the protosystem, after extensive work with psychotic or thought-disordered patients, Bion found it necessary to expand the psychoanalytic account of the origins of thinking in infancy (Bion, 1962, 1967). For Bion, the infant's ability to develop an apparatus to deal with emotion and anxiety evolves through, first, generating thoughts, and second, the ability to link them together, forming the process of thinking. Here, there are clear parallels with Lowenfeld's clusters and the network of the protosystem. Finally, a more recent area of congruence between Lowenfeld's work and this psychoanalytic tradition is in a renewed interest in the possible origins of aesthetic awareness in infancy (Meltzer, 1987; Read, 1987). These developments indicate what may be a more general resurgence of interest in the contribution of psychoanalysis as a theory of mind as well as of emotion, a broadening which promises new possibilities of dialogue with developmental psychology. It also opens channels for communication with the Lowenfeld tradition.

But despite the correspondence, it is also vital to recognize distinctive differences. All the developments in psychoanalysis mentioned above locate the processes described within the emergent relation between the infant and parents. The developing infant mind is assumed to require a relationship with another mind to receive, contain or structure its emotional experience, as a prerequisite to the baby's realizing his or her own, self-generated thoughts. Lowenfeld's theory is not a theory of interpersonal relations, and object relations are not given a theoretical priority. It remains to some extent an open question as to whether Lowenfeld's theory of the protosystem had reached an impasse, or could be developed further without a more thorough engagement with the problem of placing interpersonal experience within the overall system.

On the other hand, if the two traditions cease to dovetail after a certain point, it is also true that Lowenfeld's approach opens areas ill charted by psychoanalysis. It is worth singling out two important points of emphasis, both deriving from Lowenfeld's philosophical position, and influenced by developmental psychology. The first is on how from the outset human infants necessarily create images and symbols to mediate their own relation to the animate and inanimate environment. The second is to do with Lowenfeld's view of development itself, both within and outside a psychotherapeutic context. This is inextricably bound up with her own life history.

In giving an account of Lowenfeld's life and work we have attempted to illustrate what her own questions were when she posed her formulations or drew up her theories in the way she did. What emerges as a central question, as Lowenfeld always said it was, is: what did happen to the orphaned cattle-truck boys such that, against the odds, they survived? The paediatrician Dermod MacCarthy once said of her that the contribution of paediatric experience continued to permeate her work, leading to such questions as: what are the relations between psyche and soma, what is health, and what is the drive for life? In her early work with very ill children,

> She saw, she discovered for herself, that what determined whether a child died of heart failure or recovered was (in

> some cases) the hold the child retained on life through having what we observe in a child using the 'World technique', the capacity to *express* (with pleasure, with absorption, even with passion) what is his or her inner vision of things. (Dermod MacCarthy, personal communication to Kate MacSorley, 21 June 1980)

Alongside the commitment to the expression of an 'inner vision' was a lifelong absorption in relations between cultural products and the minds of people using them: how culture can be both an impediment to development and an absolute necessity: what mitigates against or makes possible movement from one system of cultural meanings to another. Throughout, Lowenfeld's multicultural background and her aesthetic appreciation were integral to her attempts to understand the developmental tasks facing children, and how she saw her contribution as a psychiatrist, psychotherapist, and researcher for the future. Experiences of war and questions to do with why horrors and disasters in the social world repeat themselves remained a central focus, in the face of the environmental optimism apparently attached to much reconstruction after the Second World War.

In attempting to understand the questions in Margaret Lowenfeld's own mind, very broadly we could be said to have followed Collingwood's philosophical method in which the aim is to interrogate evidence in such a way as to reveal the purposes and modes of action operating in the people acting in the past, and the thoughts which governed their actions. In so far as we have adopted this approach, we have aimed to illustrate the congruence between Collingwood's line of argument and Lowenfeld's methodological presuppositions and assumptions about the nature of development and possible goals of therapy. It is from this conviction that she asserted the fundamental principle of her therapy: to understand the meaning of what was expressed in the actions and symbols *from the point of view of the adult or child expressing it*. A similar set of assumptions applies in the case of Mosaics and other techniques in cross-cultural research. For Lowenfeld the aim was not simply to make comparisons for the sake of it, but to view the significance of symbolic forms in relation to the patterns of thought of the culture in question. To illuminate this, a whole range of other sources of information on the social, political and interpersonal habits of the community would be drawn upon for evidence, in the manner of the archaeologist who attempts to make sense of artefacts from the past. By implication, the mental activity of the individual engaged in therapy or research parallels that of the historian, who, on the one hand, rethinks the thoughts of actors in the past and, on the other hand, maintains a separation in time and circumstances, and in the process finds out 'what kind of a man he is' (Collingwood, 1939, p. 81 above). The key to the therapist or investigator's active engagement and involvement must lie in an openness to the emotional impact of the material, whether pleasurable or unpleasurable, shocking or beautiful, and to the primacy of aesthetic experience. It is essential to retain the capacity to be surprised. In evaluating effects produced within the self from the point of view of the patient or research subject, the therapist or investigator must find a new relation to them. The dialectical method thus opens possibilities for the patients or subjects to discover, create or re-create their own truth through self-reflection and/or the expression and assimilation of experience, and for therapists and investigators to achieve new understanding.

Lowenfeld's methodology cuts across the form of objectivity insisted on by much contemporary psychology, and the clinical methodology of psychoanalysis. It is influenced by if not modelled on Collingwood's account of history as science. This brings with it radical implications for the conceptualization of development and the location of what goes on between child and therapist in the consulting room. Of all therapeutic traditions Lowenfeld's is perhaps the most explicitly socio-historical. Throughout, Lowenfeld herself continually explicitly stressed the social and historical conjuncture in which her theories, presuppositions and approach were grounded. By implication the symbolic material produced by children using her techniques is determined not simply by vicissitudes of individual biography, but through the social and historical processes in which their development is located. Though universal processes, the protosystem and the regulation of 'E' are assumed as fundamental, content is variable, unpredictable, owing to idiosyncrasies of personal experience, the specifics of cultural location, and the fact that children are developing in an ever changing universe, outside individual human control and the limits of scientific prediction.

Cathy Urwin

Editors' Note

The papers in Part Two are a section of Lowenfeld's total output. The medical research in Chapter 7, for example, resulted in nine publications, singly or jointly authored. The papers in the remaining chapters are selected from fifty or more articles and unpublished presentations concerned with psychological theory and psychotherapeutic technique. We based our choice on how far they illuminate Lowenfeld's approach or particular concepts and their relative clarity. Lowenfeld also wrote many papers of a more practical nature which have not been included here.

In our presentation, some small alterations have been made in the unpublished papers to accommodate the fact that they were originally prepared to be read aloud. In general, unless otherwise stated, papers here are in the form which Lowenfeld originally intended. This results in some repetition but has the advantage of illuminating gradual shifts in emphasis or subtlety. The place of each paper in the overall framework of her life and work is discussed in introductions to each chapter, which also clarify the contemporary relevance of some of the more unfamiliar ideas. Where possible we have reproduced Lowenfeld's original illustrations.

PART TWO
Selected Papers

7 The Background in Research

It would probably be true to say that Lowenfeld's training in medicine and research provided the backbone rather than the background to the development of her approach to emotional problems of childhood. The papers in this chapter were written in the period of her life when medical research was her major activity (see Chapter 2).

'Organization and the Rheumatic Child' first appeared in the *Lancet* on 4 June 1927, p. 1177. Here Lowenfeld presented a synthesis of some of the findings of the study of acute rheumatism and home conditions described previously (pp. 37–8), together with observations on the value of a clinic for actual sufferers, where the progress of the disease could be carefully monitored. Many of the views presented here were shared by Lowenfeld's supervisor in Glasgow, Leonard Findlay, and by G. F. Still, who wrote the original foreword and concluding summary to the report eventually submitted to the Medical Research Council.

As Lowenfeld stressed, the major dangers associated with rheumatism in childhood at that time were not simply to do with the cost in terms of school absence and childhood illness, but with the known association with heart disease in later life. Although the original survey had been remarkably thorough, it did not produce simple answers as to cause and effect; the pattern of aetiology was extremely complex. Yet, as Lowenfeld pointed out, what view was taken on the cause of the illness would have crucial implications for treatment, prevention and eventual eradication. Here she discussed pros and cons of two major hypotheses. One favoured the existence of a particular organism, yet to be identified; the other, the 'constitution' hypothesis, favoured the idea that at issue was some disturbance, possibly biochemical, in the metabolism of the individual. This might be triggered by specific environmental circumstances.

Lowenfeld clearly favoured the latter alternative. Apart from the fact that an organism had yet to be identified, there were cases of diseases which had not been eradicated even where this information was available; there were also cases, like leprosy and typhus in Europe, where eradication had been achieved without an exact knowledge of causation. Moreover, pursuing the infection hypothesis would require isolating material from the individual, rendering the care of the latter person irrelevant. Pursuing the constitution hypothesis, on the other hand, would focus on the 'whole' individual in relation to his or her environment. Lowenfeld went on to sketch the advantages of the clinic organization as a way of combining careful monitoring of the phases of the disease or its life history with alerting parents, providing advice and treatment where necessary and possible.

Thus, Lowenfeld's commitments to a holistic approach and the idea of a clinic organization for combining research and treatment were already well established before she started psychotherapy. Since Lowenfeld's time, relatively little more has been established about the condition of rheumatism, except that it is now known that, contrary to the original survey's assumption, tonsillar infection cannot be recognized simply by inspection, which Lowenfeld suspected, and that a particular organism, the beta-haemolitic streptococcus, is in fact involved. (We are indebted to Professor John Davis for this information.) This does not detract from the pertinence of Lowenfeld's observations on the value of a holistic approach; indeed, the likelihood is that understanding the life history of the disease, the associated bodily changes and relations to environment played a major role in its eradication.

The rheumatism work also promoted Lowenfeld's interest in biochemical testing, which she insisted on doggedly in the early days of the Children's Clinic. Biochemical research was also a major aspect of the work on lactation, illustrated in the second paper in this chapter. Where the research training in the rheumatism study was by and large in interviewing and other techniques of the survey associated with epidemiological research, the lactation study required acute observation and the development of subtle techniques of measurement and recording.

 'Researches in Lactation' was first published in the *Journal of*

Obstetrics and Gynaecology of the British Empire (vol. 35, no. 1, pp. 114–30), in 1928. The paper was co-authored by Sibyl Taite Widdows, BSc, FIC, from the Chemical and Physiological Department of the London (Royal Free Hospital) School of Medicine for Women. She was responsible for the biochemical side of the work.

Lowenfeld's responsibility was with collecting samples of milk produced over the first fourteen days following childbirth, with the aim of studying the course of milk production and variations in nutritional content and their implications for infant feeding. This involved devising adequate sampling techniques, and means for assessing variations in nutritional content over the course of a single feed. Here, again, there was an obvious continuity between the fascination and ingenuity which Lowenfeld showed in devising research techniques in this study and the later fascination in techniques shown in her psychological work. There was also a continuity in her insistence on the importance of observation and keeping records.

In the present paper, findings of interest included the apparently obvious but highly important observation that in no two women was the course of lactation the same, though particular patterns were more or less likely to be associated with multiparity or primaparity, that is, whether the mother had given birth to more than one baby or this was her first delivery. Particularly interesting was the demonstration that the fat content of breast milk varied not only in accord with the point in the feed when the sample was taken, but that it also varied according to the amount of pressure used to obtain it. In consequence, distribution of fat in the food intake would be differentially affected according to whether the infant was a 'poor' sucker or had strong jaws, as well as according to the actual content of fat in the mother's milk. Various practical recommendations followed from the study. Here, for reasons of length, a discussion on colostrum and the summary at the end of the paper have been omitted.

In this paper, and in some of the others in the following chapters, there are statements about mothers which are jarring to a contemporary readership; for example, here, amongst mothers in the hospital classes, one could not always tell if an unmarried mother was, in fact, primaparous (this volume, p. 162). As a piece of research, however, the present paper remains valuable by today's standards (Elsie Widdowson, personal communication), not least because of the relative novelty of the research field in Lowenfeld's time. Even in 1928 Lowenfeld was hinting at a psychological factor influencing the course of an infant's feeding. Given that variations could additionally be found in mothers' milk production, as well as in babies' willingness or ability to suck, it was also possible that, in some cases, psychological factors within the mother–baby relationship were at issue. However, Lowenfeld did not draw out this implication.

Organization and the Rheumatic Child [1927]

Rheumatism in childhood has been known since the early nineteenth century, but it is only within recent years that the numerical extent of the disease has been ascertained and its significance appreciated. The position which now confronts us can be summarized as follows. From the statistics of 1926, 500,000 of the schoolchildren of the country are estimated to suffer from rheumatism, 10,000 of the children of school age in London are known to be rheumatic, and the vital statistics of 1924 showed that the deaths from heart disease exceeded those from either tuberculosis or cancer.

This incidence of disease in the community has two consequences. The first is the recurring periods of ill-health and loss of education to the child. This is a feature difficult to realize and it is something of a shock to read in a recent report (London County Council, 1925) that a quarter of the chronic ill-health of schoolchildren of the country is estimated to be due to rheumatism. The second effect is the adult carditis resulting from the disease. The extent of this is indicated by the estimation that 60 per cent of rheumatic children ultimately develop heart disease. These facts represent one of the many baffling problems confronting medicine today. It is a problem, however, which is fortunately attracting considerable attention, and the past year has seen the publication of two authoritative reports concerning it and one containing suggestions with regard to its prevention. It is the purpose of this paper to attempt to summarize the present position as regards our knowledge of the disease, and to examine the grounds upon which hope of control and of understanding may fairly be based.

THREE MAIN FACTS

If the disease be considered as a whole, three main facts become evident. The first is a marked lack of definition in the clinical outline. Only a short time ago, acute and subacute rheumatic fever, chorea, tonsillitis, and carditis were held to cover the manifestations of rheumatism in childhood. As these are well-defined conditions, the features of the disease appeared to be clear and easily recognizable. But, within recent years, it has been argued that many forms of debility, anaemia, vague muscular pains, dyspepsias, and general irritability should also be considered as of rheumatic origin. Furthermore, there is a good deal of evidence which goes to show that carditis can result equally from these as from the more definite forms of the disease, although this is a point upon which unequivocal proof is still needed.

The second fact is that the greater significance of rheumatism in childhood does not lie in the typical manifestations to which the name is given, and from which the child can be seen to be suffering, but in a single feature of these – i.e. heart disease. This, in any but its later stages, is not to be detected by the general public. Yet, as is the case with all diseases of children, it is on parents as part of the public that we must rely for the making of the contact between patient and physician. The peculiar situation, therefore, arises that the significance of the disease is in a region inaccessible to the observation of patient or mother, and without relation to the severity of the symptoms appreciable by either.

Third, we have no certain knowledge of the actual cause and nature of the disease. Two views are current. By the early observers, rheumatism, or more strictly, those manifestations of it that had so far been identified, was looked upon as evidence of a particular constitution of the body. Somewhat later, a specific infection seemed the more probable explanation. It is on this hypothesis, put forward and developed by F. J. Poynton and A. Paine (1913), that nearly all modern conceptions have been based.

INFECTION OR DIATHESIS?

To tne practical aspect of the question the choice of hypothesis is crucial. If it be granted that a given disease be the result, or the result mainly, of a specific micro-organism, then effective measures against the disease must wait upon the successful isolation of the organism, or the practical application of immunological processes yet to be discovered. In the period before this has occurred the lines of work most likely to be fruitful will be those directed towards the modification of conditions within and around the child that favour infection with this organism. If, on the other hand, the diathesis theory be assumed, other lines of approach to the problem come into view. In the disease under review during the past two years certain evidence has been adduced to suggest the value once more of considering the constitutional or diathesis hypothesis (Llewellyn, 1926). According to this view, the outbreak of the disease would depend rather upon constitutional modification of the bodily habit than an 'infection' with a specific organism.

The importance of this point cannot be exaggerated. If the constitutional view be conceded, the emphasis of study, and ultimately of treatment, is thereby shifted. The dependence of treatment upon identification of the organism becomes greatly diminished, and the inquiry shifts to points concerning the endocrine and biochemical make-up of the individual. For the designing of work either with regard to the study of the disease or to the devising of means for its control, the choice of hypothesis is of fundamental importance.

BEARING ON THE STUDY OF THE DISEASE

Hitherto, all inquiry into the nature of the disease has been conducted by separate investigations specifically designed and carried out alongside of the ordinary clinical work. That is to say, while nearly all workers in this field have been keenly interested in the problems of the disease, and have contributed much of great value to our knowledge of its clinical course and manifestations, when a specific aspect has come to be investigated, a separate effort has been needed to examine and report on the material available. Two examples of this kind have recently been provided by the reports of the BMA and MRC Committees. Just so long as the infective theory of the disease exclusively dominates our conception of it this system is inevitable. Bacteriological and statistical work have no bearing upon the treatment of the individual patient at the time concerned until their goal has been reached.

If, however, the alternative hypothesis be taken for examination, a different type of attack is possible. Here the nature of the disease is conceived as within the constitution of the patient himself, as has been brought out recently by Hurst (1927).

According to this view, the whole individual is the subject of inquiry and this inquiry can only be carried out by observation of the individual, whereas by an infection theory the subject of inquiry has to be isolated from material supplied by the patient. It is therefore necessary, if this hypothesis be held, to devise methods of study which shall concern themselves with the life-history of the patient, his biochemical and endocrine processes, his response to specific rheumatic infections, and to circumstances of his daily life. Considered from this point of view, no attempt has yet been made to carry out exhaustive research, although, as will be seen later, some tentative beginnings are already in being. The obstacle to all work of this kind is the nature of the contact at present existing between child and physician. It has been abundantly proved that acute rheumatism shows its main prevalence among children of the hospital classes. The contact of the profession with these children is through the work of the general practitioner and the hospital out-patient and in-patient departments. All these are heavily burdened with work, so that, on the one hand, it is only the child who is really ill – that is to say, who is suffering an exacerbation of his condition – who is brought for the treatment. On the other hand, it is only possible by the undertaking of special and arduous work to correlate the records of these children. There is, therefore, in the system at present in force no facility for the continuous study of children from the constitutional point of view, and if this is to be undertaken some other machinery must be devised.

BEARING ON PREVENTION AND CONTROL

It is in a sense true in this, as in all diseases, that the problem of prevention and control is dependent upon the discovery of the cause or causes of the disease. But it is perhaps worth remembering, in the face of the difficulty of the problem, that the elimination of a disease can be achieved without an exact knowledge of its causation, as in the case of leprosy and typhus in Europe, and that the discovery of the Klebs-Löffler bacillus has not been followed by the disappearance of diphtheria.

In rheumatism it is clear that there are two aspects to the problem, each of which requires separate consideration. The one, that to which attention is increasingly being directed, is the care of the heart of the already rheumatic child. The other is the attempt to control the incidence of the disease itself, and to achieve means for the prevention of its appearance in children who can be expected to become rheumatic. These problems, though intimately related, and common in origin, need to be kept very carefully distinct. All chances of success depend upon their separate consideration, and it is the failure to do so that determines the ineffectiveness of so many of the proposals at present current.

It is obvious that any scheme, either for the care of children already rheumatic, or for the study of the disease, must be based upon a definite hypothesis of the nature of the disease. Up to 1922, as has already been pointed out, work upon rheumatism has been conceived from the infective point of view and the results have been, on the whole, disappointing. In America a new step was taken with the formation of the Association for the Relief and Prevention of Heart Disease. This was intended primarily for adults, and embraced all forms of heart disease, but in 1915, W. St Lawrence (1920) adapted these methods to the study of the effect of rheumatism in childhood, and the first children's cardiac clinic was opened at St Luke's Hospital, New York. The aim of this clinic was the continuous treatment and observation, upon a classified system, of rheumatic children, with special reference to their heart condition.

In this country nothing of the kind was attempted until 1923. In this year, interested by St Lawrence's work, Professor Leonard Findlay and the present writer organized a clinic at the Royal Hospital for Sick Children, Glasgow, for the continuous supervision of rheumatic children attending that hospital (Lowenfeld, 1926). As a result of this work certain facts became clear. It appeared that the manifestations of rheumatism in childhood, usually covered by such terms as the acute and convalescent stages, needed the addition of a third term for a complete description – that of the quiescent stage. Under this head is considered the period between attacks, when the disease smoulders, but is not apparent. Upon the conception of this quiescent stage the whole work of a supervisory clinic is based.

A NEW BASIS OF CLASSIFICATION

The second point of note arising out of the clinic is that of the importance of the basis of classification of these children. Hitherto, all classification of rheumatic children, whether explicit in records, or implicit in the mind of the observer has been based upon the clinical form of the disease – e.g. rheumatic fever, chorea, tonsillitis. It has, however, been agreed that the significance of the disease does not lie here, but in its tendency to cardiac involvement. These terms, therefore, offer no help to the observer in his attempt to protect the future of the child. The use of them, moreover, necessitates a somewhat lengthy and detailed note on the cardiac condition being added to each case, and renders very difficult any survey of a number of cases.

For the working of this clinic the emphasis was shifted, and a classification was devised upon the basis of the children's cardiac history. Since the clinical findings by different observers in any given cardiac case are not always necessarily identical, an endeavour was made to arrange the classes so the discrepancies arising from this source should be reduced to a minimum. The classification finally adopted was as follows:

Class P	Potential heart cases – that is, cases with definite rheumatic history who have never had cardiac involvement, and are now well.
A	Cases with a history of definite rheumatism with cardiac involvement, which has now disappeared.
B	Cases with a definite rheumatic history and present signs of cardiac involvement, but no symptoms referable to the heart.
C	Children with a definite rheumatic history and present signs and symptoms of cardiac involvement, but no disability for ordinary life.
D1	Cases with a definite rheumatic history, present signs and symptoms of cardiac involvement, and definite disability for ordinary life.
D2	Cases without a rheumatic history, but showing signs of a cardiac lesion, and with some definite disability for ordinary life.
Miscellaneous	Cardiac irregularities, effort syndrome and cutaneous eruptions supposed to be of rheumatic origin.

From a practical point of view such a classification has the following advantages. When the original classification has been made, subsequent notes are reduced to a minimum. 'Mild Class B', for instance, can describe all the essential points about a case. Whether this lesion is the result of an acute rheumatic fever, of growing pains, or of tonsillitis, though of interest from the point of view of immediate treatment prognosis or recommendations to the mother, is of comparatively little significance. It also makes possible a rapid survey of a large number of cases without elaborate cross-indexing. By collection of those children whose classes have been changed during the year, immediate information is given regarding percentage improvement or deterioration in cardiac condition of the children. Further, any class of child can be quickly and easily isolated for reference, examination, or experimental therapeutics.

It will be noted that this classification embraces only children already the subject of a *definite* rheumatic condition. This was deliberate, because the original clinic was devised to study the possibilities of prevention and control of heart disease in children who were already rheumatic. In other words, to keep Class P children from moving into any other class, and to move as many of those in the other categories as possible to Class A.

AN ATTACK UPON THE RHEUMATIC CONSTITUTION

Another fact stands out clearly as the result of the work of this clinic – namely, that while work of this kind is very useful and effective within its own limits, if an attempt is to be made to achieve the *prevention* of rheumatism, a still earlier attack must be made upon the disease. But since all signs of rheumatism in children, other than those of acute rheumatic fever, chorea, and tonsillitis are ill-defined and susceptible of varying interpretation, the formation of a clinic upon this basis will involve the assumption of the existence of a rheumatic constitution. That is to say, children of rheumatic stock and those children who are subject to all forms of vague and indefinite rheumatism will also need to be included. Not only must the basis of the clinic be thus widened, but the treatment of these children must follow different lines, and be directed as much towards raising the child's general resistance as to combating his definitely rheumatic tendencies.

These are as yet hypothetical conceptions and need wide testing before their acceptance. One attempt to do so is already in existence in the form of a 'children's cardiac clinic' at the St Marylebone General Dispensary, which has been in operation since 1926. At this clinic children, whether definitely or possibly rheumatic, are received from the age of two years, and supervised until puberty, when they join one of the adult clinics of the dispensary. The modifications introduced into the classification are as follows:

Class P — becomes subdivided into:

- P1 — Children with history and complaints suggestive of rheumatism, no cardiac involvement, and *no* disability for ordinary life.
- P2 — Children with history and complaints suggestive of rheumatism, no cardiac involvement, and *some* disability for ordinary life.
- P3 — As in original classification.

Class B — becomes subdivided into:

- B1 — As in original classification.
- B2 — Children with a history suggestive of rheumatism, present signs of cardiac involvement, but no symptoms referable to the heart.

The standardization of the classification with that already in use elsewhere allows both accurate comparison of results, and full development of preventive measures in either.

Since the publication of the report of the Glasgow Clinic, the Science Committee of the British Medical Association have sat for a further consideration of the problem, and have issued a second report on the Prevention and Control of Juvenile Rheumatic Infection (British Medical Association, 1927). In this communication the existence of the quiescent stage is accepted, and the principle of continuous medical supervision emphatically recommended. The details of the one centre to which reference is made in the report are, however, so unsubstantial that it is impossible to discover upon what lines it is organized, what class of child is accepted, and how classified, and upon what lines the suggestions of treatment are made. The actual proposals of the report also suffer from the same vagueness; and this is unfortunate, because in the medical supervision of rheumatic children we have not only a method of treatment but also an instrument which can be used for both the examination of the effects of treatment and the study of the disease itself. At present treatment of the disease and inquiry into its nature are far too apt to be kept in watertight compartments. What is needed is a method by which the natural history of the disease, the factors influencing or retarding its development, the effect of attempts to modify the constitutional habit, can be provided in a large number of cases in such a form as to be readily and easily manipulated and studied. It should be possible to achieve this and simultaneously to provide abundant material for aetiological and therapeutic research.

It is clear that work of this kind opens new avenues for correlated research, while it demands some modification in our attitude to systems for control of disease. Such methods, by providing material for investigation upon any desired lines, and by demonstrating the life-history of the disease, will exactly fill the obvious gap in our present system. It is true that there may be difficulties in associating these principles with the work of a voluntary hospital, but they are, I am confident, not insuperable. On the other hand, by work of this kind a weapon can be forged for the study of the constitutional hypothesis of rheumatism, which, it is contended, is the next and most hopeful step to be taken towards an understanding of the disease.

Researches in Lactation (with Sibyl Taite Widdows) [1928]

Although a considerable amount of work has been done and recorded on the subject of milk, lactation in women has received scant attention, and we are in possession of very little accurate knowledge. It was therefore decided to undertake a study of lactation in normal women in the Obstetric Unit and the Royal Free Hospital under the direction of Professor Louise McIlroy.

Investigations were directed to discover the manner in which the milk appeared and lactation developed during the first fourteen days of the puerperium. All the clinical observations were made by MFL as also the collection of samples in the wards. The biochemical work, which was under the charge of STW, was carried out in the Science Laboratories of the London School of Medicine for Women with the co-operation of Miss M. Bond and Mrs E. I. Taylor. We are also indebted to the Medical Research Council for support and financial assistance.

The samples of milk were collected by different methods according to the point under investigation, and were taken, immediately after collection, to the laboratories where the appropriate analyses were carried out. In no case was the milk allowed to stand over night. Sugar, fat, protein, calcium and ash were the constituents chosen for study. Sixty-three samples were analysed for all these substances, and 140 for four or less. Total solids were estimated in sixty-five samples.

The mothers selected for observation in this section were all normal in-patients of the Obstetrical Department of the Royal Free Hospital. In a few instances women admitted to the VD wards for gonorrhoea were included, but none with a history of syphilis. A continuous series of observations was made on every woman from the morning after parturition until her discharge from the ward.

At the outset it was found that observations needed to be made according to a method which standardized itself. On the usual clinical charts observations on the infant's weight, condition of the mother's breasts, quantity and nature of the fluid secreted and the amounts taken by the infant cannot be recorded. These matters were essential to the investigation, and a single chart (Table 1) was therefore constructed to enable such points to be conveniently noted.

On this chart on the right-hand side, the infant's chart, the infant's weight, the nature of its motions, whether it had vomited or not and, if so, the nature of the ejected material and the number of feeds, were entered daily. The number of ounces of milk taken in the day, as ascertained by a test weighing chart (Table 2) was written on the chart above the daily weight together with the caloric value of the food taken, if desired, calculated from the weighing chart and the biochemical results. Morning and evening temperature and pulse-rate, should circumstances make the record of these desirable, could also be noted in this part of the chart. Owing to the universal use in this country of the ounce measure, records were necessarily made by

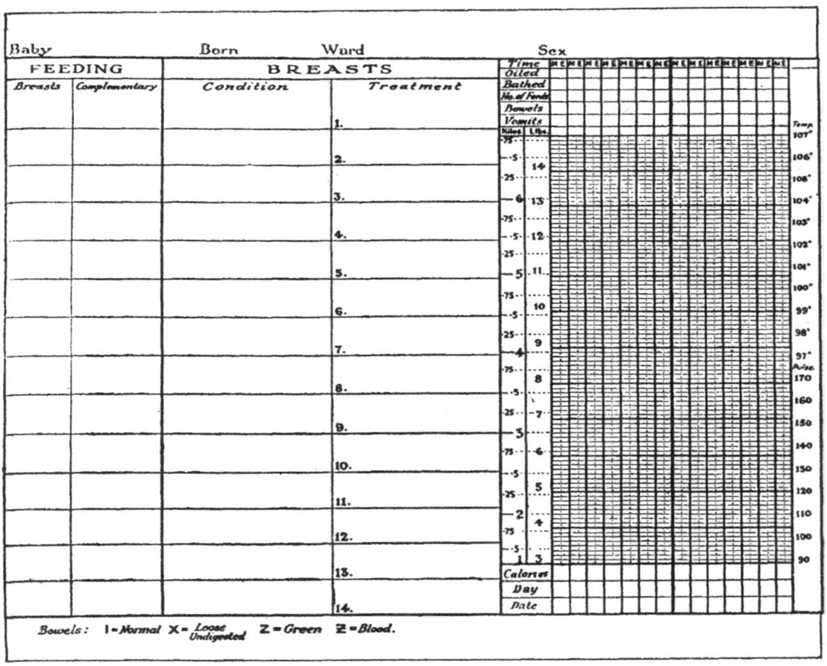

 Table 1 *Lactation chart*

these weights, but by the provision of an additional table in the metric system, the results can be compared with those of Continental workers. The central part of the chart is used for recording the nature and condition of the breasts and milk supply, and also for the prescribing of treatment. The left-hand column indicates the feeding methods in use for each particular

Date		Name		
	Time.	Weight Before Feeding.	Weight After Feeding.	Difference.
A.M.	4.30			
	7.30			
	10.30			
P.M.	1.30			
	4.30			
	7.30			
	10.30			
	TOTAL ...			

Table 2 *Babies' test weighing chart*

case. In combination with this chart, the accompanying scheme for test weighing was devised.

Six days charted in this manner can be conveniently grouped together on the same sheet.

With a little practice the nursing staff found this method easy to use. During the observation of each case, the chart remained in the neighbourhood of the weighing scales, and was inspected daily by the observer responsible for the ward work (MFL) and checked and compared with the condition of the infant and mother.

By use of these charts and the biochemical results given by the analyses of samples obtained (Lowenfeld and Widdows, 1927) the following series of observations was made.

1. *Variations in inception of lactation in different women*. The course of lactation in twenty-three individuals was studied, six for ten to thirteen days, five for five to nine days and twelve for one to five days. This forms, except for the work of Woodward (1897), a study of the milk of six cases from the first to the seventh day, and Hammett (1917), a series of five daily samples of milk from eight women from the third to the eleventh day, the first complete and continuous study of lactation in individual women during the puerperium.

The first question taken for consideration was to what extent was the development of lactation in all women uniform.

As far as the women under observation can be taken as typical, it appears that lactation in no two individuals develops in exactly the same way. The rate and character of development, however, fall into consistent patterns, of which there appear to be two main types. Under one or other of these the majority of women can be classified.

The *first type* shows the following characteristics: An early production of milk of a kind which is homogeneous in character, ample in quantity and of a colour never deepening beyond a primrose yellow. This type is found mainly in multiparae. The *second type* shows a longer latent period before the appearance of the milk, which when it comes is not homogeneous, is very viscid, scanty in quantity and often has a deep yellow colour. This type occurs mainly in primiparae. The course of lactation in an individual of each type will be described in illustration.

First type. FJ, a multipara thirty-nine years of age, in hospital for her fourth confinement. Labour had been spontaneous and normal, the mother was healthy, with large, well-shaped breasts and good nipples. The infant weighed 9lb 11oz at birth, was normal in every way, and a good sucker.

The development of lactation proceeded as follows: FJ's breasts had been secreting a small amount of fluid daily for the last two months of her pregnancy. About eight hours after delivery the infant was put to both breasts, and then six-hourly for 24 hours, after that a three-hourly fifteen to twenty minutes feed from one breast was given for the rest of her stay in hospital. The fluid expressed from the breasts within the first twenty-four hours was homogeneous, thin, faintly yellow, and easily obtained. Forty-eight hours after delivery 2oz or 60 cc were obtained from one breast partly by the infant, as ascertained by test weighing, and partly by suction with a breast pump. In physical qualities this fluid was not viscid, was quite homogeneous, and had somewhat the appearance of mature milk. By the fourth morning three ounces could be obtained at a feed from either breast, and the fluid had the thin bluish appearance of normal breast milk. This was maintained during the rest of her stay in hospital.

Second type. HP, a primipara twenty-five years of age. Labour had been spontaneous and normal, the mother was healthy, breasts large and well-shaped. The infant weighed 7lb 8oz at birth, and was normal in every way. The one difference between the two cases was that the infant of HP was a less efficient sucker than the infant of FJ, but as this is apt to occur in first children, it cannot be regarded as an abnormality. The routine treatment was the same. During the first twenty-four hours, practically no fluid was expressible from HP's breasts. At thirty-six hours 0·7 cc was obtained by expression from the right side before the infant was put to it, 2 drachms as ascertained by test weighing was taken by the infant and 1·6 cc by digital expression after feeding, totalling in all 9·5 cc. From the left side 1 cc was expressed before the infant was put to the breast, 2 drachms taken by the infant, and 2 cc by expression after feeding, totallying in all 10·2 cc. The fluid up to this date was very viscid and dense, and of a deep yellow colour at the bottom of the measuring glass. As the fluid left the nipple and streamed down the side of the glass, it was not homogeneous, but was made up of streaks having different colours. This point is relevant to the question of colostrum. On the third day the fluid was still very viscid, but had become a pale yellow colour and was much more homogeneous in character. A total of 3 cc was obtained on this day by expression from one breast, the infant having taken 2 drachms or 7·2 cc from the other. On the fourth and fifth days the amount obtained by expression increased to 10 cc and 25 cc respectively, and by the eighth day to 73 cc. By this time the fluid had the appearance of rich cow's milk. It was not till the ninth day that the milk reached the usual thin, bluish appearance of normal human milk.

The biochemical content of the milk of the two women showed also a wide difference, parallel in nature to the physical appearances. The protein content of the milk of FJ never rose above 2·2 percent and from the second day to the tenth day showed a curve from 2·2 percent to 1·63 percent. In contrast with this, the protein percentage of HP began at 7·65 percent on the second day (the first on which an adequate sample could be obtained) and fell on the eighth day to 2·0 percent, reaching on the eleventh 1·73 percent only. The ash content of the milk, as has been recorded already in dealing with the biochemical side of the work, displayed a tendency to be higher in the first type than in the second. The sugar percentage in both types was about the same. As will be shown later, the percentage of fat in the milk was found to depend upon a different set of factors altogether, these factors remaining constant for either type.

The differentiation between these two types, as might be expected, is not absolute, and cases occurred which could not be placed definitely in either group.

In all cases the appearances of the milk and the biochemical findings corresponded in the manner described above, but it was not invariable that the subjects were respectively multiparae or primiparae. In one case, that of CB, a multipara, aged twenty-eight, in hospital for her second confinement, the milk on the first day after delivery showed the physical appearances described for primiparae, with a protein content of 7·06 percent and an ash of 0·4 percent. Both percentages, however, fell more rapidly than is usual with primiparae, giving on the sixth day a protein content of 1·58 percent with a yield of 22 cc of milk. Correspondingly, it does occasionally happen that a primipara, if young and full-breasted and possessed of a vigorously sucking infant, will show a development approximating to the multiparous type. The caution in this case must be admitted that, with the unmarried mother, information regarding these points cannot be altogether relied upon.

From this evidence it is suggested that if milk samples be collected from different women on the same date of the puerperium they will have no necessary relation in composition to one another. This fact accounts for the remarkable variations found in the biochemical milk estimations of many observers. The method of averaging single samples from different women taken at the same date after parturition is that which has been almost universally employed. But as the composition of these samples will vary widely according to the type of woman chosen, this method cannot be asked to give relevant results.

In the second place, the actual amount ingested by the infant in the early days of lactation becomes of less importance. Because of the difference in composition of the fluids secreted, the higher food-values of the one type of milk compensate for the larger available quantity of the other, and a satisfactory gain by the infant can be made on either.

Third, owing to the high food-value of such milk as appears in cases of slow development, delay in appearance of mature milk does not necessarily imply failure in ability to feed.

A further point of interest between these two groups is to be found in the appearance of the early milk of primiparae. If, during the early days of lactation, the nipple of a primipara be carefully inspected while the areola is compressed, different types of fluid will be observed on the surface of the nipple emerging from the different ducts. It has been possible to distinguish four of these kinds. A clear, glairy fluid of very high viscosity, a non-viscid fluid, brown in colour, a thick cheesy-like substance and a thin, limpid, clear fluid resembling a watery solution. All these will be seen flowing from different ducts in the nipple at the same time, and joining in a streaky manner on the edge of the collecting-glass, down which they stream to mix at the bottom. In the multiparous type this does not occur, and the milk presents a homogeneous appearance from the beginning. It is possible that it is due to a lack of distinction between these two types of secretion that the divergences in the descriptions of colostrum have arisen.

2. *Relation of the time in the feeding at which the sample is taken to the composition of the milk resulting.* At which the possibility of an association between the time in the feed the sample is taken and the manner of extraction of the milk with the composition of the resulting sample is suggested by the experience both of dairy farmers and clinicians. It has long been known that the fat content of the milk rises at the end of suckling both in the case of cows and of women. It has also been suggested by Denis and

Talbot (1919), Hunnaeus (1909) and Schabad (1911) that the sugar and the calcium content respectively of the milk vary according to the time in the feed when the milk for examination is taken. To elucidate this point the comparative proportions of the different constituents of milk at the beginning, at the middle and at the end of a feed were considered. Samples were taken before and after the infant had fed from the same breast, in some cases and in other cases for comparison, the whole available supply at one feed was taken from one breast, while the infant was fed from the other. This milk was collected into three glasses *seriatim*, and a full chemical analysis was carried out on each part. When the results obtained were grouped together and studied, the following points emerged:

The *lactose* content, in agreement with the results of Denis and Talbot, appeared to be higher at the beginning than at the end of a feed.

The *protein* content of the milk, on the other hand, appeared to rise slightly at the end of a feed. This difference was greater when the samples were taken in relation to an actual feed than when only the first and last portions of an artificially emptied breast were considered. The differences in percentages found in either constituent are probably not of clinical significance. In the case of the sugar content the variation was the difference between 0·2 percent and 0·8 percent and in that of the protein between 0·05 percent and 0·6 percent.

The *calcium* and the *ash* percentage did not differ between the beginning and end of the feed.

The *fat* content, however, was found to be profoundly affected by this and by the next factor to be considered and the key to its variations lies in a combination of the two factors.

3. *The relation of the manner of extraction of the sample upon the resulting composition of the milk obtained.* It is obviously impossible to obtain for analysis at any time an exact sample of the milk that would have been actually ingested by an infant. No procedure has yet been devised which accurately reproduces the sucking action of the infant. But by varying the method of extraction, a series of samples was obtained which can be considered as approximating to that probably obtained by the infant.

As has already been described, milk was taken both with a breast pump and by digital expression. A difference was made and noted between a vigorous and gentle use of either method.

The biochemical results obtained were grouped in such a way that the effect of all four degrees, i.e. very gentle use of pump (e.g. suction only), firm use of pump, gentle expression (e.g. pressure only) and vigorous expression could be compared, and associated with the effect of the beginning or end of the feed. All constituents considered were examined in this way, but the most definite results were found in regard to the fat. Although it has long been agreed in clinical practice that the fat content of the milk is higher at the end of a feed than at the beginning, the figures of investigators have not always shown this rise. Indeed, it has been the common impression of most milk investigators that no rule could be laid down which would entirely govern the percentage of fat in milk. It has, in addition, been assumed clinically that the milk obtained in similar circumstances by different infants from the same mother would be identical in composition.

In order to investigate this point a series of samples of milk was taken, first before the feed by use of a pump and by digital expression after the infant had fed. The procedure was then reversed, digital expression being used for the sample before the feed, and the breast pump for that obtained after. To compare with these, a second series of samples was then obtained from the first and last parts of the whole available content of a single breast of the same individual, in the same manner. In all cases the quantity of the fluid obtained was noted. These two groups of figures were tabulated in series and studied. The resulting tables, an example of which is given here (see Table 3), showed that the high percentages of fat in the milk occurred in the relatively small amounts of fluid, while the low percentages of fat in the milk were found in the large amounts of fluid. Further, the higher percentages occurred in samples obtained with maximum pressure (e.g. vigorous digital expression) and the lower percentages in samples extracted with minimal pressure (e.g. gentle use of a pump). On consideration, this would appear a reasonable result since fat in milk is present in the form of an emulsion. All fats tend to emulsify more successfully under greater pressure, and percentage emulsification of any fat is increased as the proportion of suspensory fluid decreases. To illustrate this point, the fat percentages of HP are given in Table 3. In another case it was possible to deliberate the usual difference and to obtain a minus figure.

It would appear therefore that the percentage of fat in milk depends upon two factors, the one directly and the other

Case HP

	Before feed	*After feed*	*Difference*
Procedure I	Extraction by pump, minimal pressure	Digital expression, maximal pressure	—
	4·36	6·30	+1·94
	3·64	9·02	+5·38
	3·78	7·16	+3·38
Procedure II	Digital expression, maximal pressure	Extraction by pump, minimal pressure	—
	5·44	5·60	+0·16
	4·64	5·20	+0·56

Table 3 *Percentage of fat in milk in relation to feed*

inversely. It will depend inversely upon the amount of fluid available in the breast at the time the sample is taken, and directly upon the degree of pressure put upon the breast in the process of extraction. The final percentage will depend upon the balance of these two factors. These results are paralleled by the experience of dairy farmers, who find that an excess supply of fluid to the cows diminishes the fat content of the milk, and that variation in efficiency of milking results in different percentages of fat from the same cow under otherwise identical conditions.

Clinically, these facts suggest certain conclusions. The importance of the fat element in milk in relation to the nutritional disturbances of childhood has long been appreciated. Attempts are very generally made to arrive at some estimate of the fat content of the milk of unsatisfactory cases. If the above deductions be true, this is not a factor which has any existence apart from the individual infant obtaining the milk. That is to say, unless the action of the infant be watched and note taken of the vigour of its sucking, it is unlikely that a sample obtained artificially for examination as to the fat content will resemble at all, in this particular, the milk ingested by it. In other words, it is the degree of pressure of the jaws of the infant upon the areola and nipple, as well as the length of the feed, which determines the amount of fat obtained in the milk.

POINTS IN MANAGEMENT SUGGESTED BY THESE RESULTS

The advisability, if fat dyspepsia is suspected, of putting the infant, as a routine, to both breasts rather than one. In this way the fore milk of both breasts, which is poor in fat, is obtained, and only little of the rich after milk.

The advisability, if the fat still remains too high, of giving water immediately before the feed, as a dilution of the fat content.

The possibility with an infant of feeble jaw action of starting the flow of milk with the fingers or pump before putting the child to the breast. By this means the available energy in the infant can be conserved to obtain the highest fat content possible. In some cases it may even be wise to draw off and discard the fore milk from either breast so as to give the infant the chance of obtaining the later and richer part only of the milk from both breasts.

The importance of diagnosis in all cases of digestive disturbance in breast-fed infants and of observing the type of action of the infant in sucking.

As a corollary to these general observations, a curious fact was observed during the first days after parturition. Here, until the fluid became homogeneous, the fat content at the beginning of a feed was *higher* than that at the end. This is of physiological rather than of clinical interest, and would appear to be caused by the initial breakdown of the cells lining the ducts and potential ducts of the glands. Table 4 illustrates this point (see p. 168).

THE INFLUENCE UPON THE COMPOSITION OF THE MILK OF MORBID STATES OF THE BREAST

The range of experiences of this nature embraced by the work was small, since it was in the main an endeavour to study the development of normal lactation. But in one or two instances in the cases under observation the breasts at one time or another showed mild morbid states. In connection with this point the composition of the milk taken simultaneously from either breast was considered. So long as the condition of the breasts was normal the variations in composition between the milk from either breast were slight. When, however, any morbid condition appeared in either breast, a disturbance was observed in the sugar values. Table 5 gives the comparative sugar values of either breast in a number of different women. Numbers 1 to 8 are in cases in which the breasts were normal, and 9 to 13 in

Case	*Sample in cc* Before feed	After feed	Parity	Day	*Grams of fat per 100 cc* Before feed	After feed	Difference	Amount taken by infant (cc)
HP	1·0	2·0	P	2	7·14	5·02R	−2·12	7·5
	0·7	1·6	P	2	6·92	5·74L	−1·18	7·5
	1·5	5·0	P	2	9·98	8·66L*	−1·32	45.0
	1·3	8·5	P	7	5·44	5·6R*	+0·16	45·0
	1·8	2·5	P	8	4·36	6.3L	+1.94	67·5
	2·8	3·3	P	8	3·64	9·02R	+5·38	67·5
RP	1·7	1·5	P	1	0·95	0·53R	−0·42	Nil
	1·7	2·3	P	2	1·66	1·26L	−0·39	0·25
	3·3	5·5	P	3	2·73	3·35L	+0·62	1·25
	20·0	11·0	P	4	1·52	2·86L	+1·34	2·5

Table 4 *Sample results*

*These samples were taken at the same feed from right and left breasts respectively. They show the appearance of homogeneous milk later in the one breast than in the other. It will be noted that by the next day the usual rise occurs.

			RIGHT			*LEFT*		
No.	*Preg.*	*Day*	*Notes, sample*	*Sugar (gm per 100 cc)*	*Notes mother*	*Notes sample*	*Sugar (gm per 100 cc)*	*Notes mother*
			Total			*Total*		
1	P	4	1 oz	5·10	Normal	1 oz	5·12	Normal
2	P	4	Same day 4.30	5·14	Normal	As other	5·12	Normal
3	P	6	Whole	5·65	Normal	Bef. Aft.	5·67	Normal
4	P	7	Bef. Aft.	5·75	Normal	Bef. Aft.	5·71	Normal
5	P	7	Whole	6·61	Normal	Bef. Aft.	6·62	Normal
6	P	8	Bef. Aft.	6·13	Normal	Bef. Aft.	6·09	Normal
7	P	10	Bef. Aft.	6·21	Normal	Bef. Aft.	6·15	Normal
8	P	9	Bef. Aft.	6·11	Normal	Bef. Aft.	6·20	Normal
9	P	6	Bef.	6·19	V. Full	Bef.	6·00	V. Full
10	P	7	Bef. Aft.	6·19	Engorged	Bef. Aft.	6·30	Engorged
11	P	5	Mainly Aft.	4·64	V. Hard	Mainly Aft.	4·32	V. Hard
12	M	5	Bef. Aft.	5·69	Engorged	Whole	5·92	Engorged
13	HH	3	1, 3	5·49	Flushed	1, 3	6·03	Flushed

Table 5 *Sugar comparison between breasts*

which some disturbance was evident. It will be noted that from 1 to 8 the variation shown ranges from 0·02 percent to 0·09 percent with an average of 0·046 percent whereas from 9 to 13 the differences shown range from 0·19 percent to 0·46 percent with an average of 0·286 percent.

In this table 'Bef. Aft.' means that equal volumes of milk were taken before and after feed, mixed and analysed. '1, 3' means that equal volumes of the first and last milk without the baby feeding were mixed and analysed. The sugar percentage is given in grams per 100 cc milk.

In connection with this point the case of FJ is of interest. Although cited as an example of normality in the physical appearances and development of her milk, she gave a very peculiar curve in the development of her sugar values (see Table 6). After the seventh day the sugar percentage became normal. On the fifth day lactose, identified by a lactosazone, was identified in the urine, but unfortunately no further specimens were obtained. There was here no clinical disturbance in infant or mother.

Reference to curve in the *Biochemical Journal* will show one individual, HH, whose curve for sugar from the second day to the fourth day showed an inversion of the usual order. In all other cases, both of our own and of the series of other observers, the course of development of the sugar value in milk is a steady rise from a value lying between 5 percent and 6 percent on the second day to between 6·8 percent and 7 percent between the

Day	*Time*	*Relation to feed*	*Percentage of sugar*	*Breast*
2	10 a.m.	Before	5·47	
		After	5·70	
4	10 a.m.	Before and After	6·20	
4	1 p.m.	Before	8·90	
		After	10·00	Right
4	4 p.m.	Before and After	10·40	Left
5	1 p.m.	Before and After	7·50	Left
5	4 p.m.	Before and After	9·60	Right
6	10 a.m.	Before and After	5·95	Left
6	4 p.m.	Before and After	5·97	
7	10 p.m.	Before and After	5·72	

Table 6 *Case of FJ*

tenth and fourteen days. But with HH the initial value of 5·25 percent on the second day was not maintained, but showed a steep decline to 3·67 percent on the fourth day. This patient had been admitted to the Venereal Disease Ward for gonorrhea, and the investigation had to be discontinued owing to the development of acute mastitis in the mother and ophthalmia neonatorum in the child.

It would appear therefore that disturbances in the normal function of the breast are reflected by an alteration in the sugar content of the milk, but we have no evidence at present to suggest that any other constituents in the milk are affected.

In all reports of work upon lactation the use of the phrase 'to empty the breast' is customary, but in practice this is illusory. As a result of many experiments it has become a matter of considerable doubt in the minds of the authors if this can ever be accomplished. The regulation of milk supply in the breast is under the control of factors as yet only partially understood. Cases in this series have been observed in which, in spite of obvious engorgement of the breasts, it has been impossible by any procedure to obtain more than a very small quantity of milk; cases in which the infant is able to obtain one or two ounces of fluid after all attempts at digital expression or pump extraction had reported an 'empty' breast; and very occasional examples of the reverse occurrence. This experience will be borne out by all workers in this field. It is paralleled by the phenomenon known to every farmer of the difference in yield obtained from the same cow by different milkers, and by the occasional apparent refusal of the cow to 'give down' her milk to any, though the udders may be full.

Formerly in the Obstetrical Unit of the Royal Free Hospital caesarean section, when necessary, was performed in the majority of cases prior to the onset of labour. For several days following the operation supplementary feeds had to be given to the infant owing to the scarcity of milk in the breasts. During the last two years it has been the practice of Professor McIlroy to operate after labour has begun, and it is now found that lactation becomes established earlier than formerly. This suggests that labour in itself is a preparation for lactation. Further investigations are being continued on this point.

8 From Medicine to Child Psychology

This chapter presents two of Lowenfeld's first clinical papers based on work at the Children's Clinic (see Chapter 3). 'A New Approach to the Problem of Psychoneurosis in Childhood' was the most extensive account of her methods to date. It was originally read before the Medical Section of the British Psychological Society on 25 March 1931, and was published in the *British Journal of Medical Psychology* (vol. 1, part 3, pp. 194–227) in the same year.

Lowenfeld outlined the aims of the clinic, the kinds of children seen and the range of problems, and explained the basis of her holistic approach. She stressed the importance of tackling environmental, physical and individual aspects of each child's predicament, and the need for working with parents and the home situation as well as with the child. The account given of the contribution of social work, which appeared to include arranging time off for exhausted parents or children, was more detailed than in many subsequent papers. The main bulk of the paper, however, was concerned with presenting case histories and accounts of the therapeutic work with children who illustrated, in various ways, relationships between physical ailments and mental complaints. The cases were presented in pairs to highlight how similar symptoms or physical conditions can be associated with contrasting psychological characteristics or circumstances. Though they were given different pseudonyms, some of the children described here are clearly the same ones mentioned in the clinical vignettes attached to the *Annual Report* of the Children's Clinic, 1929–30, discussed in Chapter 3 (pp. 41–59).

The clinic at this time was clearly in full swing and having demonstrable success in terms of removing symptoms. However, in other respects it was still finding its feet and what eventually became central aspects of Lowenfeld's approach had yet to be crystallized. What became the 'World' was mentioned almost in passing, including the curious note that, amongst the toys provided with it, 'Trains are absent' (this volume, p 182). This omission was not explained, and appears to have been temporary. There were also emphases which were later modified, if not reversed. For example, Lowenfeld stressed disadvantages in having children of different ages all together in the same play room; later she stressed the advantages of this, adopting it as deliberate policy (see Chapter 11). In 1931, however, Lowenfeld was also stressing the deliberate intention to avoid fostering the transference, which remained a hallmark of her approach. At this time Lowenfeld appears to have taken major responsibility for providing children with comments on their difficulties and the meaning of their phantasies, pulling on diverse sources, from psychoanalysis and folklore to the work of Piaget, in a rather exploratory way. Here she expressed a greater sympathy with psychoanalysis, and an admiration for the work of Melanie Klein in particular, than in any subsequent papers.

At that time, of course, Klein's work was only just becoming known in Britain, and in many respects all work on emotional problems of children was to some extent under trial. Given this, Lowenfeld's careful discussion at the end of the paper of the nature of the therapeutic agency and what constitutes 'cure' is particularly interesting and reflective. For Lowenfeld, what provided relief in the particular cases she described was the opportunity for the expression of intense feelings, fears and phantasies which would otherwise overwhelm the young child. In discussing the nature of the 'cure', she stressed the problem of how we could know that a cure had been effected, and that a decision had to be made about where to locate ourselves, whether on the side of the child or of the social order.

Like the first, the second paper in this chapter, 'Psychogenic Factors in Chronic Disease in Childhood', took relations between physical and emotional process as a major theme. This paper, however, was originally intended for a primarily medical readership. It was published in the *Medical Women's Federation Newsletter* in July 1934 (pp. 1–18). Lowenfeld's aim was to open the issue of the contribution of emotional and mental phenomena to disease, which orthodox medicine understood in purely physical terms. She pointed out that while in adult medicine an interaction between emotional and bodily conditions was now widely accepted, this was not yet so for children. Although paediatrics was now flourishing there was little place for the emotional. As the exception she cited Winnicott's (1931) medical textbook, *Clinical Notes on Disorders of Childhood*. For this state of affairs, Lowenfeld blamed, amongst other things, the lack of adequate instruments for assessing the emotional situation of the young child or infant. Noting Cannon's work on homeostasis, in particular, she cited contemporary biochemical, psychological and anthropological evidence of the ability to judge emotional states in others, and on biochemical changes and bodily conditions which accompany these states, to render plausible the claim that even in infants bodily changes might be affected by emotion.

Much of the paper was concerned with presenting case histories which in various ways illustrated the complex interactions between bodily functions and emotion over the course of development. It includes the first explicit reference to the 'world' (p. 229). Lowenfeld deliberately concentrated on cases exhibiting problems in which, in adults, an emotional factor had been admitted in some cases: the epilepsies, asthma, eating disturbances, and disturbances in bladder and bowel functioning. As in the previous paper, in presenting these case histories, attention was given to the contribution of home circumstances and the role of the social worker. Here, though, particular attention was also given to describing the physical and biochemical assessments provided at the clinic. As noted previously, this paper was produced when Leonard Findlay was the senior physician (this volume, p. 59). The strengths of the multidisciplinary approach were self-evident. These included, for example, in the case of Richard and Joyce Harris, the ruling out of congenital syphilis on the father's side as a major cause of the children's complaints. In all cases, however, the rule was to assume multiple determination in understanding causes of the children's predicaments and, whether or not additional medical treatment was discovered to be necessary or advisable, amelioration of troublesome symptomatology was greatly aided by working through in play.

As in the previous paper, Lowenfeld concluded by exploring how and why all these children responded to a treatment method that entailed combining physical and psychological processes, and by considering the functions of play and the nature of young children's emotional experience. In particular, she speculated on the implications for the young child of having ill-formed avenues for expressing emotion, of being dominated by subjective experience, and the implications of his or her inability fully to differentiate between stimuli coming from inside or outside the body.

As we shall see, these ideas become central in Lowenfeld's later theory of the protosystem (see Chapter 9). But at this time, Lowenfeld was more interested in linking her ideas to what she knew of body chemistry and psychology, in order to account for psychosomatic effects. Using a kind of tension reduction model based on Cannon's work, she assumed that in the young child neurological pathways for the distribution or discharge of energy had not yet been fully formed, so that emotional discharge could not be fully regulated. In consequence, psychological concomitants to emotion would have maximum effects, such that the young child, for example, would be particularly likely to react with diarrhoea or a temperature to emotional disturbances like jealousy or acute disappointment. Furthermore, the young child would also be particularly vulnerable to adult disapproval or condemnation, since he or she would lack mental equipment with which to defend against it. In consequence, the little child is 'utterly helpless in the face of condemnation . . . which produces within the child a disproportionate disapproval of the self, or a violent reaction against authority as represented in the disapproving adult' (this volume, p. 232). Here she was talking in another way about the potentially crippling infantile super-ego described by Melanie Klein (1932).

At this point Lowenfeld's theorization of relations between emotion and bodily processes had some of the problems for which Freud's early use of an 'energy model' in psychological theorizing has been criticized. In Lowenfeld's case, there was a particular problem in assuming that psychological concomitants to infantile experiences could remain to effect events later on without specifying how or in what way these were stored. It was this problem, amongst others, that Freud (1911) was addressing in proposing a distinction between primary and secondary modes of mental functioning. Though implicit in her case histories, and in the accounts of development through play, Lowenfeld as yet did not have a theory of mental representations. This emerged in the papers that are printed here in the next two chapters. Nevertheless, the present paper is an invaluable account of the modification of physical symptomatology through psychotherapy. Interestingly, in delineating psychosomatic disorders in terms of an attack on the self by one part of the personality, Lowenfeld's observations are remarkably consistent with current formulations put forward by psychoanalysts in the Kleinian or object-relations traditions.

A New Approach to the Problem of Psychoneurosis in Childhood [1931]

In this paper I give an outline of some cases of psychoneurosis in children treated at the Children's Clinic for the Treatment and Study of Nervous and Delicate Children, and a sketch of the methods by which they are treated. Since these methods are new and are put into practice through a rather unusual machinery, in order to understand the cases it is necessary that I should describe what these methods are, and how and where they are carried out.

The Children's Clinic is an out-patient institution which treats children suffering from psychoneurosis and conduct problems and some forms of physical illness. During the current year the complaints for which children were referred included: anxiety, arson, backwardness, cruelty, debility, enuresis, epilepsy, insomnia, loss of voice, mutism, nervousness, night terrors, pilfering, post-concussion character change, sleep-walking, truancy and unmanageableness. To these have since been added asthma and claustrophobia. No mentally deficient child is accepted. The social class of the children received is similar to that of children attending the out-patient department of any specialist hospital. The aim of the clinic is to give continuous treatment combined with observation and study. Very careful records are kept of each case.

Now the basis of every attack upon a problem must be a conception of the nature of the problem. Such a conception, in the case of so wide a list of troubles within the narrow range of childhood, trespasses inevitably into the question of the nature of disease itself. It is possible and it is our hope that study of children's disease undertaken from the angle of this work may in the end throw light upon that problem also. It is for this reason that I have chosen to present cases of physical ailments and mental states rather than conduct problems.

The standpoint from which this work is undertaken is that a neurosis represents the reaction of the whole child to his whole circumstances. To be effective, an attack which arises out of such a conception of the nature of neurosis must therefore concern itself equally with all the factors that make up the situation. The circumstances of a child include his home and school environment, his economic situation, and the permissions and prohibitions of the section of society into which he has been born. The child himself consists of his physical heredity, his bodily constitution, his mental endowment, and the emotions and desires with which he has come into the world. These various forces can for convenience be grouped as environmental, physical and individual.

It is a commonplace that a child is the product of his environment. No child can give us an account of his environment. It is necessary to have experienced two states before one can be aware of either, and having known one state only, his own, a child is totally unaware of much of that which actually forms the colour and background of his life. A child has no knowledge of social behaviour, of ethical ideas, of ways of life, other than those of the family within which he is brought up. He has no standards for comparison, no way of escape from what he sees and hears. Inescapably and inevitably, parents are equated for him with absolutes, and what exists in his home becomes to him of the very nature of the universe. To a burglar's son, burglary is work; to a gipsy family, movement, to a yeoman, stability, are of the nature of the universe. Some grasp, therefore, of the character of the family group from which a child comes is a necessary preliminary to an understanding of that child: and information to this end must be collected apart from the child, and by a worker specially trained to an understanding of this type of work.

The next factor to be considered is the physical: and there are certain characteristics of childhood that make the physical background to a neurosis in childhood of peculiar importance.

About the physical constitution of childhood there is a remarkable fluidity: metabolic factors, comparatively stable in the adult, can swing from one extreme to the other in a child, with startling rapidity; disappointment can be the cause of a severe rise in temperature, and the onset of organic disease can be shown, not in pain, but in depression and tears. It is often in the case of a child exceptionally difficult to separate a physical from an emotional cause. A child is not, as is an adult, aware of himself as a consciousness apart from his body: a pain felt by a young child is a pain felt by the whole of his body; he is unable to describe it, very often unable to locate it correctly. Mental and physical pain tend to be identified, and the child can give no accurate description of either. Moreover, children, having no standard of a norm, do not know when they are being different, and are apt to accept as normal whatever happens to them, however abnormal it may actually be. Not only is this true, but the processes of growth are still largely unknown to us. We have little idea as yet of the mechanisms of interaction of the different factors: thymus retraction, skeletal development, co-ordination of involuntary muscle, sexual development, all are forces we inadequately comprehend. We have so little knowledge of the normal that we are unable to appreciate small departures from the norm. In too many cases it is gross disease alone that we are able to recognize.

Similarly diet and hygiene have more influence on health and disease in childhood than at any other time. With the depression of repeated infectious illness upon the mental health and vigour of a child every educationist is only too familiar. It appears, for instance, from recent work, that so simple a thing as extra milk can affect this infectivity and, through it, the child's whole attitude to life. Metabolic factors also have a far greater significance in the child than in the adult. Alkalosis and acidosis, anomalies of the calcium or phosphorus metabolism are, under conditions of stress, capable in children of precipitating a neurosis. In some cases they are even able in themselves to produce the whole phenomena of neurosis. Every neurosis contains elements from each of these sources, and each element needs to be studied and evaluated separately.

But when all has been done that can be done on these sides, there remains untouched the kernel of all neurotic problems, the child's own mind. Whatever a child feels or thinks, it is impossible for him to give an adult an account of it and, moreover, if he should try to do so, his words will in all probability mean to him something quite different from what they convey to us.

Eric, a small boy of four with a severe neurosis, was piling wet sand into an enamel ring, and patting it down firmly with his hands. He then made a hole with his finger right down the centre, withdrew it slowly, looked down the hole saying, 'What a deep dark hole.' The worker playing with him said, 'Is there anything at the bottom?' Eric: 'No.' Worker: 'Would you find anything if you went down the hole?' Eric: 'Yes, I should find myself at the bottom.' He then emptied the sand out and it became a pudding. Worker: 'Do you boil your pudding?' Eric: 'Yes, in the boiler of my engine. I am going to make a very large pudding and if I can make the very largest pudding in the world then' – in a low, deep, portentous voice as though it had terrific meaning – 'then a horrible, fierce ugly world will come and eat – (pause) the piano.' Worker: 'Have you a piano at home?' Eric: 'Oh, not our piano (pause), no, not a piano, the chairs.' Worker: 'Then there would be no chairs to sit on.' Eric: 'They would all be melted away.' Worker: 'Why melted away?' Eric: 'Because the world would eat them up, and it is very hot inside.' Worker: 'What sort of world?' Eric: 'The big world that is round and turns round.'

To a small child words are playthings. He likes the sound of them, he will experiment with the meaning of them: but when it comes to serious communication, words in the way we use them are of very little use to him. If we are to get in touch directly with a child's mind, if we are to know what it is really feeling and thinking, we need to learn to understand the child's natural idiom, and that is not speech but play and action. Speech considered as a logical structure is not spontaneous in children; action is. A child is not a logical, reflecting being – he does not when he is by himself use his brain for connected thought. Instead he plays out his ideas as they leap up in him in pictures, and uses for that play any material that comes to hand. If we are to understand him at all and understand the conflicts that come in his mental life, we must find a way in which his play can be shared and understood, and the thoughts that lie behind it gradually pieced together. Until we can do this, the kernel of every neurosis will elude us.

In order to make possible an approach to the problem of psychoneurosis in children that would contain all three factors, the social, the physical and that of the child's own outlook, the clinic from which these cases are drawn was created. In that clinic the social environment of the children is studied by a worker with six years' experience of children's social work in England, and an American training in mental hygiene. The family side of the case is in her hands.

A very thorough physical examination is made of every child on entrance, and any morbid features promptly dealt with. Diet and hygiene are carefully revised, and a record of these kept. On certain carefully selected cases, biochemical studies in the laboratories of Dr Edgar Obermer are carried out. The doctor under whose charge the child has originally come for his physical examination supervises his physical well-being throughout his stay in the clinic, and keeps closely in touch with him throughout his attendance. He has no share in the psychological treatment. This is carried out in the play room by a special staff.

A rhythm department helps in the treatment in all cases, and gives great assistance from time to time in diagnosis. Every child goes to dancing at some time during every session.

Although the clinic is open every day for office work, the children and their parents attend on only two days in the week, from 2.30 to 5 p.m. Each child is expected to attend twice a week, though for some the distance that they come makes this impossible, and once a week is perforce accepted.

The difficulties and limitations of continuous psychological work in circumstances of this kind are very great and need to be taken very carefully into account in evaluating the results. Outbreaks of infectious illness in the home, the arrival of a new baby, washing day, coughs and colds, or a school treat, all tend to interrupt attendance. Long distances, cost of fares, unemployment, all make for irregularity. Limitations of parental outlook make difficult or impossible much that we should like to do with the children, and often greatly delay results, particularly in the case of sex difficulties and sex instruction. Furthermore, the school child is the property, as it were, of the school attendance officer, and severe pressure is always there to return the child to school – that is, to discontinue attendance at the clinic at the earliest possible moment. Finally, the child is brought for the symptom, not the underlying difficulty; once the symptom has disappeared, or even become so much lessened as not any longer to cause acute difficulty at home or school, the tendency is for the child to be withdrawn from the clinic. One has to be content with the best that one can do, taking all the circumstances into account.

As understanding of the cases to be presented depends upon the work in the playroom, something must be said about its nature and technique.

The room itself is large, furnished with tables of varying heights, and tiny, medium, and normal sized chairs; and upon these a quantity of very varied play material is set out. There are also two or three zinc trays about 2 ft 3 in. by 1 ft 6 in., and 2½ in. deep, on tables fitted with castors, which offer scope for work with dry sand, wet sand, and water. For use with them, miniature models of the components of an ordinary and a savage world – houses, trees, transport, people, animals, etc. – stand beside them in nests of drawers. Trains are absent. Coloured blocks of various sizes, mosaics, stencils, paints, carpentry materials, construction toys of many sorts, Meccano, Kliptiko models, a coffee-grinding machine and other domestic articles are also provided and continuously used.

Water can be obtained outside the room and there is a lavatory near by.

With very few exceptions no suggestion is made to the children as to the material they shall choose for play. Each child is free to choose what he will. For every session a record book is kept, in which are noted the time devoted to each occupation and the order in which each child chooses its occupations.

Children from one year to school-leaving age at present work together in the same room. This is undesirable and will be changed as soon as possible. The handling of older children with younger children is exceedingly difficult – it is only the existence of some overflow space that makes it possible.

The atmosphere of work in the room has the following characteristics:

1. Individual difference between workers is minimized as far as possible, and all workers are dressed alike. No worker is allowed to develop a particular relation to any child, and the assignment of children to workers changes frequently. The transference factor is thus reduced to a minimum.

2. Every worker is trained to accommodate his body to the child's, so that his head will be on a level with the child's. Size by itself in an adult is terrifying to a child.

3. No prohibition or condemnation – in spite of the sternest provocation – may be used with any child. The worker plays and works under the direction of the child. Everything done or said by the child is accepted without remark or comment as natural and inevitable. It is difficult not to react to sudden plasticine thrown at one's head, water squirted in one's face, or sand poured down one's neck, but in the end each worker learns to control such reaction.

4. Only two unbreakable rules exist. That no child may injure another, and no harm may be done to clinic property.

5. Explanations to the children of their conduct or of phantasies are given by me only, since it is here the danger point lies, and I am alone responsible for the psychological welfare of

the children. For the understanding that lies behind such explanations, myth, folk tale, fairy tale, and legend are good allies; peasant customs, anthropological reports, psychoanalytic research, the work of Piaget, ritual magic, animism, and isolated biographies all give clues. In child analysis of any kind we are at the beginning of a new study; nothing is certain, nothing can be predetermined. We grope in a dense mist, knowledge of one's self and experience with childhood are perhaps the best guides to groping in the right direction.

Although my admiration for the work of Mrs Klein and her group is very great, and in spite of the fact that without it my own work would not be possible, not being a trained psychoanalyst, I do not feel myself qualified to use with the children directly psychoanalytic interpretation, however much I may myself benefit in my understanding of them by a knowledge of psychoanalytic findings. Interpretation of symbols by that theory is a very strong explosive to the mind of a child, and I feel convinced should not be used by others than those properly trained in its technique. There is of necessity some relation between my mode of approach and the psychoanalytic play technique, though the angle of attack is different, and it is, I think, worthy of note that in spite of this fact, the phenomena produced by my children in such very different circumstances are so often closely akin to those described by Mrs Klein (Klein, 1927). But in evaluating the phenomena, though I find myself very greatly indebted to Mrs Klein's work and to her group, it does not seem to me possible, until there is full publication of the child material from which these conclusions are drawn, to form any definite opinion as to the ultimate validity of the interpretations given by her to them.

For the rest, play with a child in suitable setting will often give, in a simple drama, a picture of the conditions at home that hours of conversation with the adults concerned will hardly amplify.

What then occurs in a room of this kind? The children come in one by one and take curiously little interest in each other. Each child, with very little help, selects the occupation that interests him, and sets to work in a group or with a worker, careless on the whole of what goes on around him. Very careful notes are made by each worker at the end of each session, of what he or she has observed. These notes are revised by me twice weekly in conjunction with the head of the playroom.

Now let us turn to the cases themselves, and see how this

works out and what actually happens. In all instances names given are fictitious.

The first case we will take is that of Richard Ford, who was referred from a hospital as suffering from epilepsy. He was a well-grown intelligent lad, eleven years old, and of a prepossessing appearance. His mother was a caretaker, living with her own mother in good-class West End houses and, owing to her constant moves, the boy had been to nine schools. The father was an interpreter, a very irresponsible man, moody and unreliable, who, at the time Richard attended the clinic, was living abroad and refusing to come back to his wife.

The mother's mother was Irish, a well-balanced and normal individual, but her father – who had been at one time well off – died in an asylum at forty-eight and had had GPI at the time of his marriage. Richard's mother was convinced that Richard's condition was due to inheritance from this grandparent. The father's people were Dutch and of good stock, but he himself had had venereal disease and been unfaithful to his wife since 1918. He was 'gassed' in the war. He is said to be very silent, to bite his nails and pick his fingers and to smoke to excess.

The mother, the only parent with whom the clinic came into contact, was a genteel woman of very slow mind and quite extraordinary stupidity. She had a way of finding the simplest situation difficult, and in spite of superficial friendliness proved very resistant to co-operation. She deeply resented her husband's attitude to her and her son's illness, and combined exaggerated devotion to Richard and spoiling of him with ingrained disapproval and the constant expectation of disgrace. She had no control over the boy, and expressed herself as being exasperated with him. She looked upon the epilepsy as incurable and, in a sense, as an obscure form of judgement upon herself. According to the mother's account, the boy had no respect for his father, who had no control over him at all. Richard is said, however, to be afraid of his father, who had little understanding of the way to deal with children and would, for instance, suddenly give him a severe smack for no particular reason and badly startle him. Everything he said and did that adversely affected the father personally was regarded by the father as a serious offence – everything else a matter of indifference.

The mother describes the boy's attitude to her 'as if he had a dual personality'. One day he would be very loving to her and on another day would rush at her and bite her arm, shake her, hit her, and have fits of leering at her, which he owned he did to annoy her. There would be violent scenes in the home if anything occurred to thwart him.

The boy's relation to his grandmother was much better than to his mother.

These three people lived together in empty houses. The economic resources were adequate.

The *physical history* of the boy was a disturbed one. His mother had had a fall during pregnancy and a severe shock. Labour and feeding had been normal except for an early weaning, and development was normal. He was circumcised at two years. At two he had a severe fall; at three and a half he was delirious from a scald on the chest. Whooping-cough, chicken-pox, measles and tonsillitis followed each other rapidly and he was said to have frequent headaches. After X-ray treatment for ring-worm at seven he was said to have facial twitchings; at eight after a fall from a hayrick he had slight concussion; at ten was treated at Tite Street Hospital for another heavy fall and a bad cut on the left knee. In October 1928 and in the following April, he fainted in the street and was grey and cold for a long time after.

Psychological history up to the onset of fits was as follows:

A happy infancy; easily trained and clean at six months. Very destructive and fond of pots and pans and things that jingled or made a noise. Between two and three years said to be 'pedantic'; a solitary child, always on the go, always occupied; with a tendency to domination and cruelty. He liked pulling off the wings of flies and being cruel to the kitten. But he enjoyed helping in the house. At eleven he was described by his mother as a born snob and a born sergeant. If with people he looks down on, such as workmen, he is odious; if with people of culture, charming. During the last two years a change is said to have come over his character: he has taken to being only in the company of small boys whom he enjoys terrifying, and shuns the company of boys of his own age. Since about the same date he has become very restless, and when he goes to the park he dashes about, waving his arms up and down with very rapid movements and running in a circle, pretending with such conviction to be an aeroplane or motor-car that his mother says she 'sometimes thinks he *is* an engine'.

Onset of fits. About nine months before he began attendance at the clinic, failing all other attempts to discipline or control him, his mother sent him to an RC school noted for its strict discipline. This school he hated. For a time he was allowed to go home at weekends, and then every Monday there would be a scene when he would lie on the floor and cling to his mother and beseech her not to send him back again. He walked away from the school twice and his mother took him back. At 7.30 a.m. on 7 April, while the boys were forming up to go to chapel, he became unconscious, and fell down a flight of stone steps. He was put to bed and shortly afterwards was taken from the school. The first actual fit occurred a month later, in his sleep, and had all the characteristics of definite epilepsy. There was general twitching, he frothed and bit his tongue, rolled his eyes and was quite unconscious. Between that date and the date of his first attendance at the clinic (19.9.29) he had ten fits in all. The characteristics were the same. They occurred in sleep; he usually passed water. The fit lasted from three to five minutes. He was drowsy for eight hours and when he waked, complained of headache in the back of the head, but was not aware that anything had happened. He then sat up and vomited copiously (green and frothy). When he got up he was normal and wanted to run about. He complained of feeling top-heavy when he had to stand still, or in school, and sometimes he got an attack of laughing and being exalted. No *petit mal* was noted, though the doctor who referred the child to the clinic reported that Richard gave an account every now and then of not being quite aware of himself.

Throughout his attendance at the clinic the boy presented quite a remarkable picture of emotional ambivalence. The shyness inseparable from a first attendance at any new place disappeared on the second session, and a mood of violent activity took its place, but balanced in its turn by a feeling of order so exacting as to give a sense of compulsion.

A note on the first day of attendance says:

> Richard became interested in toys and set about to mend, with a hammer and tacks, a lid which was broken. Rather clumsy at it, did not at first realize that his tools and bits of wood were inadequate, but was persistent and methodical: finally came to the worker and said that the job was impossible as it would need finer nails. As the cupboard was being tidied he arranged the box wood excessively neatly, fitting the little bits at the bottom with great care; he grew tired of this and threw the rest on top, shaking them down. This was really all that was necessary. Built a fortress with a single tall tower in the centre, out of big blocks: well done,

> and he enjoyed this. He then tidied everything up in sight very methodically, evidently enjoying this, and having a compulsive sense of order.

On the second day:

> Good sense of how to use tools, etc. Evidently fond of mechanical toys, clockwork and so on, but when asked whether he was going to be an engineer he said he was going to be a carpenter, engineering was too dirty. Asked whether it wasn't rather fun to get dirty occasionally, he said half-heartedly, 'Yes.' Very gentle and kind to Michael (aged two), takes him and shows him his clockwork toys. Settled to make elaborate matador engine. Very difficult, but Richard was persistent and would not give it up. Still much interested in Michael's doings.

This relation was in direct contrast to the account given of him from the outside. The quiet fit soon passed (26.9.29):

> Had a ball and threw it rather hard at one of the workers. Stood with the ball poised to destroy another child's building. Worker said 'Why not destroy your farm?' Evaded and danced about, throwing the ball as near the other child's work as he 'accidentally' could.

His aversion to messy substances came out strongly (14.10.29):

> Richard said he did not feel like doing anything, he was so tired. Said he had slept most of the day before. Decided to play with the sand-tray. Made a sea with clay walls, but did not like touching the clay and each time he touched it, rinsed his fingers. Finally he asked worker to do the wall while he banked up the sand. Later he got more used to the clay and helped. He made harbours with wooden ships to sail. Seemed interested and worked at it for 1½ hours till called off for dancing. Made rocks of clay in the middle and built a wooden lighthouse on it. Very anxious because a little clay got on his trousers.

In the fifty-four hours previous to this visit he had had two fits. *These were the last fits he had.*

The aversion from messy substances changed very rapidly and on 24.10.29,

> Asked for clay and said in a surprised voice, 'I rather like clay now.' Made much the same as before – a sea with a pier going

> into it, a lighthouse and various harbours. He shut these off at first and let the water through, sometimes with a rush and sometimes through a tunnel under the clay. Had a bridge made in wood to put across, and tried to place a little figure on it, but it was too unsteady.

During this time he showed in conversation his sorrow at not having brothers and sisters of his own:

> Talks with imaginary boys in bed about all the events of the day. They don't talk to him – just act as listeners. He does not see their faces.
>
> In conversation he says sadly that he is an only child and has no brothers or sisters.

The rhythm reports are interesting:

> 10.10.29. On his arrival at the Clinic he was extremely happy and eager. Very stiff movements in the upper part of his body, dragged his feet in marching and lurched along as if it were an effort to walk. Used the right side of his body when possible. No freedom of movement at all. Most pleasant child to deal with, a happy disposition and anxious to please. Gets no free movement at home. Body seems thoroughly unbalanced.
>
> 24.10.19. Irritated by mother's presence. Movements becoming steadier. (Third attendance.) Does his best; has admiration for beauty. Generous and kind and always ready to praise work of other children.
>
> 28.11.29. Stance becoming more manly and movements much freer. Time and rhythm good. Can co-ordinate with arms and legs.

In general reaction to work of the clinic Richard showed as it were two layers: on one he was a dignified, well-mannered, intelligent boy, well up to the standard for his age: on the other, a rebellious, impulsive, entirely uncontrolled child of three or four. These alternated, and we allowed them to express themselves freely without comment.

After a little while, when a certain amount of material had collected, I had several long talks with Richard, in which the material was examined and commented on, and explanations given to Richard of the way human character was built up, grew and developed, and why discipline was necessary.

In the meantime the reports from his mother showed steady improvement. 12 October was the date of the last fit that he had.

On 7 January he went back to school. In March of next year he was able to take a holiday at Hindhead, and thoroughly enjoyed it. His mother moved their address again and the boy went to St Michael's School, Westminster. The head teacher reported to Mrs Ford that his work was good and that he was making satisfactory progress. As no more fits occurred and the boy seemed physically well, and was settling down at school, the mother ceased attendance. From our point of view this was a pity because at home his conduct was still unsatisfactory and we would have liked to have kept him long enough to have got this in order also.

> At home Mrs Ford complained that Richard was incapable of accepting responsibility even for obvious matters. He forgot to clean his teeth, brush his hair, etc. and had little concentration. He was passionately fond of woodwork and was given plenty of scope for this at home. It was suggested to her that she should try to give him ample praise for the things he did well in order to counteract the amount of correction and the reminders that she felt it necessary to administer to him. She maintained that she did so and was careful not to let the boy get a feeling of hopelessness and discouragement.

The striking fact about this case is of course the shortness of treatment – the boy attended altogether eleven times. No medicines were given. In spite of this short period of treatment, to date – eighteen months from the last fit – no fits have recurred and he has become adjusted to school life and discipline.

The second point of interest, especially in contrast to the next case – also of an epileptic, a girl of the same age of eleven – is its ambivalence, and what one might call its lack of shape. There is no particular order or sense about what he does, and on one afternoon many varying activities may be attempted and violent changes of mood shown. After the first day there was no inhibition and his emotional release, which was wild, slowly came down to normal. He showed little or no phantasy and what he did was of an objective kind – e.g. reproduction of scenes seen – but on the other hand his understanding of tools was good.

Contrast this case with Mary Clark, aged eleven, referred to us on 16 November 1929 for a complaint of 'losing herself for a moment'. When the child first attended she was having definite attacks of *petit mal*:

> She began to nod her head and upper part of her body forward in jerks, definite but not violent, hands curled in but not clenched, eyes vague. After about half-a-minute to one minute she sighed and relaxed and looked up as if to orientate herself as to where she was.

Because it was thought desirable that she should cease for a time to attend school, and we could bring this about only by recommending convalescence involving absence from London, convalescence was recommended for Mary and she went for a month into the country to stay with an aunt. Mary was well while away, and was not brought back to us on her return. But shortly after, one evening at the Brownies, she was taken suddenly ill with a definite epileptic fit.

Her history was as follows:

Mary is the third child of a family of three – the other two being brothers. Her father – a man of forty-two – was born in London of a Sussex family, general health and intelligence very good. Entered fishmonger's trade at the age of eleven and, except for the war, has remained in it ever since. Had rheumatic fever twice – heart not affected, but acute arthritis in one leg has crippled him since 1910. His parents still living, but in 1923 he quarrelled with them and did not see his mother for a year. They are of normal stock, with no nervous trouble in them or the rest of the family.

Her mother, a woman of forty-six, was born on a Berkshire farm – educated in a country school – in service until her marriage. Health good – no history of nervous or mental trouble. Well-balanced, very sensible, high standard of morality and honesty, very self-denying and hardworking and generous to a fault. Her own mother, who died recently, used to have crying fits and could not keep quiet. Was always on the look-out for danger and expecting accidents to happen to the children.

The family live in three rooms at the top of a three-storeyed house, sparsely furnished but scrupulously clean, situated in a fairly quiet street having a small yard at the back. Of the two brothers, Fred, a boy of fifteen, did very well at school and now is apprenticed to a plumber and keeping on his education by attendance at evening classes. George, thirteen, is at the Regent Street Polytechnic on a scholarship and has done excellently in every way. He is said to have been nervy as a little boy but now to have grown out of it – to have had fears of water at first, but now to be a competent swimmer. The family atmosphere is good, except for one period of stress before the father went to hospital, when his temper was unbearable.

Mary's physical history was uneventful. An easy confinement, breast-fed for three months and weaned gradually. Very severe pneumonia and bronchitis at two, measles at seven, and scarlet fever at eleven. Lately complained of headaches. Good appetite, sleeps well, bowels regular, no enuresis. Her *psychological history* showed the history of the 'model child'. She was a happy infant, never naughty, did everything normally, played well. Always very clean, no enuresis, as soon as she walked wanted to play with water. Never frightened. Has slept in a separate room since she was two years old.

At four and three-quarters started school. Always good reports; enjoyed school; always truthful, never got into trouble, no tempers; was very often teased by her brothers but stood up to them. The only bad point admitted by anyone about her was that she was lazy at home and rather spoiled and did not like helping in the house.

The only anomalous event was that, when fifteen months old, suddenly she shut her eyes and refused to open them for three days.

The onset of trouble came in the following way. In May 1929, Mary started working for a Junior County Scholarship. Both her brothers had done well in scholarships. At midnight one night at this time the mother was awakened by hearing the door open. Mary came in in her night-dress, came straight up to the bed and said, 'You always make me get the water.' The mother said, 'I don't know what you are talking about.' Mary said in a rude, abrupt manner, very unlike her, 'Yes, you do.' The mother took her back to her own room, saying 'Whatever made you do that?' and Mary said, 'You came out here first, didn't you?' in the same rude manner. She then got into bed and did not remember anything about it in the morning.

Head-nodding was first noted in June. In September she had scarlet fever and in January was moved up three classes, and found the work very hard. At this point, on Wednesday, 29 January, the first fit occurred. On the Sunday following she had a second fit at home and on the Monday resumed attendance at the clinic. She continued to attend until October of that year, and fits ceased by June. Each fit had the same characteristics. She would be sitting quietly at home, suddenly fall back, cry out, become cyanosed and quite unconscious, this would last two minutes, she would go into a deep sleep afterwards, sleep six to eight hours and wake in the morning knowing nothing about it.

In character Mary was the exact reverse of Richard. Where he was wild and uncontrolled, she was the picture of quietness and obedience. Where he was uncoordinated and lacking in integration, she showed a character of monotonous evenness. My description of her first attendance was:

> A very good quiet little girl, rather stout, has a way of bending her head slightly down and looking up at one. Talked re scholarship and she showed a clear feeling of burdensomeness about this and about school work.

Her work at the Clinic falls into four periods. Period I. During this period she was a shy quiet little girl, occupied with normal tasks, and with puzzles. Strong inhibitions.

> 18.11.29. Free design on a sheet of paper. Began with red square. At first had evidently no ideas and just sat looking at the pieces, then fumbling with them.
>
> 17.2.30. Helped Nellie Smith with jigsaw puzzle, then cut out crêpe paper dresses for dolls, very neatly. Made a man with the grotesque mosaics which she drew on paper and coloured. It was a little difficult to draw her out, but at last she said she would really like to make a bag with beads.

Very occasionally vindictiveness appeared.

> 26.11.29. Indians had landed in England, had no home, went to people's houses and if they couldn't have their homes, they would shoot the English people. One Indian had been captured and strung up on a tree until the English had finished their work when they were going to shoot him. Another Indian was shooting a turkey for food. Dreamed of Indians, one and a half years ago, Indians coming into the kitchen.

Her attitude to the work and herself was a discouraged one:

> 27.2.30. In conversation she said, (a) 'I don't like this work,' (b) to Reggie, 'It don't matter what you do, it only gets knocked down or broken up.' Worker said, 'I don't agree. You might as well say it's no use making a cake, it only gets eaten up.' This made her think a bit, then 'A cake isn't wasted when you have eaten it.' Worker: 'Neither is a beautiful thing if it gave you pleasure to look at it. I like to see beautiful things, don't you?' Mary: 'Yes, I like ugly faces. You've got a nice face, mine's ugly. I *like* ugly faces.'

Four fits altogether occurred during this period. About March her demeanour changed and Period II (3 March to 7 April 1930) showed an entirely different picture. The 'goodness', which had been wearing thin just before this, broke up and a wild period of uproariousness set in, together with an interest in aggression and destructiveness.

> 27.3.30. This child is untidy and behaving in a very hoydenish fashion. She does a 'Bunny Race', squatting, about the clinic, climbs over obstacles fearlessly, and begs to dance and play ball. She wheedles for more time for rough games, and talks of dancing as, 'Oh, oh, just lovely.' She is difficult to keep at any occupation for long unless it is very active or rather messy, like sand pies.

Delight in messy substances appeared also:

> 24.3.30. Finding another child playing with wet sand, joined in, saying, 'I like this,' and rubbed her hands in it, becoming rapidly dishevelled and dirty. Played with sand, got hands dirty, and enjoyed making a mess. Was delighted at being allowed to make mud pies and clay work and made herself thoroughly messy and dirty.

Also an interest in food:

> 27.3.30. Playing with plasticine or sand, she makes toffee apples or fish cakes, or other edibles, and says lusciously, 'Um, don't talk to me about fish cakes, makes my mouth water – um'm,' smacking lips.

And in body shapes:

> 10.3.30. Made a grotesque figure finally called a woman, though not originally intended for either sex, naked but with a hat. The size of the nose and lips much too large for the face. Small arms and legs, enormously long thick tail. Afterwards made equally grotesque man with long arms and legs and no tail. She enjoyed doing this immensely.

You will note the contrast between her flow of ideas at this period, and her original inhibition. *Two fits occurred in this period*, and both near the beginning. Meantime, at home the following changes were taking place:

> 6.3.30. Mother complains of Mary becoming cheeky and was encouraged to feel that this is a good sign. Mary does not like helping with the housework.

> 10.3.30. Parents giving Mary more freedom.
> 13.3.30. Mary seems to be better in every way.
> 20.3.30. Mother reports that Mary's behaviour is 'nearly normal'.

Twenty-five days after the last fit, the clinic was closed for Easter and for the reorganization of the case records system. During this period of six weeks, Mary had seven fits. She returned to the clinic on 2 June, and a period of listlessness alternating with wild spirits kept her till August. Fits ceased with her return.

Her former delight in messy substances turned to a negative reaction against them, but a new main motif showed itself in an interest in the other sex, in boys and girls, and in the appearance of masochism.

> 16.6.30. She suddenly asked me [male] if I would like to be a girl. I asked why. She said she would like to be a boy so as to be able to play football and cricket in the street so that the 'copper could run after her'.
>
> 3.7.30. While painting, Mary discussed with another child caning at school. Both said they had never been caned. Mary said she would like to be caned.

Physically she showed signs of approaching puberty. The fits did not recur and, as the mother reported:

> 22.9.30. Mary was much fitter physically; more alert, more mature in taste and reactions; knows her own mind better and strives to achieve her end.
>
> 4.12.30. Mary continues to make good progress; is more responsible and very helpful in the house, is now going to cookery and housewifery courses at school; plays netball at school; goes to the Guides.

The fits having disappeared, she ceased to attend the clinic, in spite of the fact that head-nodding occurred occasionally.

On the physical side Mary was seen by Dr Obermer, who made a careful metabolic study. His diagnosis was as follows:

> The basis of the condition was that of a labile thyroid, undergoing extra pre-pubertal strain, as shown by an extraordinarily high iodine figure up to 64·6 grams.

(Two complete tests were carried out; one in between fits and one immediately after a fit.) On first test:

> 12.2.30. There was a certain degree of acidosis with lowered alkali reserve. I think that any extra external or internal strain will show in this child disproportionate acceleration of metabolism for a short period, during which time there will be an excretion of excessive quantities of phosphorous and possibly calcium. This is followed by a period of thyroid exhaustion correlating with a deviation of the acid base equilibrium to the alkaline side, and until this retarded metabolism, with diminished excretion of calcium and phosphorous, has lasted long enough to restore the balance, she is in danger of a convulsive explosion.

Whereas previously Mary had had no idea what she wanted to do in life, she now decided for herself that she wished to work in a florist's, and was able to adhere to this desire until her mother became adjusted to it and gave up her idea of scholastic distinction for her daughter.

We see therefore a child whose primitive emotional drives have been regarded by herself with such fear and dislike that they have been put under undue repression, with a resulting stultification of character development. Everything had been concentrated upon the desire to win approval, to emulate the brothers, to be better than they. The prospect of a final demonstration of her inadequacy by the inescapable scholarship examination was intolerable to her, and the 'epilepsy' occurred.

Release of the primitive trends in a permissive atmosphere set free the machinery of growth. A removal from the horizon of the (unconsciously) so-much-dreaded examination released her from this threat to her ego; a way of escape was no longer necessary, she could allow herself to be well. On the physical side this was supplemented by Ac.Phos.Dil.m.xv t.d.s. over an extensive period, but with no appreciable result. Previously she had iodine for a short time, but this seemed to aggravate the condition. No bromide was given. The mother had a bromide prescription for use in emergency, but it was never used.

We have therefore apparently in these two cases an identical pathological phenomenon arising from opposite sets of emotional factors, and as far as the psychology of the children is concerned, passing through opposite mechanisms for relief.

Let us now take two parallel cases of enuresis, and consider the same factors.

Eric Compton was a small boy of four, referred to the clinic for night terrors, a shut-in personality, passionate anger fits, and enuresis from birth. He was the elder of two, the second child being a girl, and came of comparatively well-to-do parents. The mother had been poorly during pregnancy, had jaundice just before his birth, difficult labour, twilight sleep, instrumental birth, the baby's head being badly bruised with forceps. Breast-fed three to four days only, because of jaundice in mother and baby. Development normal, circumcision at six weeks. Always very difficult to get him to give up faeces and urine, had constipated stools and much wind. He was a clean baby, never dirty, always careful and serious, only really laughed at two and a half years. He had never ceased to wet his bed.

His little sister was born when Eric was thirteen months old. He gave no indication of his feelings, but has had violent fits of jealousy since. Made up an imaginary playmate called Joan (his sister's name is Margery).

Father aged thirty-nine, one of five, very healthy, started as a teacher but gave it up for city business. Gave the impression of severe habitual restraint, sense of humour remarkably deficient, outlook on life very serious; undemonstrative, attached to wife and children, has a certain degree of insight, but little intuition.

Mother was severely neurotic and received treatment from a psychological physician in the parents' department at the same time. She was thirty-seven years of age, one of four. Suffered from nightmares and sleep-walking in childhood, still wakes at night, shouting. Fears of black cats, and of being chased and falling down wells. Temperamentally irritable with children, weepy, no energy, but a competent attractive woman, depressed with her own failure and determined to do all she can to get it remedied.

Eric on his first appearance:

> 26.9.29. Was a well-developed child with an alert adult manner, frowning expression, and an air of being in-turned, e.g. his remark at the first session, 'Leave me alone, I have a great deal to think about.' He appeared as though he never smiled and certainly never romped as a child of his age usually does. Solid and heavy in all his movements, does and says everything with great emphasis.

Eric attended the clinic altogether thirty-one times spread over intervals of eleven months. During his first period – September to January – with the exception of work with Montessori apparatus, his whole energy was absorbed in water-play. During this time, enuresis was diminishing but present. He was an exceedingly interesting child. Much of his work is of serious symbolic value, but unfortunately too long to quote here.

Examples of his play are as follows:

> 17.10.29. Had fish, swans, tins and frog. Worker had a can of water. Eric got banana squirt and spent whole time in filling it and squirting, and would scarcely pay any attention to anything else. Finally played game with worker of squirting at far edge of tray (he was not interested in squirting at any of the animals) and on to the floor beyond. This gave him great pleasure.
>
> 25.11.29. Eric was playing with a toy lavatory; he placed it on a heap of sand and said, 'It's a pump on a mountain.' He filled and refilled the cistern and pulled the plug, then filled the pan itself and watched the water running down, saying, 'It's going down the pipe.' When asked what he was putting in the pan he said, 'I put the water in and it goes rumpety, rumpety, rumpety, rumpety, and comes out lemonade.'

His general demeanour at this time was as follows:

> 3.10.29. Worker saw him sitting on the seat, having refused to dance with the others. Went and asked him if he would sit on the floor with her and copy what the others were doing. He replied, 'Must sit on the seat. I have such a lot to think about.' At that minute dancing finished, and being told he could go, he dashed off his seat and to the door alone.

His inhibitions slowly broke up and a certain amount of emotional freedom appeared. The enuresis began to lessen and by the middle of February had entirely disappeared. It has never reappeared. The faults of character, the lack of contact between himself and his family showed little change, but screaming fits were fewer.

At the end of this period, and just before the cessation of the enuresis, an identification with a train appeared. Eric became a train continually, both at home and at the clinic, and carried it out to the minutest detail.

> 22.3.30. Came into the room and as usual just stood and looked round. On being spoken to made a sh-sh-ing noise. Said he was a steam-engine. When asked what he would like to do, could not think until suggested to him to make a mountain for the engine to go up.
>
> 5.6.30. Announced in the room that all his coal and steam

> had given out. He had no more. Repeated this, saying it was because he had come so far. Began hissing and shuffling several times on the way to the playroom but checked himself.
>
> 12.6.30. Responded with enthusiasm to suggestion of playing at trains, beginning at once to puff and make movements with his arms to and fro. Explained this quite clearly; he was the whole engine; steam came out of the funnel, his mouth; his arms were the connecting rods. Seemed very sure of mechanical details. Said he was not always an engine, sometimes a tram.

This lasted through an attack of measles, and after he returned to the clinic, only disappearing six months later (mid-July).

At the same time he began suddenly to make tunnels and put 'trains' made of any material through them, and also chimneys.

> 5.6.30. Eric was building houses with chimneys. The great point all the time was height. 'Look how tall.' 'This is going to be very tall.' Talked incessantly, and would not allow additions or assistance with his work. No order and no scheme in his work. In some instances it did not faintly resemble a house, but the idea of height, chimneys and smoke ran throughout. For smoke he put large solid cubes. He did not like smoke, he said, but liked the fires inside.
>
> 12.6.30. Came into the room as steam engine. Got tired of trying to make an engine with bricks, and said, 'I will make a lovely tall house.' Frequently he said, 'A tall, tall house with chimneys,' in a far-away voice.
>
> 3.7.30. When playing with steamboat and water said steamboat was in Looking-Glass Land. When asked what Looking-Glass Land was like, he said it was all chimneys and chimneys and chimneys, even chimneys to eat with. He eats and drinks these, but does not like to drink, it makes him hot.

About this time his manner altogether changed and aggression and contempt appeared, together with wildness of behaviour.

> 20.1.30. Eric was running backwards and forwards in the room, rushing at the workers in turn, banging into them shouting 'Biff, biff,' laughing as he did so: was wild and enjoying himself, but not vindictive.

Here the conversation came about the fierce, destroying world, quoted earlier. Mention of the family, and aggression against the family began to appear:

> 31.7.30. He made a tram which had to travel under the sea completely closed up. In it were his own people, father, mother and sister. Later the tram went to a town called Puddin or Poison. Presently, playing skittles, he wanted to hurt me very much because he thought I was his sister 'Marj'.

But at the same time the cessation of night terrors was reported, and at home a much better adjustment to the family was being achieved. Eric began to be more spontaneous in every way, and to show affection to his parents. He was on holiday from the end of July to September, and when he returned was much more normal in behaviour, both at clinic and home. Aggressive play was much less marked, the train phantasy had disappeared, but a new feature, a love of messy substances appeared:

> 2.10.30. With both hands he got going with sand and water, pouring on the water in one corner till he had got a slosh and saying over and over again, 'But it is lovely to make a mess,' and dabbling in the mud, but only with the tips of his fingers.
>
> 20.10.30. Eric made circular islands with his fingers in the sand, and now and again, burying his hands in the sand with evident joy, he announced 'Now I am the dirtiest boy in the world.'

As his mother had now nothing she wished to complain of, Eric was discharged, and on his discharge the mother reported that Eric was behaving like a normal boy in every way. Enuresis completely cleared up, no screaming fits or night terrors, plays happily with his sister, no longer any train play. When in tears they soon disappear, the child has his own way of coping with his difficulties. When he is angry, Eric says to his mother, 'I want to hit you but cannot, so have to cry.'

The characteristic features of this boy as seen in the play room were the wealth of his phantasy and its dominating power over him; the repetitive nature of his play, and his tendency to repeat over and over again the same phrase; and his detachment from what is going on around him. His first remark when asked to go to dancing was characteristic of him.

Let us now take another case of enuresis, also a small boy:

Ian Baker, five and a half years old, suffered from screaming fits and enuresis. He had also had epileptic attacks, and was under treatment at the West London Hospital for them at the time of his coming to us. These had cleared up before he began attendance and he was transferred from the West London Hospital to the clinic.

The boy was the ninth living of fifteen pregnancies. One maternal aunt died in an asylum and there is considerable alcoholism on the father's side. The child was sent to the infirmary at two and a half months for wasting, and remained there till fourteen months, as a congenital heart defect was suspected. On discharge he still did not thrive. At two and a half years the question of fits was raised; his last fit occurred on 28 June, two days before his first attendance at the clinic.

The child was a miniature replica of Richard Ford. He was entirely uncontrolled, unable to settle to anything for longer than a few minutes, running wildly from one occupation to another, in each case showing quite remarkable mastery of tools and constructive material. Tunnels and holes appeared in his play, but water-play was not so persistent as in the case of Eric Compton.

During November and December, owing to the circumstances at home, we sent him away to a convalescent home which works in connection with us, where he remained for two and a half months. During the last month there the enuresis entirely disappeared, the character difficulties lessened considerably. This however does not help the difficulty; to be able to adjust to life when one's mother is not present is useful, but carries a human being only a very little way. It is the task of psychological medicine to help such a child to adjust to life when his mother is present as well, and this we attempted.

As with Richard, no co-ordination appeared in his activities. His attitude to life was determined to a very large extent by his mother's attitude to him. His father was a man of violent temper, brutal and alcoholic, and neurotically jealous of his wife. He would allow her to do nothing and go nowhere that was not connected with the care of her family and her home. Ian's fits had been a godsend to the mother as, since they tended to occur at night, she had been able to take him into her room and make the care of him a protection against the exigent sexual demands of her husband, and he had become the apple of her eye. Meanwhile her own state of health became very bad. Concentration on our part on her health gradually weaned her from exclusive concentration upon Ian, and began to give him a chance to develop on his own. Gradual progress began to show. Through allowing his wildness full outlet without reaction a certain interest in and desire for concentration began to appear. Enuresis lessened. From having been constant, it is now only twice in ten days.

Screaming fits have disappeared. The schoolteacher reports:

> 4.3.31. Steady progress. There is a great difference in Ian. He is more amenable, shows more interest and concentration, is more ready to settle down to steady work, and much more tranquil.

The conduct difficulty at home nevertheless persists.

The interest in this case lies in the parallelism with Richard Ford, and the contrast of both phenomena shown and progress of improvement with Eric Compton and Mary Clark. Where Eric found himself through emotional release, Ian will do so through progress into co-ordination of his primitive drives and integration of his ego. Where Eric and Mary are over-integrated, Ian has not integrated at all. Where Eric and Mary show abundant and ready phantasy, Richard and Ian are devoid of it. Both show ability with the manipulation of objects, and in both cases the character difficulty at home has remained unresolved.

A similar parallelism can be shown also for speech defects. Time makes it impossible to give you both cases. One was a boy with aphonia referred to us from King's College Hospital Speech Department for acute anxiety and inability to face life. This boy had to be restrained, before he left us, from fearlessly hanging head downwards from iron railings over a stone court, and his chart shows the same general characteristics as Richard and Eric's.

Grace Carter, the uncoordinated member of the two, is the more interesting, and shows certain features which may throw light on the mechanism of certain inexplicable murders which have been reported in the press of late.

Grace was a little girl of seven and a half, referred to us by an exemplary family for failure to speak intelligibly. There was always difficulty with her speech from when she first began to speak at the age of two, and it was reported from the school to which she first went that she gave the appearance of a deaf-mute. She was fond of singing, and would sing about the house, though it was not stated whether or not she used words to do so. The paternal grandmother had also been backward in talking, and at the age of four was still unable to make herself understood.

The father was a government servant, a hard, silent, reserved man, unapproachable, very conscientious and with a high moral standard for himself and his family, no spontaneity, and no sense of humour.

The mother, aged thirty-four, was a fair, cheerful French woman, who gave the impression of trying very hard by discipline of her own nature to live up to her husband's standard, but of being herself in reality much more spontaneous and cheerful.

There was one other child, a boy of thirteen, healthy and active, not intellectual, but unusually good at games and mechanical pursuits, in striking contrast to his sister's clumsiness. The academic ambitions of the father for his children had been disappointed by the son, and he turned to Grace in expectation of their fulfilment. This she was unable to do, being of slow mentality, and having no particular intellectual gifts.

Grace's psychological history was that of a placid and amenable infant, and a happy and contented child. She was stated by her mother to have been very active, very clean, very particular, very good. Apart from acute jealousy of her brother, which seemed to amuse rather than trouble the parents, she had never given her family any trouble, and neither father nor mother had any complaint whatever, apart from the speech difficulty, to make concerning her.

The physical history was uneventful, apart from the significant factor of constipation which had existed from infancy in a more or less intractable form, showed no abnormality, and physical examination revealed nothing of interest.

I saw her for the first time on 28 October 1929, and dictated afterwards a note to say that in all probability her first plain-spoken words or vigorous action would be of a kind displaying a violent aggressive or murderous quality.

On 31.10.29, at the end of the second day she had been with us,

> Grace suddenly waved in the air a wooden revolver that she had made out of Kliptiko, and then rushed round the room with a beaming face, shooting everybody. She drew in her arm and then flung it out at each person, with a stabbing movement. All her movements were very quick. She ran forward, rather bent up, again when she had to go, and this time she rushed round – with no revolver in her hand – and shot everyone, grown-ups and children alike, then shot herself and fell dead.

Her characteristic form of release was now in full swing. Whenever Grace became excited she ran round the room killing people, holding out her hand as a pistol; or showed her desires in another manner, as follows:

> 4.11.29. Came up, put her arm round my neck and squeezed with all her might, then squeezed with both hands round my throat.

There was no doubt at all of her intention in this act, as although she was only eight she had quite remarkable muscular strength, the force of the action was for a time actually embarrassing and needed deliberate and careful disentangling. The intention behind, however, was never univalent. At the same time, on most occasions, the opposite emotion would appear, as for instance:

> 7.11.29. Flung her arms round and kissed Miss B several times, and then went and hit other people with equal abandon.
> 2.12.29. She flung herself on LW and hugged and throttled her several times. This alternated with play at killing herself and being dead.

Notwithstanding this aggression in action she was negative to the *idea* of cutting up, and to handling or moulding soft material.

> 4.11.29. At first Grace persistently said 'No' to plasticine . . . I continued to make shapes in plasticine and cut them out. Grace asked me not to, but I continued, and finally, as if roused to action, she took the tool, her manner changing from negative to positive, and said, 'Very well, we will cut it all up, and then it will be finished.' This she did, almost with passion, until all was finished, placed in the box and the lid shut down.

Her time, when it was not given to running violently about, nor to speech tests nor rhythm classes, was occupied in constructive work. She was different from the other two in that her object-interest was poor, and her movements and muscular control, or eye–hand co-ordination, clumsy and unbalanced.

The necessary movement of aggressive impulses from action in reality to action in phantasy, which is part of our usual technique, was very difficult to accomplish in this child, and never really succeeded.

During this whole time, her mother when questioned, stated that she continued at home to be the good little girl, *and that no rudeness or violence of any kind appeared in her home life.*

In the meantime speech steadily improved, and on 14.7.30 had become so far normal that her mother discontinued her attendance at the clinic. On 4.10.30 when the social worker called to ascertain how matters were going, the mother reported that:

> Grace is at school. She is talking quite normally, and gets along very well. She is slightly more naughty, but Mrs Carter seemed to expect this. They were trying to give her more play-outlet with clubs, etc. At home there was less trouble between Grace and the brother; they seemed more engrossed in their own pursuits and on the whole Grace was becoming more mature in her behaviour.

This child thus shows a third type. She is uncoordinated, like Richard, and violent, like Ian. She is dissociated into two layers, as Richard was, but to a much more severe degree. She is capable, as he was not, of replacing her mask entire as she left the clinic. In contrast to either of these, however, her phantasy capacity was sound, only it must be a phantasy capacity she acted out – she was negative to the idea of playing it symbolically. So heavy was the charge of emotion behind her drama that it made all precision of movement impossible, she was very clumsy.

A very marked point of contrast with both Eric and Mary lay in her affective capacity. Whereas they were withdrawn from their parents and showed no affection to parent substitutes (ourselves), once the ban against emotion current in the Carter household was removed, Grace's affection poured out like Niagara – both components, the hate and the love, being equally unmanageable in strength.

It is not at all necessary that a case should take this kind of course. For instance with Foster Cook, a boy of four who was referred for poor health, depression, weeping, lack of appetite and occasional vomiting.

The father had asthma badly and was subject to hay fever. The mother as a child had had fainting fits and bilious attacks. She was now healthy, but a very foolish woman. Foster was her only child, and her whole life centred in him. He had had a tonsillectomy performed at hospital eighteen months before coming to us, and was said by the mother to have wasted away, and never to have been the same again. He cried at the smallest thing, fainted when knocked – according to his mother – and at the sight of blood, and even at that of a bandage.

The child attended the clinic four times altogether and then returned to school well. During the first two of these he was inseparable from his mother, refused to take part in anything going on around him, or show any initiative or enjoyment. In the interval, urine tests and a careful physical examination having been carried out, a diagnosis was made of 'a condition of acidosis, cause unknown', with the recommendation of glucose and alkalis, accompanied by restriction of fat in the diet. These were prescribed and put faithfully into practice by the mother, and as a result the symptoms complained of disappeared. By the fourth visit the condition was reported to have cleared up. The child was back at his nursery school, looking well, and behaving normally. This is an instance of an apparent neurosis arising from a physical condition which was resolved by physical means.

Another child of three, Susie Appleyard, who was referred to us for screaming attacks, showed an interesting course. She was the elder of two children, and came of working-class parents.

Her father and mother had been living together before Susie's birth, and her advent is said to have had a great effect upon Mrs Appleyard's character. The house they lived in was in a low neighbourhood, and the family living above them was disreputable and drank heavily. Mrs Appleyard was said to have been a very slovenly mother and to have left the children screaming for hours together. It seems fairly certain that Susie was frightened by a drunken lodger found lying in the passage. The father was a steeplejack, and had a good character. He seems to have had little to do with the children, and his wife to have been very fond of him.

After a second child was born they moved to a better quarter.

The mother is said to have had two falls while carrying Susie, and birth was instrumental with a long labour. The baby had a black eye owing to the forceps, but was normal and weighed 9 lb at birth. Breast-fed for four weeks, and rapidly weaned. Throve well. It is said that she had several bad falls in her first year, but she developed rapidly, no illnesses. According to both Mrs Appleyard and her neighbour, the child was always grizzly, always bad-tempered, and 'never seemed a proper baby'. She was easy to train, napkins were left off at nine months, and no interest in faeces noted. She was a very destructive child and loved tearing things to pieces, but was particularly clean and very particular 'how she ate'. She did not have a crawling stage, walked suddenly and was very independent.

When George, the second child, was born she was eleven months old. She took his arrival well and up to six months was very fond of him. When, however, he began to sit up in a high chair, and appear as a rival instead of a plaything, her affection turned to hate, and she was always wanting to hurt him. Mrs Appleyard complained that she bit him. She went to school very early and was said to be stubborn and to take all the teacher's attention. If she was the centre of attention she was good, if not she screamed. She picked her nose, sucked her thumb, and bit her nails. A few weeks before she started attending the clinic she began to scream at night also. After a fit of screaming she would lie down and go to sleep again. The other fits of screaming occurred in the day and she could go on for three or four hours. No means were effective for checking her. By the time she came to the clinic both parents were worn out with the strain of coping with her.

Her relation to her father was ambivalent. Sometimes she would let him caress her and would play with him, at other times she would scream and kick if he touched her, and say, 'Jesus will never love you, he will love me but not you.' To the mother her reaction was similarly uneven. Sometimes she loved her and sometimes ignored her. She did not seem ever to be actively hostile. Both children slept in the parents' room.

Susie attended the clinic twenty-two times from 29 September to the end of January 1930; then, as her parents said she had become perfectly normal in behaviour, she ceased to attend. This we very much regretted, as there was still a great deal that needed to be done before I could in any way feel her to be secure against a future breakdown.

During her first attendance a certain shyness showed, but this gave way rapidly to violence.

> 3.10.29 (2nd attendance). When the worker who had been playing with her left her, Susie went 'mad dog' through the clinic. Knocked down her own blocks and those of another child, which amused him, and the two played at throwing things about. Great noise, Susie ring-leading. Went to table where plasticine knobs were, and house, and garden and little fat man. Crushed house, and worker encouraged her to cut up little man and knobs. Frightened at this, then descended upon it.

Her activities were destructive rather than aggressive. She did not attack the children themselves or the worker, as Grace

Carter had done, but did everything in her power to be offensive to them and destroy their work. Her movements were very swift, and in a couple of minutes she was capable of destroying the work of four or five children.

> 10.10.29. Susie came in from dancing and destroyed the work of three children on two different tables in less than five seconds, scattering mosaics right and left. As these were collected she scattered them again.

Destruction took two forms: actual aggressive destruction in relation to other people's toys in reality; and phantasy destruction chiefly directed towards a certain person called Charlie.

> 20.9.29. She played for a long time burying a goose and a little chicken which she called Charlie. Kept on burying Charlie, and then all the animals, calling them all Charlie. Worker was not to help bury the animals. 'Why was Charlie buried?' 'Because he had taken off pins from piggy's legs.' She then emptied and filled pails with sand, took a bottle and filled it with sand.
>
> 3.10.29. Susie began playing with rabbits and buried them one by one. Mother, father and little girl and baby rabbit, because they had spilt something over the tortoise. They were buried 'as if they had never been'. Then she buried rabbits again. The policeman would take them away because they had been rude. Called him nasty and evil and began spitting.
>
> 7.10.30. Susie took other people's things for the sake of taking them, not using them. Then a rabbit was buried in sand 'because he's naughty, he's smacked little —' (worker's writing here undecipherable). Then a fish is dead 'because he's got water in his eyes'. Another fish is dead 'because he's got water in his eyes'. Susie put clay on top of it, saying 'let me do it'.

The idea of guilt was tremendously strong with her, and appeared constantly in her play. The worker was naughty, the baby naughty, the rabbit had to be buried because it was naughty, her left hand was naughty. There must quite clearly have been some incident concerned with an individual called Charlie and a lavatory at some early stage.

> 3.10.29 (going to lavatory). She pretended worker was a naughty old man. Susie spat at her and hit her and locked her outside and made noises with her mouth at her. 'Why was he

> naughty?' 'He wanted to come in there.' 'What would he do?' 'He would put on a light.'

The situation to which this referred was very difficult to clear up in the time that she was with us, as insufficient material appeared. Her mother said she had always referred to herself as Charlie: there had been a drunken man in the former lodgings, and there was some idea that his name was Charlie, although her mother on another occasion called him George. There was also an Uncle Charlie in the Navy, a harmless, jovial fellow usually away, to whom Susie had an ambivalent attitude.

There was throughout her stay continual play with the lavatory, chiefly centred in the idea of locking in. Her mother could remember no incident to which this might refer, and the time was too short to allow the incident to develop fully in play.

Screaming fits, which occurred from time to time at the clinic, had always the same characteristics: something would rouse a state of anxiety within her and she would begin to scream. It was never possible to have her mother far away for long. She would demand to go to her mother, dart to her, bury her face in her skirt and continue to scream – the note rising, if nothing was done to relieve her, to one of pure terror with an acute feeling of imminent disaster, where it showed every evidence of remaining for a long time. As work at the clinic progressed, these attacks grew fewer and fewer.

This child was too young to carry out much in the way of constructive phantasy, and the urgency of her emotion was too great to allow of the formation of any elaboration of phantasy.

Her mouth sensations were intense:

> 30.9.29. Susie left her mother fairly early, sucking her thumb vigorously, absorbed in this and paid little attention to coloured blocks. Worker drew her hands down gently. She did not resist, but went on sucking her lips. Intense absorption, to point of trembling, in this sensation. Ran hands over lips, which she extended as if sucking an orange.
>
> 4.11.29. Didn't want to play at anything. Kept amused a little time with sucking toffee, showing it in her mouth and letting water dribble out.

Also her dislike of dirt.

She was apt to use obscene names for the workers.

Withal she was a delightful child, small and well-made, with periwinkle blue eyes, and a face of remarkable intelligence. For the whole of the first part of her attendance, this was entirely spoiled by her expression, which showed a degree of malignity very strange for a small child. Her mouth was always shut in a hard line and, for the greater part of the time, fists tightly clenched.

Water play occurred, but was usually associated with the lavatory, or with watering a garden.

> 18.11.29. A little toy lavatory was produced, complete with plug. On seeing it, she seemed to be a little anxious and said, 'What's that?' She was asked what she thought it was, and replied, 'It's a pail?' We said, 'Is it?' Then with considerable joy she said, 'It's a lavatory,' and began filling the cistern. When she had made it flush over once or twice she asked me particularly to fill the pan and hold it up so that the water could run out on to the tray, 'So that I can water my garden.'
>
> 21.11.29. Went to lavatory with her mother and returned to play with toy lavatory. Filled cistern gingerly and put little girl doll on seat, and looked to see if plug water had wetted doll's bottom after she had pulled plug.

No pleasure in just pouring, as occurs in the enuresis children, and which would have been normal for her age.

Behaviour at school improved first (about 10 October 1929), but behaviour at home was exceptionally bad. She had on one weekend torn up paper with the parents' consent until they could bear it no longer, and then screamed to excess.

About this time interest in colours and in paint appeared:

> 17.10.29. Desired to paint. Wanted lots of water, poured it deliberately over all the paints; preferred red to all other colours, painted daubs of red over figures in advertisement book, over sheets of plain paper and finally painted her left hand red, carefully and with interest. Evident horror fascination for the colour. When her hand was thoroughly red, she called it dirty. Worker asked if blue paint was dirty too. Susie (daubing in blue), 'Yes, very dirty.' She then discovered brown, and daubed it on her hands. Evident horror. She repeated, 'Dirty, dirty, dirty.' Soon went to wash her hands, came back and continued painting but kept hands clean. Seems to get sensational pleasure in cleaning up red paint spilt on table and floor.

Some weeks later it became clear that we had arrived at a standstill. Susie's power of concentration, which had been steadily improving, had begun to wane, anxiety attacks to become more frequent, and I took her myself for three interviews. Owing to the difficulty of separating her from her mother, Mrs Appleyard was allowed to be present at these, but instructed to remain entirely neutral, which instructions she faithfully carried out. Susie and I then faced each other.

It is difficult to give an impression of the delicacy of touch with which work of this kind must be carried on. Anxiety in a child is a very acute experience, and capable of exceeding any suffering of the body. I am continually being impressed with the extraordinary courage of children, and the astonishing way they will face and attempt to deal with their own anxieties. To be able to succeed with a child of this kind, it is necessary at all times to sense fairly accurately the wax and wane of anxiety and to deal with it accordingly.

Susie was at first placid and then terrified at finding herself alone with me. We played grotesques and water games for a while, then she started throwing down towers erected on the floor. Security was what she was so acutely needing, but at a level which would touch her real anxiety, and up to this date that level had not been accessible. Gradually it began to appear. At this point the attitude of the worker is of central importance. The slightest feeling in oneself of fear or of anxiety, irritation or annoyance, impatience or lack of kindliness, and the frail bridge is broken, the child is alone with its anxiety once more. In this case the bridge did not break down, and slowly in this atmosphere of protection a very orgy of destruction overcame Susie. I assembled material systematically, and with as little variation as possible, and presented her interminably with the same row of scarlet bricks poised on a blue board. These she hurled to the floor.

After twenty to twenty-five minutes of concentrated annihilation, she burst into tears – real tears this time of simple weariness and affection, and climbed on to her mother's lap and hid her face in her shoulder. Our task was more or less done, and although there was, by the conditions of treatment, necessarily no outgoing of affection between Susie and myself, we felt as we left the room that we understood one another.

Progress from here was rapid. In the play room aggression ceased altogether: at home, the arrangement we had just completed for Susie's removal to a Babies' Hospital, to give her parents a rest, was refused, because 'Daddy was so pleased with Susie he would not let her go from him'. Her relation to her small brother entirely changed. The centre of interest shifted, from aggression, to what Susie was and was not a big enough girl to do. At her own request she was allowed to bring her small brother into the play room, and played with him sympathetically.

Early in December the class mistress states that the limelight tendency has almost faded away. Susie is friendly, more peaceful, obedient, and child-like.

The end of January and February 1930 was occupied with measles. Susie attended only once in March, when her mother remarked that she had become more like a normal child.

In the meantime another child had appeared – this time a sister – and on 13.10.30 the following report was made.

> Susie was behaving very well indeed. There were no outbursts of temper, and Susie was amenable and very easily handled. The same story is told at school. There they had found the child had a passion for writing. She was given every opportunity for this both at home and at school. The mother could report nothing abnormal. The child appeared to be making a very good adjustment.

The expression on Susie's face changed, and the hardness went out of it: in its place an extraordinarily lovable little girl appeared. She attended once to report in October 1930, and was so changed as not to be recognized by some of the workers who had known her well before. But her sense of guilt is still strong, and I regret that we have had no opportunity to do more for her.

It is often held that the unconscious symbolism demonstrated by psychoanalysis arises from the conviction of the analyst. That may be so, but it is a very curious and striking fact to find the same symbols as are said to appear constantly in dreams and phantasies occurring regularly and spontaneously in children as widely different as ours, and under circumstances where so little of the psychoanalytical situation exists.

It is impossible in so small a compass, and where selection has had to be made out of so large a mass of material, to give any idea of the wealth of phantasy, both acted and in speech, that these children produce, but I hope later on to be able to make a collection of symbols which constantly recur, to estimate their frequency of appearance, and the mental conditions with which they correlate. For the present, one has only the impression that the material produced does bear striking resemblance to that with which one is familiar in the symbolism of dreams and the unconscious phantasies of adults.

It would seem irrational on the face of it that play in a pleasant room could have any effect at all upon so deep-seated a trouble as a character defect, or touch in any way a condition such as epilepsy. What then is the mechanism at work in these cases? The reply is not easy, and I think it can only be found in the nature of childhood itself.

It is a commonplace of adult analysis that relief only takes place through emotional realization, or the conscious and comprehending re-living by the patient of the experiences that lie at the root of his neurosis. It is the combination of repetitive experience with understanding of experience which is the lever of cure.

In our children rarely, and that only in the dissociated or uncoordinated group of cases, is any attempt made to give the children comprehension of what they are experiencing. With others, as for instance, with Susie and Grace, no explanation is given and yet relief takes place. This is not what one would expect, and therefore some mechanism other than that usually accepted must be at work.

The clue to this strange state of affairs to me lies in certain characteristics of childhood. The emotions of a child are intense and overwhelming, the possibilities of expression open to him very poor. The child is terrified by the furies he feels rising within him, frightened of his own aggression, cramped by the impossibility of the expression of his love life, confused by his own ignorance of his own phantasies. He stands in an impossible situation. Parental prohibition has led him by introjection to condemn large pieces of himself, but these pieces do not die, they remain active within him. Parental or educational limitation on the other side too often give only scant material and opportunity for expression of the good powers he feels surging within him. Lack of understanding, of knowledge of life, make it exceedingly difficult for him to find satisfactory substitutes for pleasures he has progressively to relinquish; a chance cold or vitamin deficiency lowers his vitality and makes him tired and out of sorts and unable to deal with life. The total conflict is too severe and a neurosis is the result.

But the major part of these factors are temporary; the child grows all the time, he becomes able to do a great many things he cannot do now, to become capable of adjustments far beyond any that are within his reach earlier, to have knowledge and understanding that he cannot at present imagine.

What I would suggest is, that in this way of working I have described, we first lessen his anxiety by the provision of security – that security being given by our acceptance of everything he produced, and our lack of reaction to it; second, we draw off some of the excess of emotional energy which has become dammed up behind the neurosis, by giving it outlet in symbolic play, leaving only such a charge as can be dealt with in the natural process of growth. Third, we give him a framework of stability that reinforces the child's own struggles to achieve interior stability, and reassure him as to the non-reality of his own aggressive impulses.

But here one doubt arises. What *is* cure, and have we really cured our child when its symptoms are removed? With an adult this problem is not so difficult. Even if we do not succeed in fundamentally freeing him, when we remove a symptom, it is only very rarely that we do him any *harm*. But with a child the issue is not so simple. It is quite definitely possible that the disappearance of a symptom may be brought about by the operation of forces which will mean a limitation of possibilities of growth for that child in afterlife. Truancy, stammering, a nervous tic, may be evidence of a refusal of the best part of the child to submit to the machinery of circumstance. Disappearance of the symptom can be brought about as much by a deeper repression as by a resolution of the conflict that lies behind it. How are we to know which has happened?

Susie, for instance, stopped screaming, she became adjusted to her school conditions and to her home, but her face wears a wistful expression; the source of her anxieties about Charlie was not found, nor the deeper roots of her distress. By what wisdom can we know whether we have really helped this child, judging from the standpoint of her afterlife? Or whether we have so reinforced the socialized part of her as to repress her anti-social impulses beyond the levels to which possible expression can at present be given in symptoms, only to find at adolescence or later life she pays the price of this added repression in depression or neurasthenia?

This is not a bogy that I am raising in order to be depressing, but a very real and acute problem that I feel should be faced. The child who is neurotic, whether his trouble be asthma or delinquency, is a part of a necessary contest – child versus the social order. In which side of this contest are we most interested? It has been said by Ernest Jones that

> neurosis is an expression of the same forces and conflicts that have led to the loftiest aspirations and profoundest achievements of our race, and that neurotics are often the torch-bearers of civilization,

and this I feel to be true.

To take away a child's suffering by making him good can very often be achieved by superficial means, but when we do so are we doing the best for ourselves and him? We stand at a stage in the world's history when the moulds in which society is cast are wearing thin. The pressure of the machine is upon all of us. Social experiments in this and other countries are continually reminding us how little it is possible to forecast the kind of society our children will grow up to share.

Neurosis developing in the child means that he and social life are not fitting well together. The fault may be on either side.

I am in most profound disagreement with Dr Adler in his conception of the neurotic as lacking in courage. The qualities in a child that prevent him from fitting into the forms of society he knows are frequently precisely the qualities that, once realized and controlled, may ultimately enable him to do his part in the re-creation of social forms.

What we hear called for on all sides today is creative ability and individuality. What we need is not a greater power to conform but a greater power to re-create our society; and what we are attempting to do in this approach that I have tried to put before you is to set these individual children free and in touch with their whole personality, so that they may find their way to full and voluntary service of the best ends of society; not necessarily by repetition of the character of their parentage, but by finding their way to new values undreamed of by their parents and which will be fit vehicles for the new life they find welling up within them.

I have a profound belief in the neurotic child; well handled, I believe he is excellent material for the well-being of the next generation.

Psychogenic Factors in Chronic Disease in Childhood [1934]

Consideration of the attitude of mankind towards disease and physical suffering shows the existence of two streams of thought. In early days religion and, in savage peoples, the witch doctor regarded disease as the punishment of sin, and the measures taken to combat it were measures concerned with the spiritual condition of the sufferer. Parallel with this conception, common usage and the outlook of the barber surgeon interpreted illness as the logical result of mistakes in diet and in the hygiene of living.

The great development of physical science which has taken place during the past century has given rise to a formulation of medicine as the observation and mastery of physical law in its relation to human physique. The researches of Harvey, the work of Lister, Pasteur or of MacKenzie have presented the physician with a defined series of observable facts and provided a training in the observation of fact out of which the science of modern experimental and clinical medicine has grown. It would at first appear that we have here the whole of the situation as regards present-day man's attitude to disease, but the existence of Lourdes, the work of Charcot, of Janet and of the faith healers maintain a tradition of interest in the possibility, at any rate, of the mind and emotions of the patient as a causative factor in disease. The fact that the study of insanity and of mental defect comes among the subjects proper to the curriculum of the student of medicine has kept the door permanently open in orthodox medicine for ultimate inclusion within its province of the study of mental and emotional processes of other than insane and defective persons. Moreover, the stress that has come to be laid recently upon the Binet–Simon and other similar tests for intellectual gradation, and the success that has attended their use, has made more possible the idea of a relevance between the study of normal psychology and medicine.

During the past fifty years attention in adult medicine has increasingly been drawn to the interaction of emotional and bodily conditions, and this is now very generally admitted. But in the regions of children's disease this is not yet the case. The absence of any instrument for the intelligent estimation of the emotional situation of the child, and the impossibility of cross-questioning the infant, is in part probably responsible for this state of affairs, and has resulted in heavy emphasis being laid in all considerations of children's disease upon the objective factor. Particularly is this true of organized medicine as it is applied to paediatrics; see the proceedings of the third International Paediatric Congress held in London in 1933 whose transactions have just been published. It will be noted, for example, that although 'Diastolization for nasal blockage' and a consideration of apples in diet occur as separate entries in the subject index, there is no mention of any theme even remotely suggestive of the study of emotional disturbance in childhood. Children's medicine, which has made surprising strides during the past half century, has become a subject in which full use is made of the armoury of methods of physical investigation that have arisen during the last century, but among this armoury as it is at present conceived, and with the single exception of Dr Winnicott's book, no place exists for psychological considerations (Winnicott, 1931).

It would seem absurd to suggest, in the larger number of cases of acute disease in infancy, that anything in the nature of emotional considerations could have the smallest bearing upon the case. The age of the patient, the acuteness and complexity of the disease, the small margin of life, and the only too frequent obscurity of the aetiological factors, render it in the highest degree unlikely at the first glance, if not actually grotesque, that these diseases, their course, their prognosis or their cure could be in any degree influenced by such intangible subtleties as the emotional or psychological condition of the child. Nevertheless in certain groups of phenomena such as asthma, the epilepsies, eczemas, failure in eating, in defaecating and in gaining control of the bladder, the existence of an emotional factor has long been admitted. Kinnier Wilson in his study of the epilepsies, and O'Donovan and many others in work upon skin diseases, now freely admit that some connection exists between the conditions that they are studying and the emotions of the patient, and that without some consideration of the emotional factor, the physical condition cannot be understood. It is an extension of this point of view that I now wish to put before you.

In 1915 and again in 1929 it was argued by Cannon that strong and primary emotions are accompanied in the body by general physiological changes (Cannon, 1915). He states for example that in one experiment four out of nine medical students, all normally without sugar in their urine, had glycosuria after a hard examination, while only one had glycosuria after an easier examination. Furthermore that in an examination of twenty-five members of a football squad immediately after a final and very exciting contest, sugar was found in twelve cases, five of whom were substitutes who had not been called upon to play. A similar study was made upon second-year students at a women's college, with analogous results. In another section of his work he demonstrates the pouring into the bloodstream, with all the far-reaching effects that such an output would cause, of an increased amount of secretion from the adrenal bodies during strong emotion. He presents data showing that such stimulation as in the unanaesthetised animal would cause pain, and also such emotions as fear and rage are capable of greatly shortening the coagulation time of blood; and shows that after emotions such as fear and rage the erythrocyte count in the blood increases. Not only can changes of this kind be scientifically demonstrated, but even very low types of savage in the presence of a stranger with whose language they are entirely unfamiliar are able by observation to tell an angry man from a peaceful one, a hostile from a friendly visitor. That is to say that there are definite and regular physical changes of no insignificant kind that can be relied upon to show themselves as the concomitant of well-defined emotional states in all individuals under suitable stimuli. Very little attention is paid, particularly within the realm of medicine, to these facts, yet the common intercourse of mankind is conducted upon the basis of this common knowledge and assumption. Whether we know it or not, it is implicitly agreed by everyone in the common conduct of their everyday life that the muscles of the face, the colour, shape and behaviour of the eye, general tone of the body muscles, the colour of the skin, take a characteristic and changing stamp from the emotions passing through the individual owning them.

If this fact be carefully considered and the physiological paths by which such a change can be brought about be taken into account, such as for example the inhibition of the salivary glands in fear, the contraction and expansion of the terminal blood-vessels in rage, fear or modesty, it will not seem to be altogether so far-fetched a proposition that there should be a very intimate and widespread connection between mental phenomena, such as emotions may be considered to be, and the actual physical or physiological behaviour of the body tissues. If to this line of observation we now add those facts which can be observed and used in connection with the action of the endocrine secretions, the association of lethargy and anxiety with hypothyroidism or insufficiency of adrenal secretion, the excitablity of hyperthyroidism and the sexual disturbances of progeria or of Fröhlich's syndrome, the ground will be prepared for at least a consideration of the possible interaction of physical and emotional states at all ages.

Where adult medicine is concerned means have already been found for investigating the emotional circumstances and tendencies of the patient. In children it would appear that such investigation would be impossible, and, in the series of cases which I wish to set before you, a method of examination of the emotional situation and tendencies of the patient has been undertaken which it is outside the scope of this paper to describe. Certain indications will be given in the course of the cases themselves, but any full description, dependent as it is upon consideration of the nature of the emotional life of the child and of the theories of play upon which this treatment is based, is impossible in the present paper. The cases I wish to submit are cases of children treated at the Institute of Child Psychology and taken from the notes made on the child during the course of treatment.

Richard and Joyce Harris were referred to the Institute of Child Psychology in September (1929) by the School Care Committee. Richard was stated to suffer from nervousness, trembling of the hands, and 'getting dull'. Joyce for night terrors. Richard was ten and Joyce eight and both were the children of a respectable young widow of thirty-two.

The history behind the complaints was as follows: Mr and Mrs Harris had married in 1912 and Mr Harris died in 1923. There was one other child of the marriage, Mary, now twelve years old. The following history of the parents was obtained from Mrs Harris.

Mr Harris was British and had been brought up by an aunt. Went to work early and became a coal carman, an exceptionally fit and strongly-built man. He early married a widow with one child Ted, and his wife died soon after. About three years later he married Mrs Harris. He was two and a half years in the army during the war and attained the rank of lance-corporal and during the last part of this time began to complain that his legs felt numb as if wrapped in puttees. After a time he went to see his panel doctor, who arranged for him to be admitted to the infirmary. Here he remained one year and a diagnosis was made of locomotive ataxis resulting from congenital syphilis although a negative result was obtained from a Wassermann. Richard was at this time one year old. After a year Mr Harris discharged himself to go home and two years later in 1923 he was taken ill with pneumonia and died in hospital one week later.

Mrs Harris was British and the eldest of a family of ten of whom all were living. She had a hard childhood and owing to the economic straits of her parents was brought up largely by the grandmother, a woman of stern and puritan views. She married very young and took over the care of her husband's stepson and was happy with her husband. Four years after he died she had unpremeditatedly an illegitimate child with a man she did not see again, this being her one lapse from chastity – this child subsequently died at three years old, of pneumonia. The family have always been very poor and at the time of the children's arrival at the institute their economic circumstances were distressingly bad. Of the three children of the marriage, Mary was a healthy, well-grown, thick-set child, with a round face, bright eyes and a brisk and capable manner. She is sturdy in health and nerves and maintains a reasonably good position at school.

Of Richard's early life we obtained the following account: During the pregnancy Mrs Harris had vomited persistently and suffered from faintness. Richard was jaundiced at birth, development was normal and except for bad sleeping there was nothing to note for the first four years. At this date he fell down the area steps and cut his head badly enough to carry a permanent scar but does not seem to have suffered from concussion. At five he was admitted to St Mary Abbot's Hospital with pains in the abdomen, hips and legs which seem to have been accompanied by a pseudo-paralysis. A dog had shortly before given him a severe fright and the doctor thought that the condition was associated with this. He was sent away for convalescence and made a complete recovery.

He had chicken-pox at two and a half, whooping cough at three and measles and pneumonia at three and a quarter. It was difficult to get a history of the onset of the tremor, his mother only being able to state that it had steadily been getting worse; he is said never to have had a sense of balance. His hands fumble badly first thing in the morning and improve later, chiefly noticeable when handling small objects. He had steadily been growing duller at school.

Joyce was also jaundiced at birth; there was nothing to note during the mother's pregnancy and labour was spontaneous. She had diarrhoea and bronchitis while teething; whooping cough at one and German measles at seven. Was subject to tonsillitis. Went to school at four and a half and did very well. Night terrors began at seven and a half, two–three times weekly between 11 p.m. and 5 a.m. and had grown steadily worse. She had a tendency to fall to the right side and during the first few weeks of her attendance had a permanent bruise on her right temple. She was a round faced little girl with very bright coloured deep-set eyes and a determined chin. She was a cheerful child, always happy and smiling, intelligent and painstaking, devoted to Richard and they played well together. She is finicky over food but otherwise quite ordinary and normal in behaviour.

When Richard was examined large pustules were discovered on either buttock and ankle jerks were doubtful, otherwise nothing definite was discovered. The tremor was indistinct and variable and followed no rule.

In Joyce the knee jerks were not elicited, her skin was found to be rough, elasticity diminished and much fine hair over the whole body; no pathological signs were found to suggest a cause for her condition. Both children appeared highly nervous. Both were duly admitted to the play room of the institute for observation. During work in the rhythm room the rhythm mistress drew attention to the peculiarity of the gait of both children in that both appeared to walk as if the soles of their shoes were too thick and showed a curious rubbing movement with each foot.

It was decided that both children should be referred to the consulting neurologist to the institute. His report was that both children showed some degree of incoordination to special tests and light ankle jerks and concluded that the condition was undoubtedly organic indicating early and slight degeneration of the posterior columns and direct cerebellar tracts of the spinal cord. Blood was taken from all three children and the mother and the elder girl examined; she was found to be quite normal. An examination was also instituted into the exact nature of the father's condition. The Wassermann reaction of all members of the family was negative, and re-examination of the father's hospital history suggested Friedreich's ataxia, and this appeared to confirm the original diagnosis made for the children of early heredito-familial ataxia.

From 23.9.29 to 7.4.30 Joyce attended the institute, coming twice a week for two hours, Richard from 21.10.29 to November 1933. Joyce showed herself quick and intelligent, interested in her work and particularly in colours and shapes. She was very neat and tidy, totally lacking in initiative and very suggestible. When the other children became rather boisterous she was wide-eyed with astonishment that such behaviour should be allowed and did not join in. On 14.10.29, her fifth attendance, a change showed; she became slightly destructive and made a mocking grown-up figure, enjoying the absurdity of it very much, and gradually began to loosen out, and by 7.11.29 we had definite evidence of quantities of pent-up emotion connected with her brother. She would turn to him compulsively whenever he was in the room and seemed to have a constant guilty feeling in connection with him, and would suddenly take to beating a doll with persistence and vindictiveness. Richard on the other hand had a more obscure reaction to Joyce; although apparently devoted it was noted by all workers that on all occasions when the possibility occurred he threw blame for any small contretemps on Joyce. Much violent emotion began to come up in the play room. About this time Mrs Harris reported great improvement, no screaming attack for three–four weeks, sleeping well except for talking and giggling in her sleep.

Richard was then sent away to a convalescent home and we had Joyce alone and her general behaviour began to change. She became very rowdy, knocking things about and making much noise, became very boisterous, wanting to play and romp all the time and showing a marked lack of any kind of concentrated attention. It was found also that at school she was working beyond her powers and talked and muttered of her work in her sleep. 27 January 1930 she said she wished she was a boy and could go and fight, and by March we had the picture clear. On one side of her she was good, obedient, timorous, inert, but when this gave at all she became boisterous, destructive and unmanageable. About this time their dilapidated, noisy and verminous rooms were exchanged for a flat in one of the new flat dwellings. It was noted on 14.2.30 that falling was very much improved both at home, at dancing, and at school. The night terrors, which had already greatly diminished in force and frequency before the family's removal, ceased altogether after they settled into their new flat, no new falls were reported and as Joyce seemed in every way normal, in the middle of April 1930, six months after her referral to the institute, she was discharged to come again in six months and report.

Richard in the meanwhile had been away from home and returned in March 1930. In the play room a number of curious characteristics appeared in this boy; he was fascinated by water and sticky clay, developed a ritual of repeated movements, talked with great affect at odd intervals of religion and seemed to be suffering from some deep-seated emotional disturbance. His mother clearly adored him to the detriment of his sister, and he seemed to be out to grasp everything he could and to turn it to his own advantage. It seemed possible that the tie between him and his sister was as much the fascination of hate as love. His absence away from home and the family move did much towards mollifying this tie. When he came back he drew violent pictures of the devil which he turned into a dragon and showed obscure signs of interior struggle. His tremor had disappeared on his return, and as his general condition was good, it was not possible to keep him any longer.

In November 1930 both children were examined by Dr Leonard Findlay and were found to be absolutely normal; this finding was confirmed on 23.10.33 by the neurologist who first saw them. The final report runs:

'Richard in the first place now shows that his knee-jerks (formerly not elicited) are quite definitely present, especially on reinforcement. Further, in 1929 his arm-jerks were not elicited, but they are now quite definitely present; further, his co-ordination, previously defective, is now comparatively normal.

'As regards Joyce, the only abnormalities noted in 1929 were absent ankle-jerks and some degree of inco-ordination. Her ankle-jerks, though still very sluggish, can now be obtained. There is no definite abnormality of co-ordination.'

Both children were therefore discharged and up to the date of writing have remained well.

Arthur Marsh was referred to the institute by a physician from a London chest hospital on 16.1.33 for eczema which had lasted since birth and asthma of more recent origin. Arthur was a boy of twelve and brought to the institute by his mother. His history was as follows:

He was the middle of three boys of a moderately well-to-do artisan family, and according to his mother's account had suffered from eczema since birth. He was born in hospital and his mother states that when she took the baby home the inside of both heels were raw where they had been rubbed and that his buttocks were also raw. When three weeks old there was a skin outbreak in front of both ears which continued for several months. He attended hospital for this and it ultimately cleared up. He walked at thirteen months and shortly after this eczema started behind the knees and he was taken to the doctor. At eighteen months as he was no better he went to hospital for treatment for his skin but once again without result. A private doctor took an interest in him and for two years took a very great deal of trouble over his treatment, doing for him everything that he could think of. During these years for a period of three weeks after his whole body had been covered in ointment and bandages for some considerable time the eczema disappeared, but at the end of three weeks it reappeared as badly as ever. Throughout the period between this date and that of his referral to the institute he was under constant treatment from hospitals and private doctors but with no appreciable result.

When he appeared at the institute he was a tall well-grown boy with bright eyes and a good colour, red nose and ears, good physique, pleasant appearance and good teeth. The whole of his skin was dry and thick with patches of eczema on the hands and the popliteal spaces. The knees were bandaged and the question of their bandaging and her hopeless attempt to prevent the boy scratching the skin occupied the whole forefront of his mother's mind in regard to him. The asthma was of more recent date. It had appeared first when he went to the seaside on a school journey in 1931 and at rare intervals since; the attacks were apparently associated either with the seaside or with a boy friend who had been with him when the first attack broke out. The parents were very confused about these attacks and constantly contradicted one another. In addition to these there were other symptoms of an undue sensitiveness of constitution; he had diarrhoea or else a bout of loose stools whenever emotionally upset, he fainted on the slightest provocation such as the sight of any obnoxious object or being in impure atmosphere. His sleep was poor and at one time his restlessness was so bad that his parents had hardly more than three hours' sleep at night owing to the constant need to go into his room and pacify him. In character he was a somewhat morose child with a tendency to break out into violent attacks of irritability. The Binet–Simon test gave his IQ as 97.

His family history yielded the following facts: the paternal great-grandfather had been a severe drunkard; the paternal great-grandmother had had eczema for twenty-five years; a great uncle had had hay fever for many years and among the other uncles and aunts there was acute rheumatism and also a fatal case of tuberculosis. The father was healthy, slightly rheumatic and in his youth had been a great athlete; on the mother's side the great-aunt had had eczema, another aunt migraine; one great-cousin had been tubercular and an aunt was very nervous. The social situation was good, the home was comfortable and clean and reasonably large. The economic situation was adequate. The emotional atmosphere of the home was good; the father was kind, easygoing and jolly, but with somewhat set views about the children. The mother kept herself very much to herself, mixed very little with her neighbours and concentrated all her attention upon the family situation; her main interest is needlework.

Of the children, the elder boy, Harold, aged thirteen, was a thorough success, a jolly, friendly boy, clever at school, quick to make friends and liked by everyone. Bertie, the third child, aged seven, is also a success, a cheerful, jolly little boy, not as good at school as Harold, but popular and contented. Arthur got on reasonably well with Bertie, but quarrelled perpetually with Harold, and hours are needed after each quarrel to quieten him. At school, Arthur was unexceptional.

On his first appearance at the institute, Arthur was a very quiet and polite, well-mannered boy. It was noteworthy that when asked for an account of his asthma or for particulars of his eczema, he began always with the words, 'Mum says . . .' and then would follow an account of his mother's opinion

concerning the situation. He was quite incapable of giving an account of his own troubles on his own initiative.
Conversation with his mother revealed that she was at the end of her patience with the boy, and that the condition of his skin had been for some time an obsession with her. She stated that she got on well with the other two boys but that Arthur exasperated her beyond bearing, and that she could see no reason for his quarrelsomeness and general tiresomeness. The general method of the institute was then explained to her and she promised all the co-operation of which she was capable.

Work began in the play room, Arthur being asked what sort of things he most liked to do. The answer was Meccano, and later careful drawing of ships with a ruler. During these occupations his manner was meticulously polite, he spoke little, always said please and thank you and was courteous to all the grown-up people; the other children he hardly seemed to notice. About the end of three weeks he was invited to join a group of other children who were playing charades and quite suddenly an astounding change came over the boy. As soon as the smallest part was given him or he was asked to take a share in any group physical movement he lost all control of himself, began to make peculiar noises more like an animal than a human, to throw himself about and to become entirely unmanageable. At this time his imaginative work was exceedingly poor, he gave the impression of being unable to do anything spontaneously. Outside the institute his favourite occupation was cycling, which he preferred to do alone. There was always a reason why he could not do anything that would bring him in contact with other people. Inside the institute the same general attitude manifested itself: he could not play with sand, it would hurt his fingers, he couldn't do something else because he wasn't good at it. He was difficult to please and hard to move away from Meccano. It was found very difficult to reassure him concerning the institute and the very small physical treatment (monthly injections of old tuberculin carried on from his favourite hospital) being given him. After some time more imaginative work began to appear. About this time a new type of drawing appeared, very free, done in single heavy colours, usually of grotesque or obscene figures, the drawing of the figure accompanied by coarse bursts of laughter. In this mood it was impossible to allow him to mix with the other children as he became so coarse and boisterous. It was necessary to restrict his play with them to very short periods of time.

We then had by the end of his second month's attendance a record of an almost complete double-type of behaviour. On the one hand a quiet, well-behaved, well-mannered boy, speaking in a low voice, behaving politely and doing meticulous work of a stereotyped kind. On the other side almost an animal creature, full of primitive interest, coarse laughter, rowdy behaviour and an uncontrollable excitement in company. When sufficient material had accumulated with regard to this contrast to make the situation clear its existence was pointed out to Arthur. He was very much astonished but after a time he accepted the truth of this statement. At the same time the eczema began to improve and his mother reported that he was very much easier to get on with at home. His imaginative work developed and was of an extraordinarily fantastic nature: jungles where snakes are frightened by a man with a big nose and enormous ears; where hippopotamuses rise through the air and make a noise like an aeroplane, where possible and impossible objects are mixed and the boy seems unaware of their inappropriateness. As his freedom in developing these phantasies increased his shyness began to go. The anxiety over the physical side of his treatment diminished and finally it was possible to stop it altogether. About this time (fourth to fifth month of treatment) it became possible to get the following additional history from the mother: (1) The earliest outbreak on his skin, at three weeks, had not been irritating. It seems very unlikely that this was eczema, as the main characteristic of the later condition was its extreme irritation. (2) As an infant he had been an eager sucker with an enormous appetite and for the whole of his infancy a good sleeper. It was when he began to run about and come into active competition with his brother that the eczema began. The elder boy was adored by his mother and had never given trouble. Arthur had nocturnal enuresis until four, and having found that calling out to his parents when his eczema first began to irritate him at night brought them in to him and gave him control of the situation, he increased this to such a point that he had to be taken away by an aunt periodically, in order for his mother to have a night's rest. It seemed pretty clear that the eczema was related to the emotional situation within the family.

By the seventh month after beginning of treatment, the eczema had entirely disappeared and the boy had become practically normal in behaviour, both at the institute and at home. During the summer holidays, Arthur went to a summer camp of boys of better social status than himself and had felt acutely inferior. The eczema returned and he had an attack of asthma, but of short duration, the emotional origin of which he was himself able to see. Again, the double-sidedness of his nature reappeared and it was possible to point this out to the boy, and for him to accept it. By the ninth month the eczema had entirely cleared up and the boy's behaviour was normal; this continued until after Christmas, when it was decided to wean him from the institute. At this time an outbreak of scabies occurred on his hands with a recurrence of the anxiety concerning treatment on the part of his mother. The Easter holiday supervened and he returned to the institute with a recurrence of eczema. A refusal to accept this on the physical basis induced an examination into the psychological situation and revealed a hidden state of exasperation over recent incidents at school which he had not allowed himself to express. A thorough working through of his feelings concerning the situation and a readjustment of his hobbies and other outlets has been followed by a disappearance of the eczema, and the boy feels confident that in future he will be able to control the condition. He is now anticipating his discharge to work from school on reaching the age of fourteen and is a cheerful and normal boy of average temperament and behaviour.

No medicinal treatment was used after the termination of the injections at the end of the fifth month at the Institute.

Bessie King was a little girl of five and a quarter who was referred to the Institute of Child Psychology in the spring of 1930 for persistent wetting of herself both day and night. Born in December 1924, she had had measles at one year, chicken-pox at one and a quarter years, whooping cough at one and a half years, gastric influenza at one year ten months; mumps at three years, German measles at four years, influenza at four years; and in between had had bronchitis. Her wetting of herself had persisted since birth. In appearance she was of normal height but markedly underweight and with dark rings under her eyes and an appearance of constant strain. Her voice was so low as hardly to be audible at all, and when in company with other ordinarily noisy children she would make no move at all. Careful medical examination of the child revealed no organic disease but hypotension everywhere, marked lack of vitality at every point and hypoplasia of the teeth. The mother was an anaemic, excessively depressed individual, and the economic position such as made any radical alteration of her general hygiene and environment impossible. She was therefore as hard a case as we could put to ourselves for the study of this kind of condition. The study of the family history revealed that the maternal grandfather had died of a stroke in 1921, and the maternal grandmother was alive and working but chronically ill with heart disease, this with gallstone trouble making her nervy and irritable. She lived with the Kings. Of the paternal grandfather little was known, the paternal grandmother had died of tuberculosis in 1916. The father had a poor physical heredity, and himself suffered from a persistent cough (the result of a cold caught on war service) for which he refused advice or help. When finally persuaded to consult a doctor he was found to be tubercular and sent to a convalescent home for three months. He then felt better and insisted on coming home against orders (this at about the time of Bessie's birth), and five months later had a relapse and died. Before this Mrs King had lost her father and her second child (a boy) at ten months of TB meningitis. There were two other children, both older than Bessie, and both boys. The home was poor but very clean. They occupied two rooms at the back on the ground floor, and the grandmother lived upstairs. Though poor and overcrowded, they obviously did all they could to keep the rooms clean, bright and attractive. The atmosphere of the family was good. Bessie was breast-fed for one month, a happy baby who developed normally, was exceptionally clean (except that she had never been successfully trained off napkins), quiet, intelligent and shy, anxious to go to school, but did not do well when there owing to excessive shyness and worry over her bladder trouble; even-tempered and persevering, adoring her elder brother and teased by the younger; had never been to the country or sea or had any contact with animals or younger children.

When she first came to the institute, she was a neat, well-mannered little girl, clean and well-kept, with a soft shy little voice; showing no reaction to anything and taking everything as it came with the same demeanour; easy to manage and settling down wherever she was put. She was quiet, only spoke when spoken to, and seemed afraid of saying the wrong thing; did not seem particularly interested in anything that she did, but seemed to be observing everything. My theory of this child was that the extreme quiet was associated with the lassitude and failure to resist disease, and that release of one would improve the other.

After her first few attendances the institute closed for the Easter holiday, and though her diet was altered as much as possible to benefit her vitamin and calcium deficiency, and a week's rest in bed was given her, after the holidays Mrs King reported that her enuresis was as bad as ever, though she had been better at the end of term. She was still shy and uncommunicative, but found evident pleasure cutting up plasticine, and in June began to co-operate better with other children and to seem less like a baby and do things on her own initiative, and with her change (by request for the first time) to sand and water and making a 'world', she had four dry nights, the longest period of dryness since birth.

It was clear that part of Bessie's difficulties was the absence in any part of her conscious and expressed emotional life of the aggressive tendency which had shown distinct evidence of being present.

She had a relapse following a fright caused by a thunderbolt falling near the home, and diurnal as well as nocturnal enuresis appeared. At the same time questions about birth and babies and the meaning of physical differences began to give themselves form in her play. She became decided in her opinions, determined as to what she wanted, and successful in obtaining it, and began to fend for herself and become aggressive. During August we managed to secure a holiday for the family, and Bessie was dry for some time and much better physically, but enuresis recommenced again before the beginning of the autumn term. Her work now began to change, to show observance and a spirit of mockery and she became freer in movement. Her physical condition showed all-round improvement, and Mrs King reported that she was showing interest in things generally and particularly in books and reading. Her school report in November stated that she had improved a good deal and was becoming more friendly and trusting; at the institute she began to chatter and play easily and to be boisterous, and at the end of December had the first dry week. In the eleventh month of treatment, the energy release reached its peak and the building up of control was begun, and in June 1931 she was a healthy sturdy little

> girl, and resisted successfully several epidemics that were prevalent in her street, but the enuresis partly remained.
>
> I became convinced that this arose out of the deep-seated imaginings that she played with inside herself, and which related themselves to her relationships with the family, and this turned out to be the case. She began to do phantasy work, and to draw, and by working out her two phantasies embodying her need for reassurance, particularly in regard to her fear of men (due to the absence of a father and to another terrifying male who existed in her life) she became conscious of them. The enuresis showed marked improvement, and for a while spasmodic vomiting took its place (this was in November 1931). In March 1932, just two years after admission, the father appeared for the first time in her play, in which at last the maleness began to vanish and 'ladies' to enter into it. At home she was becoming naughty and boisterous. The enuresis returned, further exploration showing its root to be real shrinking from the brothers' teasing; this was dealt with and proved the last obstacle. The mother was given a holiday and came back well and cheerful, and Bessie was discharged from regular attendance. She came back to report a short time later and was friendly and independent and self-confident; her imagination flowed freely from one idea to another, and she chattered confidently.
>
> The last report received last month stated that she remained entirely well, had had no illness at all, no return of bed-wetting, and was getting on well at school.

It will be noted that there are certain common factors in these cases: (1) The very ordinary nature – the Harrises excepted – of the physical complaint involved in each case and its chronicity. (2) The absence of any startling aetiological factors in the heredity of the cases. (3) The fact that these conditions have arisen alongside of and to a certain degree in spite of the use of ordinary, and in some cases even of special, measures for their cure. (4) The fact that they have all responded to treatment along a combined medical and psychological approach, and that this improvement has been maintained.

It now becomes necessary to examine in some detail the probable nature of the curative process which has taken place, and to see what can be deduced from our observations as to the possible relation of psychogenic factors to chronic disease in childhood. There is no easy answer to the question as to the nature of the process that has been at work, and to pretend that I can put before you anything complete or defined is to assume a knowledge that we are very far from possessing. The practice of medicine has always found a marked disproportion between the certainty with which a favourable outcome for any given line of treatment can be deduced, and the accuracy and knowledge of the processes by which improvement is brought about, nor are we here in any different case. The tentative hypotheses that I wish to put before you have been drawn from a fair number of years of experiment with this method, and of comparison and standardization of results gained both in private and in the Institute of Child Psychology, but I can claim only for the theories that I put before you that they are a tentative hypothesis.

In order to put before you this hypothesis, it is necessary to go back a little and to discuss very briefly certain facts concerning the nature of emotion itself as it occurs in childhood. Emotion in childhood has certain peculiar characteristics. Whereas the adult is convinced that the material things of life are real and solid and is apt to give to his emotional experience a second place in the scale of reality, the child feels his emotions as the real world and the only world with which he is familiar, and tends to regard the constantly changing outer world instead as unreal. The emotional life and experiences of children fall into three groups: (1) Direct likes and dislikes, hates and loves. Of these the child himself is aware and gives to the observer direct evidence by word and gesture. (2) Intimate and changing actions and reactions between the child and the members of his family group and those with whom he is brought intimately in contact. Of part of these the child is aware, but much of his emotional life in relation to his most intimate circle is hidden in regions below his personal knowledge of himself. Upon these reactions and interreactions his later relations to society will be built up. (3) Needs and hungers concerning the world around him which are implicit in the child's situation, and of which he is unable to give an account. Their existence needs to be deduced from the general facts and behaviours of child life. Such a need, for example, is the need of the young infant for physical security in early days and emotional security in later life: or its need of reasonable consistency and firmness of handling. No child can state to himself or to any adult that he needs security or dislikes a loud noise, yet recent work shows that absence of loud and sudden noises in infancy and quiet and secure handling are cardinal requisites for development of successful reactions to later life and confidence in it.

Emotion is a universal experience both in mammals and in man, and the life of a child consists in the passing continuously from one emotion to another. An emotion arises in answer to a stimulus which itself comes either from outside, as a sound heard or an object seen; or from within the body or mind, as a hunger, or a thought; an instinct stimulated or a memory aroused. Once aroused, emotion causes in the individual a feeling of tension; tension being unpleasant seeks for itself an appropriate action by which the force inherent in it may be discharged. Once found the tension disappears and the whole being sinks to quiescence again. The stimulus may be strong or weak, and emotion aroused over-powering or so insignificant as hardly to pass the threshold of consciousness; the response of the total personality can be of infinite variety; but the pattern of events is always the same. Let us take for example the simplest form of such a sequence. A gnat bites one, irritation is felt, a quick motor movement and the gnat is eliminated.

In all small children, the paths by which in an adult a charge of emotion can be dispersed, deflected or its direction changed, are not yet formed. Consciousness is rudimentary and dissimulation has hardly come into being. Strong emotion, therefore, when it occurs in childhood has very few lines along which discharge is possible, and the physiological concomitants to emotion, noted by Cannon, have their maximum effect. Indeed, so striking is this fact that all wide-awake observers of childhood have continuously noted that a bout of diarrhoea, vomiting, or a rise of temperature in a small child can be as easily brought about by jealousy or acute disappointment as by the onset of one of the exanthemata. Furthermore, the impact upon a child of adult disapproval cannot be met as it can in later life from within the child by criticism of the disapproval or a reassuring counter-approval of the self. Lack of experience, the small stature and helplessness of the child, the overpowering authority of its elders, suggestibility and fear combine to make the child utterly helpless in the face of condemnation. Such condemnation produces within the child a disproportionate disapproval of the self, or a violent reaction against authority as represented in the disapproving adult; both emotions consistently accompanied, as can be seen in manic and depressive states in the adult, by physiological changes.

Here again a universal psychological law comes into force. It is a common experience of all of us that however much we may ourselves disapprove of appetites or desires that exist strongly within us, or however these may meet with external disapproval, the disapproval, while it may entirely restrain us from outward expression of the desires or hungers in question, is totally incapable of changing or of materially altering the force of the wish itself. Whether in consciousness or unconsciousness this desire persists, and until some way of discharge is found, remains a permanent part of the individual's emotional life. Now, if the wish remains, the emotion connected with it remains also, and by definition, with it the physiological concomitants. On the other hand, so urgent is the child's need for approval and for the reinstating of himself in family life, that all the forces of his nature are ultimately brought into play to bring about in normal children some approximation to the outer conduct desired by authority. By this means the wishes themselves that run counter to the standards prescribed by authority are pushed deep into the unconscious regions of the mind. It is, however, a tenet of all modern dynamic psychology that whether they come to expression or not, such wishes persist in the deeper regions of the mind and exert there a continual and characteristic pressure. It is at least reasonable to assume that the physiological concomitants remain in operation also, and as continuously exert their characteristic pressure. Unless some form of discharge is found, this pressure will continue and will gradually bring about actual changes in the self.

The rationale of all these cases then is the same. The child, faced with a situation which normally arouses strong emotion, finds himself in a situation in which the emotion aroused conflicts with another emotion of equal strength, both seeking expression. Expression to either would involve the annihilation of the other; a satisfactory solution is not possible. The general feeling of the situation becomes that of acute tension and exasperation against life, such an exasperation as might well be expressed by drawing one's nails as it were down the face of life. But the mere concept of such a wish or the idea of such an injury carried out against members of the family to whom he is bound by all the ties of love, habit and affection would immediately call out a condemnation of such a desire. The child, forced to attack someone, behaves as a small child who is seen slapping herself or her doll in imitation of Nanny's condemnation of herself. Prevented from scratching others by his love of those others, the child turns upon the self that harbours such a desire, and inflicts upon it, in detestation of it, just that punishment which one part of the child wishes to inflict upon its surroundings.

It will remain for the biochemistry of the future to explain by what paths the cellular condition of the skin can be so altered by chronic emotional tension and, the inevitable concomitant, chronic physiological stimuli, that an irritative eczema could result. But the fact remains that once the emotional tangle lying behind the eczema, for example, is brought to light, realized and exploded, the eczema dies away, and the child states himself as having come into conscious possession and therefore control of the mechanism which gave rise to it.

Every individual child is only possessed of a certain amount of total energy. Energy which is absorbed in the maintenance of desires which remain unexpressed within the personality is energy withdrawn from normal life. If much of the instinctive and primary emotional energy of the individual be denied expression, a great part of the remainder of the energy of the child is occupied in keeping this insurgent section of the personality under control, and the result is the child with whom we are so familiar, who is limp, bored, open to all infection, unable to be interested for long in anything. Skilful teaching may modify this condition, and alleviate the child's own sense of dryness, but it does not do this any more than temporarily, the fundamental inertia remains. The one thing that can be satisfactory is a removal of this condition, and the restoration to the total conscious economy of the child of that part of the mental energy which has been withdrawn from it by emotional conflict. It is this restoration to the total economy of the personality of energy that has been withdrawn by interior emotional conflict that is the role of psychological medicine in the diseases of childhood.

9 The Need for a New Method in the Treatment of Emotionally Disturbed Children

Despite the financial difficulties of the depression years, in many respects the papers presented in this chapter, and first produced shortly before the outbreak of the Second World War, reflect the ICP in its heyday. But as noted (this volume, pp. 72–4) psychoanalysis with children was also moving forward. So were the tensions in the psychoanalytic movement. From 1933 onwards Melanie Klein was regularly and vehemently attacked within the British Psycho-Analytical Society by her daughter Melitta Schmideberg. There had also been rancour between Melanie Klein and Anna Freud, initially coming to a head over Anna Freud's (1927) first major publication, *Einführung in die Technik der Kinderanalyse*, leading to the attempt to clarify theoretical and technical differences in the Symposium on Child Analysis organized by the British Psycho-Analytical Society later in the same year (Grosskurth, 1986). Working relations proved more difficult rather than easier after the Freuds' arrival in London in 1938, paving the way for the famous 'Controversial Discussions' between 1942 and 1944. This culminated, in 1946, in the establishment of two major groups within the British Psycho-Analytical Society, associated with different theoretical tendencies. Eventually a third group, the 'middle' group, or the 'independents', also evolved (Kohon, 1986).

But in the 1930s rivalry between Klein and Lowenfeld also existed, as is indicated in a brief note published in 1937 in the April edition of the Institute of Child Psychiatry *News Bulletin*. This reported on proceedings of the Child Guidance Inter-Clinic Conference held in January of that year. Apparently a discussion on play was opened by Klein, who gave a paper on the psychoanalytic point of view, claiming that 'only by this method could the different anxieties in the child be modified'. Lowenfeld spoke next and found herself 'unable to accept this point of view and stated briefly that which forms the basis of the approach to the problem by the Institute of Child Psychology' (ICP *News Bulletin*, vol. 1, no. 6, p. 5). Ethel Dukes's editorial in the same issue reported with pleasure that the child guidance clinics' conference approved play therapy and advocated that play therapists should be attached to all teams undertaking the psychological treatment of maladjusted children. At that time, the editorial stressed, the ICP was the only institute offering a training in this profession.

Lowenfeld's report went on to announce the presentation of the first paper in this chapter, 'A Thesis Concerning the Fundamental Structure of the Mento-emotional Processes in Children'. This paper (henceforth 'the Manchester paper') was given in Manchester at the annual meeting of the General Section of the British Psychological Society on 18 April 1937. Though it was never published and its theoretical speculations are clearly incomplete, the paper introduces what was arguably Lowenfeld's most interesting and important theoretical concept: the existence of a primary, non-verbal form of thought, later called the 'protosystem', which cuts across the usual distinctions between unconscious/conscious, emotion and cognition, and phantasy and reality testing, though it shares properties with Freud's 'unconscious' and Klein's 'unconscious phantasy' (see this volume, pp. 94–9).

Lowenfeld's discovery of the protosystem hinged crucially on her methods, the World technique and the use of mosaics, which are visual, plastic and multidimensional. For this reason a large part of this paper, and of the one which follows in this chapter, was concerned with presenting the World technique as a research and therapeutic tool. Lowenfeld began the Manchester paper by setting out a position midway between what were then two dominant traditions within psychology: psychometric research, then gaining momentum through the work of Cyril Burt and others, concerned with plotting conscious faculties and delineating variance amongst normal populations; and the discoveries of those working with so-called emotionally disturbed individuals within the confines of the consulting room. She challenged the latter tradition on the grounds of inaccessibility and dogmatism, adding some obvious critical references to Melanie Klein's work, 'elaborate cannibalistic phantasies in the recently born' (this volume, p. 254). This scepticism may be surprising, given the tentative appreciation expressed earlier, in 'A New Approach to the Problem of Psychoneurosis in Childhood' in 1931 (this volume, p. 177). In the Manchester paper she referred, elliptically, to her failing to make the psychoanalytic approach work for her, but stressed that her aim was not necessarily to dispute the existence of processes described by psychoanalysis. Rather, she was putting forward an approach which would make those processes more generally available to scientific scrutiny. Indeed, the contribution which her own work could make to establishing their validity was all the stronger because she deliberately set out to minimize the effects of factors which psychoanalysis deemed essential, notably the relationship between a patient and a particular therapist with privileged theoretical knowledge, and the fostering of the transference (see Chapter 11).

None the less, it was Lowenfeld's contention (using illustrations of children's Worlds which are unfortunately no longer available) that children's Worlds gave access to a form of pre-verbal thought which falls outside the terrain of psychoanalysis. She introduced her idea of the protosystem by pointing to difficulties in using the distinction *unconscious/ conscious* in referring to young children's thought. Lowenfeld proposed to start with the child rather than referring backwards from the adult, and to replace the emphasis on unconscious/ conscious with a distinction between 'primary' and 'secondary' systems of thought.

Freud (1911), of course, had made a similar distinction between 'primary' and 'secondary' mental processes. As noted previously (this volume, p. 96), it was to avoid confusion that Lowenfeld eventually introduced the term 'protosystem'. Later in the Manchester paper she points to the overlap between her 'secondary system', or the rational, organized mental activity of the older child and adult, and Freud's secondary process, concerned with rational thought and the monitoring of external reality. It is worth noting that the distinction between primary and secondary forms of mental activity actually pre-dates Freud (another well-known use of the distinction is in the secondary signalling system found in the work of the Russian physiologist, Pavlov).

Though at this time Lowenfeld's account of the protosystem was incomplete there were several features which differentiated it from Freud's 'primary process'. In the Manchester paper

Lowenfeld's main aim was to emphasize that, though distinguishable from conscious, rational thought, this pre-verbal mental activity was none the less 'thought'. In consequence, it must be governed by regular, lawful principles, as contemporary psychology was claiming for conscious, cognitive activity. From this viewpoint this system was not, in contrast to Freud's primary process, a system concerned with the regulation of pleasure/unpleasure *per se*. Rather, it was one which demonstrated something more like a primary drive towards pattern, to make links between perceptual and sensory experiences, producing subjective effects which might be aesthetically pleasurable and intensely personal.

To investigate organizing principles underlying this primitive thought, as Lowenfeld noted, you have to start somewhere. For Lowenfeld the starting-point was not Freud but the theoretical writings of the British psychologist, Charles Spearman (1863–1945). Originally a student of Wundt and one of the major figures in British psychology, Spearman was the Grote Professor of Mind and Logic at University College, London University, from 1911 until 1931. In this position he was a successor to Sully and was followed himself by his erstwhile student, Cyril Burt.

Spearman is best known for his work on intelligence testing and, in particular, for the theory of the dominant factor '*g*', or 'general ability', which was presumed to exist in individuals to a varying degree, contributing to measurable differences in intelligence (Spearman, 1923). But Spearman was by no means exclusively a factor analyst. Like many of the pioneer psychologists aiming to put the study of mental processes on a clearer, less mythological footing, he was deeply immersed in philosophy. His intention was to take philosophical arguments, based on introspection and observation, as a starting-point in formulating generalizations about the nature of mind, whether or not these generalizations were amenable to experimentation subsequently.

Thus, in addition to his factor theory, Spearman also proposed subsidiary laws intended to capture regularities in mental functioning. These included an attempt to encompass 'orectic' processes, or such problematic issues as will, desire and emotion (Spearman, 1937). More relevant here are the 'laws of noegenesis', referred to in the two papers which follow, which are concerned with the creation of knowledge, or the means by which the mind creatively organizes, makes connections between sensory experiences, makes comparisons across different fields and creatively perceives relations between them (Spearman, 1937). These ideas require some explication.

Spearman's noegenetic laws were heavily based on the philosophy of Locke and included, first, the law of 'awareness of experience', second, the law of 'eduction of relations' and, third, the law of the 'education of correlates'. The first law refers to the fact that 'a person tends to know himself and items of his own experience', that is, as locatable within the self; the second is expressed in the principle that 'on the presentation of two or more items, a person tends to know relations between them'; while according to the third law 'on the presentation of an item, together with a relation, a person tends to conceive the correlative item' (Spearman, 1937, pp. 125–9).

The processes described in the second law are embodied in the kinds of intelligence-test items of the form '*X* is to *y* as *a* is to . . . ?' where the individual is required to choose the appropriate item from the list. The education of correlates, on the other hand, enables the individual to predict a precise relation. For example:

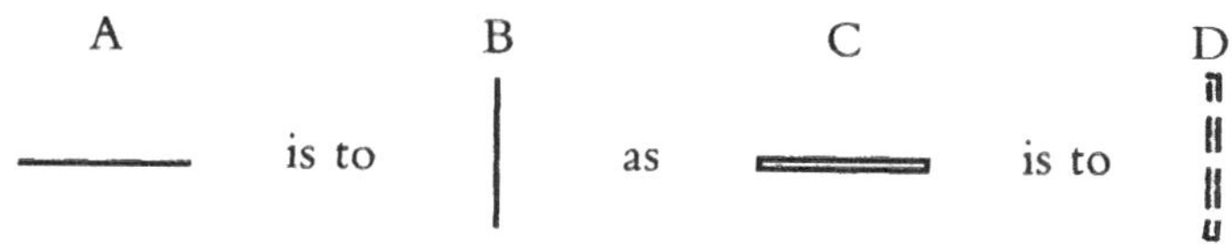

(Spearman, 1937, p. 141)

For Spearman the mental processes embodied in these laws were not encompassed by the association of ideas nor could they be reduced to logic. The emphasis was on the creative aspect of mental functioning, as distinct from blind habit or mechanical reliance on memory. However, knowing relations and the ability to educe correlates would increase with age. This is embodied in the design of intelligence tests. As to how these processes might begin in infancy or early childhood, Spearman situated his position within the then dominant positions of the associationists and the gestalt psychologists. That is, in speculating on whether development proceeds via aggregating elements into wholes (the associationist doctrine), or through differentiating wholes (the gestaltist position and the position of the holistic psychology of Heinz Werner, for example), Spearman proposed that development goes in *both* directions. He added the proviso that initially mental development would be likely to start with complexes, or aggregates of perception and sensory experience, which are differentiated into finer complexes, to be built up again into larger ones. Differentiation would 'act like a lifting of a fog, whereby the spectator sees more and more clearly items as related to one another'. Aggregation, on the other hand, 'resembles more the course of a survey which first detected the related items and then notices *that* they are related' (Spearman, 1937, p. 133).

In a recent history of psychology, L. S. Hearnshaw (1987) suggests that, despite the breadth of Spearman's scheme, his noegenetic laws were 'merely descriptive generalizations' which made little impact (p. 214). However, in presenting the Manchester paper, Lowenfeld was able to assume that her audience was familiar with them, and in the discussion following the second paper presented in this chapter it is clear that Susan Isaacs, then head of the Child Development Department at the Institute of Education, knew this work and took it seriously (as she did the work of Kretschmer, 1925; this volume, pp. 294–6). In the Manchester paper, Lowenfeld aimed to illustrate that Spearman's noegenetic laws operate in the same primary system, thereby proving its status as 'thought'. But at the same time, they would result in mental products which were distinguishable from those produced by the rational processes of the secondary system.

Beginning with the law of the 'awareness of experience', which she rendered as 'Any lived experience tends to evoke immediately a knowing of its own character and the experiencer' (p. 255), Lowenfeld pointed out that, as adults, we have already elaborated systems for organizing experience and attending to features which demarcate conceptual boundaries. These are often based on functional criteria, like the answer to the question what constitutes a knife or a table. But what of the infant or young child? Lowenfeld first cited Wohlegemuth's (1919) introspective investigations of sensations of pleasure–unpleasure, which claimed to demonstrate that adults can separate out or differentiate between the contents of experience and the external object producing effects. But this differentiation could not be assumed for the infant or young child. She proposed that, whereas the use of a *me/not me* distinction would be fundamental to the secondary system, in which experience tends to be grouped round *external* objects, in the primary system mental acts were based on subjective values of experience.

Lowenfeld believed that this mental activity began at birth or earlier. It would proceed according to subjective principles until challenged by external fact, though modifications in initial products would not really begin in earnest until the third year. The latter conclusion is compatible with Piaget's (1929, 1932a, 1932b) assumptions of a move away from infantile egocentricity, in early or middle childhood. It should be noted, though, that Piaget had not yet crystallized his views on infant cognition; his infancy books were first published in English in the 1950s (Piaget, 1951, 1953, 1955). Moreover, despite similarities, in contrast to Piaget, in Lowenfeld's account affect did not simply provide 'energetics' for cognitive development (Piaget and Inhelder, 1969). Rather, it would provide a basis for making links between different kinds of experiences. But since the infant would not necessarily perceive different objects producing similar effects as *external* stimuli, stimulus object and affect aroused would be registered as a totality, the sensory experience and produced affect together making up the 'fundaments' or basic building blocks of mental activity. Because this occurs before classification based on practical function, the qualities of objects arousing the most powerful effects in the infant's mind would actually *be* the qualities arousing affect (the knife its coldness, the table its hardness, etc.).

The second and third noegenetic laws would also operate in the primary system but would again be affected by the lack of differentiation between subject and object. That is, as in adults, presenting two or more characters would evoke a knowing of a relation between them. But in the infant and young child there would not yet be an ability to detach this relation from the characters themselves; 'coldness' would not be perceived as a quality which can be separated from a knife, a stone or a block of ice. This separation is necessary before the child is able to recognize that 'coldness' is none the less a quality which all these objects share. Similar effects would be seen in the young child's way of educing correlates. Instead of applying the third principle to separate relations in order to illuminate fundaments (a process which is employed in understanding relations like 'coldness is to stone as sharpness is to tool'), the child uses the relation to bind two fundaments together to make them one experience. In some cases the child's connections are superficially similar to adults'. In other cases the relation may appear far more obscure, incomprehensible, and completely idiosyncratic.

Thus, in the primary system correlates would not be educed

on the basis of socially and culturally influenced functional criteria, but according to subjective and objective criteria, producing relations not of similarity (as in adults) but of identity. For the young child affects would dominate as organizing principles, affects which would be felt unquestionably as absolute: because the child feels them, they *are*. To this characteristic of absolutism, Lowenfeld added that in early development there is a pervasive involvement of bodily sensation in all activities of perception and idealism, giving childish thought a quality of multidimensionality not easily discerned in the conscious, functionally dominated thought of adults, constrained by convention.

Lowenfeld concluded this paper by sketching the dangers of isolation, emotional shipwreck or intellectual inhibition which can result from the social environment's inadequacy in providing means by which the child can work through the ideas contained in the primary system. Her comments on the clinical vignette presented at the end of the paper are a thinly veiled reference to the buildup of Fascism in Europe and the imminent threat of war.

At this time one of the unique things about Lowenfeld's contribution was the attempt to bridge the gulf between the study of 'normal' mental functioning and abnormal of clinical populations. While attempting to chart out pre-verbal mental activity as a form of thought was at that time a radical move, so too was the insistence on rational thought as a social product. The latter position is in many respects compatible with the 'social constructionist' tradition within contemporary developmental psychology, a tradition generally associated with reapplications of the theories of the Russian psychologist, Vygotsky, and the social psychology of the American philosopher George Herbert Mead (see Ingleby, 1986).

Here, of course, the major influence on Lowenfeld was Collingwood. It is illuminating to look at his response to the Manchester paper, given in a letter. After congratulating her on one of the best things she had written so far, he added a postscript, reproduced below, which expresses criticism of her original formulation on the nature of 'reality', and his own thoughts on the implications of the idea: what if the world as we know it and its truths are not given, but are elaborated or constructed through social invention according to designs or interests of particular social groups?

> I am really *very much worried* about the point I have raised on p. 27. We all know what kind of world it is to which you refer as the reality (or objective reality) world. But what is exactly its *title* to the name reality? I am haunted by a suspicion that it has none except the fact that adult members of modern European society (or rather, the 'educated classes' of that society) are agreed to treat it as real: that (in other words) it is the *conventional* world of a particular historically determined culture. It is *not* the world of adult human beings *as such*: not, e.g., of modern Indians or (educated) medieval Europeans. This doubt in my mind leads me to wonder whether such words as *phantasy* (p. 30, middle) aren't quite non-scientific terms, indicating merely our wish to ignore those (perfectly *real*) features of experience which we can't fit into our conventional scheme. (19 May 1937, Robin Collingwood to Margaret Lowenfeld)

Though Collingwood was critical of the insistence on objectivity, this emphasis found concordance amongst psychologists and medical colleagues present at the Manchester meeting. But given the number of explicit challenges to psychoanalysis, it is unlikely that the psychoanalytic community could take Lowenfeld's contributions lying down.

That this was the case is indicated in the second paper in this chapter, 'The World Pictures of Children'. This was first presented to the Medical rather than the General Section of the British Psycho-Analytical Society, on 23 March 1938. It was published the following year together with an ensuing discussion, in the *British Journal of Medical Psychology*, vol. 18, part 1, pp. 65–101. The main bulk of the presentation was concerned with describing the nature and functions of the World technique as a research and therapeutic tool. Again Lowenfeld stressed the value of the objective record in facilitating making comparisons over time and between individuals, and contrasted her approach with what she took as the dominant orientation within psychoanalysis. She remained consistent with her earlier emphasis on focusing on the meaning of the symbols at the point in time at which they were created and used *by the children themselves*, and finally, she stressed her emphasis on primitive thought as well as emotion.

However, here Lowenfeld's emphasis on objectivity introduced a paradox. Given that she wished to uncover the workings of mental processes which, by her account, were more or less entirely 'subjective', one must question what 'objectivity' could mean, and wonder, too, if there would not be an inevitable loss in abstracting a product, a particular World, from the dynamics of the situation in which it was produced. But where Lowenfeld stressed that the primary thinking processes she was uncovering required plastic, multidimensional media, and could not be simply translated into verbal imagery, she repeatedly stressed, here and elsewhere, that a persistent problem in putting across the power of her approach was the difficulty in reproducing the original forms, whether with drawings or photographs. On the one hand this is due to the impossibility of reproducing the totality of emotional experiences and meanings available at the time of production, which applies in any psychotherapeutic tradition. On the other hand, the power of working with Worlds comes through aesthetic experience, non-translatable but fundamental to what a World means to child and therapist. It is this which Lowenfeld had attempted to capture in the Manchester paper, in which she insisted that the products and structure arising from the primary system 'are self-evident to the mind that produces them, and absolutely satisfying' (this volume, p. 259).

Recent psychoanalytic work on infantile origins of aesthetic awareness has to some extent brought Lowenfeld's ideas and psychoanalysis closer together, as discussed previously (this volume, p. 136; Meltzer, 1987). This could not have been predicted in the 1930s, as the vehement and highly critical discussion which followed the presentation of the paper indicates (this volume, pp. 290–309). Though the arguments for an objective methodology were not lost on some of the doctors and educationists present, the main burden of the discussion consisted of vigorous attacks from Klein and her supporters. In brief, Klein accused Lowenfeld of ignoring her work and grossly misunderstanding psychoanalysis. Susan Isaacs, on the other hand, attacked Lowenfeld for ignoring the work of other developmentalists, accusing her of failing to appreciate Piaget's work, and of being confused between 'thought' and 'phantasy'. Winnicott expressed reservations about the artificiality and constriction provided by the set apparatus, and implicitly accused Lowenfeld of evading the issue of the unconscious. Winnicott's interjection appears uncharacteristically uncharitable, especially given that he had actively given support to many of the ICP's ventures. Later, of course, he acknowledged a considerable debt to Lowenfeld (Winnicott, 1971). Given the outrage expressed towards a dissenter from outside psychoanalysis, it may be relevant to note that at that time tensions within the British Psycho-Analytical Society were particularly strong, and that the arrival of the Freuds was imminent. Winnicott was at that time having supervision with Klein and had entered analysis with Joan Rivière (Grosskurth, 1986; Winnicott, 1962).

Lowenfeld's reply was detailed and cogent and included an illustration of the use of the World. She clarified the nature of her debt to Klein, whose work made her own possible. Nevertheless there were fundamental differences in emphasis which made her approach a complement rather than an alternative to psychoanalysis. In illustrating the therapeutic value of the World technique, here also referring to the 'Newspaper game' used to encourage spontaneous associations (see *The World Technique*, 1979, pp. 276–7), Lowenfeld emphasized how, rather than working with the transference, the child's emotional responses and mental activity are focused on the material itself, as an indisputable representation of part of him or herself. 'There is an extraordinary force in this confrontation' (this volume, p. 303).

In replying to Susan Isaacs, of particular interest was her rejection of the accusation that she had neglected Piaget and confused thought and phantasy. As Lowenfeld rightly pointed out, *Play in Childhood* (Lowenfeld, 1935) had included extended discussion of Piaget's work, as did her 1931 paper 'A New Approach to the Problem of Psychoneurosis in Childhood' (this volume, pp. 177–214). Neglect in fact reflected her attempt to open a new dimension. Taking the opportunity to expand the theories of the Manchester paper, Lowenfeld argued that in Worlds both primary and secondary forms of thought could exist side by side. In so far as the secondary system was drawn upon, there would be age- or stage-related differences between different children's constructions. In the primary system, on the other hand, thought is ageless.

At this time many of Lowenfeld's criticisms of psychoanalytic theorizing were well placed. For example, there were inconsistencies in the use of the terms 'unconscious' and 'phantasy' amongst child analysts as well as confusions in integrating assumptions about a normal developmental course within a psychoanalytic framework. These considerations eventually contributed to Isaac's paper on 'The Nature and Function of Phantasy', given in 1943 during the 'Controversial Discussions' and eventually published in 1948. Lowenfeld's criticisms formed part of the impetus behind this much-needed clarification. In retrospect, within the history of child psychotherapy and psychoanalysis in Britain, it may be a serious misrepresentation to assume that all there was at issue in the 'Controversial Discussions' were differences between followers of Melanie Klein and Anna Freud, ignoring the influence of Lowenfeld's extra-analytic alternative.

A Thesis Concerning the Fundamental Structure of the Mento-emotional Processes in Children [1937]

I have before me today a very difficult task and one I feel I shall only very partially be able to fill. It is with considerable diffidence I approach it at all and am doing so because I feel that the work I and a group of others have been engaged in now for a number of years has reached the stage where it is imperative, for all the soundness of its future work, that the very tentative conclusions which I have been forming in regard to the meaning of the phenomena that we are studying should be submitted to such a gathering as this for expert criticism and advice.

We are all agreed that psychology today tacitly admits of two separate groups: on the one hand those who are concerned with the study of the conscious faculties and whose endeavour is to arrive at an understanding of the norm; and on the other, medical or clinical psychology whose material is the sick person and whose work is carried out in the atmosphere and circumstances of the consulting room.

The great difficulty with which we are faced is that the material gained in the consulting room does not admit of repetition or reproduction against control groupings, and is dependent for the vast majority of its conclusions upon material gathered by memory from interviews at which there were no witnesses. Research work upon memory of conversations shows vividly how riddled with inaccuracies and fallacies such memory reproduction must inevitably be. The whole situation is peculiar, because though this material of the clinician is not available for detailed and critical examination, yet upon its evidence is based the whole of the deductions concerning what is known as the unconscious; and it is daily found that this unconscious affects wider and wider fields of consciousness.

Perhaps in no field is this situation more unfortunate than in that of child psychology. Here an authoritative educational pamphlet has recently said: 'The understanding of the child's psychic life is mainly the province of the handful of psychoanalysts . . . the psychoanalytic technique alone enables us to understand those unconscious mental processes which control the conscious flow of mental life within the child as well as the adult' [reference not given].

If we come to examine this statement, we find it to be based wholly upon the results of therapy, and that there is no opportunity whatever for the examination of these data. It is not possible in any way to get to grips with this material as it is with the material from which any other psychological deductions are made. No facts or figures as to number or type of cases treated are available for study, no independent estimate of those children, their qualities or types, by independent observers, no parallel investigations of the children from other angles, no means of discovering what the effect of the process of analysis does actually have upon the children either in the immediate or remote future. The symbols, type of play, etc. from which the deductions are made are also not available for study and comparison, and there is no opportunity or means for the observer to make contact with the process itself. Let us dispose at once of the answer that is always made to such an objection, which is the suggestion that the individual making it should submit himself to the process under consideration and then judge of this from the inside. This is no answer at all. It is impossible to evaluate it. Evaluation can only be made from without upon adequate data, and for this process, as we stand at present, all data are lacking.

The situation is therefore that either we must give up all together to attempt to understand the child's unconscious life, or we must devise some other method of making contact with it. This is the more absolute in that both Adler and Jung regard the child as forming part of a total family situation, and as I was able to substantiate some years ago in personal conversation, are not interested in an attempt to conceive of the child itself as an individual phenomenon.

Now it is agreed that man has a conscious and an unconscious life and that for the young child the unconscious or the irrational factor predominates. The question before us is, therefore, are we going to try to make contact with part of the child's mind and experience directly, that is, without the previous intervention of any dogma, such as the acceptance of the Freudian schemata, or of the analytical situation, or not? And if the answer is in the affirmative, by what means can this be accomplished? What would be the results of such an attempt when made?

I want now very briefly to put before you a description of such an attempt in which I and a group of allied workers have been engaged for the past eight years, and to offer for your criticism certain of the conclusions that very tentatively I have come to from this material.

Some nine years ago, having failed to make direct contact with the psychoanalytic material, the idea came to me that it might be possible to construct a direct approach to the disturbed child, and that moreover such an attempt might be made to serve two purposes. The first was to make such an approach in itself and the second so to construct it that it would be a direct negative to all the prerequisites of the psychoanalytic approach and so act as a negative test of their validity.

Now the principles upon which psychoanalytic child analysis are built are too well known to need repetition. The work I am about to describe carefully eliminated every one of these principles.

That is to say, instead of being treated by an analyst himself trained in the Freudian technique and accepting wholly its validity, the work was done, and is done, in public, in a group, with the frequent advent of visitors. No worker has received a psychoanalytic analysis or knows more of the theory than is common to the general reading public, though most workers have had some other form of personal dynamic psychological experience. No psychoanalytic interpretation is used and no attempt is made by the worker to avoid the reality situation. Every attempt is made to reduce the transference factor to the irreducible minimum and children in the middle of treatment are often changed from worker to worker. Parallel observations from as many different points of view as possible are made on each child by workers having different forms of training and who do not themselves take part in the play treatment, and all are carefully recorded in case sheets. All observations of the children's play are recorded in detail as soon as possible after the afternoon itself and checked carefully by time sheets and parallel observations. All case sheets are open to observation by any properly accredited observer. Careful follow-ups of the children have been made from time to time and repeat investigations of intelligence and general adaptation carried out. Intimate contact is kept with the schools throughout treatment and the school report taken into account, with the result of the intelligence test, in making an estimate of educational progress.

Taken on its scientific side there were two goals to this work. One was to see whether without the analytic situation, the transference and the acceptance of psychoanalytic doctrine direct contact could be made with the unconscious of the child; the other was to see of what nature was this part of the mind when contact had been made with it.

To these a third side must be added, which was: would the making of such a contact be beneficial to the child in his struggle to gain harmony with himself and if so, how?

Now supposing that we have succeeded in negating all features of the psychoanalytic approach, taking the opinions quoted previously as they stand, such a treatment of children should:

(a) Have no effect upon the children whatsoever.
(b) Have a definitely deleterious effect.
(c) Arouse anxieties which it is impossible to relieve by these methods.

Either such handling should have no effect upon the patient and leave him where he was, or, if chance or some accidental factor should bring about temporary alleviation, this should disappear as soon as the transitory factor ceased to operate.

It is because I wanted to have time for the proper examination of these factors that I have left a period of eight years since the beginning of the experiment elapse, before reporting upon it, in order that there might be time for the various factors to have operated adequately.

The subjects of the experiment have been children from zero to seventeen years, of both sexes, drawn, as far as the institute children were concerned, from the elementary schools and supplemented, as far as children seen in private are concerned, by children from the private and public-schools. They are children suffering from every form of disturbance of their emotional life and as far as possible the severe cases have been selected for treatment. The series includes cases of melancholy and isolation so severe as to suggest psychosis, eczemas of twelve years standing, psycholepsy, manic states, persistent antisocial behaviour lasting from early childhood, phobias and word blindness.

I want to attempt to present two things: the general results of the experiment; and certain deductions drawn from the work itself. I wish with your permission to take the second part first.

The primary difficulty, if contact is to be made, is to devise a means by which the child can make clear to us the nature of his own thought. Speech is of no use to children and their technical limitations make drawings of very limited application. We set out, therefore, to design a piece of apparatus for the expression of this non-verbal thought.

The resulting technique covers a large number of means of approach, out of which today I am selecting one to put before you.

We call it the *World*.

The apparatus consists of a metal tray 27 in by 18 in, painted blue inside and mounted upon a table. The use of two or three sorts of sand is combined with the tray and as much water as the child desires. The sands are of various colours, silver sand, brown sand, etc. and can be used for various effects. Figure 1 (see p. 252) shows a view of the cabinet which stands beside the tray. It consists of trays which draw out to their full length and can remain fully extended. Within these are small models of all the ordinary objects that fill the ordinary world, such as:

All sizes and varieties of trees and houses
Churches
Windmills, bridges, fences and gates
Market, fair and street furniture
Motor vehicles of all kinds and description
Trains, trucks and engines
Pony-traps, wagons, ploughs, etc.
Ships and lighthouses
Aeroplanes, guns
Wild and domestic animals
Soldiers and savages
People and children of all kinds and descriptions

These are all used with scoops, wooden spoons, odd bits of wood and debris of all sorts as the children happen to desire them.

This apparatus is used with children of all ages from about four to sixteen and seventeen. No difference has been found in the acceptability of the material to children of elementary-school or private-school social environment.

The child when presented with the tray is shown the cabinet and its contents and asked to do with it whatever he likes. Younger children take to it immediately; to older children it is explained that there are many things in one's head one cannot put into words and perhaps the use of this material may help them to make these things clear. It is particularly explained to them that reasonableness is not necessary and if they want to put things in upside down or without any particular sense they are at liberty to do so.

The time taken on the construction of a World may be twenty minutes or two to three hours. 'Worlds' may be unitary and stationary in that the whole afternoon may be given up to the elaboration of a single scene; they may be vivid and moving, suggesting a cinema film more than anything else for the rapidity of movement. The Worlds of many weeks may show a continuous story, each successive afternoon's work being the development and continuation of the previous one.

The use to which children put this material is quite unexpected. It ranges from photographically accurate transcripts of known scenes of ordinary life through every possible modification of this to the most complex and interwoven incoherence. [Here Lowenfeld put on three slides to give some indication of these varieties. They were made by a child of eight, a boy, a boy

Figure 1 *The cabinet originally used with Margaret Lowenfeld's World technique*

of fifteen at a public school and a girl of sixteen, 'all highly intelligent children'.]

A few days' work with these children, once they have found the material, convinces the observer of two things; this kind of mental functioning is entirely unrelated to reality but is not in the least unconscious.

I would submit that we have here in this material achieved the first of our tasks, in that we have now an access to the direct register of precognitive thought in the child which can be treated like any other laboratory scientific material in that it can be abstracted from the subject making it and removed for study and comparison apart from the children. Careful record is made of all these Worlds, enabling them to be set up again at will in the laboratory.

Now we are accustomed to thinking of the mind as consisting of two parts, the conscious and the unconscious. Let us for a moment see what these terms mean and how they came about.

Freud, starting his work and confronted by a human being, took for examination that which he saw, the conscious mind, taken at that time as being conterminous with mind. As he worked however, another structure began to appear which appeared to have none of the qualities of conscious mind and of which the conscious mind was unaware. It was inevitable and fitting that the term unconscious should be applied to this emergent force. This was found to be at its strongest in childhood.

But if we now turn the medal round and instead of beginning with the conscious, that is, by being confronted by the adult in whom consciousness and cognition are fully developed, and look backwards to the unconscious, we start with the infant in whom cognitive faculties are not yet developed, and look forward to cognition. Then the reverse of the picture arises. The strange part of the mind, the phantasy part, is what confronts us. This is now the norm and the problem before us, instead of being 'How and why does the unconscious part of the mind come about?' becomes, 'Here we have the phantasy part as the norm, how and why does the cognitive system arise?'

In making his Worlds the child is quite clearly aware of a great deal of what he expresses, but is unable to explain its meaning in words. This thought cannot be equated, therefore, with the unconscious of adult life, and to call it unconscious is misleading. Also, clearly, as the conscious or cognitive part in young children is so little developed, it is difficult to see how this can arise by repression out of the consciousness. Psychoanalysis has met this difficulty by calling it the Id, but that is only to dress it up in fancy dress and give the wearer an identity disc. To do so does not explain the underlying process. It is the task of science to examine its material and to examine it upon lines not of an ideology which is self-contained and peculiar to itself, but upon that which holds current in the world outside the dogma.

Once we allow ourselves to move into an ideology which is individual to its subject and has no affinities in the cognate branches of knowledge, we are off the earth and anything is possible, even elaborate cannibalistic phantasies in the recently born. I suggest therefore that the terms conscious and unconscious are, in these circumstances, misleading, particularly since consciousness, as Spearman has emphasized, is closely bound up with speech and the child has no speech when it begins its mental life (Spearman, 1937). If there is anything at all that our material has shown and shown conclusively, it is that to call a thing not conscious, i.e. outside the individual's awareness, because it is non-verbal, is an abuse of terms.

I wish to propose that we get rid of this difficulty, which is a linguistic one, and substitute the terms primary and secondary mental system for unconscious and conscious functioning.

The primary system of thought, then, describes all mental functioning between the age of nought and that when cognitive processes occupy a normal part of the mental field, and the secondary system of thought all thought that can be expressed in prose. The primary system then becomes conterminous with the unconscious and the secondary with cognition.

I should like, in putting forward this suggestion, to draw attention to the value of looking directly at material before our eyes. It does seem to me of the very greatest importance in studying children that we should have names for the facts that we study that do not pre-judge our conclusions, but which enable us to value all phenomena on an even basis, leaving pronouncements as to their ultimate nature to be made after and not before investigation.

Having arrived at this point our next task is to examine the nature of this primary system, and to subject it to the same methods of examination as we apply to the cognitive aspects of the mind. Are there any laws discoverable for this primary part of the mind, laws, that is, expressible in the terms we already have? Can we find in this region in operation any of the laws that govern the workings of the conscious mind, even if in rather different guises? I believe the answer to be in the affirmative, and I wish to put before you some of these conclusions.

Now in conducting an investigation of this kind, one has to begin somewhere and I have chosen to begin with the noegenetic laws of Spearman (Spearman, 1937). Can these be shown to operate in the primary system or can they not? I believe they can.

You will remember that these principles run as follows:

1. Any lived experience tends to evoke immediately a knowing of its own character and the experiencer.
2. The mentally presenting of any two or more characters tends to evoke immediately a knowing of a relation between them.
3. The presenting of any character together with any relation tends to evoke immediately a knowing of the correlative character.

Can these be shown to run also in the primary system? Or can they not? I believe that they can.

Spearman's classification of the material to which the first principle applies runs as follows: (a) Sensory experience. (b) Visceral. (c) Affections such as excitement, tranquillization, tension and relaxation, pleasure and unpleasure. (d) Cognition itself. (e) Himself the experiencer.

I want to take two of these, the sensory and the affective and examine them more closely.

To take the first, *the sensory*. It is interesting to note that as far as the everyday application of this principle is concerned the qualities perceived are external to the experiencer and are moreover relatively fixed and relatively agreed upon. The camera *is* black, the knife *is* sharp, etc.

There is also a further characteristic of our habits along these lines which lies in a certain economy of distribution of perceived qualities in relation to external objects. Take for example the knife. Any given knife may be lightly bluish in colour, smooth and cold to the touch, have a faintly metallic smell, in use may well make a faint and characteristic sound, but only in exceptional circumstances of specially directed interest would we perceive these qualities in its connection. For the whole, we tend to economize in emphasis and seeing a knife, to associate with it three things only: *size* – it is natural to say large or small knife; *nature*, such as pen-knife or kitchen knife; and the words *sharp* or *blunt*. That is to say, the qualities of the object normally perceived are associated with common practical experiences of the central qualities of the object, that is, experiences of the kind for which the object was created. We are *capable* of perceiving and manipulating the other qualities, but we do not do so.

Furthermore, the qualities which we perceive and use for the education of [that is, educing] relations and correlates are those agreed upon by the general opinion to *be* inherent in the stimulus object. The rest are errors.

I would like here to note that Spearman himself emphasizes the very limited number of grades of experience perceptible by the adult. Leaving sensory experience on one side for the moment, let us consider affect and use the description of Dr Wohlegemuth (1919) of the scent of heliotropine, given by Spearman.

Here is an abbreviated account:

> Sensation, at first unpleasant. The unpleasure persisted for a brief period at the same intensity. Then it increased suddenly. A moment later I detected a pleasure component in the sensation . . . It seemed to me of an exciting character which was accompanied by fairly widespread organic sensations of a typical kind. I noticed particularly a slight catch in the breath which occurred at the moment of greatest pleasure. I think the sensations might be described as thrilling, or slightly vibratory, in character . . . This high degree of pleasure persisted only for a very short time. The olfactory sensation itself became then much less pleasant and the organic sensations died down . . . This disappearance was accompanied by some disappointment and discontent.

Now there is here a very important and central fact. Dr Wohlegemuth throughout his description is immediately able to separate his own sensations from the agent arousing them. He is aware throughout of a duality, of a something exterior to himself, and that the sensations and emotions he feels are aroused in himself in response to that object. Clearly such an ability depends directly upon Dr Wohlegemuth's previous experience, upon his capacity to separate the Me from the Not Me, and his knowledge that such things as scents exist.

Had these not been present his account, given the same degree of introspective ability, would have been the same, but would have been a description of a series of affective states in which the agent was included in the state itself, as, 'I was aware at first of a general sense of unpleasure, accompanied by and specialized in my nose, which changed to' etc.

To return then to the nature of the primary system. Whereas the acts of cognition of the secondary system depend upon certain accepted *external* qualities of the experience experienced, and tend to group themselves around functional values, I wish to suggest that the mental acts of the primary system are of a similar nature but purely subjective in nature and depend solely upon subjective values of the experience.

To consider this rather further in detail:

It has been pointed out that the qualities accepted for attention in the secondary system tend to be the practical qualities of the stimulus object and that even if the other qualities are perceived they are immediately subordinated to the practical qualities. That is, an immediate automatic classification into more important and less important qualities is made in the cognizing mind. Moreover, some experience of the object must already have occurred to enable a correct classification to be made. It is upon the capacity to make this classification that tests such as 'Prison is to criminals as water is to . . .' are based. To complete such a sentence correctly one must be able to sort the perceived qualities of each object.

In the primary system such a sorting also takes place, but its basis is not objective and practical but subjective and affective.

Mental work begins with birth and has the quality throughout life of seeming conclusive and self-evident to the author until incontrovertibly challenged by external fact. Such challenge cannot occur in infancy, only in very modified form until well on in the third year. By that time there is a wide basis of interwoven belief and experience already present in the mind. It is easier to refer new experience to this than to fragmentary new objective experience.

A child has a sensory experience; the experience arouses in him an affect. Since he is as yet incapable of distinguishing between stimulus object and affect aroused, these two together are registered in his mind, but they are registered *as a total affect*, not as evidence of the existence of an external stimulus. They themselves together, the experience and the affect, indistinguishably one, make up the fundament from which the child later educes relations.

Furthermore, the child has no knowledge of the practical nature of the object producing the affect, he has also not as yet made his basic classifications; he does not know of 'scents' or 'sounds', he only knows a series of total experiences. Those qualities of the stimulus object, therefore, which arouse in him the most powerful or the clearest (here questions of habituation, etc. arise) affect *are* to him the qualities of the object arousing the affect. These may be the same as the adult would automatically perceive, or they may be different.

There is no means for the external observer to know *which* quality of the perceived object has thus reached pre-eminence, and has become joined to affect in the child's mind. For it to be 'cuttingness' for knife, one must have had that experience of the knife and found it important. To a child it may be the bluishness or the coldness. We have, therefore, a situation in which in the child's experience does tend to evoke immediately knowledge of its characters, but the nature of these characters is purely subjective.

There is, however, a further characteristic of the first principle. This is the ability possessed by the cognitive system to detach a character once it has been perceived from the stimulus object and to perceive it not *as* the object but as a character of the object.

In the primary system the presenting of two or more characters evokes equally a knowing of the relation but does not include an ability to detach this relation from the characters. For example, in order to be able to say coldness is to stone as sharpness to tool, one must be able not only to perceive the stone as cold but also to conceive of the coldness as a separate quality. Now if the qualities chosen are those which the adult would agree to as being characteristics of the objects indicated, there is no importance in the difference: the child in this case educes the relation of 'hot' between pie and, say, a bath, and the adult agrees; it does not become inconvenient to the adult that pie and a bath should have the relation of identity to the child, because the practical consequences are agreeable. This may by no means always be the case. The child, however, though he is able to educe relations and does so all the time, does not separate the relations from the fundament, but works the equation backwards. Instead of using the relation as an illumination to the fundament, he uses the relation in order to bind two fundaments together and make of them one experience. Some of the results are agreeable, some disagreeable to the adult, i.e. some are comprehensible, some not.

The relation evoked between the two fundaments is also always of a subjective kind; that is to say, *those fundaments are chosen which evoke in the experiencer a similar effect.* Supposing the affect produced is similar or analogous to that produced in the adult, the result is harmonious; suppose, however, which is far more common, the relation is one which remains unsuspected by the adult, the result is confusing. For example, if a child seeing slime on a pond and spinach on his plate evokes a relation 'green' by this perception, the slime and the spinach become actually identified; they are for him the same thing, and obviously so – but the identity is unperceivable by the adult.

The child then, in the primary system, follows the second principle, but with different fundaments and without being able to separate the relation from the fundament.

To take the third principle.

Here exactly the same follows as in the case of the first principle. The child does educe correlates, but they are according to the nature of the relation. For example, the child sees green slime on a pond and perceives the relations, green and horrid to touch. He then educes the correlate, spinach, and makes the appropriate reaction.

In every case the correlate educed is not the objective functional one of the secondary system, but the subjective affective one of the primary system.

We have, therefore, as the first analysis of the primary system, a series of relations and correlates evoked and combined in the same way as that in the secondary system, but upon a subjective and not an objective basis. These correlates and all the structure that arises from them are self-evident to the mind that produces them, and absolutely satisfying.

The essential nature of the secondary system is its 'realness', the reality principle of Freudian thought. This must not in any way be confused with the reality of philosophy as it is a purely conventional and practical reality. It is in fact no more than a current agreement, but an agreement upon which the business of practical living depends. A cognitive percept or concept is from this point of view a certain emphasis on experience arranged in such a way as to represent his individual experience.

If the hypothesis I have been putting before you is correct, then we have a structure in the child's mind alike to and yet different from the structure in the adult mind.

Now the adult reacts in certain settled ways to his mental structure. Having perceived the relation of cutting and educed numbers of correlates to them, he expresses a general affect, 'I am afraid of . . . as things which cut'. So does the child. He makes his structure of identities, differences, etc., and in the process of making it, powerful affects are aroused, much as Dr

Wohlegemuth describes the affects induced by heliotropine. These affects are absolute to the child; he would never question their absoluteness or inquire if other people also felt them. Because he feels them, to him they *are*; that is, they are characters of the universe.

He therefore reacts appropriately to his mental structure, shrinks from his mother wearing a fur coat because of the cat who scratches, bursts into tears and refuses to eat his spinach. The outside world then reacts to his action, and once again the affect induced in him becomes attached to the object from which it arises. Thus 'This hurts me', becomes 'That-is-a-hurting-me-thing-or-person': an absolute quality and an absolute experience.

From this there follows a most crucial and important characteristic of child thought. This involvement not only of affect with percept but of bodily sensation with all percept and with all ideation gives to a child's thought a quality different from that of adult thought, what we may call a multidimensional quality where adult thought may be conceived of as two-dimensional.

Thus to an adult, for example, all surfaces maintained somehow in space at a level approximately between the knees and shoulders, upon which one can put things, are grouped together, and a unitary concept made of them, to which the word 'table' becomes attached. It is immaterial to this grouping what may be the size or colour of the material of which the structure is made, how it smells, or what experience it gives to the tactile sense. These differences can, if you wish, be grouped together later and come to be subsections of the group table. They do not affect the 'tableness' of any given table. Below the knees and above the waist level of an average man a different grouping comes into force and the structure becomes either a stool or a counter.

Here it is the simplest characters that are selected and they are chosen from a practical angle. If a structure has these three qualities, it enables you to 'do' with a table the things you would want to do with a table. All the other appeals to the senses of these structures are disregarded as for the moment irrelevant.

It is, however, clear that to be able to make a grouping of this kind two basic essentials are presupposed. You must have had something which you wished to rest at some level other than the floor, and second, to have had experience not only that such a thing can be procured, but that it can be procured in different versions of itself. These experiences are entirely outside the range of the young child. Your point of view is one he cannot have since he has none of these experiences. The smooth brown curved leg of one table may be to him cool and brown and smooth and shiny, qualities possessed by his mother's silk dress. They will then combine with the dress to form one block – or the darkness and 'good-to-play-in-ness' of the space underneath may bring to mind the feeling of being curled up waiting to spring, in a landing cupboard or a space in the bushes, and join the table with that experience.

The process is a true noegenesis following accurate lines of identity, opposition, etc. and can be retraced accurately by an outside observer according to known fact if the lines are known. Herein lies its fundamental differences from the grouping by association upon which much analytic technique is based. The brown of the table leg does not 'suggest' the brown of mother's dress, it is identical with that brown, the smoothness with smoothness, etc., and would be the same for all observers if they happened to think of it.

Groupings made by association occur independently of absolute qualities and are traceable only by knowledge of the intimate history of the person concerned. Thus it might well happen that the child was looking at that leg by chance at the moment that it heard its mother fall downstairs, or the cook step on the tail of the cat, and the horror evoked by either circumstance would spill over to the leg so that in afterlife a faint distaste for polished walnut tables remained. In free association the links are individual to the subject and cannot be recovered except through the medium of his own history.

While, therefore, connections in cognitive thought are made in the main by logic and reason, and are therefore retraceable and recoverable, connection in a child's mind can be made in any of its multi-dimensions, so that structures arise such as are illustrated in Worlds.

If what has been said is true, then it would follow that if a child is to be able to reproduce its mental content, it must have material to do so which is capable of setting out constructions of this nature: material which is not only multi-dimensional, but also capable of representing movement. Such a material is provided by the Worlds as set out and much of the rest of the equipment of our playrooms. If these structures be accepted as they stand and taken to pieces according to the laws set out above, they are found to yield their meaning and, moreover, this meaning to be a sort that would be *absolutely* inexpressible in words.

I would like here to draw your attention to a certain caution and to point out that such a study demands of the observer some cheerfulness of temperament and satisfaction with his own stoutness of heart, as there is much that is shocking in the content of the primary system both of children and ourselves. It is important to realize the grimness of much of the material. No approach to childhood is going to be fruitful which is going to shirk any of the evidence produced. It is perhaps worthy of consideration, at least, whether we are not going to be able to do something fairly effective towards the prevention of the playing out of these ideas in the stuff later of reality by the adequate facing and resolution of these impulses in the primary system of childhood.

How close is the parallel between certain aspects of man's behaviour under certain circumstances and the play of these children may perhaps be indicated by the following abstract from the plasticine play of a nine-and-a-half-year-old boy from a pleasant family. In ordinary life he was the rather particularly sweet-tempered new boy at a preparatory school.

'This is going to be a man. Look – he's going to be a cannibal. He's going to be a heathen: a heathen that bows to an idol. Look – I'm going to make him kneel.' Here he makes one very long leg about twice the length of the body and half the thickness. 'Look how long his leg is: he's got to learn to kneel because he's a cannibal. Look, he's kneeling to the idol. He's the cannibal King!' Soldiers appear from nowhere and begin attacking the figure – 'He's the bad witch. He's the powerful bad one. Look, they're cutting at him.' He then begins to slash the head of the figure repeatedly; then all down the front of the chest, interspersing remarks made by the figure. '"Look", they say, "We're going to cut you up". "Don't do that, I don't like it."' By the time this is said the face of the figure is half cut away. 'Look how he's bleeding,' with ghoulish glee, 'He doesn't like being cut at all.' He is, however, completely cut to pieces, his head being cut to bits first and then the rest of his body, ending with the legs. During the whole time the figure goes on making remarks like, 'Oh I don't want to be cut up.' The figure continues to speak after his head is cut off, and the boy speaking for him says 'He doesn't like having his head cut off, he doesn't like having his arms cut off', etc.

We now come to the question of the relation between the primary and the secondary system.

 A child throughout his growing life as an individual, that is, from about his second year, is constantly coming up against the adult system of thought, the objective-reality world. The main characteristics of this world as he meets it are its unchangeability and its coldness to his own emotions (the chair-leg remains stuck however much he may hit himself against it, hate it and curse it); and the fixedness of its meaning. As a child of my acquaintance said once despairingly to its mummy, a mummy who, like Madam Montessori, disapproved of phantasy, 'Mummy, Mummy, must the chair *always* be a chair – can't it be a bear even on Sundays?' This exterior world is entirely unlike the world of his interior thinking.

The quintessence of this process is exemplified in language. Language is the flattened out, codified epitome of the cognitive experience of the race. At the beginning the acquisition of language is an acquisition of power. It is delightful, important, it brings the child into contact with his grown-ups. Very soon, however, he finds that for most of his most intimate things there are no words in the sounds offered him.

Some children meet this difficulty by making a language of their own; some by refusing to talk at all; some by trying to repress and forget their own experience and adopt wholesale the codified symbols of adult life. Whichever it is that happens it is now that the child meets a factor crucial to its whole experience. Rebecca West has written a set of masterly short stories illustrating the fact that the crucial meaning in adult relationships can so little be expressed in speech that for lack of it emotional shipwreck supervenes. This is a common experience. For all of us expression in words of the deepest features of our emotional lives is quite impossible. Very much more strongly is this the case with the child. One needs to have experience of the kind of concepts produced by children in the specialized techniques of our play rooms to appreciate the depth and immensity of the gulf between the content of the primary system of thought and that which is offered to the child by ready-made language. Similarly language is poorly polarized, is objective, factual, limited, totally unable to convey multidimensional thought. The contrast between this life of grown-ups that is offered him and the interior life of his own arouses in the child acute anxiety.

There remains the final and most important point.

Does such study of the child do harm to the children studied or does it leave them where it found them?

I have left so many years before bringing forward these

conclusions because I wanted to know the answer to that question myself.

During the eight years that the ICP has been at work, my colleague and co-director Dr Ethel Dukes and I have been unable to find any child definitely the worse for treatment at the institute. Very few were unchanged and a very substantial number appear changed for the better. A recent follow-up of the cases has shown a minimum number of relapses. In certain cases it would appear that the basis of the neurotic character has been altered. In no case has anxiety been aroused with which it was impossible to cope.

It would seem that the barrier that has been erected by psychoanalysis to the intimate study and assistance of the interior life of children by other than those trained in this special technique cannot on examination be maintained.

The World Pictures of Children A Method of Recording and Studying Them [1939]

I am going tonight to attempt a very difficult task.

For some years I have had as my goal the achievement of an approach to the child's mind which shall be both objective in itself and susceptible of record. I have desired to become able to review freshly the whole question of the child's mental and emotional nature and its development, and to bring to light such manifestation of their nature as will carry their own conviction and be themselves grounds for further study.

I wish tonight to attempt to put before you some of the results I have obtained. These form part of a considered point of view about the nature of the mind, a point of view which embodies particular pieces of apparatus and their use, and certain deductions drawn from the material produced by children with this apparatus as to the structure of the mind in childhood.

I have delayed presentation of this concept until I should be able to demonstrate also the nature of the evidence which had given rise to it. The moving next month of the Institute of Child Psychology into its own freehold quarters at 6 Pembridge Villas, W11 will now enable me and my co-workers to make available, to any members of our profession who may desire to see it, the clinical material which has formed the basis of these deductions, of which the slides I wish to put before you are a part.

As I have said, my views consist of a method of approach and of deductions drawn from material produced by that method. These two aspects stand separately, and tonight's paper is concerned only with the presentation of part of this method and the results which can be achieved by it.

Owing to the fact that I wish to occupy the main part of our time with the actual presentation of material, I propose in the place of the historical review that customarily precedes the presentation of a new method, to take two considerations only – the origin of play, and the relation between the methods employed in the treatment of children at the Institute of Child Psychology, of which the one under consideration is a part, and the work of Freudian child analysts.

Now it is perfectly clear that children have played since the beginning of time and archaeological diggings show us that every civilization has provided toys for their use. The loving care expended upon these toys in all human groups shows that grown-up human beings since the beginning of historical times have understood that the way to make contact with a child and to understand his way of thought is to play with him.

Play in childhood is a function of childhood, none can discover it. Toys to children are like culinary implements to the kitchen, every kitchen has them and has also the elements of food. It is what the cook does with these implements and elements that determines the dish. My own approach to the use of a toy apparatus with children derives from a memory of H. G. Wells's *Floor Games*, the first edition of which had made a deep impression upon my youth (Wells, 1911). When, therefore, in 1925 I came from orthodox paediatrics to the associated study of emotional conditions in childhood, I began to put this memory to use. I collected first a miscellaneous mass of material, coloured sticks and shapes, beads, small toys of all sorts, paper shapes and match boxes, and kept them in what came to be known by my children as the 'Wonder Box'; with this I began to experiment with my children patients.

My approach to the work was that of a clinician, and my aim was to endeavour to devise a method by which direct contact could be made, without interference from the adult, with the mental and emotional life of a child. I set myself as a goal to work out an apparatus which would put into the child's hand a means of directly expressing his ideas and emotions, which would allow of the record of his creations and their abstraction for study. I had at that date no theory of the mind and was determined to avoid making or accepting one until I should have achieved objective records from which a theory could be built or checked. Apart from a sporadic reading of Freud's own works and occasional personal and friendly contacts with some British psychoanalysts, I had not at the time any knowledge of psychoanalytic theory or practice, and was unaware that any special approach was being made by this group to children.

It was in 1927 that I first came into contact with the work of Melanie Klein, on the occasion of a paper read by her to this section of this Society (Klein, 1927). After that paper I had the opportunity of a short conversation with Mrs Klein and some slight subsequent correspondence. This paper and my subsequent contact with Mrs Klein made it perfectly clear to me that the child analyst brings to her work with children an *already formed* outline of a doctrine concerning the structure of the mental and emotional life of children which is implicitly accepted, and that the treatment of children, for the origination of which Mrs Klein was responsible, was derived from the main body of psychoanalytic theory and was an extension of it to children. This has recently been confirmed by Mrs Klein in a private letter to myself.

Child analysis is, therefore, an adaptation of psychoanalytic principles to the treatment of children, implying the acceptance beforehand in the analyst practising it of the psychoanalytic view of the mind. This is further borne out by the regulations for training child analysts, whereby the candidate must himself have received a full psychoanalysis and have gained experience in the analysis of adults before he is allowed to begin work with children. The child psychoanalyst therefore uses toys as a means of gaining contact with the child's mind in order that that mind may be dealt with on lines indicated by psychoanalytic theory: the child's use of toys is interpreted symbolically in harmony with that theory. Now without entering at all into the question of the validity of psychoanalytic thought, which is far from my purpose, I wish to point out as clearly as I am able that this is a totally different dish from that which I aim to cook with approximately the same materials.

We both use toys, as does everyone who plays with children, or children who play with themselves. My own endeavour in my work with children is to devise an instrument with which a child can demonstrate his own emotional and mental state without the necessary intervention of an adult either by transference or interpretation, and which will allow of a record being made of such a demonstration. My objective is to help children to produce something which will stand by itself and be independent of any theory as to its nature.

The central task of psychotherapy is that of making contact with the whole of the patient's mind, not only by intuition but by direct and conscious knowledge and understanding of the laws of mind. There are certain points about the nature of children's thought that make this task particularly difficult. A child does not think linearly as the adult is capable of doing: thought, feeling, sensations, concept and memory are all inextricably interwoven. A child's thought is fluid and movement can take place on several planes at once. A child's feeling is absolute in that any emotion, while it is present, holds the whole field of consciousness. Finally, a child's concepts have no relation to what we call, in our view of the world, external reality.

An apparatus, therefore, which will give a child power to express his ideas and feelings, must be independent of knowledge or skill, must be capable of the representation of thought simultaneously in several planes at once, must allow of representation of movement and yet be sufficiently circumscribed to make a complete whole, must combine elements of touch and sensation, as well as of sight, and be entirely free from a necessary relation to reality.

Another aspect of the necessity for some such apparatus is that not only child psychotherapy but psychotherapy and psychopathology as a whole suffer from a difficulty not now shared by any other branch of medicine, in that it is impossible to abstract clinical material for independent consideration apart from the circumstances in which it is produced.

We cannot examine the mental and emotional products of other physicians' patients without first understanding in full the psychotherapeutic hypotheses upon which the treatment has been based, and second having, by courtesy of the physician, access to the whole of the case notes of the patient. Even then, the personality of the physician must be taken into account in evaluating the facts, since what is available even in these ideal conditions is not the material produced by the patient himself, but this material seen through the eyes of the physician.

Physical science has progressed in strict accord with the development of possibilities of precise investigation and direct record of the facts observed, and their abstraction for study from the circumstances of production. The dish therefore that I wish to cook with our common implements is one in which all these elements are present and which can be used, if you wish it, as check or proof of any system of psychotherapy, but which, although it is the source from which my own theory of child psychotherapy has been drawn, is independent of it as of other theories.

This apparatus I have called 'the World' from the feeling the children have about it. It came into existence in 1929 and has been in constant use since that date both in the Institute of Child Psychology and in my private work. Children of all ages from four to late adolescence have worked with it, suffering from complaints comprising somatic disorders, educational difficulties, personality deviations and social maladjustments. Many hundreds of these 'Worlds' have been made and recorded, and it is a selection of these I wish to put before you.

Perhaps a word of comment is due upon the name of the apparatus. Very recently my attention has been drawn to the fact that Anna Freud, writing in 1927 in her book *Einführung in die Technik der Kinderanalyse*, describes Mrs Melanie Klein's work as 'a little world in miniature' (Freud, A., 1927). Now I believe it is true that this phrase does occur in Anna Freud's work, but it is equally true that I did not myself know of this fact until the pertinent extract was sent to me by Dr Charlotte Bühler. This ignorance is partly sheer failure to keep abreast of reading, and partly deliberate policy. Every scientist will know how great are the difficulties that beset the mind which is trying to look at a common object freshly, and for many years now, while studying the bulky material which crowds in on me and my group daily from the use of this and other forms of apparatus, it has been my deliberate endeavour not to read the writings of other workers until I had the outlines of my own theory clear. I offer my apologies for this ignorance, but know no other way of working.

The World apparatus is not a test, except in the sense that the electrocardiogram is a test, and beyond a tentative investigation of the use of the apparatus by normal children in elementary schools, which is being carried out by one of my own co-workers, no comparison of the use of it by normal and disturbed children has yet been attempted by us.

In May 1934 Dr Charlotte Bühler visited the Institute of Child Psychology and, becoming interested in the World, in agreement with ourselves has embarked upon the investigation of the use made by normal children in relation to age, of a modified form of this apparatus. When completed, this investigation will give a useful basis for comparison of the nature of the material selected by normal and emotionally disturbed children of different ages.

We will now turn to the apparatus itself and to a consideration of the material produced with it by children.

1 REALISTIC WORLDS

Figure 1. Depicted is a tray by a boy of nine years. This is an actual photograph taken of the World as it was made, and reproduced directly.

This photograph illustrates the first difficulty in the presentation of this piece of apparatus, which is the means of reproduction. The obvious method for the reproduction of scenes of this kind is that of photography, and my first attempts to present this material were by taking photographs of the actual World made. After a certain number of these had been taken, however, the following difficulties presented themselves.

(a) All photography, however well done, is the taking of a given scene from a given viewpoint. As an inevitable result of this, objects nearer at hand are larger than those further away:

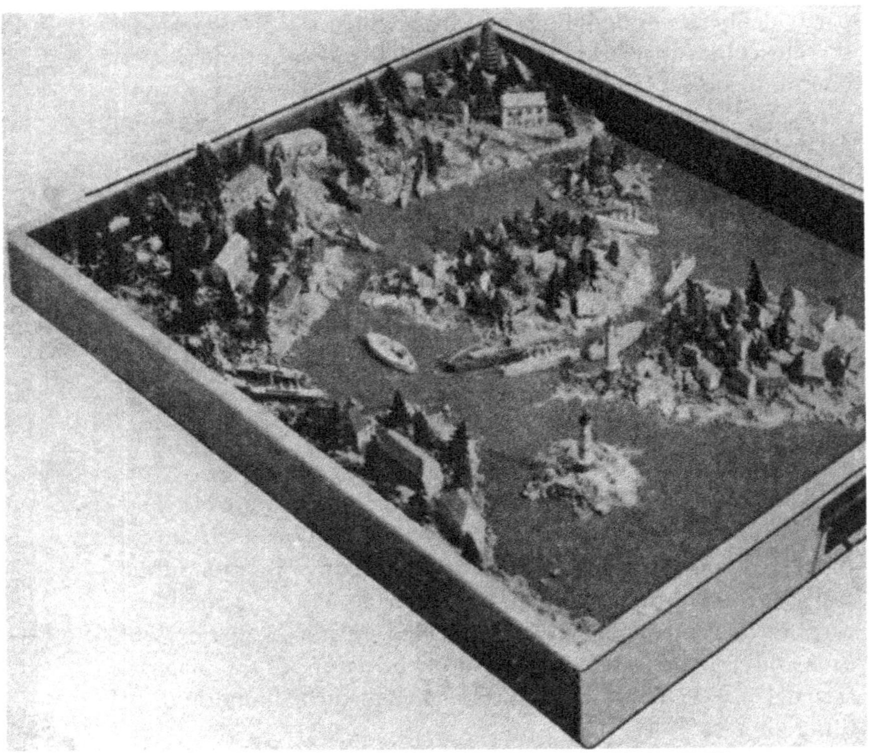

 Figure 1 *An island scene*

smaller objects are hidden behind larger ones and the relative emphasis given by the actual scene to different parts of the scene photographed is inevitably altered.

(b) Our second proposal to circumvent this difficulty was to take photographs from the air, having the camera in a standard position, facing downwards, and the Worlds placed always in the same relation to the camera. This, however, proved equally unsatisfactory owing to the high degree of distortion of objects photographed from the air. Several photographs of this kind were made of Worlds, but when submitted to independent observers unfamiliar with the actual material, it was found that the distortion was so serious as to make recognition of the objects photographed in many cases impossible.

(c) A further difficulty soon appeared, in that the Worlds are made upon a tray oblong in shape and the conventional form of lantern slide is square. Not only, therefore, was it necessary that the above two difficulties should be overcome, but there was a further obstacle in that in order to present photographs of an oblong tray within a square, parts had to be excluded or the whole thing reduced to such a scale as would tend to make it unrecognizable.

Figure 1 illustrates these difficulties. This has been taken at an angle and in so far as it gives a general picture of the scene, is attractive and has actually been selected in order to give some idea of the picturesque possibilities of the apparatus. It will be seen, however, that one corner has had to be omitted and that all details occurring on the opposite side of the central islands, should such have been present, would have had to be hidden.

After many months of experiment of this kind, it was decided to attempt drawings instead. In this way it is possible both to emphasize those points which are of importance to the child who has made the World, and to eliminate the detail which is to him of no importance. As you will see, this technique is still in the experimental stage and far from being satisfactory in every way, but we are obliged to use it until such a time as some better solution of these difficulties is reached.

The apparatus consists of a big metal tray on a table of medium height; it is painted black outside and blue in. It contains sand (three sorts of sand are provided, fine and coarse brown sand and silver sand): also as much water as the child desires. Silver sand is used for snow on mountains. The tray can also be used empty of sand. Some children use quite dry sand, some wet enough to be mouldable, some a great deal of water in which sand is a negligible factor. Some Worlds are made almost or entirely without the addition of any toy objects, the relation between water and sand fully satisfying the child. I have known boys play elaborate and exciting dramas for many sessions, using the 'eating' qualities of water on islands of sand and the mopping up qualities of sand in water. Some examples of this are given in my book *Play in Childhood* (Lowenfeld, 1935).

Standing beside the tray is a cabinet: it contains small objects of every kind, as varied and accurate as the manufacturers will give us, of all the things commonly to be found in a world; houses, trees, people, both ordinary and military, animals, wild and tame; transport of all sorts, ice-cream men, fences, lamp-posts, garden chairs, etc., and with it are used coloured paper, coloured and plain sticks, plasticine and glitter-wax, and anything else the ingenuity of the observer can suggest to supply the need of any particular child.

Figure 2 illustrates the method of record that has been adopted, by which drawings made first of the scene can be photographed and from these slides made.

Figure 2 *Street scene and railway station*

In regard to realistic Worlds there is not very much to be said in so brief a summary; the significance of such Worlds to the child making them is only revealed by very close and detailed study of each World. They are shown here only to show the range possible in this apparatus.

The instructions which are given the children are that they are to make on the tray whatever they wish and to pay no attention to external reality. If they have an impulse to put a tree in upside-down or to make a train go on top of houses, they are to do so. With children of junior-school age, the apparatus needs no introduction, the attractiveness of the material makes its own appeal. With the older child or young adolescent an explanation of some sort is given – that we all have pictures in our heads that we cannot put into words; that it is fun sometimes to make things anyhow without bothering whether they are really so or not – or some such phrase. With the older adolescent or young adult the simile of a Japanese garden is used and they are asked to see if anything in any rough way similar occurs to them.

Once started on the work, introduction becomes superfluous, the interest of the creation itself is its own explanation.

In the ordinary course of treatment, children use this apparatus indifferently with other forms of material. Sometimes they act, sometimes they play, sometimes they recount dreams or paint, write stories or recount phantasies that come into their heads. I hope to show later in this paper the intimate connection that exists between all these products. The World takes its place among other pieces of apparatus and forms of expression as a clinical instrument used in the process of treatment and study of the child, but upon which the whole burden of treatment does not rest.

Some children keep up a running commentary on their work as they do it: some invoke the help of the physician with them throughout, some work absorbedly at their Worlds in silence till they are completed and seem oblivious of the presence of any other person.

Some children take immediately to this form of expression and hail it with delight, saying, as did one very verbalized boy of fourteen, 'I never expected this to be like that! One really *can* express onself in that – it's all living – just like we are.' Some come to it later, some children after the first day do not use it at all.

It has been usually assumed that the deeper thoughts of children, what have been called their unconscious phantasies, are not expressed because of a mental mechanism which keeps them out of consciousness. My own view is more nearly that certain essential qualities of those experiences make it impossible in the truest sense of that word for them to be represented in speech – they are of a kind which speech cannot convey. It is towards this odd nature of the thought of childhood that this apparatus is directed, and the sand and water, the three-dimensional and sensory nature of these component parts are of the essential nature of the apparatus.

Every child, either seen in private or in attendance at the Institute of Child Psychology, is given an opportunity on entering into treatment to make a World if he wishes to, and every World that is made is carefully recorded.

2 FANTASTIC WORLDS

Illustrations have been chosen to illustrate the fact that this apparatus is capable of expressing ideas of pure phantasy.

Figure 3. Here the ring of houses is partly the right way up, partly upside-down; on top of the houses runs traffic and on top of the traffic again people stride from car to car. In the entrance to the dell a bus runs over a person and in the foreground a policeman is pinned under an ambulance. This was made by a highly intelligent public-school boy with a phobia of chickens. Fantastic as this appears, it proved under analysis to be a very perfect structure in which each component part exactly fitted. He felt the World to be a satisfactory expression but could give no account in words of what it expressed.

Figure 3 *A topsy-turvy town round a dell*

Figure 4. In this scene a rhinoceros pushes over a house, there is a tree with a snake on top and one at the bottom, many crashes on the roads, houses placed anywhere and anyhow, trees anywhere, one house upon two fences with a boat upside-down on the roof and an ostrich hiding its head under the boat, etc., etc. This was made by an elementary-school girl of fourteen, referred for bouts of extreme apathy interspersed with bouts of violent activity.

Figure 5. Here is a bull on the top of a post about to leap on a man below who is singing and suspecting nothing; an elephant is up a telegraph pole falling towards a woman who is trying to escape; a lion is being speared by a knight and an isolated charabanc crashing into a beacon. This was made by a boy of eleven, who was extremely backward at school, though of average intelligence, and who took three hours to dress himself in the morning if left unaided.

The above pictures are purely fantastic and do not contain any coherent concept. The maker in describing them talks about each item in turn but does not consciously weave them into a whole, although on further consideration with him or her they

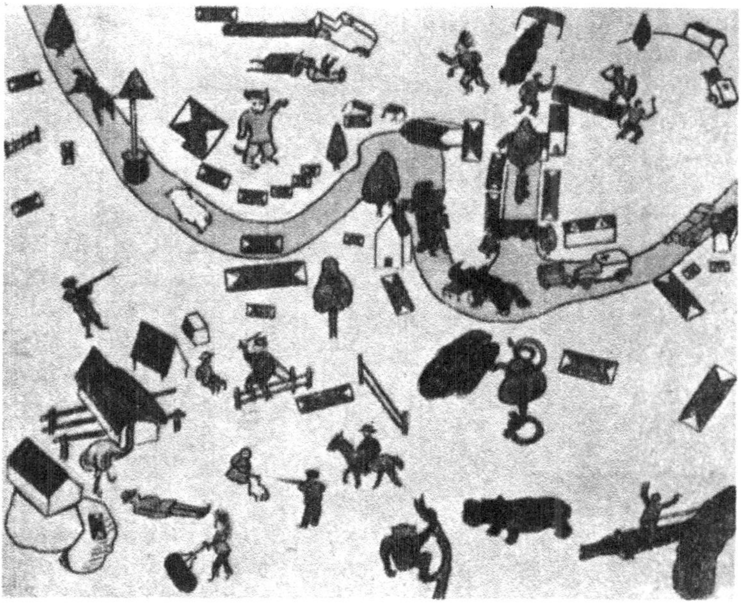

Figure 4 *A medley scene*

Figure 5 *More medley*

turn out to be representative of a connected mental and emotional state.

We now come to a group of illustrations which show an affective side combined with a conscious concept.

3 COMBINATION OF AFFECT AND CONCEPT

Figure 6. This was made by a very intelligent and musical girl of seventeen, referred for unmanageableness and irresponsible behaviour while abroad. In the top corner is the snake's house with the snake just going into it. Next door is another house. Close by is a wood where lives the 'horror'. Here is the snake's boat. Down below you see the tortoise at home to his musical friends. Still on the same side of the river which divides the world into two halves is the snake singing to the microphone and surrounded by a group of Important People listening to him. In the centre on the other side of the river is a committee discussing what the snake is to have for his birthday. Behind is a neutral house.

Figure 6 *The snake's birthday*

Here, as in dreams, two positions of the same thing are represented simultaneously. The snake on the right and on the left is the same snake. The scene contains two aspects of the snake's day presented simultaneously.

Figure 7. This World was made by an elementary-school girl of eight, referred for functional paralysis of one leg. Here on the right is a cave; in it is a 'small animal' with some eggs – but a man came and killed the animal and the eggs were never hatched. Here in the centre is the mound, hollow inside. Up in the sky it is foggy and the aeroplanes cannot see one another. Only aeroplanes can reach the top and one has brought eggs and placed them at the bottom of the hole in the mound where no one can see them. Some horsemen are riding round the mound to keep people away. When the eggs are hatched robins will come out. Here in front are some people who want to poison the sand and they are emptying bottles of poison about and in the water so that the children may drink it. Across the corner is a strong parapet with a space for children to play in inside it. The entrance is guarded by a soldier and there is another one at the side to prevent people getting over the top. The children had to pay a penny to get in – and here are three fathers coming to fetch the children home.

Figure 7 *The mound 'So high that it reaches up to the sky where Jesus and God are'*

4 PSYCHO-SOMA AND AFFECT

Not only do some Worlds relate affect to concept, but there are others which depict exactly a somatic state and put this among scenes expressive of the corresponding affect.

For reasons of time I am showing only one slide in this group. I am indebted to my colleague Dr P. C. Castell for this World and the account of it.

Figure 8. In the centre you will see a man in the grip of a bear. The boy's comment on this was, 'He can't get away.' The boy himself suffers from a feeling of constriction in the chest when his anxiety is acute. All around this man are scenes depicting terrifying situations – animals kill and eat men and a child. Then a woman is approached by a lion and gradually surrounded by a crowd of animals: the lion, a crocodile, two cows, an elephant, a horse, a lamb, two donkeys, a bison, a bear, a tiger, a seal and a pig. 'They did nothing, but she was horribly frightened.'

5 WORLDS SHOWING IDEAS OF MOVEMENT

I will give but one example, by the same child as the previous illustration.

Figure 9. This is a stage at the beginning of an afternoon's use of the World during which violent movement was represented. Belisha beacons were blown down by the wind; there was a collision between a car and a tip-up lorry. Two planes crashed and a dead airman lay by one of them. Cars and trees were added, a decrepit fence, half falling over. A man was mending the top of a lamp-standard – a lion climbs up the ladder after

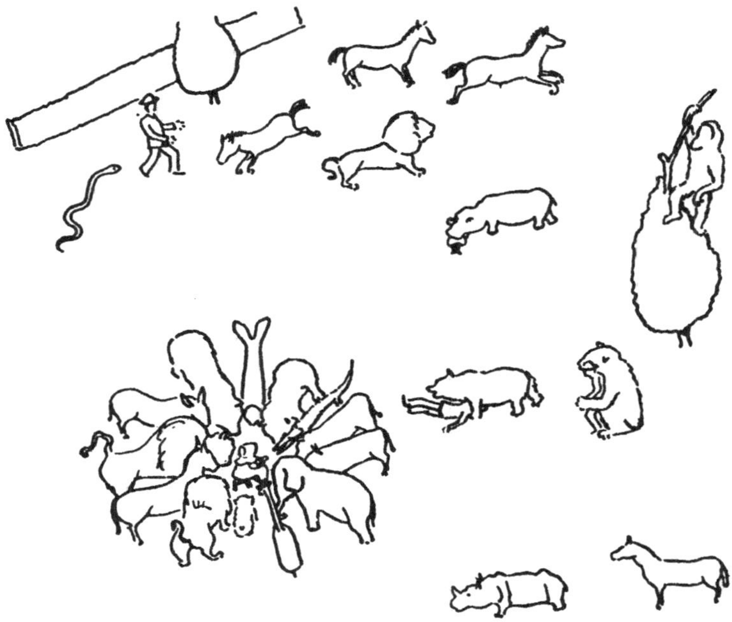

Figure 8 *'He can't get away'*

 Figure 9 *'England – London'*

him, seizes the man and eats him. The lion then nearly decides to jump over the crashed vehicles, or to jump over a horse – but does neither and finds himself on his back with his legs in the air, the mounted knight stabbing him with his lance. Part of a broken lamp-post is about to fall on the knight. A bull now gets up to the top of the lamp standard in order to jump down on the man passing below, who is singing and suspecting nothing. A pair of telegraph poles appear with an elephant on top of one of them and falling off towards a woman who is trying to escape. A charabanc is going too fast and is about to knock down the surviving beacon. 'This', the boy said, 'was England – London.' (See also Figure 5.)

There are certain common types of Worlds, the question of time prevents my being able to show them to you tonight.

These are:

(a) Worlds made by mentally defective children.
(b) Worlds made by very young children.
(c) Worlds made by children in high states of excitement, where intensity of affect has temporarily disorganized cognitive consciousness.
(d) Worlds made by children in obsessional states.
(e) Purely plastic Worlds.
(f) Worlds in which common objects are used but where a quite personal and unusual meaning is given to each object, a milk-can used as a gun, or, as we have seen in the slide of the houses round the dell, houses can be employed quite out of their ordinary context.

We will now consider of what nature are these products and what relation they bear to other productions of the mind. We will consider first the relation of 'World' to drawing, and continue with the boy we have just been studying so as to give a rather more complete picture of a single case. (See Figures 5 and 9.)

You will note that in these Worlds considerable emphasis is laid upon height and the up and down of height. The Worlds were also prefaced with the remark, 'This is London.' I will now show you two drawings made by the same boy.

(a) *Figure 10.* This shows a part of London as you would see it from near the top of the tower of Big Ben.
(b) *Figure 11* shows the Monument seen from half-way up,

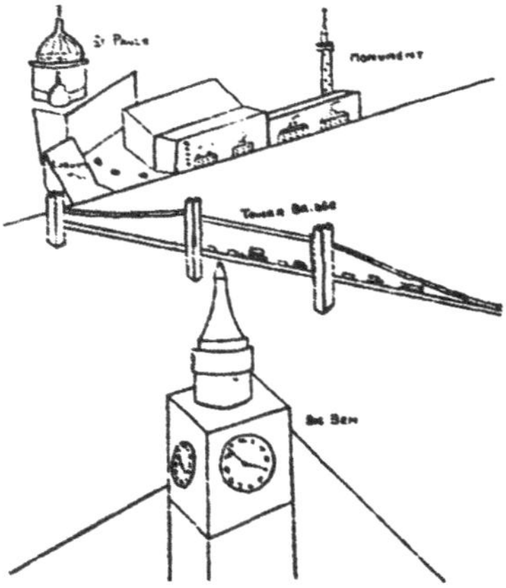

Figure 10 *London from the top of Big Ben*

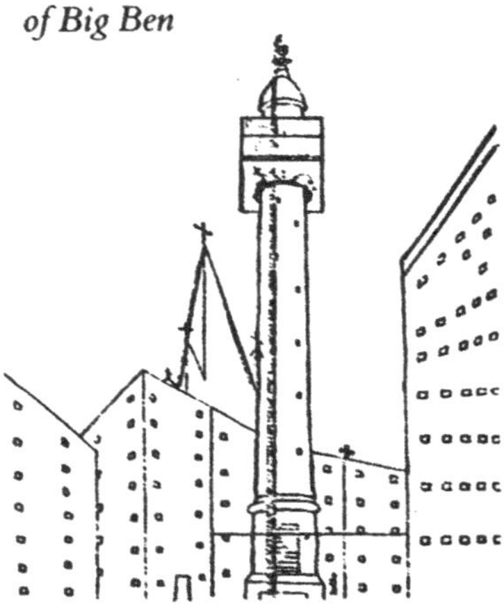

Figure 11 *The Monument, London*

Figure 12 *British United: London Main*

looking up and looking down. The line across the tower, the boy said, was the street and the dot was a Belisha beacon seen from above and so upside-down. He felt himself obliged continuously to make draw ings of this kind but could get no further than the actual buildings. When given the World material he was able to represent not only what obsessed his interest, but also the affect with which it was associated.

6 RELATION OF WORLD TO DREAM

Figure 12. This was a very elaborate construction, taking several days to make and representing an underground station with a town on top. On the night of the day following the beginning of the World the boy – aged eleven, and referred for a very noisy stammer – dreamed as follows: 'I was going to have another mother with whom I was going to do all the things I do at Jane's, like smoking and gurking (belching).' On the night of the day the World was completed he dreamed: 'I was going along in a train when we came to a tunnel. We went through it, then afterwards I went to stay at a place near the tunnel and I found that the place above the tunnel had been on fire while we were going under it, and still was on fire in a horrible creepy kind of way. I think it was called "The Manor House". Just as we went in some sparks seemed to come out of the side.' (Manor House was the name of a temporary home where his mother was living.)

The dream, it will be seen, carries on the thought which has been expressed in the World and gives additional material which would be impossible to represent even in so plastic a material as this apparatus affords.

In this case the dream and the World illustrate and enlarge each other, making together a more complete concept. The dream allowed for the addition of the fire and the feeling of creepiness, and also the connection with his mother; the World on the other hand allowed this thought to be connected up with a number of other lines of development which he had worked out in previous 'Worlds' and gave the explanation of his relation to the whole of his social life, showing that the apparent excellence of his outward adaptation was of a neurotic kind.

There remains to be considered the central question which may perhaps be stated thus. Of what nature is the thought depicted in Worlds? Does it develop from World to World of the same child? What relation does it bear to cognitive processes?

7 CONTRIBUTION MADE BY CHILDREN'S WORLDS TO PROBLEMS OF DIAGNOSIS

Let us approach this point first by considering the question of the relation of making a World to the problems of diagnosis.

Figure 13. Here is a World made by a girl of nineteen on her

Figure 13 *A man threatening a giraffe*

first visit for consultation. She was brought by her mother for advice on choice of a career, as the mother, who was a very serious woman, had been troubled by her daughter's frivolity and lack of concentration. From the history and outward behaviour of the girl there was nothing to suggest the presence of any neurosis. While I was talking with the mother, the girl was asked to make a World – this is the one that resulted.

Here you will see a man brandishing a stick and threatening a giraffe who is looking over the hillock at him. The other animals were on their way down to the pond in the centre to have a drink, but when the giraffe caused this disturbance, they all turned to watch. The only person not watching is the man in the top right-hand corner who is walking away and cannot see because of the bundle he is carrying.

It is clear that underneath the girl's apparent adaptation lay ideas of a paranoic quality. The girl herself felt the World as absolutely normal and usual, and could see nothing in it that was peculiar in any way. The existence of this World, however, made it possible to convince both her and her mother of the necessity for treatment.

Figure 14. Here is the World of a case illustrating the opposite

 Figure 14 *Empty house with town and harbour*

pole of difficulty. This was made by a girl of seventeen, brought by her family as an 'emergency' for advice under conditions of great excitement, with an account of having recently made a serious bodily attack upon a relative in circumstances suggestive of a manic state. This World, as you will agree, is childish in construction and considerably inferior to Worlds usually constructed by a seventeen-year-old girl of good intelligence. When asked to talk about it, she felt it satisfactory, but could give almost no account of its nature. The central building is a dwelling house, but it is empty: it has no connection with the pump. The trains are just going but not going anywhere, the same is true of the aeroplanes and cars. The only part of the World with coherence and purpose is the town and harbour in the top right-hand corner: from here ships are going to a town (not shown) further up the coast.

Figure 15. This was made at the next interview and made the situation clear. In the left-hand corner there is a piece of jungle. Tigers are creeping round trees here to attack the deer. The lion is looking on. He will join the meal later. In the centre bison are being rounded up by cowboys and the tiger is preparing to attack them. The elephant at the back is really representative of a

Figure 15 *A jungle scene*

herd of elephants who have come a long journey but have come through safely. They are purposeful. The elephants in the bottom right-hand corner, on the other hand, are just standing about. The two giraffes and the zebra are safe as long as they avoid the rattlesnake. The giraffe nearest the snake knows about him – the other does not.

Whereas in the first girl outwardly normal behaviour was correlated with real interior abnormality, in the second, outwardly very abnormal behaviour turned out to be the expression of an immature and entirely undisciplined nature, but of relatively normal emotional construction. In both cases the Worlds were definitive in diagnosis, prognosis, and the construction for the relatives of an outline of treatment.

8 WORLDS SHOWING DEVELOPMENT OF HYPO-NOIC THOUGHT

You will note I have not raised the question of conscious or unconscious thought in relation to these Worlds. I have not done so because I find myself unable to fit the material produced by them into these concepts. I do not know if this material is conscious or unconscious, and I hope later to have an opportunity of putting forward an alternative view of mental structure in which these two divisions do not occur. For the moment I would prefer to refer to the series of slides I am now going to show you – in Kretschmer's term, as an illustration of *hypo-noic* thought (but without implying a necessary acceptance of that which Kretschmer expresses by this word).

Figures 16–19. Made in sequence in one week.

Figure 16. Here you see a very competently carried out reality demonstration of a country house. The only moving figure is a gardener mowing the lawn. The execution of this World and Figure 4 are almost on an adult level.

Figure 17. Here is a purely phantasy World, about on the level of a small boy playing trains. The water flows both ways at once and the trains go both ways.

Figure 18 is on the same level as Figure 15. Here there is movement up the road and down the river to its mouth. The boy himself, who had had many breathing exercises for speech trouble, referred to it as representing breathing. The trains cut across the opening.

Figure 19. Here we are back on the level of Figure 1. This is a garden town. When we came to consider the time of day represented, we found that there was no time, as the boy himself

Figure 16 *A country house*

Figure 17 *Water and trains go both ways*

Figure 18 *Breathing*

volunteered that if it were night there would be a cat. This is then the perfect or ideal town, looked at, as he himself said, by the eye of God: a God who enforced absolute order on his creatures. Figure 16 represents the same conception, only less completely. The contrast between these two Worlds and those in between in the series expressed an actual objective picture of the boy's own state: the centre very much retarded in development, full of undirected, undifferentiated force, the outside compulsive and static, an antithetical formation to the crude retardation of the interior. As he himself had made these Worlds in this exact sequence, he found himself confronted inescapably by his own problem, the part of the grown-up being only that of the naturalist examining a beetle with his student.

We will now take a similar series produced by an undergraduate referred for inability to work.

Figure 20. Here we have a World divided into two halves by a pond. On the left-hand side is a tableau, representing war – you will note that the guns fire themselves – and in front, figures, illustrative, so the maker described them, of the idea of death. In the top right-hand corner – the idea of a holiday; and in the centre – a peaceful pond. When asked if the village on the right knew of the war, the answer was in the negative. When asked if the sharpshooters on the left knew of the village, the answer was also 'No'.

Figure 21. This was the next World to follow. Here the theme has developed. The single source of anxiety in the World preceding this one has split into three. You will observe in this World a peaceful village in the centre and an ice-cream man: a mountain at the back suggesting to him his summer holidays, and a charabanc in the foreground, suggesting to him conviviality and sightseeing.

The pond has now moved to the left-bottom corner: out of it comes a sea serpent of a deadly kind. Behind the mountain a firing party fires at a man. To the right, wild animals emerge behind the hill to attack the charabanc. Here there is some connection between the two parts of the picture. The animals are dimly aware of the charabanc, which is unaware of them. The maker of this World was widely read and thoughtful and the serpent was a rich symbol to him, meaning a wide variety of concepts related to ancient wisdom, sexual knowledge and the mythic side of life. He had not seen till it was pointed out that there was no one keeping the man before the firing party and he could have run away. He had a great respect for rifles as evidence

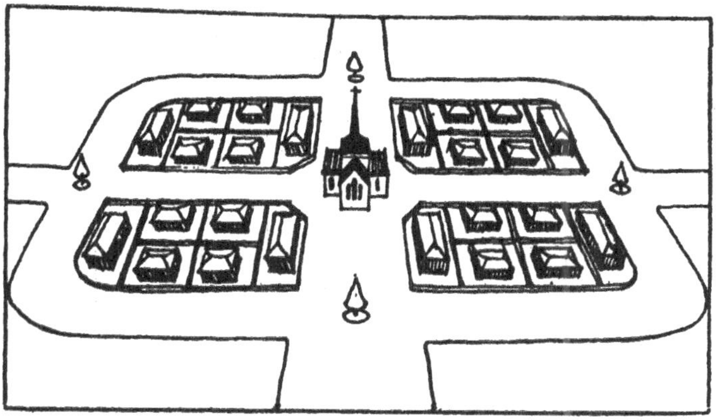

Figure 19 *The perfect town*

Figure 20 *War and a peaceful village*

Figure 21 *A firing party and a peaceful village*

of man's taming to his will the forces of inorganic science – the wild animals were to him the wildness of natural things.

You will note in this World there is no real relation between the two halves and no concept of defence against the danger.

Figure 22 was the next of this series. Here we have a meeting of the two ideas – danger coming from the air has now struck the houses and a scene of desolation results. Some men have survived, however, and they are marching gaily along: these are soldiers, and the maker of the World felt that they were safe, they understood the dangers and were not in danger from them: they were not afraid either of the destruction around them. Safety lay in aggression activity.

These two groups are tiny excerpts from series made by numberless patients in the course of treatment. You will note that in the first set the four Worlds taken together complete the picture of a total state. They are susceptible of almost unlimited analysis, as each object used, the grouping of the objects and the interrelation combined with each other to present a total picture, which, I believe, would be impossible to express in words.

In the second series each World takes up and develops the theme expressed in the World before, so that the whole develops like an argument. The contents of these Worlds also were

 Figure 22 *Danger from the air*

exceedingly rich in meaning and also like the first series entirely impossible of total expression in words. Confrontation with the World he had himself made brought the contents of it forcibly to the mind of the maker. This total representation is neither conscious nor unconscious, but truly non-cognitive in either case, or, to use Kretschmer's term, below the level of consciousness, hypo-noic.

One word now as to my own handling of World material.

It is perfectly clear that, confronted with this material, anyone who wills will be able to read into these World representations components derived from his personal conviction, and that not merely as a result of wish fulfilment, but because they are almost certainly to be present there. A psychoanalyst will find sexual themes, sometimes overtly, sometimes symbolically represented there, for the reason that sexuality does play a part in a child's World picture. The Adlerian will undoubtedly find the power complex and its derivatives represented in this hypo-noic language. The World apparatus should appeal to the heart of the Jungian, seeing that the World cabinet is richly furnished with already completed archetype symbols.

My own direct use of the material in the presence of the child is to treat it like a cipher language, and concentrate my attention on an endeavour to discover what exactly the objects used represent to *the child who uses them*. Thus I explain to each child that a horse for example may be to one child a representation of a thing it fears, to another its dearest friend, to a third, as one said, 'A strong thing which runs', to another 'What Daddy rides', and so on; and then we imagine I am a South Sea Islander having never seen Europe and the child explains to me what each object actually is, that is, is to him.

Having drawn the World we then substitute in it the *qualities and concepts the child has given*. When these are reassembled together the result is a picture of affect, concept, memory and experience inextricably woven together into the presentation of a total state.

May I then sum up the qualities and advantages of the method I have tried to put before you?

1. It is in the nature of an experiment which can be repeated.
2. It permits of continuity from one session to another without imposing a strain on the therapeutic situation.
3. It permits of accurate record.
4. The personal factor enters to a minimum extent.

In short, this apparatus enables representation of the total content of a mind at a given moment in time, which can be separated from the therapeutic situation and thought about and analysed in an atmosphere of emotional neutrality. 'World' can be compared with World and findings checked. And although, as I have already said, it is impossible for me in the limits of this paper even to indicate my own conclusions as to the structure of the child's mind, or the theory which underlies both this use of the material or which in my view should underlie child psychotherapy, yet I would like to say that my study of many hundreds of World pictures, obtained in the way described, has led me to the conviction that the hypo-noic levels of the child's mind, and therefore presumably of the adult mind as well, are concerned with profoundly metaphysical problems, such as the nature of time, of movement and of relations of perception and sensation, and of the nature of reality both interior and exterior, and that these matters are of greater moment in the emotional and mental development of normal and disturbed children than is the working out of an arbitrarily abstracted concept, such as the pleasure–pain principle.

At a later date, if this Society is interested and indulgent, I should like to present for its consideration some of the principles of mental life which I have come to formulate as a result of ten years' study of material such as I have been endeavouring to demonstrate tonight, and which have formed the experimental basis of not too unsuccessful psychotherapy. I have only been able to present to you a methodological paper which leaves all fundamental considerations untouched.

Discussion

In opening the discussion Dr Grace Calver said: I think we should all be most grateful to Dr Lowenfeld for her most interesting paper and also for trying to devise a method of play which can be studied objectively and where comparisons between the work of different children can be made. One point which has always appeared of great importance to me and which had so far been overlooked by Dr Lowenfeld, but which, from her paper, I understand she is now studying, is the observation of the use that normal children of different ages would make of this material. Dr Charlotte Bühler and her assistants have made careful studies of the behaviour of children at different phases of development and have drawn attention to the fact that there are certain activities of childhood that are age characteristic. In dealing with the World material of Dr Lowenfeld I think it is of the utmost importance that we observe the age characteristic layout before making any interpretations in relation to this or neurotic behaviour. As an example, a six-year-old using the World material would perfectly naturally place wild animals and domestic animals in a field together. This would not be in him any sign of conflict or neurosis. The same layout in a child of ten would definitely be a sign of some emotional abnormality, as by that age a child should use the material in a way much more consistent with reality situation.

The value of the use of this World material seems to me to lie in the fact that we can have these layouts for comparison by other therapists. They are of the utmost value in the diagnosis of particular behaviour problems and are a means whereby the child can express objectively a subjective feeling which because of its inability to express feelings verbally it would be otherwise unable to communicate to us.

Mrs Melanie Klein: Mr Chairman, Ladies and Gentlemen, I wish to make some remarks about two aspects of Dr Lowenfeld's paper. First, some comments on what she has said as to the historical relation between her work and my own; and second, upon the nature of her work.

From Dr Lowenfeld's account of the child analyst's approach, it would appear that this is an extremely rigid and limited one, and as if the analyst were more concerned with applying and confirming his theories dogmatically than with getting into full contact with everything that goes on in the child's mind and feelings, and with curing him. From a study of various papers written by child psychoanalysts and of my book (*The Psychoanalysis of Children*) it will be seen that Dr Lowenfeld's description does not meet the facts. I shall confine myself here to quoting from the paper which I read to this section in 1927 and to which Dr Lowenfeld has referred this evening. I made it clear that the aim of the psychoanalytic play technique with children is to discover the child's emotional life, his wishes, phantasies and thoughts. I will quote what I said then: 'Slowly the analyst, by interpreting to the child what his play, drawings and whole behaviour means, resolves the repressions against the phantasies behind the play and liberates those phantasies. Tiny dolls, men, women, animals, cars, trains and so on, enable the child to represent various persons, mother, father, brothers and sisters, and by means of the toys to act all his most repressed unconscious material . . . When from our psychoanalytic point of view we watch the child at play and use special technical measures to diminish his inhibition, we can bring out his phantasies [and theories], find out the experiences the child has had, and see all the child's impulses and its reacting criticizing faculties both at work' [Klein, 1927].

Some of these aims and some details of the psychoanalytic play technique have influenced many psychotherapists working with children. Dr Lowenfeld tries to dissociate herself entirely from the influence upon her work of the psychoanalytic play technique and its principles. I would like, however, to remind her of a passage in a former paper of her own, which I came across only today, and which was addressed to this Society in 1931; that is to say, four years subsequently to my own paper referred to before. She writes: 'Although my admiration for the work of Mrs Klein and her group is very great, and in spite of the fact that without it my own work would not be possible, not being a trained psychoanalyst, I do not feel myself qualified to use with the children directly psychoanalytic interpretation, however much I may myself benefit in my understanding of them by a knowledge of psychoanalytic findings. Interpretation of symbols by that theory is a very strong explosive to the mind of a child, and I feel convinced should not be used by others than those properly trained in its technique. There is of necessity some relation between my mode of approach and the psychoanalytic play technique, though the angle of attack is different, and it is, I think, worthy of note that, in spite of this fact, the phenomena produced by my children in such very different circumstances are so often closely akin to those described by Mrs Klein. But in evaluating the phenomena, though I find myself very greatly indebted to Mrs Klein's work and to her group, it does not seem to me possible, until there is full publication of the child material from which these conclusions are drawn, to form any definite opinion as to the ultimate validity of the interpretations given by her to them' [Lowenfeld, 1931; this volume, p. 183].

It would thus appear that in her own special method, Dr Lowenfeld has drawn upon psychoanalytic research and technique much more freely than she now seems to remember. It seems clear that Dr Lowenfeld, in spite of her repudiation of the psychoanalytic method, tries to achieve certain of the aims which underlie the psychoanalytic work. As she said tonight, 'to devise an instrument by which the child can demonstrate his own emotional and mental state'. She also wishes to make direct contact with the whole of the child's mind – a thing which cannot be done without understanding and dealing with the unconscious part of the mind: and for that the psychoanalytic approach is essential.

She stresses, however, that she wants to achieve her aim 'without the necessary intervention of an adult either by transference or interpretation'. Now this obvious wish to keep away from one of the fundamental principles of psychoanalysis, namely the transference, leads to a dead end. Freud has discovered that the phenomenon of transferring one's early feelings in relation to parents and brothers and sisters enters to some extent into all human relationships, and plays a special and very important part in the relation of the patient to the physician. The psychoanalyst makes use of the patient's transference feelings in a specific way for the purpose of helping the child – and for that matter the grown-up also – to express what his phantasies are, and to experience them and his feelings and impulses in relation to a real and helpful person. But as I said before, transference feelings, even if they are not dealt with in this specific psychoanalytic way, still enter into every relationship, and therefore also into the relation with any psychotherapist. If he tries to avoid the transference, he cannot in fact achieve this, but in trying to do so, he necessarily impedes his work and creates a false situation. In this respect, therefore, Dr Lowenfeld's work seems to me to suffer a serious disadvantage as compared with the work of many other child psychotherapists, in so far as these make a sensible and careful use of the transference. Dr Lowenfeld, however, seems to sacrifice the valuable possibilities inherent in the transference for the sake of a polished academic finish and an effort to fit psychological science into the mould of physics. As she says: 'Physical science has progressed in strict accord with the development of possibilities of precise investigation and direct record of the facts observed, and their abstraction for study from the circumstances of production.'

I do not believe that the feelings, wishes and phantasies of children can usefully be abstracted from their human context in this artificial way.

DR SUSAN ISAACS: Mr Chairman, Ladies and Gentlemen, I have listened, as I am sure we have all listened, with the greatest interest to the fascinating material which Dr Lowenfeld has brought before us. The glimpses of the feelings and phantasies in the minds of the children who constructed these various Worlds have indeed been fascinating, as any direct material from children themselves is bound to be. It is, however, specifically as a contribution to scientific method that Dr Lowenfeld has brought forward her material tonight. Throughout her paper, she has emphasized this aspect of her contribution, and it is from this point of view that I would like to make some remarks.

Dr Lowenfeld has emphatically stated tonight that her studies have been independent of other people's investigations. Not only so; she has taken the line that this is the right, indeed the only, way to do research: to work alone, without knowing what other people have done in the same field. Now in the first place I do not believe this to be a sound scientific doctrine. One has only to imagine what would happen if some investigator at this time of day set out to create a new method of studying intelligence, say, a new scale of intelligence tests, without knowing anything about or making any reference to the work of, for example, Binet, Terman and Burt and Spearman, in order to see how inappropriate and extravagant, how foolish, such an approach would be. The originality of our contributions in the scientific field does not rest upon our ignorance, but upon a creative assimilation, and if necessary, criticism, of other people's thinking.

In the second place, moreover, Dr Lowenfeld's work has not in fact been so much in the dark as she has suggested tonight. In Dr Lowenfeld's own previous paper to this Section in 1931, from which Mrs Klein has just quoted, she not only made full acknowledgement of the extent to which her own work depended upon the previous investigations of psychoanalysis in general and Mrs Klein's researches in particular, but also acknowledged what she had gained from Piaget's studies. Probably many of you who have heard Dr Lowenfeld tonight and her remarks about the child's concern with the fundamental problems of time, movement, the nature of things, will have remembered the major contributions of Piaget in this field. In the five most important volumes of Piaget's work, which were published in this country a number of years ago, he has shown in great detail the way in which at successive ages the child's thought about the movements of bodies, the nature of life, of consciousness, of thought, of dreams, the different forms of causality, and so on and so forth, develops and changes until it approximates more and more closely to the relational thinking of the adult.

There is, however, one fundamental point in which, judging by her remarks on this subject, Dr Lowenfeld has failed to appreciate Piaget's work, namely, the changes in the child's mode of thinking according to his age. Dr Lowenfeld's own statements tonight have been entirely without reference to age: 'A child does not think linearly as the adult is capable of doing: thought, feeling, sensations, concept and memory are all inextricably interwoven. A child's thought is fluid and movement can take place on several planes at once . . . Finally, a child's concepts have no relation to what we call, in our view of the world, external reality.'

She thus speaks of 'a child' as if in this respect children of all ages thought in exactly the same way, even including boys of nineteen, since one or two of her slides showed the World of an undergraduate of nineteen. I confess that this seems to me a surprising oversight. It is surely nonsense to suggest that the *thought* of a boy of nineteen, a child of ten, and one of four years or less is as she has described it in the sentences I quote. There are very few generalizations which one can make about children's minds without any reference to differences due to age, since surely one of the fundamental facts is the fact of growth and development.

It is not even true of the very little child, say the child of two years, that his concepts have 'no relation to external reality'. Even then he is in his aims vitally concerned with the real qualities of things, and relates himself to reality, within the limits of his knowledge and experience; but of course his perception of reality is limited, and liable to be distorted by his feelings and phantasies. Even with the older child and the adult, well adjusted to reality in his relational thinking, this is liable to happen where feeling is intense.

The error surely springs from Dr Lowenfeld's misconception that in her Worlds she is dealing with the child's thought as such, and her wish to reject the psychoanalytic discovery of phantasy – conscious and unconscious phantasy. In her Worlds it is surely the child's feelings and phantasies that are involved, not his thought. It is certainly true that phantasy has very little relation to age, the unconscious phantasies of adolescents and adults being very little if at all different from those of the infant and young child. As we know, the unconscious mind takes no account of time, and is incapable of differentiated relational thinking. Dr Lowenfeld is right therefore in assuming that her Worlds reveal mental processes which are constant at all ages. But she is wrong in calling these 'thought', and is surely wrong in attempting to blur the distinction between unconscious phantasy and noesis. It is a great pity if she has to cling to such a confusion in order to support her contention that her own work is original and unrelated to that of other people.

Again, in another sentence, Dr Lowenfeld said: 'A child's feeling is absolute in that any emotion, while it is present, holds the whole field of consciousness.' But one of the striking and outstanding facts revealed by the material she showed us this evening is the existence of a *conflict* of feelings – of contrary feelings occurring in the child's mind at the same time. Her Worlds are a useful way of enabling the child to express these opposing and conflicting feelings and the enormous inner tension which results from conflict. And, as we all remember, it was Mrs Klein who first taught us that in his use of toys and play material the child can show us his conflict of feeling, his love, his fear, his hate, his guilt, his anxiety, and his phantasies, in a way and to an extent that he cannot express in words, without our technical help in analysis.

DR R.F. BARBOUR: In psychological work the need for some objective form of record has long been felt – something that will permit of examination by more than one person – something that will allow comparison of different children at different times and places. The drawback of most records is that we are too dependent on the bias of the observer. Dr Lowenfeld is attempting to provide an impartial type of record and for that we are grateful, it is a step in the right direction. In her present paper she is not attempting to define a form of therapy, but merely to describe a method of recording children's play and it is on this basis that we must judge it.

 DR D.W. WINNICOTT said that when he had recovered from

enjoying the lantern slides he had tried to understand what was the aim of the work. He felt a sense of constriction at the provision of set apparatus and he was sure that anyone who had developed a personal freedom of technique would wish to be assured of some very definite gain by the use of Dr Lowenfeld's apparatus before being happy about its employment. The gain from this or any set technique might arise from the fact that many beginners felt anxious or guilty at enjoying play with children; for them any set technique would come as a sort of sanction which might carry them over till they had become less frightened of the intimate emotional relationship with children which play with them entails.

But there seemed to be some larger aim implied by Dr Lowenfeld, as if someone was trying to prove something to someone. Who is trying to prove what to whom? Could Dr Lowenfeld be trying to prove to those who do not believe it that there is an inner fantasy world of every child? This existed whether it could be demonstrated or not, and it seems unlikely that those who denied it could be altered in their view by this means; or, alternately, if they came to recognize the existence of fantasy they would fail to see its essential significance, or its movement, or its relation to the child's past and present history and to his appreciation of the external (shared) world.

One interesting feature of this apparatus was the way in which it provided reassurances, for instance the reassurance against part-objects-shapes, unnamed terrors, long-leggedy-beasties and so on. The toys provided were so designed that the resulting Worlds gave a much greater appearance of integrating power and reality appreciation than one would get without set technique (drawings, for instance, may show a person with no belly or with an exaggerated phallus); the differences here would be due not to a difference between groups of children but to a limitation imposed by the apparatus.

To get an idea in one consultation of the psychiatric condition of a child one could get more without the use of the apparatus than with it. But Dr Lowenfeld's object was not so much this as to prove something to someone, to someone very sceptical and inhibited if so restricted an apparatus must be used. And who could this sceptical person be?

A criticism that could be made of the apparatus as such was

that such a great variety of toys as were available would bewilder many children – children who, with a few little people and a house and a railway train, or with a pencil and paper, would be capable of displaying a whole range of inner- and outer-world hopes and fears to anyone who was not afraid to learn how to see.

MISS M.N. SEARL: I should like to pay a full tribute to the interest and clarity of the presentation of the material Dr Lowenfeld has given us, and also to the care expended on the records. Any difficulty I have on the subject of the lecture is of a different kind from that expressed by the previous speakers. It sometimes seems to me that such comparison of records leading to classification in terms of neuroses tends to a standardizing which may overshadow the understanding of the individual child with his great variety of individual problems, dispositions, capacities, etc. One would naturally expect that the childhood of poets, explorers, practical men of affairs and so forth would show great divergencies both in accomplishment and in failure. Every gift has its own particular possibilities of defect, and too much regard to standardizing in terms of the latter *may* hinder both the awareness of the former and the help for its development.

REPLY TO THE DISCUSSION BY DR LOWENFELD: There is one very great difficulty which has to be faced but which cannot be surmounted by the writer of a paper on a new piece of apparatus. This difficulty is the iron limitation imposed by the shortness of the available time. In one hour, if sufficient material is to be presented to make the subject intelligible, the surrounding issues have to be neglected. I would like now to take this opportunity to supplement the serious gaps in the paper itself of which I myself am only too conscious.

First, about the *method of reproduction of World material*. It is clear to anyone who has seen the actual Worlds made by children that the drawings reproduced here give on the whole a very poor idea of them. Photographs of actual Worlds would seem to be a better way, and direct photography was the first method tried. In practice difficulties arose, as have been cited. To these may be added the following. The whole of any World is equally important and the sand is only occasionally kept level. A photograph, therefore, from one side of a tray containing, for example, a hill, can show only the side of the hill facing the camera: a second one must be taken for the other side. To represent some Worlds adequately four photographs would be necessary. Even so, considerable effort of imagination would be required to combine them in the mind so that the whole World is seen. By this means the Worlds can be reconstructed for further detailed study.

As a result of these objections the photographic method of record was discontinued and the really rather unsatisfactory alternative of drawings has been adopted instead *faute de mieux*, since by this method all items on the tray can be shown, their relative importance indicated and the ground plan of the tray set out.

The Age Factor. Had time permitted I would very much have liked to have dealt fully with the question of age in relation to the Worlds of children as this factor enters into the question in rather a curious way. Dr Charlotte Bühler has, since she first met my World apparatus in 1934, been particularly interested in the question of the relation of age to the *selection* of material, and decided to undertake an investigation with normal children of this point. Any detailed information that can be obtained as to the behaviour of children must be of value, but the information obtained in this way will not, I am afraid, be of much assistance in elucidating the questions raised by Dr Calver and Dr Isaacs. In Dr Bühler's experiments the choice of materials offered to the children was fixed and standardized, and I understand that no sand is included: the possibilities, therefore, of three-dimensional presentation, which is an essential quality of the apparatus, are removed, and only the most superficial aspects of the material are considered.

As far as my own observations go the age of the World maker affects the World in two ways. Below a certain age, the limit probably being between four and six, 'World' material is not suitable. The child of this age is interested in each piece separately and in the relation of one or two pieces to each other, but has not reached a stage of development where combination of many objects is possible. Also, as Dr Calver points out, animals tend to be 'animals' to him and he hardly differentiates wild from tame.

From this date onwards, age affects and does not affect the World material according as to which part of the mind is presented. Here may I answer Dr Isaac's very interesting and important observations. Dr Isaacs states that it is a confusion to call the World product 'thought', and that I should call it phantasy instead. Professor Collingwood in an *Essay on Philosophic Method* deals at length with this very difficulty, pointing out that values lie on a scale, the one below partaking of so many qualities of the one above that we are often forced to use the same word for it as for the next value above it in the scale, though clearly the main characters are different [Collingwood, 1933]. Thus all psychologists are agreed that there are two forms of cerebration to be observed in the human race, one which is reasonable, consciously directed and as we say 'cognitive', and another which does not seem to partake of these qualities. To this other part of the mind and its products many names are given, chief among them being 'unconscious' and 'phantasy'. But since these parts of the mind have a structure (see such books as the *Logic of the Unconscious*, for example, etc.) they are also thought – that is if thought is to be defined as the product of the mind in action. They are different in quality and structure from cognitive (or 'conscious') thought, but what I contend is that they are no less 'thought' though of a different nature from conscious thought. This difficulty, as Collingwood has pointed out, is a common difficulty and in no way peculiar to psychology. I would propose to surmount the difficulty by alluding to a primary and secondary system of thought, in which the primary system would cover all forms of thought described more usually as phantasy, and the secondary system, cognition.

In as far as a World represents the thought of the primary system, it is, as Dr Isaacs has pointed out, ageless: in as far as it contains elements of thought from the secondary system, age is a most important factor. Here comes in also the 'Work Maturity' of Charlotte Bühler and all the observations of Piaget. Let us take the subject of a feeling of interior danger arising from an uncontrollable source: an eight-year-old child will, perhaps, put three figures on the sand, and two lions, and have one lion jumping at a figure and another running after a human who is running away. An eleven-year-old boy will perhaps have a sailing boat at sea suddenly finding itself surrounded by sharks: a nineteen-year-old girl might have an aeroplane having made a forced landing by an oasis in a desert with hostile Zulus hiding in the scrub around them: an undergraduate can make the Worlds already shown.

In each of these a comparable 'thought' of the primary system is shown: the relative age development in the secondary system is active, however, in choosing the form in which this is displayed. It is possible to have Worlds in which there is no element of the secondary system, as Worlds in which the secondary system predominates, where at first sight it would appear that the primary (or phantasy) element was absent. When the secondary system is considered, all those changes in a child's mode of thinking to which Dr Isaacs refers are perceivable.

I am very sorry I did not foresee and so attempt in the paper to clarify this confusion. It lies in the definition of thought. Taken as 'cognitive' thought, everything Dr Isaacs points out is most clearly true, but if I am allowed my contention of a primary system of thought, then what has been said in my paper stands.

In the primary system of 'thought', as in a paper entitled 'A Thesis Concerning the Fundamental Structure of the Mento-emotional Processes in Children' [in this volume, see p. 247 above] read to the General Section of the British Psychological Society in April 1937, I made an attempt to outline, feeling and sensation are inextricably involved and with memory and the concepts belonging to that region make up what I am putting forward as this system of primary thought. If it be asked, why reject the term 'phantasy' or 'unconscious', the answer is that the interaction between this part of the mind and that of cognitive thought which the study of Worlds has brought to light suggests that this is too vague a definition to carry the weight of the material revealed and leaves unanswered the questions fundamental to all psychotherapy: What is meant by the word phantasy? What kind of an activity is it? What parts of the mind take part in its production?

Here perhaps it is best to reply to Dr Isaac's query concerning Piaget. The writing and the reading of books is a great labour and it is possibly arguable that too many are written, but they do serve the purpose of getting said, and therefore out of the way, a number of questions that are permanent and so leaving freedom for other matter. The question of Piaget and of many other important works on the observation side of child psychology is of great weight for all observation of children and in order to set the way free for reports on experiment was dealt with in my book *Play in Childhood* [Lowenfeld, 1935].

Considering the matter of the relation of this work to child psychoanalysis, Mrs Klein has in her opening paper stated exactly and clearly where the difference lies. As Mrs Klein states, the analyst by '*interpreting to the child* what his play, drawings, and whole behaviour mean, resolves the *repressions* against the *phantasies behind the play* and *liberates* those phantasies. Tiny dolls, men, women, animals, cars, trains and so on, enable the child to present various persons, mother, father, brothers and sisters, and by means of the toys to act all his *most repressed unconscious* material . . .' (my italics).

Clearly that is, as stated in my paper, the analyst on approaching the child at play has already accepted the validity of the theses of 'conscious' and 'unconscious' repression' and 'repressed phantasies', and the operation of these in the child's psyche. That is to say he has already in his mind a mass of dogma concerning the nature of the mind of which, as I stated and as Mrs Klein restates, he makes use to 'interpret' his play to the child. Now one can only interpret into a language one already knows oneself and this language must be known beforehand. The child analyst, therefore, assumes on approaching a child at play that he already knows in general terms the probable structure of that play and so of the child's own mind; which is the point I was trying to make and in which I see Mrs Klein concurs. Now I wish to state as clearly and definitely as print or language will enable me, that in setting out to make independent observations of the products of the child's mind and to devise apparatus by which this may be done, I am not designing an attack upon the doctrines or the procedure of psychoanalysis. As the universe presents itself to me, the human mind is too wide for any one system of thought or observation to exhaust its meaning. My own work is complementary to and not in opposition to the work of psychoanalysis. I look forward to a time when there will be enough psychoanalytic material: material produced by my own and by many other forms of approach available for their contradictions to be resolved in a higher synthesis. This is the method of all progress in thought. I would not even contend with Mrs Klein's statement that for the understanding of what she terms the unconscious part of the mind the psychoanalytic approach is essential. I am not yet clear what part of the mind this is and would not venture an opinion upon it. The presentation of these Worlds is an endeavour to produce a means by which the theories of psychoanalysis, of

Adler, of Jung, of myself, and of any other form of thought, may be studied concretely. No two people will regard a World exactly in the same way, but so long as the given World has been recorded their different points of view can meet and their differences be thrashed out over a fixed phenomenon and thus perhaps ultimately some mutual understanding be achieved.

To take the question of the transference and of the points which have been raised as to the use of the World apparatus in treatment:

Once again I regret that the time limit and the desire to show you some width of material made it impossible to include also in this paper the question of the relations of Worlds to therapy.

The aim of the World as a research instrument is to give material for objective study of mental states. The aim of the World in treatment is to confront the child with himself. Such is the aim of psychoanalysis. As I have said above, they go side by side by different routes to a common goal. In the psychoanalytic approach the analyst is the agent confronting the child with the 'meaning' of his play by the interpretation given by her to it. In Worlds the child is confronted by a piece of his own feeling, thinking, remembering-life set out by himself for his own study. A transference situation, that is a transference to the physician rather than to the material, is an intervention between the part of the child which made the World and the part that regards it. The work of the physician in reference to a world is to assist the secondary system (the conscious) in the mind of the maker to grasp what has been stated by the primary. There is an extraordinary force in this confrontation: the child having made the picture has to accept it as his own: the force of the statement brings home to him its reality.

It needs to be stressed that on the other hand the making of Worlds is only *part* of a psychotherapeutic treatment, and that much else occurs in the course of any such. All I am concerned here to claim is that certain problems (not all problems) can be better stated in this way and that such statement gives valuable evidence concerning the nature of this primary-system part of the mind, and the relation of it to other parts, which has not been available before. At the end of this paper I have put out very shortly an account of a case which may perhaps make this point clearer.

It is sad also that time prevented a proper consideration of the relation of World, drawing and dream.

My own thesis, which I hope to have the opportunity to set out at length in another place, is that from the date of birth, and possibly and indeed very probably from before birth, the consciousness of a child begins to record its experience: that this experience in the early stages of life is composed of sensation, feeling, emotion and rudimentary thought inextricably bound together; that it has a multidimensional quality (where cognitive thought may be thought of as two-dimensional) and is bound together by certain laws; that the emotional element in this complex gives it a dynamic quality which seeks always for expression. When in later months or years the beginnings are made of the cognitive system, the elements of this (as I tried to show in the paper read to the Manchester conference) are fundamentally different from and incompatible with the primary system, and there remains a permanent state of tension between these two.

The nature of the primary system precludes the possibility of its expression in words as normally used, though the essence of the poetic genius is that he can bend this instrument to portray primary thought. The primary system therefore presses for expression and finds it among other ways in dream, children's (non-objective) drawings and in Worlds, which appear all to be products of the same nature. The essence of the quality of a dream, the combination of feeling, affect and sensation with movement and idea can with difficulty be reproduced in a drawing since the drawing is forcedly two-dimensional. Still, young children's drawings have often, as set out in my book, a three-dimensional quality to the child who draws them. Examination of Worlds and the accounts given of them by the children who make them show that those qualities of the dream described by Freud, condensation, displacement, etc., are also present in them, not, I would suggest, owing to the action of repression, but because they are intrinsic qualities of the primary system.

I am sorry that Dr Winnicott should feel that the use of any means by which a child can represent to himself the content of his own 'phantasy' should imply, in the adult helping him in his use of the material, inhibition and anxiety, and blindness to the existence of that world of thought and feeling which the material is specifically designed to enable the child to represent. Dr Winnicott brings forward an interesting point in drawing attention to the reassurances and at the same time the limitations imposed on the child's thought by set and apparently complete objects. This is more apparent than real, since in actual work with this material certain pieces inevitably quickly become damaged and losing their heads or limbs become defective in every conceivable way. The child has also at his disposal plasticine and a drawer of shapeless objects, and can and does use them to represent those odd and partial concepts to which Dr Winnicott refers.

I think it is true that presentation simultaneously of a large number of objects to a child may bewilder it and that this is a real danger. I endeavour to guard against it by the use of a cabinet in which the pulling out of one drawer obscures all others.

I feel that Miss Searl in her comment has brought up a most valuable point. I would regret exceedingly if the introduction of records such as these were to lead, as she suggests, to classification in terms of neuroses, and I feel acutely that far greater knowledge than we at present possess of the nature of temperament, disposition and innate capacity is needed before a final word can be said about any series of Worlds. The mere fact of the existence of records of a large number of widely differing children with whom I hope to be able to keep loosely in touch, suggests the hope that future correlation of developed character and attainments with early Worlds may throw light upon this very problem. As regards classification, I look upon the classifications which can usefully be made of this material in terms of themes stated, rather than the condition of the child stating them. One of the absorbingly interesting features already revealed by this material is the occurrence over and over again of Worlds or parts of Worlds of exactly the same character, made by children differing widely in age or temperament, in type of complaint and in the point in the treatment at which the World was made. It is these spontaneous groupings which are valuable and I hope it will be long before we impose upon collections of World material any arbitrary classifications from outside.

I would like in closing this part of my reply to return to the question raised by both Mrs Klein and Dr Isaacs of the relation of this part of my work to that of other people. Mrs Klein draws attention in her opening remarks to a paragraph in an earlier paper of my own in this journal which at first sight would appear to contradict some of what I have said here. This contradiction is, however, more apparent than real. In the paper of 1931, I was attempting to describe the work of a group of people in making a new approach to child psychotherapy and in this case what was stated is correct. It was owing to the interest aroused in free work with children and the possibilities that the interested public were coming to see in it (all of which was related to Mrs Klein's publications) that the existence of such a group as I was describing became possible.

Although I myself have not found it possible to accept Mrs Klein's views on the play of children and have in this paper endeavoured to state the source of my own views, that does not in the least detract from my admiration of Mrs Klein's courageous pioneering efforts. It is not necessary to agree with a person to admire them. In 1931 I was still groping in the dark as to the relation between psychoanalytic findings and the phenomena I was daily observing, and thought at that time I was going to find it far more possible than has subsequently proved the case to accept the point of view put forward by Mrs Klein. I now see that the attempts I made then to accept this point of view were, for me, in a wrong direction, and the account at the beginning of this paper is an attempt to state the history, not of temporary excursions into other regions, but of the genesis of the point of view I now hold and have endeavoured in this paper to indicate.

Finally I propose to give brief notes of a short case, using Worlds already illustrated in order to attempt to show the general relation of Worlds to other therapeutic procedures in treatment. To do this adequately in the reply to a discussion is not possible, as the ground covered by any one normal treatment is too extensive. I propose, therefore, to take for consideration the case whose Worlds Nos. 20 to 22 are given in this series.

The patient was a young man of nineteen referred by his family for help in connection with failure in school work. He had left his public school one year before treatment and was due to go the following October to a university. His school reports throughout his school years stated uniformly that he was capable of brilliance but that his results were always seriously marred by carelessness and lack of concentration. Owing to the financial circumstances of his family, success at the university was very important, but these characteristics showing an increase rather than diminution had in the last year caused his parents grave anxiety. Treatment occupied fourteen interviews. On the first interview it became evident in conversation that there was considerable underlying opposition and resentment both to the idea of education and to the proposed treatment. Superficially, however, there was a certain interest. From the beginning he impressed me as being courageous and remarkably honest. The treatment was divided into two blocks by the summer holidays, two interviews taking place before and twelve after. The first interview was occupied with discussion of his present position which disclosed geology and politics as his main interests – the curious point about this which became clear was their divorce from affairs of the present day. Modern geography and modern politics were of secondary interest, his political interest being absorbed in the devising of future utopias.

In the second interview the family situation was explored and certain significant facts came to light. He had been told that a certain condition present in a near relative was often hereditary. A direct venture on my part that possibly his geological and political views were pictures of anxieties which centred really in perplexities concerning his own birth and the fate of his future children was met first by dumbfounded surprise, and then with keenly interested acceptance. The rest of this interview was taken in dealing with this problem on a basis of reality.

After the summer holidays he returned. The previous conversations had greatly cleared his mind and brought about a significant change in the direction of his interests, but had not altered the reluctance concerning work.

World 20 was made in this interview. I then explained to him very briefly my views concerning the existence of two systems of thought in the mind and how a 'World' was a valid product of the mind, but represents, in the main, material from the primary system and asked him to use his secondary system, i.e. cognitive and critical faculties, in evaluation of it. He worked out for himself what is stated in the text in regard to this World. We agreed that a unified attack upon any task would be impossible for a person whose interior self felt as was represented in this world.

The making and study of this World was a psychic event of great moment for him. By it his problem became to him 'reasonable', that is to say, he could see that he had a problem – his resentment against being called lazy, etc. and so against me as representative of the adult world dropped away and considerable reassurance and interest took its place. I assured him that such states were usual and familiar to people doing my kind of work and that they would, by goodwill and courage on his part and conscientious hard work on mine, resolve themselves.

Five days later he made World 21 and once again worked out the comments as given in the text. He saw for himself that this represented a fact of which he was dimly aware – i.e. that underneath his well-socialized exterior there was a hidden layer of anxiety and that it was this anxiety that prevented him from working. The content of this anxiety he himself suggested might be a terror of the force and effect of his own emotions.

Two days later he made World 22. This he stated was 'Everytown' and that there was an aeroplane suspended over the village. The stationary aeroplanes on the right (not represented in the drawing) were part of the village (defence) army. The making of this World occupied most of the hour and entirely absorbed him. He himself pointed out that the only safe people were people in action.

On the next day we began to examine the content of his anxiety and he did a piece of technique which I have not yet published but which is known as the Newspaper Game. From this and subsequent discussion of it and material brought up by it the next day, it became clear to him that his relationships to other people were on a very childish level. This was an astonishment to him but so clearly depicted in the results of the Newspaper Game that there was no escape from them. The next four interviews were spent dealing with the flood of problems and difficulties that came up regarding relationships, and in going over the three Worlds in relation to them. What became clear was that he was in a state of isolation, unnatural and undesirable for an adolescent. In particular there had been a barrier between him and his parents that had made it impossible for him to ask for exact information about his own background. In the middle of these interviews he became able to make direct contact with his parents and to clear away an accumulation of bogies, also to establish a natural relationship with his mother in relation to their common reality situation.

About this time it became possible for preliminary interviews to take place with the authorities of his college and for arrangements concerning his work to be made which greatly diminished his apprehension of scholastic failure.

This interview was the last and after it he entered the university. Months after he wrote: 'I am looking forward a lot to starting *X* next term, though I understand it as one of the hardest working schools.'

This improvement has so far been maintained and he is working well and with enjoyment.

The 'Worlds', therefore, in this case played the following part:

(a) They eliminated resistance to the psychotherapeutic process.

(b) They confronted the patient with irrefutable evidence of the existence and reality of his own difficulties.

(c) They gave him an opportunity to use his own brain in understanding his own difficulties.

(d) They stated for him in general terms the nature of his difficulties.

10 Theoretical Concepts Developed

Partly in consequence of the uncomfortable reception given to 'The World Pictures of Children', Lowenfeld's subsequent papers tended to accentuate differences between her approach and the psychoanalytic tradition. She saw her work as redressing an imbalance in psychoanalysis and analytical psychology. As she put it in the second paper in this chapter, the latter traditions had concentrated on the dynamics of desire and the emotional life, giving less attention to the 'intellectual' or 'conceptual' aspect of the pictures in the mind. 'Yet it is the two, the picture *plus* the urge . . . that make the complete phenomenon' (Lowenfeld, 1948; this volume, p. 327). Her intention, in the first instance, was to elucidate the 'conceptual factor', expanding the account of the nature of pre-verbal thought introduced in the Manchester paper before the war.

Previously unpublished, the first paper in this chapter, 'Direct Projective Therapy', was read to the annual meeting of the General Section of the British Psychological Society in Glasgow, in April 1944. Lowenfeld recognized the interdependence between the discovery of this form of thought and the methods she had devised to investigate it, and noted the close relationship which exists between the development of method and the production of knowledge in all scientific investigation. By implication, this would include psychoanalysis. Though she identified a distance between her account and existing approaches, perhaps because of the criticism following 'The World Pictures of Children', she was careful to cite the work of Piaget, Freud and Jung, referring additionally to the Jungian influence in the educational journal *Child Life*, which ran for a time through the 1930s and 40s. She also expressed an interest in the work of Erikson, which became clearer in subsequent papers (see Chapters 11 and 12).

The main body of the paper was concerned with elaborating the thesis of the Manchester paper by writing, as it were, from the point of view of an imaginary infant dealing with the world for the first time. Here she assumed that the infant would lack clear boundaries between what was inside and what was outside the body, and that it would be difficult to distinguish the source of a perception from its subjective effects. The infant would not be aware of a distinction between self and other, or rather, would lack knowledge of the external world as shared by others. On the other hand Lowenfeld assumed that principles of organization would exist in the human mind from the word go. In line with the Manchester paper and her application of Spearman's laws, here she focused on the interlinking of experiences according to subjective qualities by a process of 'identification', to form, in the infant's mind, new wholes or preconceptual structures which at this point she called 'conglomerates'; she noted similarities with Piaget's 'syncretism'. Through a case history, she illustrated how a particular child's symptoms could be understood in terms of confusions in the protosystem, or primary conglomerate or 'jelly'. Disentangling these confusions in therapy would increase the energy available to the child, enabling him or her to relate more effectively to the external world known by other people.

Thus Lowenfeld's theory of the nature of pre-verbal thought influenced her clinical practice, making processes which she had already been working with intuitively more accessible to further analysis. At the end of the paper, she discussed the problem of how you know when the meaning you have assigned to a piece of material is right for the child who has produced it, and explained the title of her paper. Through the provision of suitable materials within a permissive atmosphere, children will seek means for expressing their experience of their own selves. Thus, 'What is attempted is direct contact with the child's intimate structure of experience by means of projection by the child of this interior jelly-like thought into external material' (this volume, pp. 322–3). Although 'direct projective therapy' was a reasonably apt description of the approach, in fact Lowenfeld soon stopped using this nomenclature because of the likelihood of confusion between her use of the term 'projection' and the concept of projection as a defence mechanism in psychoanalysis. She also wished to avoid a too-ready assimilation of her approach to projective testing, which was increasingly in vogue in clinical psychology.

By the time that Lowenfeld wrote the second paper in this chapter, 'The Nature of the Primary System', given to the ICP conference in July 1948, links between the theory of the protosystem and her approach to psychotherapy were even sharper. The paper was first published in the report on the conference by the ICP and has been discussed in Chapter 5. What was added to the theory was the idea of 'clusters' and the protosystem network, now recognizable as replacing the 'conglomerates' or 'jelly' of the previous paper. She also differentiated four major patterns of maladaptation which could occur in development, resulting in the persistence of confusions or blocking of energy, and the four major types of difficulty seen in the child patients at the ICP (see this volume, pp. 343–4), and indeed, in the social world outside. The paper concludes with an application of the theory to the situation produced by Nazi domination during the Second World War.

But this paper was also particularly interesting because of the use which Lowenfeld made of references to painting and the metaphoric use of language to illustrate the nature of mental functioning and the region of the mind that she was exploring, thus taking advantage of the fact that the phenomena found in Worlds can be identified by all of us outside the clinical context. In doing so she explicitly linked her account to the question of the possibility of aesthetic appreciation and experience in all of us, and of great artistic achievement in a few. In particular, Lowenfeld made great use of the work of Chagall, which had just become known to her. Chagall's creations appeared to come straight out of the protosystem. As she noted, the unconventional combinations of parts of bodies, to produce forms which coalesce, linked to places according to subjective tone and which invert usual spatial boundaries, are extraordinarily reminiscent of the clusters of the young child. Again, Lowenfeld's theoretical account concentrated particularly on the formation of pre-verbal concepts according to principles whereby perceptions would be *identified* with each other to form a new totality. As she stressed, correctly, this is not the same as 'association' of two or more ideas or experiences. The recognition of this process remained Lowenfeld's most important, and unique, contribution. It lies at the heart of all metaphor and the possibility for symbolic expression.

To all intents and purposes the account which Lowenfeld (1979) gave of the protosystem in *The World Technique* is the same as that presented in this paper. (Here two of the drawings she referred to are unfortunately no longer available.) It is the fullest account of the system which she produced. As she herself recognized, there was much left unexplored and explained. The question has already been raised as to whether the theoretical scheme could develop further without a fuller engagement with the findings and concepts of psychoanalysis (Chapters 5 and 6). One might also ask how far Lowenfeld's account is compatible with recent developments in developmental psychology, and work on perception and cognition in infancy in particular.

Given the sophistication of much of the experimental work in this area (see, for example, Bower, 1982), by current standards some of Lowenfeld's statements on the infant's mind may appear over-speculative or unnecessarily vague. Even within her own framework, there are some odd inconsistencies, particularly around the relationship between the primary and secondary system and the development of the latter. Given that, under usual circumstances, primary concepts are eventually modified through the secondary system, thereby releasing energy into it, there is something lacking in Lowenfeld's claim that 'Already a great deal is known about this [the secondary system] and there is nothing new to add here' (this volume, p. 342)'. Similarly, for a psychologist today, it may be hard to square Lowenfeld's view of the human infant as apparently disorganized, incapable of differentiating inside and outside, with contemporary views on the neonate's sophistication and, indeed, Lowenfeld's own claim that organizing principles operate from the start.

On the other hand, Lowenfeld was not alone in having to reckon with contrastive viewpoints on infant abilities. Despite current views on infant competence, there is much that is obscure about the process of development itself (see Urwin, 1986). Lowenfeld's approach points to the possibility that several forms of thought exist in the infant, side by side. More specifically, Lowenfeld proposed that mental development proceeds both through establishing relations with the external world and through building relations internally; producing mental representations of bodily and perceptual experience provides the core of mind itself. It is this dimension which is lacking in developmental psychology. Moreover, there are phenomena which Lowenfeld identified as crucial which developmental psychology has only just begun to recognize. These include phenomena illustrated in the now numerous experiments which demonstrate the ability in young infants to match sensory and perceptual experience cross-modally, from sight to sound, tempo to texture, as Lowenfeld's emphasis on subjective linking would suggest. (For a useful review of this research from a clinical perspective, see Stern, 1985.)

But despite these grounds for interchange between Lowenfeld's ideas and developmental psychology, there remains a fundamental difference. On the whole psychology has retained an emphasis on charting infant achievements, according to the normative tradition through which it began, and re-rendering these in terms of some underlying cognitive structure. For Lowenfeld, the process of link-making and imaging remains uppermost, and it is the latter that drives the development of thought rather than the other way round. In some respects this brings her approach nearer to the idea of symbol formation enhancing the development of ego functioning to be found in the work of Melanie Klein (1930; see Segal, 1986). But whereas in psychoanalytic theory symbol formation involves a loss of the object for which the symbol is a substitute, for Lowenfeld the production of symbols was in the first instance a creative process through which subjective experience was assimilated to the self, making relations with others possible.

Direct Projective Therapy [1944]

Advance in objective investigation can only be made through limitation of inquiry to specific fields. To be fruitful, an inquiry into any aspect of human behaviour needs instruments capable of revealing facts relevant to the nature of the inquiry. There is an intimate connection in the progress of all forms of objective study between instruments used in an investigation and the achievement of a new understanding of the subject investigated.

Much knowledge has already been won in the fields of child psychology and child psychotherapy and we already possess a considerable store of information concerning the relation of children to their human environment, to their own developing physical powers, to each other and to external objects. The psychotherapies of Freud, Jung and Adler have brought us information concerning the development of the instinctive drives and their relation to the ego components, concerning the influence upon a child of factors of racial and parental emotion and of the effect upon a child's life of his own self-valuation.

I want today to direct your attention to a sphere which is outside all of these and which, I believe, lies below or around them: this is the sphere of the child's non-verbal thoughts about his own intimate experience, and the effect they have upon his later development.

In such reading as the limitations of life as a practising physician allows, I have been able to find no direct reference to this region of the mind as such. But I think Piaget's 'syncretism' (Piaget, 1929) and Freud's conception of 'condensation and displacement' in dreams (Freud, S., 1900), passages in Ruth Griffiths' and Dr Michael Fordham's *Child Life*, and passages in Herbert Read's *Education Through Art* (Read, 1943) touch upon the same region.

In the USA, Erik Homburger Erikson seems to be investigating some of the same facts as I am, and in a very difficult monograph suggests a terminology to describe them. Had there been time I should have liked to discuss his suggestions today and to have made use of some of them. But this is not possible; I will do my best with our terminology.

I must return to the reasons why this part of the personality has so far escaped observation.

Before lenses were discovered and made available to scientists, the facts about the universe which the microscope and the telescope have revealed were inaccessible to men and, because inaccessible, unimaginable. The same is surely true of the human mind. Without instruments suitable for the observation of an aspect of mental functioning, the existence of such functions must escape observation. The two are bound together. So too, unfortunately, is the case of the expositor in exposition. Description of the instrument and of the region brought to light through use of the instrument are inextricably blended and until each listener has tried himself to work with the instrument, description is apt to be incomprehensible or to sound too improbable to carry conviction. For this reason I had hoped it might have been possible to bring drawings of material for display by epidiascope, but the latter being unobtainable, and as time is too short for discussion of drawings passed around, I propose to do what I can with words, but with acute consciousness of their limitations.

Let us take first the question, to what problem is this work upon which I wish to report, the answer? And the query 'What goes on in the *mind* of the child before speech becomes an instrument of thought?' Now I would like to draw attention to the point that the word used here is *mind*, not heart, if the word heart is taken as symbolic seat of the emotions. It is not the instinctive part of the child's experience upon which I want to focus attention, but the child's interior early mental or reasoning processes. And again not these processes as applied to the outside world but as they deal with processes and experiences occurring *within* the self.

The question naturally arises as to how these can be investigated, since speech is here essentially irrelevant. Speech is a system of abstract symbols which need general external agreement to make them relevant and these are by definition concerned with experiences common to all. How difficult the

 voicing is of passionate or individual experience in the common coin of speech everyone in love and every poet is aware, though perhaps the work of James Joyce and Gertrude Stein are the only attempts we have to transcend it. To understand this region we need an instrument by which it can be reached and demonstrated, and by means of such demonstration analysed and understood. It has been my work for the last twenty years to forge such an instrument.

For some time now it has been an accepted fact that a child's relation to toys and his form of play with them reveals a great deal concerning his interior experience. But the points to which attention has been directed in the study of this material, and therefore the deductions which have been drawn, have been almost exclusively concerned with the affective life of the child and his relation either to affects within himself or to those of other people, together with his concept of the nature of those affects.

This valuable work I can now supplement with observations directed to another aspect. This aspect is to be found to some extent, if looked for, in all children's use of all play material and especially in any child's use of the particular play material I have devised. But to some extent if it is to be recognized it must be understood beforehand, a fact which is true of all scientific observation, namely that we must know something of the nature of what we are looking for in order to be able to perceive it.

To indicate therefore the sort of material we are investigating, let us take the question of movement and of space. To an adult or an older child it is perfectly clear that there is a difference, for example, between movement *up* and movement *down*, that *within* is not the same as *without*, that the glove is not the same as the hand. We know these things because they are external happenings; they are relations in the world outside us and relations that we constantly experience. Similarly we know that our body trunk intervenes between our head and our nether end and that these two are different in function and in character. We know further that, if we vomit, matter rushes from within us to without and if we swallow, it goes from without within; that if we fall into a rage, feeling wells up within us but nothing material leaps out, and that if we are hurt with an unkind word or look, nothing material again goes from without within us. *Our knowledge of the external world makes a distinction clear to us.*

Now a small child, when he has recovered from the trauma of birth, begins his conscious life in mid-air. He is carried from place to place and for him there is no 'above' or 'below', only motion or lack of motion, appearance or disappearance. Things appear within his area of sight, smell, taste or touch, and disappear again. He has no notion of the causality of either. They are; they are pleasant, neutral, unpleasant, they have certain qualities which his senses register, and then they are not. They have vanished, slipped, as far as he is concerned totally out of existence. Similarly with states within his own body (only he does not know these are 'within'), they are, and they are not, they come and go, as external objects come and go, only as we well know there is no difference as yet to his awareness between 'within' him and 'without'. There is in him a centre of awareness with a relation to things that happen, and, I submit, the nature of these happenings to that centre is indistinguishable the one from the other.

Similarly when he gains the personal power of movement this is for him for a long time only in one place, the horizontal. Here things roll away but do not come back, though a cry will bring larger human objects back, the cry having apparently power over their movement and that perhaps of household pets, but not of other objects. Similarly he begins to find certain 'inside' feelings can be called up by personal attempts, cries and so on, and certain others, hunger, sleepiness, anger, come and go on their own. There is no order and no coherence in this universe.

There is, however, in every sane human mind an imperative need to reduce to some kind of order its own experience and it is here the first relevance of this work appears. It appears from the type of investigation about to be described that there is a form of synthesis of experience which has not yet been identified and which is additional to and earlier than the form we already know, which is that of combination through association (in all its forms) of words, objects, ideas and experiences. This mode of mental functioning was discussed at length some years ago in a paper read to this Society in Manchester, and it is upon this that I wish now to build (Lowenfeld, 1937; this volume, pp. 247–64).

This form of organization I suggest takes place through *identification* of experiences with each other so that they become part of a new whole. That which results, I believe, forms the core of every human mind. The differences between the two modes of mental function is that in the usual process of association, mental object *A* remains unaltered as object *A* (such as for example a pillar-box calling up the idea of a red dahlia).

The dahlia becomes mental object *B*, some characteristic of *A* leading to the mental image of another object *B*. This characteristic selected here is the colour of redness. Thought of *A* (or of *B*) will bring up the idea of *B* (or part of *A* or *B*) or vice versa through the selected characteristic, here the idea of redness. *But in this process* A *and* B *remain themselves unaltered,* and clearly distinguishable from each other.

In the process I have called the formation of 'identities' this does not happen. Here the possession by *A* and *B* of a common characteristic *X* results in the fusion of *A* with *B so that they become part of a new whole* Z which once joined is in future evermore inseparable into its component elements. It becomes therefore impossible in the future, except by special apparatus and long experience, to diagnose in the fused conglomerate what originally was *A* or *B*, or to distinguish the linking characteristic *X*. *A*, *X* and *B* now become qualities of a new whole, *Z*. That *Z* may not exist or be capable of existing in any 'real' world makes no difference whatever to the creator of *Z*, since to him *Z* is real, being his own experience, and the 'real' world unreal.

If this be admitted the question immediately arises: according to what rules does this identification take place, that is, what brings about such a fusion of experience?

The essential quality of the mass of material made by fusion of this kind is that it is purely *subjective* and relates wholly and entirely to subjective experience, where the more usual form of association with which we are familiar is mainly concerned with relations in the external world. How then does identification take place? It appears that the essential quality which brings about fusion of two experiences is a similarity of subjective tone; ideas, objects or experiences become fused together which rouse the same subjective experience. When one thinks this over it becomes natural that this should be so since a young child possesses no other criterion. At the time fusion begins to take place the child possesses no knowledge of the external world which is shared by others that it can use as a criterion. If similar experiences are to be selected it must be by subjective criteria.

It is because of these two characteristics that fusion of this kind cannot be observed by other human beings. For something of the same reason these fusions are taken for granted by the child himself and become later invisible to him as well.

To go a step further, it is a commonplace of popular speech that emotional experiences are portrayed by physical analogy, as 'a sickening thought', 'he gives me a pain in the neck', 'You could have knocked me down with a feather', and so on, which is to say that, since certain personal experiences are incommunicable in direct speech, knowledge of them can only be conveyed indirectly through analogy with bodily states having a similar subjective content.

This is universal in early childhood. A child, being unable to separate bodily subjective experiences from emotional ones, combines both in a single concept and the central self uses either indifferently to express the other. So I have found vomiting, diarrhoea, constipation, pyrexia, skin eruptions, coughs, cold and a host of other apparently physical happenings can be merely the physical side of a mass of fused experiences containing physical as well as *mental* experiences. Being 'identified', physiological process and mental idea become inseparable. Here the syncretism of Piaget, the 'condensation' and 'displacement of affect' of Freud and much of gestalt psychology are relevant.

There are many other elements in this most delicate and intricate process which time does not allow even of mention. Thus the whole makes up a structureless mass which I have hitherto termed the 'primary system' and which I now want to propose to call the primal or primary conglomerate or jelly. This, I believe, exists as part of the matrix of personality in all children, normal and neurotic. The difference between them is that in the 'normal' child, or perhaps we should say the happy child, with a satisfactory background, the matter composing the primal conglomerate is sufficiently similar to that of other people and sufficiently akin to external reality for the ordinary processes of mental, emotional and physical growth and development, together with the bridges of myth, fairy-tale etc. to enable him to pull his main forces out of it and to apply them to real life.

In neurotic children or children from an obstinately neurotic background, it appears that the composing elements of the conglomerate are at once too strange and their implications too threatening for him to be able to extricate his energy. Too much of it remains therefore entangled in the web of the primary conglomerate and development is hindered or ceases.

Let us now consider an illustration.

A well-brought-up dainty little girl suffers from an attack of acute anxiety if undressed by any but very familiar people. She is very fussy about her clothes and will make a scene unless very nicely dressed. She is a pretty girl and her parents amuse themselves and her by great emphasis upon pretty clothes. She has also been anaemic and been given an iron tonic which turned her excreta black. One day her favourite tortoise died, and she found it later in the garden half eaten by maggots. The soil of the garden of the house in which she lived was very black. She was not allowed to play with it, as she wanted to, because it 'spoiled her clothes'. Later she suffered from intestinal worms and her mother appeared to her to be very revolted about this, as she was with dirty clothes.

We have here several subjective similarities. First, soil is black, often moist and also mouldable; a substance comes out of her which has the same qualities. She would like to play with the soil and may not because it 'spoils' or dirties things. She has at one time also shown a similar relation to her own stools and been trained out of this desire. Soil and stools, therefore, look alike, may be presumed to feel alike and have the similar quality that handling either is forbidden pleasure which has become something from which we must turn away. Since there is no difference, as we have explained, to a small child between inside and outside, soil and 'inside' become fused and the result runs, 'I have black soil inside me, dirty, spoils things, mustn't touch.'

This is followed by a horrifying experience of seeing something that was alive, moving and beloved, stationary, eaten away and full with maggots and that at a time when the word 'dead' conveyed no meaning. Passing excreta gives to most children a feeling of there being something inside moving out; this time, in her experience, worms like maggots come out. Both are horrifying experiences and the similar horror makes of these a fusion also. As a result it became clear to her that she was full of black earth, riddled with worms, as the tortoise had been with maggots. She then had a short bout of diarrhoea in which faeces 'rushed out of her', as she felt. This set up an acute and perfectly logical anxiety, lest at any moment the wormy earth inside might rush out of her and make clear to everyone the horrible nature of her own body. The only possible response to her was to refuse to allow anyone to see her body lest they might see the horrible inside of it, always remembering that inside and outside are continuous, and to redress the balance by concentrating attention upon exterior clothes to distract people's attention from thinking about or wanting to look at the child within.

Two other questions here arise: What is the relation of this part or aspect of the mind to the rest of the mind and what effect has it upon development?

Time does not allow of more than a sentence or two in answer to either query.

The answer I would like to give to the first is intricate and complicated as it involves consideration of how much of what is normally called the unconscious comes in here. But it cannot be attempted here. Very briefly it appears to persist through life, to have an intimate connection with bodily illness and to vary greatly in importance in different individuals according to individual constitution, temperament and the relation of the individual to the external world.

The second query involves the equally important and also complicated question of the relation to growth and how human beings normally escape from identification of the self with the primary conglomerate. All I can say today is that here is involved the question of the individual's relation to words and of the type of education he receives. There is also involved his active and affective experiences and what happens to the rest of his personality, each part interpenetrating the other.

We have in this short exposition two remaining points to deal with: (a) by what means can this conglomerate be investigated; and (b) how do we know when our reading of it is correct?

To take (a) first.

I have drawn attention to the fact that to the small child internal and external are either identical or continuous. There is further a dynamic drive in all children to get away from that which torments them, to set a distance between it and them, and so to regard it objectively. It is upon this dynamic that the design and operation of our technical instrument is built. This instrument is the provision in sizes and consistencies suitable for use by a child's small fingers of material objects in which he can express the curious ideas he has in himself. The process of investigation or treatment is the analysis of these into elements of his probable experiences and concepts.

It is essential that this material should be able to express all the elements of space, time and movement, should be capable of being both ways at the same time, in and out, up and down, of being glove and hand, bottle and contents, and that its elements should easily represent both fragmentation and fusion and be taken *at the value the child gives it*. There is no attempt in this method to import into analysis of the child's production anything from knowledge the observer may have from theoretical psychology except as a corollary to what the child himself shows or does. What is attempted is direct contact with the child's intimate structure of experience by means of projection by the child of this interior jelly-like thought into external material.

How then do we know when we are drawing the correct conclusion? The answer is simple. The child tells one. We must remember that to a child his interior world is the only one existing. As to the average Englishman English ways are 'normal' and other forms of behaviour 'foreign', so to a child his interior concepts *are* and others are odd, queer, or just Olympian. So if we analyse a structure produced by a child and tell him what we find, he will nod and smile as if the result of our sweating labour and thought is the easiest and most obvious thing in the world and say 'yes' or 'of course' or else just look up and nod and go swiftly to the next stage. Once experienced, there is no doubt about this criterion; the child knows whether we are right or not and if right most clearly tells us. If he does not agree with what is put to him, I think it is rarely sound to postulate 'resistance' and instead usually find it is due to lack of understanding on the part of the adult. The child here probably is right and the adult wrong.

Now when a child agrees with you that a certain piece of play or a certain structure that he has made has the nature that you suggest, this piece of his explanation to himself of his own experience comes into focus and a process takes place which is familiar in all education. His intelligence can then get to work upon it and with your help he can test out this conception and compare it with reality and so dissolve it. As in all education true knowledge dissolves error and misconception. This false part of the conglomerate then disappears with all its consequences and the energy caught up in it is freed for growth.

It is for these reasons therefore that *direct projective psychotherapy* has been chosen to describe this method of approach to the child's problems.

The Nature of the Primary System [1948]

For the past twenty years, we have been studying children by methods the aim of which was to enable the children to talk, as it were, without the use of language. A careful and detailed analysis of the productions the children have made, with materials specially designed for their use, has brought to light an aspect of the human psyche which so far has not been described. To this the name of the Primary System has been given, since it is a systematized region of the psyche, appears first, and remains for life in the core of the psyche. It is with this system that the following paper deals.

To give an account in words of this system is a task set about with great difficulties. The difficulties will be stated first, to show why it is that many gaps must appear in the account. To give a complete account of this part of the psyche, one should first describe the system itself, then show how it operates in normal healthy childhood, say what happens to it in adult life, and against that background describe the Primary System as we see it in our patients. But this would be a matter of intolerable length and quite outside the limits of this paper. Moreover, there has been no opportunity to study this region of the psyche in normal children, in anything resembling the same detail as has been possible with the disturbed child. Also, the amount of available evidence as to the behaviour of this part of the personality in later life is too scanty to give more than indications of probability. Thus all that can be done here is to put forward some of the evidence which has been collected as to the existence of this part of the psyche, and then to describe it as it has appeared in child patients.

It must first be noted that psychiatry and psychotherapy have hitherto, in the main, been occupied with adult life and experience and with childhood as it has been recovered or re-created by the adult through the techniques of psychoanalysis. In the analytic study of children, it is the material obtained primarily from adults which forms the basis of the interpretation given to children of the meaning of their play. In the work with adults, it has been taken for granted that language, supplemented by drawings, gestures, tones of voice and movements, all combined together in a specialized relation to the physician, formed tools by means of which the whole of the psyche could be investigated. But in this assumption certain important considerations have been omitted. First, European educationists tell us that children cannot use words as tools to think with, until the age of about seven or eight; before that time, their use of language is similar to that of adults speaking a tongue which is only slightly known to them. Before that age, children are unable to manipulate language as, for example, to write a letter or an essay that has a beginning, a middle and an end. On the other hand, we have Freud's discovery, and the knowledge poets have always had, that early childhood is the time of the most vivid impressions, and of emotional experience which is crucial for the whole of later life. Furthermore, in adult life, language is the tool used to realize, within the self, by interior speech, the individual's own experience and to communicate with his fellows – unless the individual is an artist, a point which will be dealt with later.

Now, R. G. Collingwood, the English philosopher whose work underlies so much of this study, used to teach that all thought began with putting a question. The question put by the writer some twenty years ago could be formulated as follows. Since the parts of the brain with which one thinks are formed and active long before seven, when language is not available for thought, in what way do children, before they reach this age, think and register and group their experience?

Here we find ourselves in the same difficulty that the child finds in his communication with adults. The thesis we wish to present has several facets which should be presented simultaneously, since they are each part of a single whole – but though it is possible to present many aspects of the same feeling or thought in the use of the Lowenfeld World material, it is not possible in speech. There only one aspect can be described at one time, and one must rely upon the memory of the reader which must combine the different elements for himself.

 Study of the interior life and experience of man, by the

processes either of psychoanalysis or analytical psychology, has hitherto concentrated its attention upon the aspect of desire and of emotional life. To the pictures that arise in the mind as the goals of these interior urges, the term 'fantasy', whether conscious or unconscious, has been given. But little attention has been paid, so far that is, to the intellectual or conceptual aspect of the pictures which appear. It is to the nature of the dynamic behind the picture, to the wish or urge which has appeared to call the pictured goal into being, that attention has been directed. Yet it is the two, the picture *plus* the urge that brings it into being, that make the complete phenomenon. It is with the first element, the conceptual factor, that this paper is concerned and which it sets out to examine.

Take the simplest of all human urges, the drive of appetite – the desire to eat which arises from the reality of the body's need for sustenance. This desire, because of the physiological substratum from which it arises, would, in its simplest form, seem to give rise to the most obvious and direct kind of activity. One is hungry and one eats. But even here, experience with primitive people has shown that, in the relief of famine, the dominant factor in the situation is not, as would be imagined, the physiological need, but instead, the intellectual concept that accompanies it. Hunger alone, and the organic need behind it, is not sufficient by itself to bring about eating. There must also be, in the minds of the hungry, a concept of 'food', which corresponds to the foodstuffs available. It is no rare thing for large numbers of adults – men and women – to die, for instance in India, or among the Indians of Canada, because the food offered them, maize, for example, in the place of rice, was not seen by the hungry as food – and this refusal to accept the unknown, even when the preservation of life depended on it, has been persisted in, until death supervened.

The conceptual element is, therefore, at least *as* important as the element of desire, and worthy of the same attention. But if it proves difficult to understand this element in adults, and in adults who share a common language, how is such contact to be made with the inner life of children and particularly of young children or of infants?

To answer this question, means must be found for making contacts with children which are independent of speech. Tools must be created with which children can describe to themselves and to adults the nature of their own experience; methods must be devised to make it possible, as it were, to watch a child think.

Once it became clear that something real was emerging through use of the, at that time very primitive, tools designed by the author, the next step was to secure companions in the search and adequate material to make genuine study possible. This was necessary to cope with a difficulty which had begun to appear very clearly. For Freud, without realizing it, had made in his work a certain basic assumption, which it was not possible for him to realize as an assumption, because it was accepted by all the men of his time. This was, that there exists a common plan of development in the emotional sphere of human beings which parallels physiological and anatomical law. Working on this assumption, he felt justified in drawing deductions of universal application from the study even of single individuals. This assumption is continued by present-day psychoanalysts, namely, that what occurs in a small group of individuals, or even in a single individual, if sufficiently carefully studied and rightly understood, can be taken as generally applicable to all individuals. But although this belief is very strongly held, no evidence has been deduced in support of it. The cautious individual would prefer not to assume anything, but to leave it to the material to demonstrate whether this conception was true or not.

The next question to be tackled was that of the checking of observations and the recording of facts, and to do this a system was devised by which every fact was cross-referenced and checked, and, later, charts were drawn up of the data obtained. A paper on the first findings was read to the Medical Section of the British Psychological Society and published in their journal, entitled: 'A New Approach to the Problem of Psychoneurosis in Childhood' (Lowenfeld, 1931, this volume, p. 177).

At that time it was possible only to see dimly what can now be understood far more clearly. This was that there is a region of the mind which has so far been inadequately observed and understood, and that because it is inexpressible in language. But it is in language ultimately that all discoveries have to be communicated, and this accounts for the delay that has occurred in the presentation of these findings. Moreover, it seemed best to wait until a certain number of the children treated in youth had gone out into the world as adults in order to see whether the benefits which appeared to accrue from this type of treatment in childhood, produced in reality, in later life, the results that theoretically it seemed likely it would do.

 A series of some two thousand cases has now been treated and studied in this way, and a fair number of the earlier ones of these are now grown up and out in the world, as independent individuals. Wherever it has been possible, contact with them has been maintained.

It is possible, therefore, now to present a study which has a certain completeness about it.

But we must return to the matter in hand, which is to put forward some of the essential nature of that strange part of the human psyche which has emerged from these studies.

To make the matter clearer, a parable is set out, the form of which is drawn from Worlds children themselves made.

When we were children, many of us delighted in reading that mixture of fairy story and children's tale in which there was a garden surrounded by a wall, which all the grown-ups took as being really the end of the garden, but which, at a specially exciting moment in the story, the children of the house found to conceal among the bushes, which grew close up to the wall, a secret door. This door, opened only at midnight, led to a garden of delights, unsuspected by the grown-ups, and peopled with fairies and wise or prankish gnomes. This story has many forms; sometimes it is under the sea, sometimes on an island out at sea, sometimes in a lost valley in the hills. But the essence of the story is the same; the finding of a country near to home but with rules of life within it which are magical and different altogether from those which obtain at home. There are also terrible things in this garden, ogres and man-eating giants and wizards and spells; but in the end it is only the wicked who are consumed, or the careless, and if one knows the rules of life in that country, it is exciting and virile, and from it the traveller brings back treasures of gold and jewels.

It is clear that there are many ways in which these stories can be regarded, and Jung and Freud have thrown a great deal of light on them, but here they will be taken quite simply as they stand and studied in almost a literal fashion so that they may assist the understanding of what we are calling the Primary System.

For instance, there are always certain constant characteristics about these stories. There is always a key to that garden, and the key is difficult to find and to many people altogether invisible; and great efforts are called for from those who are bold enough to take the key and open the door, before they can enjoy the freedom of the secret kingdom, and of the strange things that are in it. Within that garden, or that kingdom, there are dangers also, and tests and struggles, and not all come back again. Some die, some lose their way back; perhaps these become some of those people we call insane, who never find their way back again. There are people who, having been once inside, are frightened and spend the rest of their lives denying there is any such kingdom at all; and there are some, like the painter Chagall, and James Joyce and the poet Blake, who live equally on both sides of the wall, and come and go at will; and though people find them strange, they do not call them mad. And finally there are those who take theodolites and measuring tapes and go in and out measuring and calculating and trying to learn the geography of that vast garden and how its outlines are drawn.

This is easier for the author to do personally because her childhood was spent in part in a square in London, near the Park, and partly in a quiet part of Poland. Her father was a collector, and the house in London, that formed the background to experience, was full of objects that came from faraway places and had no relation to each other. They were rich in colouring and unexpected, to a child, in character, and did not fit into the life of everyday. In Poland, the people wore brightly coloured clothes and were simple and direct in speech and thought. Several languages were talked around one normally, and so things did not have just one name by which everybody knew them, but several names, and some called them by one and some by another, so there was always a certain amount of uncertainty as to what the names really were; the word one thought of might be the one the grown-up one was talking to wanted, and then again it might not – it was difficult to be sure.

The author was also a very delicate child and spent a large part of her life in bed in illness, with long periods of solitude.

The years immediately following the 1914 war brought opportunity in Eastern Europe of seeing and experiencing famine and war and terror and isolation, but also the exhilarating experience of taking part in the rebirth of a country. With a basic training in paediatrics, return from Poland brought an opportunity of training in paediatric and biochemical research work under the late Professor Leonard Findlay, and as part of a research team at the Royal Free Hospital, London. Perhaps these experiences have made it easier to forge a key to that garden and not to be too startled at its contents.

Two characteristics of that fable must now be considered, which differentiate it in important ways from the concept (either psychoanalytic or of analytical psychology) of the unconscious.

First of all, it is quite a well-defined region, and a wall separates it from the home garden. The rules of conduct and the type of event that occur on one side of the wall are different from those on the other side. What is to be expected in one garden does not happen in the other, and in the magic garden almost anything may come about. This is not strange, because the idea of the fable has been arrived at directly from study of the actual productions many children have made with the tools supplied to them.

The second important fact about the garden is that though to some extent it looks like the outside world, there is in it neither time nor space. It is this timelessness, and this quality of being able to be at the same time in two places which may actually be far apart, that has given rise to the legends and fairy tales of Rip Van Winkle, the Magic Carpets, Seven-League Boots, the little figures that suddenly grow tall as in *Alice's Adventures in Wonderland*, and much of the paraphernalia of fairyland.

We are dealing here with something, therefore, that resembles closely what is termed the unconscious. Indeed, most of the phenomena of the Freudian and Jungian unconscious will be found within it, though with a different explanation. We need to ask ourselves, therefore, how is this garden constructed, and what do these strange features mean?

Now it is very difficult to understand this directly, it is too peculiar, and those who are not poets and artists have left it too far behind and grown into too different another world to be able to regain contact with it easily. Some artists keep a dim consciousness of it, and the work of the painter Chagall may be taken to help us in building a bridge.

It is characteristic of Chagall to paint pictures in which figures and objects appear without apparent relation to one another and without the normal relation to gravity. His method of grouping these and his skill of colouring are so aesthetically pleasing that his pictures receive a warm welcome in most countries of the world. Nevertheless, judged from a 'rational' standpoint, it is difficult to understand the rules upon which he works, why he selects just those objects that appear in his pictures, or why the ones which are included in any given picture should appear together. Moreover, the size of figures and objects and the place in the picture they occupy seem, judged from the commonsense point of view, to be completely irrational. Figures are painted within other figures and in some, large heads contain whole scenes within them. From the ordinary standpoint, this is very odd. This is not surrealism, which is an attempt to represent and to evoke in the beholder by that representation certain emotional states, but something different that stands by itself. It is, in the main, the painting of the beautiful side of the strange inner region of man, so difficult to reach in adult life but which dominates the experience of children.

As a first step may be considered the way he treated common metaphor in a concrete fashion. For example, it is quite common to speak of a 'horse-faced' woman. But in the picture called *Claire de Lune* (1944), Chagall paints a nude female figure in solid texture, and superimposes over the head of the figure a shadow painting of a horse, so that in literal fact the central figure in his picture is both woman and horse. In Figure 1 is shown for comparison a reproduction of a drawing made by a young woman patient who wished to express early confusion of thoughts about certain aspects of bodies. It is a commonplace of psychoanalytic experience that the teapot with its projecting spout and the breast-like formation of its lid can stand in symbolic fashion for a combination of male and female sexual characteristics. It is also one of the characteristics of the early confusions and identities of the Primary System that the parts of the body which contain orifices into which and from within which substances come and go, stand for and are identified with one another, the head becoming in this way confused with the excretory end of the trunk. This particular patient wished to express a concept into which these ideas had coalesced, and to combine the resultant mass with the idea of struggle for possession of the total qualities conceived of as existing both in the head and in the male and female genitalia.

It will be seen that so complex a conception is impossible to express in words, just as the complex of ideas and feelings behind the impulse to superimpose a horse upon a woman's head cannot be fully expressed in words. Both, however, can be presented in a plastic medium, if the usual concepts of 'sense' and 'possibility' are rejected. Chagall, being an artist, can blend his concepts into an artistically pleasing whole which has value in itself. This patient, having no artistic ability or desire to do anything but communicate something, has produced a drawing in which teapots formed parts of heads of pairs of people engaged in a struggle with each other. The teapots were of different colours, and the patient stated that each figure was dissatisfied with its particular coloured teapot and wished to change it for another's. The top hat, the cork seen from the side, and the third crude drawing indicating a cork stopping up a hole, fill out the genital significance of the drawing in a manner that will be familiar to all psychoanalysts (see Figure 1).

Further, those who are familiar with the paintings of Chagall will remember that, as for example in the well-known painting, *Dans Mon Village*, Chagall makes use of the device of painting scenes within scenes, small solid individuals within parts of larger figures. In particular, in the painting entitled *La Somnambule* (1945), there appears within and painted upon the crinoline skirts of a female figure a winter village scene, the floating horizontal figure of a man with a cock's head, and a quadruped minus the front legs and with human legs instead of its back legs. In the same picture, a candelabra appears in the top right-hand corner although there is a moon below it, and a man's arm in a coat sleeve is in the region of the ear of the bridal female figure. Once again, because Chagall is an artist, the total result of these compositions is enchanting, and has brought Chagall fame in all countries in which his pictures have been

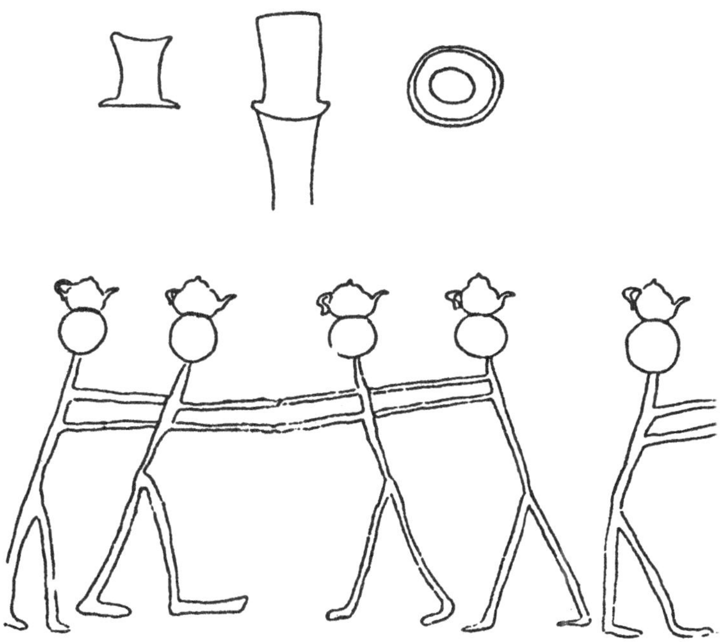

Figure 1 *Drawing made by adult patient during the course of treatment*

exhibited. But this means only that Chagall, being an artist, has chosen to use as the material for his pictures concepts and plastic forms which many experience. These are a common possession of all human beings, but of which we are at present unaware.

To make this clear, let us consider two drawings of a young woman patient. In the first, out of the mouth of a dragon's head come what she termed 'many tubes' or 'many tongues' with parts of the human body attached to the end of them. The body of the dragon curving away then becomes part of a scene of a river with a lugger on it and a camel on the bank. The end of the tail is finally looped around a kettle. At the bottom left-hand corner of the paper on which this drawing appears is a quite small scene of a prehistoric monster standing by a sheet of water; at the top of the paper is a crucifix with a charwoman prostrate before it; a lamp floats in the middle, as does Chagall's candelabra, and a crown sails away to the right on wings. In the second drawing a whole under-sea world with seaweed and sea creatures appears inside a woman's abdomen and in the place of breasts are bombs. We should here note that in the patient's drawings parts of the human body become mechanical objects where in Chagall's animal and human parts are interchanged.

We have here then drawings suggesting the 'introjected objects' of psychoanalysts. Indeed this same patient described at another session that at one time she had a vivid feeling of her father's body, diminished to something much smaller than life, present within her own body, with the face at right angles to her neck; and she maintained that the 'tickling in the throat' from which she suffered was caused by his moustache touching the sides of her throat. At the same time this patient is, as far as daily life is concerned, remarkable for her quick and correct observation of people and her sound commonsense.

Another feature of Chagall's paintings is the confusion of time and space or, to put it the other way round, the absence of the dimensions of time and space. The materials he uses appear, therefore, to be suitable for the expression of experience in which there is neither time nor space but only immediacy of experience, each experience obliterating the one before it and replacing it with itself.

Now the beauty and the harmony of Chagall's pictures, and the gulf that in that aspect separates them from the productions of patients, gives much material for thought, material which arises equally out of contemplation of the work of Blake, of Coleridge, of James Joyce, of Henry Moore or of Hieronymous

Bosch. The great artist works with the same tools as our own experience could make accessible to all of us, but he produces results which are mysterious and act powerfully upon us. Where the work of our patients very often reflects fear, horror and suffering, the work of these artists, even where we cannot understand it with our intelligence, affects some other part of our being in a way peculiar to itself, often calling out responses of which we did not previously know ourselves capable.

Here lies the key to the difference between the Primary System in health and in illness, and this difference will be described in detail later on.

The fact having been established that these strange processes exist, it is now necessary to consider the questions of how they come about and what they convey; and as to the place these processes play in the total personality. The first idea that will occur to any worker familiar with the technique of free association is that these represent the chain of free association occurring, not in sequence as it usually does, but congested or condensed, as it were, into a solid mass as indeed often occurs in psychoanalytic studies.

It will be useful, therefore, to start there and to analyse out some of these combinations. To do so we might take a hypothetical case in which a man walking down a street, undergoing emotional experiences of high significance for him, but of a type liable later to be repressed, at the same time notices idly that a woman on the opposite side of the street, wearing a red hat, is passing a pillar-box of exactly the same colour. Further, as she comes towards him, she moves in front of a small front garden to the houses on the street, in which there are some Paul Crampel geraniums. The colour of these, he casually notices, is the same as that of her hat and the pillar-box. These three as they come together make, as it were, a column of red topped with a hat and finished with fluffy flowers. It is possible that he would remember that experience exactly as he had experienced it; or the sight, on another occasion, of a component part of the combination would reproduce for him the other part; or even that when some chord in the accompanying emotional experience was touched, it would lead him to associate that with these, or the other way about. But whichever way it happened, he would at all times see the hat as a hat, and the pillar-box and flowers as a pillar-box and flowers. It is necessary to examine this fact a little closer to see why this should be. To do so, let us consider the experience of a foreigner coming to a country with the life of which he is unfamiliar, as for instance, the arrival in the seventeenth century of Europeans in China. Or let us take our own experience when moving around an exhibition of pictures of an artist with whose style we are unfamiliar; or going around a number of furnished houses looking for accommodation. When we attempt later on to remember accurately the arrangement of the items we have seen, if we make a note of what we remember and then compare with the actual facts, we shall find that we have confused the characters of the objects seen, and in memory at times attached the qualities of one part to another, and so on. It is this well-known phenomenon which renders so much legal witness, and even scientific record, on occasion unreliable.

It may then be agreed that the reason the man in the street would be unlikely to do this with the pillar-box, hat and flowers lies in his perfect familiarity with those objects and with their functions. Moreover, they have displayed themselves before him *as he is accustomed to seeing them*. He has seen many hats, knows well their purposes and cannot mix the hat, for instance, with the face of the wearer. He has posted many letters and only the swiftest glance is needed to tell him all he needs to know about the pillar-box. The same is true of the flowers, particularly if he lives in London. He is, therefore, able swiftly to abstract one quality from each of these and associate it with the same quality abstracted from the other objects, while at the same time holding each distinct in his mind. That is to say, his ability to keep these distinct while at the same time associating them through a single aspect depends *upon his previous experience*. Had he not had that experience, this would not have been possible for him, or possible only in exceptional circumstances.

But it is just this element which is missing in children, especially young children. It must be emphasized that the one essential characteristic of all children's experience is that it is new to them, and comes, in the larger number of cases, uncombined with understanding of the significance to other people of the sensorial experiences personally experienced.

Now it is one of the characteristics of intelligence that the owner attempts, as if driven by an inner need for internal economy, to group his experiences together. We all do this automatically in cataloguing. As soon as we meet some new fact, we say to ourselves in order to locate it: 'That is rather like an *X*, but with the added character of *Y*.' This impulse starts at as early an age as we have been able to gain contact with children (it may even begin pre-natally).

But in order to make a catalogue, some principle must be adopted by which events, taking that word in its most limited meaning to apply to all items of experience, may be grouped. The author had the opportunity of discussing this point with the late Professor Spearman at the General Meeting of the British Psychological Society in Manchester in 1937; he agreed with her that the usual method of grouping in the ordinary speech and usage of the adult includes a large measure of consideration of function and of common use. Thus, when thinking of a knife we tend to speak of its sharpness or bluntness, of its size and use – penknife, dinner-knife, etc., and do not use the adjectives 'cold', 'bluish', 'sour to taste', etc., which are equally appropriate to it. We do this not because we deny the existence of these qualities or could not perceive them if we desired but because they are uninteresting to us and so not noticed. Once again, the perception of these qualities we do notice involves experience of their use, and therefore is *ex hypothesi* inaccessible to young children.

By what method, therefore, do children classify their experience? This was one of the first questions that it was essential to answer, and the material collected over many years had made it quite certain that the answer is: 'By the quality of the personal experience the child has of the thing and event in question.' Thus 'things which made me feel horrid' go together, as do 'things which made me feel warm' etc., up to the greatest refinement of difference, in sensitive children, of all varieties of experience. Moreover, items when grouped together in this way do not become *associated*; they *coalesce*, the shared quality not combining them in a way that can be separated later by the owner into the component parts, but becoming entirely identified so that the original items now form part of a single whole. Here is a little story which makes this clearer. A little boy of three and a half with a pretty, social mother, had a green, smooth, shining toy duck to which he was much attached. He used to put it under his cheek when sleeping. This duck quacked. His mother used to go out a great deal in the evening, and so came up to his nursery usually wearing a green silk evening dress, to read him a good-night story. She then sat in a low chair, and being rather tall, her knees came just to the height of his cheek. It was their custom that when he had had his bath he came in from the bathroom to his nursery with his duck under one arm, paused at the door, looked at his mother, then ran forward, stroked his cheek on his mother's knee, said 'Pretty Mummy', climbed on her knee and cuddled down, and she read him his story. Every night this little ritual was carried out. But one night his mother came up wearing a red dress. The little boy paused at the door and looked at her very hard before he came forward rather slowly, did not stroke her knees with his cheek, and climbed up rather soberly on to her lap. This happened two nights, and at the third he stood at the door and burst into tears and said, 'Oh, Mummy, why do you not put on your quacking dress?' That is to say, the whole combination of affection, greenness, smoothness, cheek-stroking, etc., and *quacking* had come together into a whole, and it was a matter of chance which of this composite group of qualities he might hit upon to characterize this whole.

This is the process by which the inner experience of children becomes grouped, and to the results of this process has been given the name 'cluster'. The strange composite objects in Chagall's pictures are almost certainly clusters, though this could not be finally settled without investigating them with the artist himself. The difference is that Chagall is a great artist and children are just children. There are innumerable clusters in each child's mind. The number and variety depend upon two factors; the sensitivity and intellectual quality of the child, and the variety of its experience. Clusters are of all sizes and complexity and composed of very various material.

The formation of clusters, it would appear, is an essential process in the development of the individual personality. When the child is sensitive and intelligent, the linking together which takes place in this way, in early life, of experiences of intimacy and intensity in ways which are personal to him and which are afterwards forgotten (in a manner to be described later), gives the personality resources to be drawn upon which are of inestimable value. From this region come 'five miles meandering with a mazy motion', the 'Tiger! Tiger! burning bright, in the forests of the night', and so on, that delight us as adults. Since much of our essential experience is similar to that of the poet, musician or sculptor, in whom suddenly a cluster can burst into poetic speech, or dynamic sound, or form, the creation of an artist will express for us similar clusters in our own experience, which are inaccessible to ordinary man. In so doing, they bring about in us discharge of energy and release of tension and the experience of profound inner satisfaction.

Now two main characteristics are observable in any large collection of studies of this kind. The first is the occurrence of the same formations in Worlds made by patients who vary in every possible way in age, sex, complaint and intellectual capacity. Take for instance a relatively simple formation, that of the mound surrounded with water which is, at times, a volcano; this can occur with a number of variations in different patients, but with always the same essential features. This is a representation plastically of the kind of experience which in an artist can result, because of his temperament and ability, in the 'explosion' of a work of art, but which in a patient expresses only anxiety and neurotic tension. There are a very large number of these constant factors, but we are only at the beginning of the recognition of them and an understanding of their significance, both in themselves and in and for the patient who makes them.

The second characteristic of this type of material is the individuality of each patient's productions, when these are considered as a whole. This parallels to some extent what we all know of human life. We are all born, feed from a mother or a bottle that we suck, grow in stature with the constant change of relation to the outer world that this involves, come into full possession of our bodily powers, including those of reproduction, and finally die. Our faces and forms are made of the same features, but no two individuals and no two individuals' lives are really alike. In the same way there is a certain likeness in the material produced by patients when it is *itemized*. Were this not so it would be impossible ever to think of understanding it; but there is an infinite difference in the manner in which the material is grouped and in the individual features which are added by each individual patient.

It is quite impossible within the scope of this paper even to begin to show the range and variety and the infinite subtlety and complexity of these clusters and the light they throw upon processes of individual and of group thoughts. We must, therefore, pass on to another aspect, that of how clusters are arranged. Intensive study of material from roughly two thousand cases has brought much material on this subject to light. To arrive at an understanding of the full meaning of any Primary System production, either of Mosaics or of Worlds, a series of material of the same kind from the same individual should be studied together, because the first productions often contain, as sometimes does the first interview of a long analysis, the germ of all that comes later.

A very striking similarity between the development of Primary System material and of musical themes here appears.

The later themes emerge from elaboration of elements of the original design. It is as if the whole system were charged with power which only slowly becomes perceptible as it finds expression for itself, thus once more paralleling the process of artistic creation.

So far, the clusters have only been considered from their sensorial side. But clusters also represent, and in the most powerful way, dynamic experiences. To illustrate this, consider a very simple picture. This was made and drawn by a young woman and represents the following: at the top are, in parallel lines beneath each other, a black smear, a green hedge, and a train of trucks loaded with coal. This train is going very fast. The blackness above 'is frightening, as things pop up in it and one does not know what they are'. Below these, a child runs. She is really, the painter said, running out of the picture towards the beholder. She is running with all her might, but she does not know to where she runs – it is the running of panic, combined with the aimless running for the sake of the movement, of young children. Below on the left is a heap first of faeces and then of smoking manure with streaks of blood in it, and on the right the sound that trucks made when heard shunting in the night. This picture aroused powerful vague emotion in the painter. She described this as follows (the thoughts are given in the order they occurred):

> It is important that the manure steamed – like the train – like smoke. I loved [that is as a child] giving plants heaps of manure [pause]. The train is in pieces – like sausages. Coal burns, it leaves ash – I have often heard a lavatory [her word for faeces] referred to as ash. Yes, I remember tramps' hats popping up from behind a hedge [she later painted this incident without realizing what she was painting], it's like when a man finishes peeing, it comes in spurts. Something here is really like a face [she worked this out in great detail later], the nose area, and a little like sick. There's something somewhere about what drives a train being partly water and steam, sick comes up in jabs too and is also hot – horrible trains at night, I used to hear shunting and puffing, frightening. Peeing is like lav., coming out with a rush [here followed a reference to early childhood defaecation experiences when she had to get out of bed suddenly, from beside a heavily sleeping sister, because of a sudden onset of diarrhoea and run down a terrifying dark passage to a

> frightening lavatory]. I think of something cook told us about a man, and while he had been ill and away from home, they had built a railway and a bridge, but he had not known of it, and he said he had seen a row of houses rushing down a drain [i.e. a train going under a bridge]; if one is being upset inside, one feels one's whole inside is going to rush out, like it does down the lavatory plug – I get a feeling that if I start machining I shall get faster and faster – I shall lose control – very like running down a slope, you start all right and then you can't stop yourself later – and tobogganing.

Here then, therefore, is a cluster and in it are entangled a number of the patient's phobias, sights, sounds, sensations, memories, conceptions and motor experiences, the whole highly charged with energy. All these factors and feelings are, therefore, interrelated, and the material of this picture recurred in other forms and was combined with other material in dreams and in Worlds. If space permitted, many examples of this sort could be given where the strongest feelings form part of the clusters.

To return for a moment to the upside-down faces of Chagall. One of the most striking features of the interrelation of clusters among themselves is the interchange of positions. Clusters are not arranged flat or vertically, but apparently in a massive clumped manner. Children (and also such adults as have been studied so far) often attempt to arrange objects suspended in space above the World trays, and the relation between World and World of the same patient makes it clear that they are conceived plastically. Not only is this true, but confusion between the relation of glove and hand and that of 'inside-out' with the 'right way out' also frequently occurs.

This leads to a consideration of the relation between the clusters. How is the whole system tied together and what is the dynamic quality?

As far as it is possible to make a statement from what has been observed, it would appear that energy invests the whole of the clusters of the Primary System, but does so in an uneven fashion. Some clusters are very highly charged, some less so; and the question of what happens to this energy, and what part is played in the conscious life of the individual by the presence of these clusters, depends on the next feature of the structure of the psyche that has appeared from investigations, which is the formation of the Secondary System.

It appears that the Primary System begins with the first

beginning of sensorial experience and continues through life. But *pari passu* with the formation of the Primary System, the child begins to struggle to make contact with and to understand the world that he shares with the rest of his surroundings. To say this is only to say, in other words, what is the common ground and study of all the aspects of child development. Already a great deal is known about this, and there is nothing new to add here. The child as he grows goes through all the stages known to child psychology and shown especially by the beautiful and careful work of Gesell and his school. Through these processes he learns to gain mastery over his own body and gradually to understand and in a practical way to master his environment, adding at about the age of eight the supreme achievement of mankind, the ability to communicate with others, and with his own interior self, in language.

Thus, in every child, there are two systems. The Primary System is personal, idiosyncratic, massive and multidimensional, by its nature incommunicable in words to others. Parallel with the development of this goes the development of the Secondary System, which is reasonable, practical, governed by causality, shared with other people and to a large extent describable in language. The Primary System is non-rational, peculiarly constructed, entirely individual, and made up of groups of clusters not later separable by free association, all charged with undifferentiated energy. The Secondary System is shared, logical, reasonable, and uses language as its tool.

Now the important point is that the contents of the Primary System cannot appear in the Secondary System. Most people are, therefore, totally unaware of their existence and contemptuous about the possibility. These contents are, in this sense, truly unconscious. But they are so, not through repression, either of the Freudian or Jungian type, but for the simple reason that Primary System material as such, and in its crude state, is totally inexpressible in Secondary System terms.

In order to discover the Primary System, material has to be made accessible to the patient in which constructions of this peculiar nature can be expressed. It is the absence of such material which has prevented its discovery hitherto. Similarly, for the expression of music, instruments capable of producing certain types of sound must be available and adequate; and suitable stone must be available for the production of sculpture. What, for example, it is interesting to meditate, would have been the fate of Prokofiev or Beethoven had they been born in the Greece of classical times, or to Henry Moore if born in a desert of sand?

In collections of Mosaics made by workers as far apart as Sweden, Switzerland and central France, all the characteristics described appear; and also in Worlds made in Sweden as in those made in this country.

For development to be normal, two things are essential. First of all, there is much in the Primary System that is common to many different individuals and groups, and fairy-tales, folklore, myth and fable embody many of these elements. As the Jungian school of analysis has shown, through enjoyment of these, the energy which charges Primary clusters can find its way through the Secondary System, to expression in the outside world. Certain of the clusters even become almost tangible in solidity and form the 'introjected objects' of psychoanalysis.

The second necessity is adequate opportunity for the child to play and toleration of his play and his difficulties in adaptation, by the adults around him. Gradually, then, he corrects his interior concepts, through contact with external reality, and the energy with which the clusters in the Primary System are charged passes through to the Secondary System to find expression in the outside world.

If, however, this does not occur, for any of the many reasons that can happen to a child, then four conditions may result and these correspond to the four main disabilities of the children we treat. First, the energy may remain locked up in the Primary clusters. In this case, the child becomes listless and without interest, unable to put energy into any aspect of living; he tends to be conventional, uninteresting as a character and under the domination of outside circumstances. Second, if the amount of energy is greater and more concentrated in certain parts of the Primary System, with no outlet through the Secondary System, then the energy, finding no way out, comes to be concentrated in the body. Different organs appear to be associated with different types of cluster; thus arise the asthmas, the eczemas, the catarrhs, convulsions, disturbances of digestive and sleep habits, and so on, which have no organic basis. Third, if, on the other hand, the child takes his clusters for reality and tries to see them in the outside world, they make themselves into phobias and rituals and obsessions. And fourth if it be the type of child who cannot achieve a proper development of his Secondary System and a clear distinction between what is outside and what within, the outside world becomes for him mixed up with his inner life and his relation to reality confused. According to the content of his clusters, he may become the dreamy detached child, the child who appears to be suffering from an early psychosis, or the neurotic delinquent. A single child may even develop all four types of trouble, or varying types may appear in turn during the lifetime, or the treatment, of any single individual, depending upon his constitution and upon circumstances.

Another fate may occur in later life. The Secondary System, through some external circumstances of physical disease, may disintegrate. Then the Primary System is liable to flood over the debris, using whatever means it can to express itself, and giving the appearance with which we are familiar in several forms of psychosis, notably in some forms of schizophrenia.

This is what may, for example, have happened in Nazi Germany. The Secondary System in that country had for years previous to 1933 been more highly developed than in any country, with little opportunity in individuals for play. This steadily increased the gap, both individually and nationally, between the Primary and Secondary Systems. The lack of material in education and life for expression of the contents of the Primary System, and so for modifications to take place, kept it, in too many people, both at a primitive level and in a state of high tension. The loss of public confidence in the value of the Secondary System, consequent upon economic stress, led ultimately to a breakdown of the whole structure of the Secondary System. What then happened was a flooding of the personality of many individuals and groups with the disjointed elements of the Primary System. Within the Nazi movement, therefore, the Primary System, with its passion, cruelty and unreality, came to take the place of the Secondary System, and then through the dynamic of the leadership of Hitler, the sort of stuff we find in the Primary System of neurotic children came to be taken for reality, and ultimately given actual expression in reality.

A remarkable study of individual Nazi camp officials has recently appeared, in a book written by Dr Lingens Reiner called *Prisoners of Fear*, a description of a woman prisoner-physician's experience of Auschwitz and Dachau (Lingens Reiner, 1948). This courageous book bears out exactly what has been said, and shows the camp guards, doctors and officers not to have been organized individuals at all, but persons in whom disintegrated clusters had become animated – each taking charge in turn of the actions of the individual's body, so that guilt was evaded because one part of the personality was dissociated from the other, in the way that clusters are often separated from one another in the Primary System.

The mapping of the Primary System is only in its beginnings, and what have been set forth here are only some of the highlights, as it were, of the experience gained. It takes a full three years to train workers in the understanding of the nature of actual clusters in actual children, and in the acquiring of adequate skill in the use of this knowledge in therapy. But these scrappy notes, most inadequate to the vastness of the subject with which they attempt to cope, may have provided something to stimulate interest in this pregnant subject and perhaps to form a basis upon which to be considered later – the use of the concept of the Primary System in psychotherapy.

11 Questions of Therapeutic Technique

The first paper in this chapter is in fact compiled from two papers which Lowenfeld gave at the International Congress for Psychotherapeutics, held at Leiden-Oegstgeest, on 5–8 September 1951. Lowenfeld's original titles were, 'Some Principles of Child Psychotherapy' and 'The Problem of the Withdrawn Child'. In the latter paper she took advantage of a full description of her approach given in the former, delivered first.

Here, what has been omitted in the compilation is some description of the 'theory of E', then embryonic (see this volume, pp. 120–3), and specific references to other speakers. For example, in the first paper Lowenfeld expressed her enthusiasm for the work of Kretschmer, who gave an opening address at the congress, and used the opportunity to stress that the starting-point for her own work was the problem of relating psyche and soma. She also pointed to similarities between her work and child guidance, stressing the psychiatric social worker's role in supporting parents. Even at that time, however, it was important that the social worker at the ICP was thoroughly familiar with the principles underlying Lowenfeld's work with children, so that these could be clarified for the parents. In her first paper Lowenfeld also gave a fuller discussion of the role of the physical therapist than is reproduced here, and concluded the paper with an illustrated account of the use of Worlds.

Within this collection these papers are particularly useful in giving a detailed description of the layout and amenities at the ICP, and in illustrating what psychotherapy might have been like for a child passing through. Lowenfeld set up a contrast between her approach and the model used in psychoanalytic psychotherapy. Where the latter emphasizes the child–therapist relationship, at the ICP the centrality of that relationship was diffused. Furthermore Lowenfeld gave challenging examples of potentially therapeutic effects of children's contact with other children. She used the case of the withdrawn child to highlight the value of her approach in opening up communication within the self as well as with other people, and attempted to render 'withdrawnness' comprehensible within her theoretical scheme.

In challenging the standard psychoanalytic model, here Lowenfeld was also stressing limitations in what, in 1951, she saw as a ubiquitous focus on the family. To Lowenfeld the importance of the family was not in doubt. As she stressed in the original version of the first paper, 'growth to adulthood within the family is the norm and goal for every human child'. Rather, her argument was that concentrating on the family militated against the possible contribution of psychotherapy to understanding the developmental tasks facing children growing up in a post-war world. That is, it was no longer possible for the family to equip children with means for dealing with the aftermath of war and the effects of rapid social and political upheaval and technological change; today's children must find their answers from somewhere else.

The second paper in this chapter, 'The Structure of Transference' was also first presented at a conference, the International Congress of Psychotherapy, held in Zürich on 20–24 July 1954. It was first published in 1955 in *Acta Psychotherapeutica Psychosomatica et Orthopaedagogica* (vol. 3, pp. 502–7). Omitted here are footnotes containing a description of the World technique, and details of a discussion of the meaning of the word 'objective' which took place after the original presentation. Americans in the audience, apparently, took the term to mean 'scientific' in the narrow sense, or as implying a lack of engagement of thoughts and feelings. For Lowenfeld the intention was to convey a distinction between the experiencing subject and the existence of 'facts or objects which have their own separate existence distinct in every way from the subject who regards them' (original publication, p. 505).

That there was some confusion amongst the audience is understandable, particularly given Lowenfeld's implicit acknowledgement of the patient's subjective involvement in producing Worlds. However, what World-making does is to take the patient to a point at which reflective contemplation of the mind's products is possible. In this sense Lowenfeld's approach is 'structural'. Given the ascendancy of psychoanalytic child psychotherapy, the time was overdue for Lowenfeld to address the nature of the patient–therapist relationship, and in particular the place of transference.

There are a number of problems in placing the role of transference within Lowenfeld's scheme, made more difficult perhaps by the fact that the term has been used to carry several different emphases since Freud's original formulation. In 1905 Freud observed that patients would repeat towards their analysts impulses and feelings experienced earlier on in their relationships with significant others, such as parents. In the transference, 'a whole series of psychological experiences are revived, not as belonging to the past but as applying to the physician at the present moment' (Freud, 1905, p. 116). As Freud found that repetitions like these made it possible for earlier conflicts to be understood, facilitating psychological change in the patient, the transference eventually became a central psychotherapeutic tool. Since Freud's time the concept of transference has broadened, largely as a result of psychoanalytic work with psychotic patients and Klein's adaptations of technique in working with young children. Within the Kleinian tradition in particular, the concept of transference has been extended 'to include the transfer on to the analyst of the whole range of early emotions as well as the projection of the infantile feeling states which persist throughout life' (Miller, 1983, p. 136).

Lowenfeld's aim was not to deny the existence and value of transference. She appears to have been operating with a view based on Freud's original definition. She referred to the transference as an 'instrument' or 'tool' which, apart from being akin to her own approach, implies that she thought of it as linked concretely to particular past events rather than as a more or less continuous process. In claiming that only with difficulty can different levels of experience or fragmentation be dealt with in the transference, she appeared to ignore or be oblivious of the idea of analysing transference on a 'part object' basis, central to Klein's (1946) work with psychotic patients, for example. But Lowenfeld's preoccupation centred on what would constitute evidence for transference outside what is known between patient and therapist.

Lowenfeld repeated many of the points given earlier (see Chapter 9) on the need to back psychoanalytic assumptions with methods of validation which are external to the therapist–patient relationship. She argued that, in fact, World-making has produced powerful evidence on the existence of transference.

Her emphasis, however, is on the 'dynamisms which form the major significance of transference', which express themselves through the arrangement of inanimate objects in the World, rather than on the interpersonal relationship (see this volume, p. 366). For Lowenfeld the gradual revelation and therapeutic power of her technique come from the fact that the Worlds are the patient's own creation, accompanied by more or less assistance in understanding the inner experience provided by the therapist.

Lowenfeld's paper does not answer critics who would point out that the relationship to the therapist is left unacknowledged. In consequence, the possibility remains that the therapeutic agency comes primarily through that relationship rather than through the impact of the child's own production. Furthermore, she did not explore or acknowledge the possibility that the World produced is an expression of relationships, whether with persons present or absent. Nevertheless, in attempting to place transference within the total gamut of what may be observed during World-making, Lowenfeld's account provides a useful challenge to the assumption that everything taking place in psychotherapy can or should be understood in terms of transference. For psychoanalytic psychotherapists, it also suggests that refinement may be necessary in understanding similarities and differences in transference phenomena expressed through the use of inanimate objects as opposed to directly through interpersonal aspects of the therapeutic relationship.

Principles of Psychotherapy Applied to the Situation of the Withdrawn Child [1951]

Any speaker whose contribution falls in the latter part of the conference has the advantage of being able to make use of points of agreement with other speakers. I have been very interested in the many presentations which have dealt with the processes of child psychotherapy, and with the events, interior and exterior, which take place within the family situation or between the child and his group. But one very important reservation remains. What of the child without a family? For example, we would all stress the importance, for a child's inner development, of his acceptance by the outside world; but what of the instances where this does *not* take place? What about the cases in which because, let us say, of the shape of his nose, the colour of his hair or skin, the form of his body, the accent of his speech, the child is *not* accepted by his environment? What about the child with no family? Or the child who has not only no family to which he belongs but also no group, no citizenship to grow into, no tradition which he automatically inherits?

Europe is faced at this moment with millions of children growing up to be citizens of tomorrow who lack all of these, and I feel that, in concerning themselves exclusively with the happenings within the family circle and the immediate environment, psychotherapists are turning their eyes from this problem.

My object in this paper is to describe a form of child psychotherapy which is being carried on in London by a body called the Institute of Child Psychology (ICP). This is an out-patient clinic founded in 1928, and therefore coexistent in time with the child guidance movement in Britain. Its work has developed side by side, and on friendly relations, with the child guidance movement, and includes the activities found in every child guidance clinic. The whole programme of work of the ICP, however, is based on principles which differ from these and are expressed in new and specialized activities. Here, I shall concentrate on these differences.

In order to make clear the principles of the work at the ICP a little time must be spent on a description of the building itself. This is a four-storey building so constructed that what is the garden floor at the rear is semi-basement in front. The work done in the building is arranged in blocks and the whole of the garden floor is occupied by play rooms.

The rooms and their contents are painted gaily in the colours of southern France, and each room is designed to fulfil a particular purpose. They are as follows. Two square play rooms open out of each other from front to back. In the front play room are a built-in house (about 4 ft high with a door and two windows and walls strong enough for children to climb over them), a shop with a counter and door and windows, a large double-fronted dolls' house and a large toy cooking stove and dresser. The back play room contains a blackboard, a garage, and so on, and opens on to the garden. Both rooms are fitted with about a dozen shelves on which are bricks, blocks, runabout toys, cars and numerous boxes containing fantasy and construction materials as well as paper, pencils and paint. Down the centre of the rooms are tables of varying heights with trays of sand on them for use in the World technique, and to one side of the rooms stand the World cabinets. Next to these play rooms is a small room used for administering tests, with a corridor at right angles out of which opens the physical-activity room. This has guards over the lights and is fitted with wall bars and other gymnastic equipment. It also contains a chest for acting and dressing-up materials, a cupboard for musical instruments, and solid tables and chairs. On the other side of the play rooms there are two small rooms next door to each other, with large windows opening on the garden. These are the 'water' and 'mess' rooms. The floors of these rooms are of concrete and slope slightly towards the outside wall where a surface drain carries off water. The walls are tiled and suitable for use as painting surfaces with powder paint; the lights are waterproof.

The children referred to the ICP come from any part of the country, and occasionally from outside the country, from all social groups and from age groups ranging from infancy to eighteen years, with all types of educational background. They come for an hour at a time, once, twice or three times a week, and have free access to all the rooms, moving about among them as they will, and come and go throughout the day at the times arranged with each family, the number present at any one time varying from hour to hour. Each child is in the special care of one adult who is either a therapist or a graduate student-in-training working under the supervision of a therapist. A report on each child's activity and behaviour during the session is written immediately after the session and discussed by the whole group of workers before the child's next visit.

You will see immediately that there are here certain radical differences to the current mode. Although there are many differences in detail, on the whole most psychotherapeutic work with children has followed along the same lines as work with adults. That is to say, at the centre of the work lies a specialized relationship between patient and therapist. The content of this remains private to those two and is concerned with the use of many means through which the emotional life and development of the patient can be made clear to him and errors in it corrected through reliving in a new context. In contrast, here there is no privacy; children of widely differing ages work in the same rooms together, and the adult working with any given child often changes. These differences are based upon certain qualities of children; and in the arrangements I have described, use is made of a fundamental characteristic of neurotic children, their egocentricity. We have found in this performance of direct experiment, which we have been carrying on now for many years, that when given the opportunity to occupy themselves with activities that are vital to them, children with problems are so absorbed in their own actions and feelings that the presence of other children similarly occupied around them does not disturb them at all. It is a common experience in our play rooms to find adults discussing with individual children the most intimate aspects of their lives in a room in which several other children are actively engaged in other occupations, without any of them affecting or disturbing one another. Indeed the presence in the room of other children gives a feeling of security to many children: it makes them feel less peculiar, less isolated, to find other children also doing the queer things they long to do; and as each child discusses what he is doing with his 'worker', it seems natural to him that other children should be doing the same. If one child wanders off to watch or listen to the actions or conversation of another child, this means that the process he is involved in is not gripping him sufficiently; and as this will be immediately recorded on the reports of two workers at that session, that on the child himself and that concerning the child he has interfered with, steps can immediately be taken to remedy it.

This arrangement has an additional positive value. One of the most commonly recurring elements in a disturbed child's problem is that of uneven growth and development. Many children for a wide variety of reasons have left out important stages in their development, and ordinary life gives them no chance to make this good. But in our play rooms the presence of children of all ages gives the children in whom these gaps have occurred many opportunities, either through the device of 'helping the younger ones' or with a directness which is amazing until one has got used to it, of filling in the missing stages of development.

The second element which will appear astonishing is that the adults working with any given child change quite frequently. This procedure has a solid theoretical basis and is assisted by the fact that all women workers wear overalls of the same colour (green), and being rarely called by their names tend to blend, for many children, into a whole. Men workers wear anything they have available in the way of old clothes which do not need protection. Nothing resembling a hospital is present and white is not used anywhere in the building, because of its association with hospitals.

SPECIALIZED TECHNIQUES AND THEIR THEORETICAL UNDERPINNINGS

What then lies behind the furnishing of the play rooms, and what is the use of the physical-activity room? At this conference various speakers have laid stress on the primary importance of experience in the development of personality. This brings me to that line of approach, which is the foundation of our whole work. It is experience which is the crucial fact. Children experience the world through their senses, being dependent on them to a peculiar extent. That is, compared to the adult, the child is bounded by his whole body and its experiences and by his senses. It is by the internal and external experiences which his senses bring to him, and perhaps even more acutely by the experiences and emotions that his deliberate explorations by these senses can bring him, that a child forms his impressions of the world. Our play rooms are therefore equipped to afford him two types of experience. First, there are opportunities for the active external expression of fragmented internal impulses towards sensuous experiment with water, mess, mouldable substances, and so on; and second, the child uses instruments for the objective presentation of the *many-sidedness* and complexity of his immediate experience, in a way that can enable him and his adult companions to study it and integrate it with his conscious understanding. There are a number of these tools, but here I have only time to mention two: the Mosaic Test and the World.

The Mosaic Test gives the user, whether child or adult, the challenge of a large number of pieces of different geometrical designs and sizes and in size-different colours, with which he can construct anything he likes on a standard-sized tray. The World technique puts at his disposal a deep metal tray fitted with sand and/or as much water as he likes, together with a cabinet of many shallow drawers, each containing toy models of different types of existing objects (such as trees, animals, human figures, furniture and the like).

The Mosaic material forms a 'test' in that its constituents are fixed, and it must be administered in a uniform manner according to definite rules. The World is a 'technique' in that its constituents, although classifiable into groups, are unlimited and the child is free to make of them whatever use of them he desires.

For many children further means of expression and exploration are available in the Physical Activity Department under Miss Margaret Kirschner. Before the war when more adequate space was available, an assessment would be made in this department of every child's relation to movement, whether playful, experimental or rhythmic, and help was arranged for all who needed it. Now, in the more limited space that is all post-war conditions make available, this help can be given only to a proportion of the children and it is reserved for those who have asthma, tics, bodily inhibitions, clumsiness etc.

All our methods have evolved through practical experience. But they are also based on theoretical assumptions, developing over many years. Through the study of the material produced by these techniques I have come upon a discovery that is in the highest degree unexpected. This is that there is a structure in the interior world of the child about which we know hardly anything, but to whose clear-cut 'solidity' and the exactness of whose working much of the ineffectiveness of therapy and of education is due.

This structure is peculiar in that its linkages come about through factors which, though they follow general lines, are personal to the child himself. The emotions and drives of the child become caught in this interior network. Psychosomatic conditions, phobias, anxieties and phantasies, whether conscious or unconscious, turn out often to be the projection, either into the body or upon the outside world, of formations of this inner structure. This can only be effectively set right by separating out their elements and regrouping them in more appropriate connections. Every such separation that is carried out by the combined action of the child and therapist, working together on the material constructed by the child, brings about a release of energy in the child. His released energy then finds expression through delighted experiment with sensuous experience. The skill, understanding and enjoyment achieved through this experiment furthers the development of the self and the child's confidence in the integrity of the self.

THE WITHDRAWN CHILD

To illustrate how our approach works out in individual cases, I want to take the problem of the withdrawn child.

All psychiatrists working with children are agreed that one type of case presents difficulties of a very special kind: that is the child, of whatever age, from whom it is impossible to obtain a response. These children and young people neither like nor dislike their therapists; they give either a polite and superficial answer to all questions or attempts to elicit from them any kind of material, or they make no response whatever. Now it is generally believed by therapists that the operative mechanism in these cases is that of 'jamming', i.e. the impingement upon one another of two instinctual drives acting with equal force in opposite directions. The problem in such a situation is to separate the components of this 'jam' so that at least part of one of these forces becomes detached and available for the child to use.

It is undeniable that in a number of such cases this is the mechanism at work. It is also clear that a number of cases exist where a traumatic experience which is too painful to be touched upon forms the core of the inhibition. However, our experience suggests that in many such cases there is another factor at work.

In an examination of the concept that the amnesia for childhood events, from which we all suffer, arises from the factor of repression, Ernest Schachtel (1947) has pointed out that the main tool which has been used for the exploration of memory is language and that in any language only a few aspects of the totality of experience have found expression. This view is shared by many anthropologists who have stressed the inadequacy of ordinary language to express many of the most important aspects of human experience. In any thoughtful consideration of the world today, particularly in its international aspect, it is impossible to avoid such a disturbing consciousness of this inability of language to bridge gaps in understanding or the failure of understanding between peoples of differing social experiences. Many languages show examples of identical words or phrases, as for example 'sanctions' in French and the original English meaning, which actually convey opposite significances, and in single languages phrases occur which according to the context may have opposite meanings.

In no sphere is this difficulty more acute than in the intercourse between adults and children. We are indebted to Piaget for exhaustive study of some of these differences of meaning according to whether words are used by adults or by children. But the areas of exploration of Piaget and his co-workers are limited and devoted to such definite themes as the child's conception of causality, the language and thought of the child, and the moral judgement of the child (Piaget, 1929, 1932a, 1932b).

Action, not language, is the natural mode of expression of children and the use of objects for expression of idea and feeling is much more natural to them than the use of words. If opportunities for varied and subtle forms of action are provided for children, their use of them suggests that their difficulties in response arise from factors essentially different from those which have been suggested. Study of these children by the means I have been describing suggests that failure to achieve expression of inner experience arises not so much from the operation of expression as from sheer inability to find material in which some of the essential interior experiences of children can be expressed. Thus many of the children who we find confronting us in silence, unable to give any response to our most tactful questioning, incapable of drawing or modelling or discovering within themselves any sentiments or ideas that they can put into story or other imaginary form, are children held fast in a situation from which it is for them impossible to escape.

The dilemma that faces them may perhaps be called the dilemma of simultaneity: that is, that a number of things within them are happening at one and the same time on different planes and in differing modes. If this state is therefore to be communicated, some tool must be found which is capable of expressing complexity and simultaneity of this sort. Language cannot do it, since in language words must be strung out into grammatical form, and, even when accompanied by gestures, can only deal with one aspect of a situation at a time. It is just this analysis into aspects and their serial presentation in grammatical form which is outside the capacity of the withdrawn child. His consciousness is drowned in the situation in which he finds himself, and his misery consists precisely in the fact that he is unable to extricate his consciousness from this confusion or to stand aside and see it objectively.

Most children who come to us as patients have been a long time in this condition, and secondary effects have begun to develop. According to the nature of his condition and the origin of his troubles, by the time a child comes to us he is often immersed in a fantasy world of his own so different from our world that no bridge exists between him and us. What is needed, in order to make the process of analysis possible, is to reawaken the feeling of hope. These children are so shut up in the blackness of their own isolation that unless *hope* of communication can be aroused there is no dynamic available with which we can work.

It is here that the type of approach which I have attempted to describe begins to show its value. Children learn from each other; and a child introduced into an assembly of children for whom the help which they need is patently becoming available can catch from observation of other children that reassurance about the possibility of help that we, as adults, are incapable of giving to him. The procedure, therefore, that we have found most suitable is to explain to each child, in words, the nature and contents of the children's floor to which he is coming, and to couple this with a particular reassurance that on this floor children are safe from adult comment and interference, and that what they do or say there is not reported to their 'grown-ups'. Arrangements are then made in the usual way for the child to come to the building at times which make as little disturbance as possible in the usual rhythm of his week.

Once arrived at the ICP, in accordance with his age and degree of shrinking isolation, he is invited or coaxed to come downstairs to the play rooms. In the case of very young children it is sometimes necessary at first to invite a parent to come downstairs with the child. The parent is then accommodated with a chair in the corridor or the small interview room, and urged to become absorbed in an occupation of her own.

The child, in the meantime, is welcomed by the therapist assigned to him and told he may behave exactly as he likes, that no one expects anything of him, and he can wander where he will. As far as the child is then concerned, no further notice is ostensibly taken of him. This, however, is only apparently true as, in order to be successful with a child of this kind, the therapist in charge must maintain a constant and unobtrusive observation, even when she seems to be busy helping the other children or tidying up and putting in order some of the apparatus of the play room.

Left to himself the child will probably retreat to some chair or some corner of the room, and with tense muscles wait for the assault that previous experience has told him is certain, sooner or later, to be made upon either his feeling or his attention. At the close of the hour it should be made quite clear to him, by the therapist who has fetched him, that his presence in the play room has been appreciated and enjoyed; that no one minds or feels embarrassed by his total lack of response; that he is liked as a person, and that the therapist is looking forward to seeing him again. Other therapists working in the play rooms whom he may have met or passed in the corridor will also have given him a welcoming smile, and on his return to his waiting parent (if one has accompanied him) care is taken to avoid giving any impression at all except that of a general welcome.

When through constant repetition of this experience it has soaked into the consciousness of the child that the freedom from demand which the welcoming adult has given him is a reality and can be depended upon, the child will begin of himself to make tentative steps forward. He will gradually move out of his phase of frozen isolation towards observation of other children; he may return a ball that has arrived in his neighbourhood, poke a toy nearer to a child who clearly needs it, smile at an absurdity in the play of another child, or even take a hesitant part in some occupation that is going on. At this point the therapist may unobtrusively join him, always taking care to arrange that the child's head is on a higher level than her own so that the child, not the adult, talks down. A willingness to experiment with the material offered will then gradually appear.

It is here that the value of the World technique becomes apparent. It makes no demands on the child and presents no challenge. A withdrawn child will probably start by watching other children using the apparatus, and when he has seen one or two of them place objects in what will appear to him quite irrelevant positions, will venture himself to put one or two objects in the tray nearest to him. His therapist will then drift across to him and make a gentle comment expressing approval, and then sit down quietly to watch. The child may continue to add objects to his tray or may move away to watch other children. Which of these he does is immaterial: he is gaining confidence.

After a period, short or long according to the child and the severity of the conditions from which he suffers, the child will settle down to making a World of his own. Now a World made by a child is a presentation of an aspect of his inner state. Because of this a psychotherapist from any of the major traditions would be able to produce a formula on the nature of mental contents depicted and its determination. If the judgement and intuition of the therapist has led him to recognize some truth about the nature of the material presented and the child's relation to it, the interpretation given by the therapist will produce some relief of tension in the child, and the barrier of isolation will be to that extent diminished. This mode of treatment of the material is valid in itself. But it is not that for which the apparatus was designed, where the goal was rather different.

The essential quality of the World apparatus as designed is that it is a tool for the exploration of the total content of a child's inner experience, and studying the *structure* of this content within the personality of the child. In order to make such study possible, no more than is absolutely necessary is said to the child at each stage about the underlying significance of the World he is making; instead each world is carefully discussed with him, *as it stands*, and the exact meaning to him of each object is elicited. The World is then drawn by the therapist, mostly with the help and according to the comments of the child, and filed in his case sheet for future reference. In this way a complete series of his Worlds and records of his use of other materials is accumulated which is at a suitable moment taken from the case sheet and gone through in detail with the child. What is aimed at then, as always, with the child, is to understand exactly what the child has intended to express in the constructions he has made in the tray, and to trace from World to World the interrelations, inversions, enlargements, suppressions and developments which have taken place in the themes and statements made in his earlier Worlds.

When a range of material is treated in this way, what becomes clear is that these productions represent a very complex structure, composed of sensorial experience, observation, deduction, ideas of all kinds, simple and complex affect, individual and group phantasy, all mixed with statements about everyday happenings. The characteristic of this intricate network is that each part or aspect is, for the child who makes it, inseparably bound up with every other part, affecting it and being affected by it. Thus what this apparatus does is to make available for the child a way out of the most crucial factor in the isolation of the child: the simultaneity of the elements of his experience. For him these elements are like the individual members of a frightened flock of sheep which, when startled by a dog, crowd together in an attempt to get out of a field by a single narrow gate and end by blocking the pathway of escape altogether, perhaps trampling one another to death in the exit. But once the child has within reach an apparatus which allows the simultaneous presentation of fundamentally different and even opposite elements of his situation and dilemmas, the width of the gate as it were becomes equal to the size of the field. It is my experience that when the complexities are disentangled the 'withdrawnness' disappears, and the emerging personality is often of unusual versatility.

In making a simultaneous presentation of many different qualities of experience and *of stress* possible for the child, we are not doing for him anything that is peculiar to the process of therapy. Rather, in our endeavour to meet the urgent needs of children, we are co-operating in that struggle which is at the core of the problem of our generation. It is in an endeavour to present together the whole experience of the human being that James Joyce wrote *Ulysses*, that Gertrude Stein has written all her work, that Picasso and the Surrealists have been experimenting in painting, and that Chagall was moved to the strange composition of his pictures.

It may be asked what is the advantage of this mode of approach over the older method of direct interpretation of selected elements within the framework of an accepted school of psychopathology. A great deal of the answer to this may be found in the recent book of Erik Erikson (1951), *Childhood and Society*. We are confronted in our children by individuals who, in their adult life, will have to face, and to find their identity within, circumstances and forces totally different from those which confronted us in our childhood. It is not enough to solve for and with a child the conflicts that lie within him in his relation to the members of his family; the child needs also to find his own identity, to become familiar with his own sensuous equipment, his abilities, his constitution, his type of emotional endowment, and the possibilities of interior self-respect and satisfaction that lie within the exercise of his own individual functions.

The Structure of Transference [1954]

In the development of any science there is a peculiarly intimate relationship between the structure of new instruments of investigation and the type of knowledge which is gained thereby.

Each instrument brings to light that aspect of the total field of study which is especially related to the possibilities of the individual instrument, and for a time, when through the work of an outstanding genius a new instrument is forged, it appears that within its use will lie ultimately the solution of all the major problems of the particular field of research.

Thus when through the genius of Freud the phenomena of transference first were discovered and described, it seemed that extensive use of this tool would ultimately lead to a solution of the major problems of human personality, whether normal or disturbed. This hope, however, has only partially been realized, for, as Dr Edward Glover stated in a recent paper, 'No accurate records or after histories of psychoanalytical treatment exist: such rough figures as can be obtained do not suggest that psychoanalysis is notably more successful than other forms of therapy and in any case none of the figures is corrected for spontaneous remission or resolution of symptoms' (Glover, 1954). In his paper Dr Glover goes on to state that this fact does not invalidate the reliability of the theoretical formulations derived from psychoanalytical treatment, but does not give the grounds upon which his statement is based. In the absence of examinable evidence this affirmation becomes a statement of belief rather than of facts.

In this disappointment of the earlier hopes psychopathological research follows the normal course of all scientific advance. Each major discovery, thought at first to provide an ultimate solution, proves on further use to have defined limits of validity. Further growth in knowledge is then usually gained through more detailed examination, such as this congress is undertaking, both of the basic tool itself and of the field in which it operates.

Now in setting out to study the phenomena of transference we meet immediately a peculiar obstacle. All aspects of transference take place within a relationship of two people, the analysand and the analyst, and are immune to direct observation. Only the analyst's own experience as analysand and analyst, and the written or spoken words of his colleagues, furnish material which is accessible to direct study. To gain additional insight into the phenomenon itself and a more exact understanding of its functioning, therefore, a reconsideration is necessary of what exactly is taking place in the patient which gives rise to the phenomena of transference. In undertaking such an examination there are two facts of which we can be certain: on the one hand, that processes are at work in the patient, and older experiences are exercising power upon the thought, feeling and actions of the patient, of which he is unaware: and on the other, that behind these forces are operative which attempt to drive both factors into consciousness, nothwithstanding the obstacle to such awareness presented by other aspects of the personality.

It is these processes and experiences and the forces which animate them which the therapeutic process aims to bring into view and to understand. That is to say, put in the widest possible sense, it is a problem of communication with which we are faced. That which is at work in the patient needs to be made manifest to the therapist and, through his understanding of it, to the patient himself.

In seeking to solve this problem we are confronted therefore, as in all situations involving problems of communication, with the basic and dominating fact of the relation between medium and content. In every medium only those experiences or processes can be communicated which the intrinsic nature of the medium makes possible. It is impossible, for instance, to communicate musical experience except through the medium of sound, or the peculiar sensuous-plastic experience that lies behind the work of great sculpture, in words or in paint, or even in the phenomena of transference. If, therefore, we wish to ascertain whether the interpersonal relationship of physician and patient, regarded from whichever standpoint we choose, does in actual fact really mediate the essential forces determining human personality, then a means must be found which will allow of expression within it of other aspects of human experience also and with an equivalent emphasis, in order that the structure of these as part of what the analysand would, if he could, bring before his therapist, can be studied and its importance assessed.

Now there are two characteristics of inner experience of which we are all aware but which can only with great difficulty appear in the transference. These are in the first place the simultaneous presence in any individual of many aspects and levels of experience, and in the second the existence at certain levels and in certain persons of that fragmentation so convincingly presented in the work of Dr Winnicott and Mrs Klein.

The interchange between patient and analyst partakes, as much as any other aspect of interpersonal communication, in the limitations of time and space. No matter, for instance, how vividly the patient may be aware of a number of processes simultaneously present in himself, the communication of the larger part of them has to take place within the structure of a time sequence, and if the simultaneity of these experiences is to be realized they must be reassembled as such in the mind of the therapist. Only in dreams and to some extent in the drawings and modellings used by the school of Jung can this simultaneity be directly experienced. The same is true of the phenomenon of fragmentation. It is not by accident that realization of the importance of fragmentation in early stages of development, indeed of its existence, has waited for the work of the child analysts who use the medium of objects rather than words and gestures. To some extent fragmentation can be expressed by children through the medium of objects on a flat table, but apart from Direct Objective Therapy this help ceases with the end of childhood.

For direct study of the structure of transference to become possible a means must be found of objective expression by the analysand of all aspects of experience in a manner which will permit of detailed study and comparison in his absence. It is with such a technique that I am here concerned. In order to compress what I have to say into the limits prescribed, you will find in your seats a description of the instrument itself and of its use, and at the further end of the foyer a brief demonstration of some of the aspects of human experience which the use of the World technique brings to light.

The characteristics of this technique are that it appeals to all ages and is equally suitable for use in the therapeutic handling of adults and children, and that it makes possible the simultaneous presentation of differing aspects of the personality at one and the same time and place, even if certain of these aspects be in direct opposition to one another.

Although the significance of what he constructs is unknown to the patient at the time of presentation yet, owing to the objectivity of the tool, the exact interaction of aspect with aspect, experience with experience, can in a series of productions be most effectively presented. Since the material is recorded directly it is produced and this part of the case records is available to the patient for study with the therapist, much of the time of 'working through' is obviated, and experience has shown that all the aspects of transference as described in the three papers of yesterday afternoon's plenary session appear at one time or another in the World material.

From the point of view therefore of increase in scientific knowledge and detailed understanding of the inner processes of disturbed human beings, each therapist using this tool accumulates a wealth of directly recorded material which affords a parallel to that collection of morbid material in the Pathological Museum upon which medical and surgical understanding of physical medicine is based.

The question now arises as to whether the dynamisms which form the major significance of transference express themselves in this medium also. The answer is that they do. Twenty years of work with this tool has demonstrated beyond any possibility of doubt that the making of Worlds can be, and frequently is, to the patient a psychic experience as powerful as any known in the course of analysis in any of the standard schools. In all therapeutic procedures dreary periods occur in which little of significance appears; similarly in the course of ordinary therapy numbers of Worlds are made which have a repetitive or purely external significance to the patient, but when a dynamic example appears its dynamism can change the whole life picture of the patient. It does this because it is the creation of the patient: its power lies in the gradual revelation to the patient through his own work, accompanied by the understanding of it which is mediated to him by the therapist, of his inner experience. Because the World or series of Worlds have been produced by himself and the work upon them based upon previous work objectively recorded, resistance or denial is not possible. However long the working out of the intrinsic significance of any World may take, its validity remains unchallengeable.

To forestall misunderstanding I should state carefully that in the ordinary process of Direct Objective Therapy, Worlds form only one aspect of treatment. It is, however, not possible in the time at our disposal to do more than mention the non-exclusive aspect as, in themselves, Worlds are *capable* of expressing so wide a range of experience that it would seem, when taken alone, that the whole sphere of human experience can appear in them. This is, however, true only of the total range and obviously does not and cannot apply to any one patient.

Owing to this width of range it has been possible only to present a very small extract from this material in the demonstration which I hope will elucidate many of the points I have tried to make in this paper.

The demonstration itself has only become possible by our success at last in finding an artist who has succeeded in conveying through the medium of black and white the real structure of dynamic worlds. As to the matter of language I am glad to say that Miss Kotschnig, our artist, and Miss Andersen from Denmark, who is herself a therapist trained in this mode of therapy, can between them explain what I have been here trying to set out in English, French, German and the Scandinavian languages.

12 Later Concerns

The two papers in this chapter are amongst the last which Lowenfeld wrote after practising for nearly forty years as a child psychotherapist. They do not add to the development of her theoretical ideas, but they indicate her persistent concerns and, at the same time, a recognition of the need for psychotherapists to adapt to a rapidly changing social world. In this respect they continue the theme of the first paper in Chapter 11, where Lowenfeld challenged the major traditions in child psychotherapy for an overemphasis on the centrality of the family.

The first paper, previously unpublished, was given on 25 July at the sixth International Congress on Child Psychiatry, held in Edinburgh on 24–29 July 1966. The reference to 'identity' in the title 'The Adolescent's Search for Identity' is clearly derived from Erikson's (1951) work on the crises of identity versus role diffusion which, in his developmental account, had to be mastered in the passage through to adulthood. Erikson was a German-born psychoanalyst who emigrated to the USA between the wars, becoming associated with the American tradition of ego psychology (see Riley, 1983). He was particularly interested in problems experienced by the many groups of European emigrés in establishing an identity within the USA, and, like Lowenfeld, was highly sensitive to effects of culture. Though Lowenfeld did not refer to his work explicitly here, in considering the post-war world in the first paper in Chapter 11 she acknowledged a sympathy with some of his views.

But Lowenfeld's paper on adolescence was given in the 1960s, a period of expansion which she clearly viewed with mixed feelings. In contrast to the paper in Chapter 11, her emphasis with respect to the adolescent was less on limitations in the family than on conservative tendencies within society and their contribution to the alienation to which young people are particularly vulnerable.

The theme of alienation is also pursued in the second paper, 'Communication with Children'. This was first published in French as 'Communication avec les enfants', in *Revue de Neuropsychiatrie Infantile* (vol. 5, pp. 431–45) in 1967. Here Lowenfeld emphasized the inevitable tension and loss involved in acculturation, and the alienating effects of becoming a language user. None the less she clearly believed that it was possible to build a bridge between children and adults, using other forms of communication which would allow the simultaneity of different kinds of experience to be expressed and understood. In Lowenfeld's approach, the use of her particular techniques was central, here the Kaleidoblocs, the World technique and a version of the 'Newspaper game', described in Chapter 9, p. 245. A description of the World technique has been omitted from the original paper.

Though in describing her work as a child psychiatrist Lowenfeld now chose the word 'communication', the emphasis was as much on communication with the self as with the therapist. As in the previous paper, Lowenfeld's account illustrates how her extended experience contributed to her particular way of understanding the predicaments of children and young people. It is clear that she was, in fact, acutely aware of what they might be feeling. But her great skill was in being particularly sensitive to what they might be *thinking*, and in making this comprehensible and credible within an atmosphere relatively free of judgement or adult stricture. This sensitivity to the thought of the infant and child also underpinned her genius in devising techniques, and in bringing the pleasure of creativity alive as an integral part of the psychotherapeutic process.

The Adolescent's Search for Identity [1966]

My task is to attempt to present an approach to adolescent problems which may seem an unusual one. My theme is the adolescent in 1966: What is his situation and that of society in regard to him? How do the two interact?

In essence, the situation of the adolescent is biological in nature. With the onset of puberty the adolescent feels a surging sense of power within him. Pictures come into his mind of great achievement for himself: of reforming abuses, redressing grievances, changing world conditions. The vagueness of content and the mistiness of outline of these pictures render them absurd or incomprehensible to his surrounding adults. Their incomprehension drives him into strident battle with the members of his family, and from them to the outside world. The *feeling* of power is strong, but for this to turn into the deep satisfaction of achievement, in my view certain specific conditions are necessary: an abiding sense of acceptance within a group; participation in corporate adventures and disciplines and a long series of small acknowledged achievements, and forgiven failures, which integrate him firmly into the group and add to the attainment of the group's objectives. When these moulding conditions are absent the surge of force within an adolescent remains formless and frightening, driving him to seek the shelter of the accustomed and the safety of the known. At one and the same time therefore, he is a child seeking protection and a rebel driven by whirlwinds beyond his control.

While the dilemma of the individual adolescent is in its nature a biological one, so also, in my view, is the relation between the adolescent and society. In all periods there is a tendency for organized society to become conservative, hardened into fixed viewpoints, resistant to new conceptions and fearful of loss of power. The force, the idealism, enthusiasm, courage, endurance and imagination of the adolescent, when welcomed and gradually assimilated by society, can, by their very extravagance, renew life in society, enlarge vision and change directives.

Let us look at two examples.

In 1346 Edward III of England, marching into Normandy to fight the French, arranged his army in three corps; two in the front line and one in the rear. He gave to his eldest son, *a boy of sixteen*, command of a front-line corps and took himself command of the rear reserve. At a desperate moment in the battle, a member of the prince's retinue hurried to the rear to plead with the king to send help to his son. 'Is he dead?' asked the king. 'Or so mortally wounded that he can no longer take command?' 'No sire,' replied the messenger. 'Go back then,' said the king, 'and do not send to me again while the boy lives. I command them to let him win his spurs.' With 'terrible slaughter' the battle was won. The prince grew up to be a distinguished commander, and a wise statesman.

Four hundred years later, Marie-Angélique Arnauld, *a girl of eleven*, was made abbess of the convent of Port-Royal by Paris. After six years of experience as abbess, Marie-Angélique, now aged seventeen, started out on a reform of the convent *which was accepted by the community*. She became the leader of one of the most significant religious movements of that time and that country.

Contemporary writers make clear that these two were not exceptional. Because the structure of society in many countries was still organic it appeared natural to adults to accept the leadership of adolescents of ability; as it became for the adolescents themselves to dedicate their utmost powers to gaining the objectives of a disciplined group, which accepted and valued them, as they, in their turn, valued the opportunities the group secured for them.

How different is the situation today! We are afraid of our adolescents and being afraid, society neither welcomes their idealism nor makes room for their abilities. Untrained in living, the force within them drives them either into exacerbation of sexual urges, the one area where independent experiment is possible; into excesses of appearance or behaviour, into violent destructive action; or into near worship of those few (for example the Beatles) who have fought their way from the ground up, against social norms, to a fantastic fame.

Evidence for the view that it is not the biological state of adolescence, in itself, that turns potentially constructive energy into destructive licence, but the handling of adolescents by society, comes from those many adolescents who, having the luck to grow up in a group that respects them and a social structure that contains avenues of competitive and developing experiences, physical, intellectual, emotional, experimental and organizational, develop into effective and satisfactory young adults.

What then can be done for adolescents caught in the 1966 situation? As I see it, this is a problem of human engineering. Power when not made use of, explodes. The responsibility is partly society's and partly the adolescent's. How then is the situation to be tackled? For the therapist to whom the adolescent comes for help, a basic qualification is a vivid memory of his own adolescence and a sensitive awareness that, however disturbed a particular adolescent may appear to be, there is within him the germ of health. The task the therapist has to carry out is one which should be done by society as a whole for adolescents as a group.

The adolescent is adrift on a shoreless sea. He knows neither himself, nor anyone about him. The therapist's first task, in my view, is therefore to enable him to recognize *himself*, his specific abilities, his potentialities and his essential characteristics. How do his perceptions of the world reach him, by ear, eye, tactile sensation or what else? What does he dream about as he sits in the tube or train? If he could choose to be someone else, who would this be? For what satisfaction does he most yearn?

To discover the answers to these questions, tools are necessary which enable him to represent several aspects of an idea or emotion simultaneously, and through the use of which both the adolescent and the therapist come to see the shape of, as yet, undeveloped potentialities. Meanwhile the therapist explains to him the stresses he suffers from, and their absolute normality: opens out his concepts of life and its possibilities and makes contact for him with the satisfying aspects of normal living.

Adolescents can grow only through their own experiences and must be allowed to make their own experiments, their therapist aiding them to discover the grounds of their success or failure and by accepting these to come to respect their own individuality.

A basic knowledge of himself, when gained, gives the adolescent firm ground beneath his feet from which to tackle his deeper conflicts, experienced now within a framework of achievement and on a basis of reality.

Communication with Children [1967]

As the speed and the effectiveness of physical transit over the face of the globe increase daily, the achievement of effective communication between individuals and nations comes to occupy a place of central importance. Every development in facility of transit increases the urgency of the need for mutual understanding.

Between adult and adult and between group and group, language is the main instrument of communication. But language is a double-edged tool and can hide as well as convey exact meaning. Moreover, apart from certain philosophical groups, little attention has been given to consideration of the ability of language to convey other than descriptions and definition of fact from speaker or writer to hearer or reader. Reflection upon such words as 'democracy', 'freedom', 'security', for instance, shows how little basis there is for reliance upon language for success in conveyance of essential meaning. Moreover, adults for the most part, in their long apprenticeship in the passage from childhood to maturity, have learned to clothe their concepts, ideas and intentions in terms tradition has long rendered automatic. Very different is the position of the child, caught in a situation of pain and tension between himself and his surrounding adults and required by them to give an account of himself and his deeds to an adult audience in words.

Within a family, shared experience and shared verbal traditions can make achievement of understanding possible, even in situations of acute distress. For the psychiatrist, confronted by a child brought to him by family, school or court, the position is different. Here no undertones of common forms of phrase, no background of shared experience are available upon which to build. All the aids to understanding which are normally present when adult meets adult are here lacking. Moreover the adult himself comes from a specific background, has forms of phrase and of expectation of response which have become part of his personality. His facial expressions, pose of body, tones of voice, assumptions arising from his particular social strata, are unconscious to him. The child brings also to this confrontation his experience and expectations of adult nature and responses.

The psychiatrist will, moreover, in his professional training have accustomed himself to certain classifications of motivation, affect and behaviour, certain accepted patterns of reaction to recurring situations, and will, inevitably, look for these in considering the problem before him. To the successful handling of this common professional situation a further difficulty is added through the prevalent acceptance by psychiatrists of the psychoanalytic view of the basic importance of the affective element in personality, and the importance of the translation of affect into language.

A child's experience, however, is compounded of many different facets occurring simultaneously, and words are of little use to him. Interpretation to him, in language, of possible or actual affective states can, at times, only increase his confusion. A child thus faced by an adult he does not know tends to become an uneasy amalgam of frozen states of mind and feeling, packed into an unresponsive body. He thinks and remembers, not in words, but in scenes or pictures, conceived or performed, and knows himself only through what he hears adults say about him. If communication with him is to be established it must start from the child's point of view and in the terms in which he thinks and feels: it must meet him where he is and be expressed in modes that are natural to him. He has no experience of accepted ways of verbal expression, no sense of time, or of consequence.

In recent years great attention has been paid to a child's need of affective security, and while this in itself is true and important little thought has yet been given to the process by which that most common of civilization's distresses, the sense of alienation from one's fellows, finds its germ and its development. Faulty affective development plays most truly a large part in the germination and development of such a state, but equally potent is long experience of absence of *communication* with one's fellows.

It is to consideration of this fact that this paper is directed. Few facts in a child's life can be more important to him than an experience, even if only a brief one, of wholehearted intimacy of communication with an adult. This can be achieved in many ways, but whatever the method, the process of studying and establishing communication with a child goes through certain stages in which a bridge of understanding is built from the child to the adults around him and, with good fortune, from the parents to him. Let us look at three cases and consider first that of a boy of seven, eldest child and only son of a solid and respected family in a small thriving town. Suddenly one day some household money is found to be missing. The circumstances are such that no outsider could be involved. After an exhaustive search the missing £1 notes are found hidden under the mattress of this little boy's bed. The consternation in the family is acute, the distress extreme: not only is the whole matter most mysterious but the parents, people of exceptional rectitude, feel themselves shamed. Under questioning the boy is silent: he will neither admit nor deny. The child and parents reach my consulting room, with an atmosphere of disaster emanating from the three. It is clear to them that the boy must have taken the money, but *why*? 'Doctor, will he grow up to be a criminal?' they ask the psychiatrist. The boy is white and silent, moves slowly and stands with a look of terror and of anger in his eyes.

Here is the type situation: the adults with anguish in their souls and their minds frozen into a stereotyped repertoire of ideas and phrases and showing no concept of the personality of their child. It is not James or Andrew that they see but a little-boy-who-has-stolen-his-mother's-money-and-who-if-not-stopped-will-grow-into-an-adult-thief. Will I tell them what to do with him?

Having got rid of the parents the process of achieving communication with, let us call him Andrew, can begin. As in all negotiation there are two aspects to each stage, that experienced by the child and that carried through by the adult. For the child it is essential that all that has happened heretofore be put on one side and he become absolutely certain it will not be brought back – unless *he* wishes to, that is. For the psychiatrist the essential foundation of communication is to discover and decide what sort of a child this is.

There are, of course, a number of possible symbolic interpretations for a theft of this nature by a boy of seven, the eldest of his family: but from the point of view of communication, the first essential is to gain some idea of the nature of this particular boy as an individual. To achieve this we call Kaleidoblocs to our aid. Kaleidoblocs are a set of twenty-six coloured wooden blocks of varied size and shape closely interrelated with one another in a complex manner. To a child they are intriguing and unfamiliar: to the observer a considerable variety of varied information can be gained from the child's responses. Andrew is listless, withdrawn and bored, he moves the pieces about without interest: then his eye falls on a curved block with its suggestion of a boat, and all is changed. His hands begin to move quickly, his mouth loses its hard line, he uses his fingers deftly, he perseveres in a struggle to achieve an objective which does not come easily: he finds that formal trees can be made with the thick triangles; he constructs a scene, not original but observant: he puts one block on top of another and it makes a comic outline; he looks to me for comment; we laugh together.

As a psychiatrist, I now have a good deal of information. I know this boy is of good intelligence, that he has skilful fingers, is observant and capable of initiative; he has a sense of humour and a capacity for enjoyment. It would seem that his parents have made a good atmosphere at home since he can let himself play freely with a strange adult.

It is time to pass to the second stage. This is where, building upon what has been gained, some definite work is given to him to do. With a change in my tone of voice, some of the problems concealed in the Kaleidoblocs are put to him. His interest is caught, he can think consecutively and reason clearly. One problem concerns a birthday party; his face is now mobile and its expression quickly changing. We begin to talk about birthdays and how nice they are and about presents. When this word is mentioned the light goes out of his face, his mouth sets tightly, his whole body appears to shrink. The psychiatrist begins now to talk about parents, how they forget their own childhood, how easily important things become forgotten, how rigid their ideas are and how dully they live, doing the same things every day, seeming to have so little fun. As talk proceeds, the boy begins to relax, to nod his head in agreement, to look eager. It is probable we have now come to the core of the problem: the disaster can now be directly approached.

I say: 'Andrew, something bad has happened between you and your parents, I think it is something to do with presents. Parents are difficult people to understand. Tell me about it, I may be able to help.' Then the story comes out. Every Christmas and birthday Granny sends him some money as a present. Up till now he has bothered little about it, but this year it is different: 'I am big now, I am in the second class.' He had watched his mother opening the envelope and seen her draw out a green money note. This she said was a present from Granny: Andrew wanted to have it as his own. 'No,' she said, 'she would keep it for him and he could get nice things with it later on'; she put it in her handbag. Later in the morning he went with her shopping – as he continued his face registered increasing horror and distress – 'Do you know what she did? She went into a strange big building with a wall down the middle and some men sitting on the other side. She took my green paper out of her bag and [his voice rising to a squeaky shout] SHE GAVE IT TO A STRANGE MAN THE OTHER SIDE OF THE WALL.' 'This must have been dreadful,' I said. 'It was,' he gulped. After a short space of silence for recovery, we entered upon the third phase. I began to tell him what I had found out about him in the play with Kaleidoblocs, how well he noticed and thought, how he stuck to something he had decided upon until he had done it, how good his fingers were and what fun it was when he made the little funny man. His face by now had become quiet and concentrated: he listened intently, and when it was put to him that 'You must have felt you *had* to do *something* to show Mummy how you felt', he nodded vigorously and to the question, 'Well what did you do?' his reply came instantaneously, 'I found some green papers of hers and hid them.'

The position was clear. A point to remember is that not only was the immediate problem solved, but the depth of distress both of parents and child underlines the care that should be taken by the psychiatrist or therapist in such a situation to make every stage of their child's thinking, feeling and reasoning clear to the parents. Such an incident and its clarification can also make an important contribution to parents' understanding of themselves, and of the way adults regard and react to children. Each disaster, therefore, which is brought to a psychiatrist should make a positive contribution to the general mental health of the family and sometimes through them to the neighbourhood.

This case has been chosen as an illustration of the steps that can be taken, to create for a child some at least of the tools and advantages normal to an adult in negotiation. In this case the problem was recent, the child quick and intelligent and the core of the situation factual.

Quite different is the situation of a child patient, in trouble for a long time, and suffering from a distress for which there is no factual cause. Let us consider a boy of this sort aged nine, referred by a psychiatrist from a general hospital for stammering, being obstinate and uncooperative at home, and at school working far below his intellectual level, which on examination (L. Form Revised Stanford Binet) proved to be an IQ of 130. He had had a good deal of speech therapy without much effect.

Brought by his parents, Thomas was a stocky, well-dressed, good-looking boy with a serious expression. At the consultation interview he was silent and rather anxious. His stammer was said by the psychologist to disappear when tackling tasks he found difficult. Like Andrew he was the eldest child and only son of a solid, industrious, working-class family, apt to keep themselves to themselves. Both parents get irritated with Thomas and shout at him, complaining he is disobedient and obstinate. He was popular with the neighbourhood boys and played with them in the street.

Preliminary study of this boy's history and the family situation made it clear that the conflict was between himself and his parents, and his inability to function at the level of his inherent endowment were long-standing troubles and composed of many elements. There is no similarity between this boy and Andrew; however good the means of communication might be, neither boy nor family in Thomas's case would be able to define what was the nature of their problem.

In such a situation Kaleidoblocs would be of no value; the boy's problems lay in quite a different area of the psyche. The basic rule, however, still held that without means through which Thomas's subjective experience of himself and of the outside world could find expression, no communication with him would be possible. It is for the expression of states of this nature in particular that the World apparatus and World technique is designed. On his second treatment session Thomas constructed the World shown here (see Figure 1). This was the third World he had made; most of the themes in it had been indicated in the other two, but appeared for the first time clearly in this one.

Thomas's concentration was complete as he constructed this World. It was made, as it were, in sections, but is quite chaotic. The making fell into six sections:

1. First the soldiers (with army vehicles; the modern soldiers about to attack the old-time ones).
2. Next three buses, full of people and going along; a police car

shouting that prisoners have escaped, 'the people will then help to catch the prisoners and shut them up again'. Between these two sections the skier was put in coming down a slope (later a zebra put in his path; he knocks him down and passes over him).

3. Wild animals now appear, a giraffe, a lion and a crocodile 'just walking around' (the zebra we have already met), to these a horse is added also just walking around, another crocodile, however, is just about to get into a bus and eat all the people in it, and a snake twines around a bus so it cannot go along and then will get into the bus and eat all the people in it.

4. The next emphasis is on pigs: a mother pig is put on the top of the bus and at first a baby pig was to go with her, but Thomas decided to put it on the ground some distance away and two babies with it; a further pig suckling babies, and two mother pigs walking along. Two cows were now added, one astride the crocodile about to get into the bus, but apparently with no connection with it.

5. Finally all the trains he could find were added facing all ways and thought of as electric. Thomas did not know if they were moving or, if moving, where they were going.

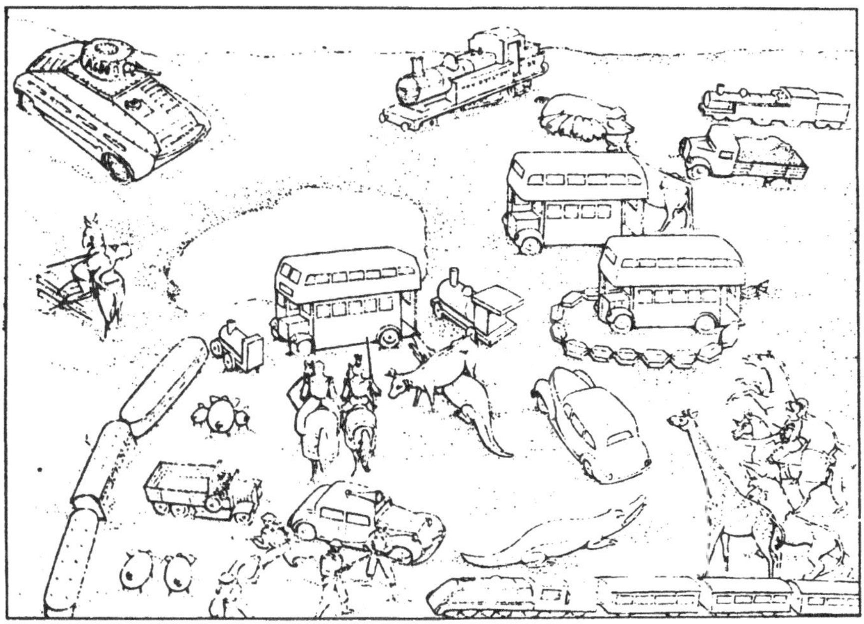

Figure 1 *World made in Thomas's second treatment session*

6. A large tank he had used in his other Worlds finished the construction 'just standing' in the further left corner.

His concentration was absolute, each item was both chosen and placed with care. The chaotic nature of the arrangement in the tray, the presentation of contradictory emotions and the clarity and definition of expression of the feeling within the boy of being 'lost' in a dangerous, incomprehensible, chaotic world, is complete. Communication here can only be developed on the basis of the boy's own type of 'speech', i.e. as if a Spaniard were faced in negotiation with the pictographs or glyphs of Aztec civilization. The one is as readable as the other – i.e. Aztec pictographs and children's (or adults' for that matter) Worlds – once the necessary work has been put in to understand them. Here we are presented with an intricate combination of feeling, experience, emotion and phantasy. Added to these all concepts of a nature basic to many children, which, for convenience in reference in my work and with my colleagues, we term the 'protosystem', as it forms the 'protoplasm' of the mind.

With the help both of World apparatus, as the 'words' of the child's language, and understanding of the 'protosystem', as the grammar of that language, a child can be brought into the normal situation of negotiator, i.e. able to talk in his own language to an adult using his, and gradually come to understand and share the understanding of himself and his problems – being progressively gained – by the psychiatrist. The particular value of the World apparatus is that it can present a subjective situation as it really is at a moment of experience, with elements of different nature and lying at different levels in the psyche actually present at the same time. The presence in the World cabinet of the same objects makes possible a sequential working out in a series of Worlds of the significances and implications of the statements and stories presented in single Worlds. (Each World, as it is completed, is drawn by the therapist and filed as material for later review and discussion with the maker of them.)

Let us turn to another situation. The parents of an eight-and-a-half-year-old boy, Ralph, urgently ask for a consultation. An emergency has arisen. The headmaster of the boarding preparatory school the boy is attending has asked them to remove him from the school. The reason is extreme aggressive behaviour against another boy and in relation to furniture of classrooms, etc. The boy's parents belong to the group where the men attend preparatory boarding schools (in this case the same one as that at which Ralph now is), go from there to one of the most prominent public schools and from there to Oxford or Cambridge. Ralph was the eldest of four children, his father a well-established civil servant. Ralph's mother was of a forceful and dominant personality very much attached to her children, but determined that they should develop the traits she felt admirable. The family was one of a large clan and Ralph as both eldest son and grandson occupied an important position. Both parents were devoted to their children, lived in a country house with large garden, spent much time with the children and always went to the sea for a family holiday. At home Ralph was inclined to fly into tempers, which were controlled by his mother, was dictatorial to the younger ones and had few if any friends outside the family. In school work he was backward, failing to read at anything like his chronological reading age, with very poor writing and spelling.

The crisis at school had developed in his second term. It proved impossible to persuade the school to keep him any longer. As this was the school his father had attended, and he had been entered for the public school to which his father had gone, dismissal from this school broke seriously into his educational career. The parents and the school were at a loss to account for his behaviour at school: to the parents it was a major tragedy. Diagnosis presented considerable difficulty. Ralph's own account of the incidents at school was as confused as was the behaviour itself. There were a number of possibilities, some of them physiological. A period of careful study was indicated. From the general situation one would have expected the boy to have absorbed the standards and conventions of the family and, in spite of his spasmodic temper tantrums at home, to have been able to fit into the normal schoolboy pattern at school without too great difficulty. This, however, was not the case. His reading was bad because he did not want to read. The same applied to writing and spelling. It seemed unwise at that moment to subject him to a standard intelligence test, so I presented him instead with Kaleidoblocs. Here his response contradicted expectation. In all the problems involving space perception and the manipulation of geometrically related objects, he showed ability far beyond his chronological age, and that of most adults.

His most surprising reaction was to the World apparatus. He made mouldable sand, selected a number of differentiated motor vehicles and studied the marks they made running in the sand. He then moulded sand contours and constructed for himself problems in speed and timing of the vehicles on the tracks as they crossed each other, demanding that each arrangement be carefully drawn. His reaction was that of a child who had been starved of something essential to his well-being.

It proved impossible to interest his parents in either of these phenomena: the matter of competence in reading, writing and adjustment to school life absorbed their attention. Gradually, with assistance from tutoring, these were brought near to normal standards, work on the general handling of the boy at home resulted in disappearance of the temper tantrums and better approximation to expected social norms.

His complete absorption to his sand-tray work, however, made exploration of the emotional aspect of his situation difficult. He would talk, when prodded, but used words either as defence or evasion with little relation to factual truth. To get any true response I felt a means of communication would need to be used where fabrication was not possible. We had recourse therefore to Pin pictures, that is, the employment of primitive figures in the current 'newspaper strip' technique to illustrate themes.

As he had complained often about being bullied at school, I suggested as a theme, 'A Nasty Fellow'. He set to work at once, obviously drawing with pleasure, and produced the set of pictures shown here (see Figure 2). Here he, Ralph, had been standing in a doorway when another boy (unidentified but from his class, therefore about nine years of age) came in through another door, walked across the room and knocked the master down. Ralph went to his assistance, helped the master up and hit the other boy. The master, then, with Ralph, took the other boy to the headmaster's study, who then beat the other boy. The story ended with Ralph and the master going out through another door in friendly fashion together. Nothing about this story struck Ralph as odd; he took it as a perfectly 'real' possibility, was proud of his own action in it and generally satisfied with himself over it. This response together with his performance with Kaleidoblocs gave the clue to the situation and the time had now come for a formal intelligence investigation. This was carried out by an unusually experienced psychologist using the Wisc form. Her report on the central matters ran as follows:

This boy is of very superior intelligence, obtaining the highest possible score on this test, for both Verbal Ability and Performance, working out slightly higher for Performance.

He is capable of creative and constructive thinking.

He has a very special gift for Mathematics; he solved all the problems including those for subjects up to 15 years 11 months in age in record time, verbalizing what he was doing when the tests became difficult. His way of solving the problems showed real understanding.

His other even more striking gift is that of constructive work with three-dimensional material.

He did all the Block Designs in under one minute each (which is a good deal less than is allowed) and he remarked when given all the blocks that he now had nine, and that knowing this was helping him with the problem as it meant that each side now had three blocks instead of two. He proceeded to kind of shove the blocks together making the right pattern after one look.

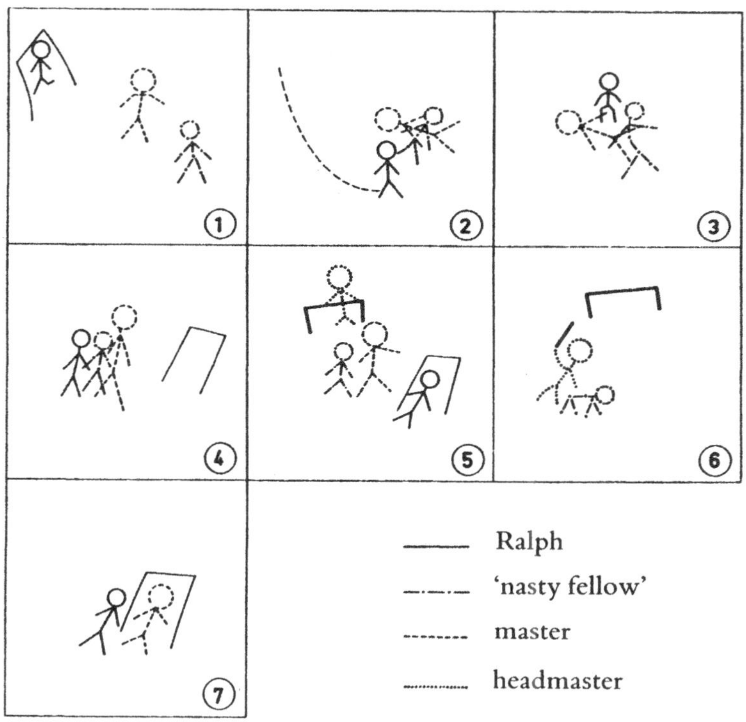

Figure 2 *Ralph's Pin picture*

Another test item which bears this out is the Object Assembly test and here again he scored the highest possible scores, never making a mistake. (Translated into the Binet–Simon scale this would give an IQ of around 168 with exceptional ability in space perception.)

Of his behaviour during the test interview the report runs as follows:

> After an initial anxiety he was very free and easy with me. The anxiety showed itself in his request that his mother should come up with us and stay for a few minutes. After the test he no longer cared. He was happily typing away when I went down to fetch his mother from the waiting room.
>
> He was extraordinarily distractable, he was also rather supercilious and much too conscious of his own cleverness. He was restless throughout, and inquisitively exploring everything in the room like a four-year-old child. At times he seemed so preoccupied with other matters, playing about with blocks, etc., that I thought he had not heard what I had asked; however, this was not so, he always answered and answered very quickly.
>
> This is a very gifted but totally undisciplined boy, used to getting his own way and making very conscious use of his power over adults who have to deal with him.
>
> His school failure is probably due to inattentiveness and 'inapplication' and his need to play about rather than work. He behaved like a boy of four, showed his inquisitiveness at about that age level in spite of his high intellectual ability.
>
> He seemed very self-willed and needed firm insistence of application to the task in hand. This could be due to thwarted creativeness and the lack of sufficient creative outlets in play.

To his parents the whole of this is incomprehensible; a boy who (at now ten) can read and write with difficulty is 'a stupid boy', one with a handicap to be taken with kindness: allowances should be made for him and he be guided slowly into the routine of school work. The double standard of behaviour, so clear to the trained eye, is invisible to them as is his increasing ability to manipulate adults. His hunger for opportunity for experiment for tasks that are, to him, really difficult enough to be worth working at misses them altogether. His emotional immaturity and need for help to 'grow up' is likewise invisible to them as is his growing hatred of the discipline which forces conformity upon him. The dangers of the situation they do not see, nor the despair of the boy when alone with his psychiatrist. There is no communication between them.

Here we have one of the problems that has true gravity. Ralph's exceptional intellectual powers and their unusual nature will inevitably bring him eventually into prominence. If time has not by then been made up on his social and emotional development, he will present, at the moment when his true abilities become evident to himself, that most dangerous of all types of human beings, the man with the ability to appear 'just like anyone else' and that in a particular type of social milieu, who in himself has the undisciplined nature of a primitive, and also resentful, child.

Note on the Dr Margaret Lowenfeld Trust

When Dr Margaret Lowenfeld died in 1973, two small trusts were set up to perpetuate and update her ideas and methods. In 1983 they were amalgamated for administrative convenience to form the Dr Margaret Lowenfeld Trust. Although this is a charitable body working with very limited resources, we are pleased with the progress made. Apart from contributing to the publication costs of the book you have just read, we have supported Dr Cathy Urwin as the Margaret Lowenfeld Research Fellow, a position held within the Child Care and Development Group and Department of Paediatrics, Cambridge University. We have also supported other research by former Institute of Child Psychology students, ensured the publication of Margaret Lowenfeld's *The World Technique* and helped to maintain and generate growing interest in Lowenfeld's methods in the UK and USA. As these selected papers and their extended introduction show, Dr Lowenfeld's ideas blend well with modern thinking and practice. Particularly interesting are the correspondences with the work of the late Dr Donald Winnicott.

The Trustees also support the annual Lowenfeld Seminar, held in Cambridge. This is a multidisciplinary event with a mixed programme which brings together researchers and practitioners in child psychotherapy who are particularly interested in relations between emotionality and non-verbal thought.

With our limited resources we would, of course, welcome further financial help. Information about the Trust, Dr Lowenfeld's work and the availability of the methods and publications may be had from:

Dr Martin Richards, Child Care and Development Group, Free School Lane, Cambridge CB2 3RF, UK, or

Dr H.B. Wright, Brudenell House, Quainton, Aylesbury, Bucks HP22 4AW, UK.

H. Beric Wright, Chairman of the Trustees

Bibliography

Reports and pamphlets are listed separately at the end of the Bibliography.

Place of publication is London, unless otherwise stated.

Adler, A. (1928) *Understanding Human Nature*. W. B. Wolfe, trans. Allen & Unwin.

Ariès, P. (1962) *Centuries of Childhood*. Cape.

Armstrong, D. (1983) *The Political Anatomy of the Body: Medical Knowledge in Britain in the Twentieth Century*. Cambridge: Cambridge University Press.

Bettelheim, B. (1960) *The Informed Heart: Autonomy in a Mass Age*. Glencoe, IL: Free Press.

Bion, W. (1962) *Learning from Experience*. Heinemann.

—— (1967) *Second Thoughts*. New York: Jason Aronson.

Boston, M. (1975) 'Recent research in developmental psychology', *J. Child Psychother.* 4: 15–34.

—— (1987) 'Splitting image? The child observed and the child within', Paper presented to British Psychological Society Medical and Psychotherapy Section, January.

Bower, T. G. R. (1982) *Development in Infancy*. San Francisco, CA: Freeman.

Bowlby, J. (1940) 'The influence of early environment in the development of neurosis and neurotic character', *Int. J. Psycho-Anal.* 21: 154–78.

—— (1944) 'Forty-four juvenile thieves: their characters and homelife', *Int. J. Psycho-Anal.* 25: 1–57.

—— (1951) *Maternal Care and Mental Health*. Geneva: WHO; London: HMSO.

—— (1953) *Child Care and the Growth of Love*. Harmondsworth: Penguin.

—— (1969) *Attachment and Loss*, vol. 1, *Attachment*. Hogarth.

Bruner, J. S. (1972) 'Nature and uses of immaturity', *Am. Psychol.* 27: 1–22.

Burke, N., and Miller, E. (1929) 'Child mental hygiene – its history, methods and problems', *Br. J. Med. Psychol.* 9: 218–42.

Burt, C. (1915) *General and Specific Factors Underlying the Primary Emotions*. Manchester: British Association.

—— (1917A) *LCC Report on the Distribution and Relations of Educational Abilities*. King.

—— (1917B) 'The unstable child', *Child Study* 10: 61–78.

—— (1923A) 'The causal factors of juvenile crime', *Br. J. Med. Psycol.* 3: 1–33.

—— (1923B) 'Delinquency and mental defect', *Br. J. Med. Psychol.* 3: 168–78.

—— (1925) *The Young Delinquent*. University of London Press.

Cannon, W. B. (1915) *Hunger, Fear and Rage: An Account of Recent Researches*. New York, London: D. Appleton. 2nd edn, 1929.

Clegg, H. (1984) *The Reparative Motif*. San Francisco, CA: Aronson.

Collingwood, R. G. (1933) *An Essay on Philosophical Method*. Oxford: Clarendon.

—— (1938) *Principles of Art*. Oxford: Clarendon.

—— (1939) *An Autobiography*. Oxford: Clarendon.

—— (1945) *The Idea of Nature*. Oxford: Clarendon.

—— (1947) *The Idea of History*. Oxford: Clarendon.

Crichton-Miller, H., ed. (1920) *Functional Nerve Disease: An Epitome of War Experience for the Practitioner*. Hodder & Stoughton.

Darwin, C. (1877) 'A biological sketch of an infant', *Mind* 2: 285–94.

Davis, M. (1988) 'Play and symbolism in Winnicott and Lowenfeld'. (Free Associations forthcoming.)

Daws, D. (1987) 'Thirty years of child psychotherapy: the psychoanalytic approach to children's problems', *Ass. Child Psychol. and Psychiat. Newsletter* 9: 3–11.

de Lissa, L. (1939) *Life in the Nursery School*. Longman.

de Mause, C. (1974) *The History of Childhood*. Souvenir Press.

Denis, M., and Talbot, F.B. (1919) 'A study of the lactose, fat and protein content of human milk', *Am. J. Diseases of Children* 18: 93.

Dicks, H. (1970) *Fifty Years of the Tavistock Clinic*. Routledge & Kegan Paul.

Donzelot, J. (1979) *The Policing of Families*. Hutchinson.

Erikson, E.H. (1951) *Childhood and Society*. Imago; Harmondsworth: Penguin, 1965.

Evans, B. (1984) *Freedom to Choose: The Life and Work of Helena Wright, Pioneer of Contraception*. Bodley Head.

Forrester, J. (1986) 'Can there be a non-psychoanalytic history of psychoanalysis? Part 1', Paper presented at Cambridge Conference on the Historiography of Psychoanalysis and Psychiatry, September.

Foucault, M. (1977) *Discipline and Punish*. Allen Lane.

Freud, A. (1927) *Einführung in die Technik der Kinderanalyse*. Leipzig: Internationaler Psychoanalytischer Verlag; London: Imago, 1949.

—— (1966) *Normality and Pathology in Childhood*. Hogarth.

—— (1973) *Infants without Families and Reports on the Hampstead Nurseries, 1939–1945*. Hogarth.

Freud, S. (1896) 'The aetiology of hysteria', in James Strachey, ed. *The Standard Edition of the Complete Psychological Works of Sigmund Freud*, 24 vols. Hogarth, 1953–73. vol. 3, pp. 191–221.

—— (1900) *The Interpretation of Dreams*. *S.E.* 4–5, pp. 1–338, 339–627.

—— (1909) 'Analysis of a phobia in a five-year-old boy'. *S.E.* 10, pp. 1–145.

—— (1911) 'Formulations on the two principles of mental functioning'. *S.E.* 12, pp. 13–226.

—— (1920) *Beyond the Pleasure Principle*. *S.E.* 18, pp. 1–64.

—— (1921) *Group Psychology and the Analysis of the Ego*. *S.E.* 18, pp. 65–143.

—— (1923) *The Ego and the Id*. *S.E.* 19, pp. 1–66.

—— (1930) *Civilization and Its Discontents*. *S.E.* 21, pp. 57–145.

Garvey, C. (1977) *Play*. Fontana.

Gesell, A. (1928) *Infancy and Human Growth*. New York: Macmillan.

Glover, E. (1954) 'The indications for psychoanalysis', *J. of Mental Science* 100: 393–401.

Grosskurth, P. (1986) *Melanie Klein: Her World and Her Work*. Hodder & Stoughton.

Hammett, F. S. (1917) 'Variations in the composition of human milk during the first eleven days after parturition', *J. Biochemistry* 24: 2.

Hardyment, C. (1983) *Dream Babies: Baby Care from Locke to Spock*. Cape.

Hearnshaw, L. S. (1987) *The Shaping of Modern Psychology: An Historical Introduction*. Routledge & Kegan Paul.

Henderson, D. K., and Gillespie, R. D. (1932) *A Textbook of Psychiatry*, 3rd edn. Oxford University Press.

Holland, R. (1977) *Self and Social Context*. Macmillan.

Hoyles, M., ed. (1979) *Changing Childhood*. Writers and Readers' Cooperative.

Hunnaeus (1909) 'Über den Kalkgehalt der Frauenmilch', *Biochemische Zeitschrift* 22: 442.

Hurst, A. F. (1927) 'An address on the constitutional factor in disease', *Brit. Med. J.* 1: 823–7.

Ingleby, D. (1986) 'Development in social context', in M. P. M. Richards and P. Light, eds *Children of Social Worlds*. Cambridge: Polity.

Isaacs, S. (1930) *Intellectual Growth in Young Children*. Routledge.

—— (1933) *Social Development in Young Children*. Routledge.

—— (1941) *The Cambridge Evacuation Survey*. Methuen.

—— (1948) 'The nature and function of phantasy', *Int. J. Psycho-Anal.* 29: 73–97.

Joyce, J. (1922) *Ulysses*. Paris: Shakespeare; Harmondsworth: Penguin, 1986.

Kalff, D. (1966) *Sandspiel*. Zürich: Rascher.

Keir, G. (1952) 'A history of child guidance' (with the assistance of Sir Cyril Burt and other members of the British Psychological Society), *Brit. J. Educational Psychology* 22: 5–29.

Klein, M. (1921–45) *The Writings of Melanie Klein*, vol. 1, *Love, Guilt and Reparation and Other Works*. Hogarth, 1975.

—— (1927) 'Criminal tendencies in normal children', *Brit. J. Med. Psychol.* 7: 177–92.

—— (1930) 'The importance of symbol formation in the development of the ego', *Int. J. Psycho-Anal.* 11: 724–39.

—— (1932) *The Psychoanalysis of Children*. Hogarth.

—— (1935) 'A contribution to the psychogenesis of manic depressive states', *Int. J. Psycho-Anal.* 16: 145–74.

—— (1946) 'Notes on some schizoid mechanisms', *Int. J. Psycho-Anal.* 28: 130–9.

Kohon, G., ed. (1986) *The British School of Psychoanalysis: The Independent Tradition*. Free Association.

Kretschmer, E. (1925) *Physique and Character: An Investigation of the Nature of Constitution and of the Theory of Temperament*. New York: Harcourt, Brace; London: Kegan Paul. (International Library of Psychological, Philosophical and Scientific Method.)

Langer, S. (1942) *Philosophy in a New Key: A Study in the Symbolism of Reason, Rite and Art*. Cambridge, MA: Harvard University Press. Revised 1951, 1957.

Lewis, J. (1980) *The Politics of Motherhood: Child and Maternal Welfare in England 1900–1939*. Croom Helm.

Lingens Reiner, E. (1948) *Prisoners of Fear* (with an introduction by A. Barea). Gollancz.

Llewellyn, L. J. (1926) *Proclamations of the Royal Society of Medicine* January: 1.

Lowenfeld, M. F. (1926) 'On the control of heart disease in childhood', *Brit. Med. J.* 8 & 15 May, 1: 817–20.

—— (1929) 'History of the clinic'. Cambridge, Lowenfeld Archive. (Unpublished MS.)

—— (1930) 'The interaction of physical and psychological factors in the causality of neurosis in children', Paper presented to London Association of the Medical Women's Association, March.

—— (1935) *Play in Childhood*. Gollancz.

—— (1950A) 'A combined approach to the study and treatment of disturbed children', *Am. J. Psychother.* 4.

—— (1950B) 'The nature and use of the Lowenfeld World technique with children and adults', *J. Psychol.* 30: 325–31.

—— (1951) 'Les images du "Monde" chez les enfants', *Sauvegarde de l'enfance* (Paris) 4: 91–319.

—— (1954) *The Lowenfeld Mosaic Test*. Newman Neame.

—— (1969) 'The Institute of Child Psychology'. Cambridge, Lowenfeld Archive. (Unpublished MS.)

—— (n.d.) 'Factors influencing "peace" and unrest in countries'. Cambridge, Lowenfeld Archive. (Unpublished MS.)

—— (1979) *The World Technique*. Allen & Unwin.

Lowenfeld, M. F., and Widdows, S. T. (1927) 'A study in the variations in the chemical composition of normal human colostrum and early milk', *Biochemical J.* 21: 1–15.

Masson, J. (1985) *The Assault on Truth: Freud's Suppression of the Seduction Theory*. Harmondsworth: Penguin.

Mead, M. (1931) *Growing Up in New Guinea*. Kegan Paul; New York: Morrow.

—— (1974) 'Obituary: Margaret Lowenfeld 1890–1973', *J. Clinical Child Psychol.* Summer, 56–7.

Meltzer, D. (1967) *The Psychoanalytic Process*. Perthshire: Clunie.

—— (1973) *Sexual States of Mind*. Perthshire: Clunie.

—— (1987) 'On aesthetic reciprocity', *J. Child Psychother.* 13: 3–14.

Metraux, R. (1976) 'Eidos and change: continuity in process, discontinuity in product', in T. Schartz, ed. *Socialization as Cultural Communication*. Berkeley, CA: University of California Press, pp. 201–16.

—— (1986) 'Margaret Lowenfeld and Margaret Mead: Mosaics, Kaleidoblocs and Worlds', Paper presented at Lowenfeld Day Conference, Cambridge, November.

Metraux, R., and Abel, T. (1957) 'Normal and deviant behaviour in a peasant community', *Am. J. Orthopsychiat.* 27: 167–87.

—— (1975) *Culture and Psychotherapy*. New Haven, CN: College and University Press.

Miller, Sheila (1983) 'Glossary', in M. Boston and R. Szur, eds *Psychotherapy with Severely Deprived Children*. Routlege & Kegan Paul, pp. 133–6.

Miller, Suzanna (1968) *The Psychology of Play*. Harmondsworth: Penguin.

Montessori, M. (1912) *The Montessori Method*. Heinemann.

Newman, G. (1920A) Quoted in Editorial, *Brit. Med. J.* 1: 646.

—— (1920B) Quoted in Editorial, *Brit. Med. J.* 2: 709.

Pearse, I. H., and Crocker, L. H. (1943) *The Peckham Experiment: A Study in the Living Structure of a Society*. Allen & Unwin.

Perticone, E., and Tembeckjian, R. (1987) *The Mosaic Technique in Personality Assessment: A Practical Guide*. New Jersey: Programs for Education Inc.

Piaget, J. (1929) *The Child's Conception of the World*. Kegan Paul.

—— (1932A) *The Language and Thought of the Child*. Kegan Paul.

—— (1932B) *The Moral Judgement of the Child*. Kegan Paul.

—— (1951) *Play, Dreams and Imitation*. Heinemann.

—— (1953) *The Origin of Intelligence in the Child*. Routledge & Kegan Paul.

—— (1955) *The Construction of Reality in the Child*. Routledge & Kegan Paul.

Piaget, J., and Inhelder, B. (1969) *The Psychology of the Child*. Routledge & Kegan Paul.

Pollock, L. (1983) *Forgotten Children, Parent–child Relations from 1500 to 1900*. Cambridge: Cambridge University Press.

Poynton, F. J., and Paine, A. (1913) *Researches on Rheumatism*. Churchill.

Read, H. E. (1943) *Education through Art*. Faber & Faber.

Read, S. (1987) 'The discovery of beauty and its importance in the psychoanalytic experience', Paper presented at Tavistock Centre Scientific Meeting, London, November.

Reynolds, P. (1972) 'Play, language and human evolution', Paper given at Annual Meeting of the American Association for the Advancement of Science, Washington DC, December. Reprinted in part in J. Bruner, A. Jolly and K. Sylva, eds *Play: Its Role in Development and Evolution*. Harmondsworth: Penguin, 1976, pp. 621–37.

Riley, D. (1983) *War in the Nursery*. Virago.

Rose, N. (1985) *The Psychological Complex: Psychology, Politics and Society in England 1869–1939*. Routledge & Kegan Paul.

St Lawrence, W. (1920) *Hospital Service Series*, May, pp. 151–81.

Samuel, R. (1987) 'History that's over'. Review of R. Hewison *The Heritage Industry: Britain in a Climate of Decline* (Methuen). *Guardian* 9 October, p. 14.

Schabad, J. A. (1911) 'Der Kalkgehalt der Frauenmilch', *Jahrbuch für Kinderheilkunde*. 24: 511.

Schachtel, E. (1947) 'On memory and childhood amnesia', *Psychiatry* 10: 1–26.

Schmideberg, M. (1934) 'The play analysis of a three-year-old girl', *Int. J. Psycho-Anal.* 15: 245–64.

—— (1935) 'The analysis of asocial children and adolescents', *Int. J. Psycho-Anal.* 16: 22–48.

Searl, N. (1927) 'Symposium on child analysis', *Int. J. Psycho-Anal.* 8: 377–9.

—— (1930) 'The roles of ego and libido in development', *Int. J. Psycho-Anal.* 11: 125–49.

—— (1933) 'A note on symbols and early intellectual activity', *Int. J. Psycho-Anal.* 14: 391–7.

Segal, H. (1986) *Introduction to the Work of Melanie Klein*. Hogarth.

Selleck, R. (1972) *English Primary Education and the Progressives, 1914–1939*. Routledge & Kegan Paul.

Sheldon, W. H. (1940) *The Variation of Human Physique: An Introduction to Constitutional Psychology* (by W. H. Sheldon in collaboration with S. S. Stevens and W. B. Tucker). New York, London: Harper.

Simon, B. (1974) *The Politics of Educational Reform 1920–1940*. Lawrence & Wishart.

Smith, L. (1985) *To Understand and to Help: The Life and Works of Susan Isaacs (1885–1948)*. New York: Associated University Press.

Spearman, C. (1923) *The Nature of Intelligence and the Principles of Cognition*. Macmillan.

—— (1927) *The Abilities of Man*. Macmillan.

—— (1937) *Psychology down the Ages*, vols 1 & 2. Macmillan.

Stern, D. (1985) *The Interpersonal World of the Infant*. New York: Basic.

Sulloway, F. (1979) *Freud, Biologist of the Mind: Beyond the Psychoanalytic Legend*. Burnett Books in association with Deutsch.

Sully, J. (1895) *Studies of Childhood*. Longman. Rev. 1903.

Sylvester Bradley, B. (1988) *Visions of Infancy*. Cambridge: Polity (in press).

Trotter, W. (1920) *The Instincts of the Herd in Peace and War*. Fisher Unwin. First pub. 1916.

Turner, C. E. H. (1948) 'Interpretation of play therapy by the psychosomatic theory of family sexuality', *J. Mental Science* 94: 718–32.

Urwin, C. (1985A) 'Constructing motherhood: the persuasion of normal development', in C. Steedman, C. Urwin and V. Walkerdine, eds *Language, Gender and Childhood*. Routledge & Kegan Paul, pp. 164–202.

—— (1985B) Review of D. Riley *War in the Nursery*. Virago, 1985. *Feminist Review* 19: 95–100.

—— (1986) 'Developmental psychology and psychoanalysis: splitting the difference', in M. P. M. Richards and P. Light, eds *Children of Social Worlds*. Cambridge: Polity, pp. 257–86.

Urwin, C., and Sharland, E. (forthcoming) 'Whatever happened to original sin? Aggressivity in childcare books post World War Two'.

Vygotsky, L. S. (1962) *Thought and Language*. Cambridge, MA: MIT Press.

Walkerdine, V. (1984) 'Developmental psychology and the child-centred pedagogy: the insertion of Piaget's theory into primary school practice', in J. Henriques, W. Hollway, C. Urwin, C. Venn and V. Walkerdine, eds *Changing the Subject*. Methuen, pp. 153–202.

Warner, F. (1890) *Lectures on Mental Faculty*. Cambridge: Cambridge University Press.

Wells, H. G. (1911) *Floor Games*. Palmer.

Wills, D. M. (1954) 'The Association for Child Psychotherapists (Non-medical)', *Bull. Brit. Psychol. Soc.* May.

—— (1978) 'Fifty years of child guidance. A psychologist's view', *J. Child Psychother.* 4: 97–102.

Winnicott, D. W. (1931) *Clinical Notes on Disorders of Childhood*. London: Heinemann.

—— (1962) 'A personal view of the Kleinian contribution', in Winnicott (1979).

—— (1964) *The Child, the Family and the Outside World.* Harmondsworth: Penguin.

—— (1971) *Playing and Reality.* Tavistock.

—— (1979) *Maturational Processes and the Facilitating Environment.* Hogarth.

Wohlegemuth, L. (1919) 'Pleasure – unpleasure', *Brit. J. Psychol. Monogr. Suppl.*

Wood, M. (1987) 'Towards thinking the unthinkable', Paper presented at Margaret Lowenfeld Day Conference, Cambridge, November.

—— (forthcoming) 'A comparative study of the imagining processes in readers and non-readers, using the Lowenfeld World technique'. University of Nottingham.

Woodcock, T. (1986A) 'The Lowenfeld Mosaic Test in the study of cultural differences', *Brit. J. Projective Psychology* 31: 25–31.

—— (1986B) 'A patchwork of mosaics', Paper presented at Margaret Lowenfeld Day Conference, Cambridge, November.

Woodward, G. (1897) 'Chemistry of colostrum milk: a study of six cases', *J. Experimental Medicine* 2: 217.

Reports and Pamphlets

Berkhamsted Children's Clinic (1946) *Story of the Berkhamsted Children's Clinic.* Pamphlet and Annual Report for 1943, 1944, 1945.

British Medical Association Science Committee Report (1927) *Brit. Med. J.* 1: 731.

Children's Clinic for the Treatment and Study of Nervous and Delicate Children (1930) *Annual Report 1929–30.*

—— *The Children's Clinic for the Treatment and Study of Nervous and Delicate Children.* (Pamphlet.)

'Clinic for nervous and difficult children' (1928) (Unpublished Report.)

Consultative Committee on Medical and Allied Services (1920) *Interim Report on the Future Provision of Medical and Allied Services.* HMSO. (Dawson Report.)

Hadow Consultative Committee of the Board of Education (1931) *The Primary School.* HMSO. (Hadow Report.)

—— (1933) *Infant and Nursery Schools.* HMSO. (Hadow Report.)

Institute of Child Psychology (1934) *Annual Report for the Year 1933*. ICP.
—— (1935) *Annual Report for the Year 1934*. ICP.
—— (1936) *Annual Report for the Year 1935*. ICP.
—— (1936) *News Bulletin* 1: 3.
—— (1937) *News Bulletin* 1: 6.
London County Council (1925) *Annual Report of the London County Council for 1925*. (Public Health Publs 3.)
MRC Child Life Investigations (1927) *Social Conditions and Acute Rheumatism* HMSO.

Index

How to obtain Lowenfeld Mosaic Sets and books by Dr Margaret Lowenfeld

The Dr Margaret Lowenfeld Trust was established after her death with the aim of ensuring the continued availability of the equipment needed to practise her methods and of the books that she authored.

Mosaic sets may be ordered from the Trust by visiting its website **<http://www.lowenfeld.org.uk>**, which also contains information about where to purchase her publications.

"Throughout her long and innovative life, Margaret Lowenfeld emphasised the development of new forms of communication with children, especially devoting herself to the diagnosis of troubled children . . . By understanding and using the tools she developed, we can experience, and so partake of, her insights." *From the Introduction by Margaret Mead, world renowned anthropologist and author of* Coming of Age in Samoa, *to Margaret Lowenfeld's* Understanding Children's Sandplay

The following books by Margaret Lowenfeld can be ordered by visiting the Press website **<http://www.sussex-academic.com>**, where information on ordering from the UK, the US and the Rest of the World, is provided.

UNDERSTANDING CHILDREN'S SANDPLAY
Lowenfeld's World Technique
ISBN 978-1-84519-082-8 £17.95/$34.95, 292 pp.

PLAY IN CHILDHOOD
ISBN 978-1-84519-300-3 £17.95/$34.95, 272 pp.

Printed and bound by CPI Group (UK) Ltd, Croydon, CR0 4YY

13/09/2026

14961101-0005